W9-CNF-253

BLAST FREEZING SYSTEM FOR QUANTITY FOODS

Eulalia L. Harder

1

BLAST FREEZING SYSTEM FOR QUANTITY FOODS

CBI PUBLISHING COMPANY, INC.
51 Sleeper Street   Boston, Massachusetts 02210

Library of Congress Cataloging in Publication Data

Harder, Eulalia L   1938–
    Blast freezing system for quantity foods.

    Bibliography: p.
    Includes index.
    1. Food, Frozen.   I.   Title.
TP372.3.H37   641.4'53   79–16832
ISBN 0–8436–2157–5 (v. 1)

Printed in the United States of America

Printing (last digit): 9 8 7 6 5 4 3 2 1

Contents

Introduction

The reasons for adopting a system of blast freezing pre-plated meals increase in importance against today's backdrop of ever higher food and labor costs. Keeping these costs under control depends on close scrutiny of current operations as compared with alternate operational options. Only by considering alternates can a foodservice operator, manager, or dietitian find out what changes will be most helpful in improving foodservice performance.

The comparisons offered in this book make it easier to determine what a different system can offer an existing operation. Increasing labor costs may well justify the equipment investment needed for blast freezing pre-plated meals on-premise. A five-day, one-shift work week scheduled to produce meals for seven days may provide hourly savings that offset equipment costs. Experience with such a system has also demonstrated that productivity increases when tasks are clearly defined. With each task programmed, the worker learns new skills more readily. Supervisors know what to expect and can spend time in preventing waste motion on the part of employees and in further improving the system.

The pre-plate blast freezing system for quantity food production must be scaled to the specific needs of the operation, to its purchasing opportunities, and to its ultimate goals. Working out such a system requires the kind of background knowledge this book provides.

Operations of all sizes can profit from a system of preparing foods on-premise for blast freezing. At Hennepin County Medical Center we found the system works very well in smaller hospitals where maximum productivity in terms of meals per labor hour is generally very low. Due to their limited culinary crew, small hospitals usually cannot afford to offer a selective menu.

With preparation and freezing done on-premise, they can produce several entrees using continuous production scheduling which will enable them to make the more popular selective menus available.

But why bother setting up an on-premise, pre-plated blast freezing system? Why not just purchase prepared convenience foods? Analysis of convenience food programs does illustrate that it is possible to achieve the same desirable results. But one has to analyze various cost ramifications as well. Convenience foods have built-in labor costs plus the added labor costs of reconstitution. What staff reductions could be made to offset the additional cost of purchasing these convenience foods? The quality factor must also be considered, undoubtedly as a value judgment made by the potential consumers of foods to be presented in each system.

In a Ready Foods System (the on-premise preparation, packaging, and freezing of foods) all processes can take place on a five-day, one-shift basis. With this type of production, the "ups" and "downs" normally encountered between breakfast and supper are minimized. Instead, in continuous preparation, the cooking and freezing of two or three entrees—with appropriate modifications—is done during each shift for freezer inventory. Patient demands for special diet foods can be met from either a frozen or thawed inventory.

When the demand is properly related to inventory, this can be done without loss of time or effort. Wastage from over-production or the difficulties of underproduction are eliminated. In this system, food production is divorced from the actual meal-to-meal demand from the patient galleys. With a tight product inventory control, there is better cost accountability in relation to number of portions used and number of portions on hand. This, in turn, determines the production scheduling two weeks hence (if two weeks is the storage time allocated for freezer space).

Perhaps the greatest advantage of a Ready Foods System for hotels and restaurants is the possibility of production scheduling which allows weekends off. Qualified chefs are scarce even though the pay scale is high. Often this is due to the long hours required not only for the preparation of regular meals, but for banquets and special parties. Many chef's specialties lend themselves to freezing with only a modification in thickening agents for their basic sauces and gravies. Freezing cream sauce is no longer a problem since the advent of spray dried whey. With this in mind, the master chef can really offer a wide array of choices on his menu. Another advantage of uniform production scheduling is the possibility of reducing the number of chefs necessary. Perhaps duties that now require an assistant chef can be relegated to a kitchen or pantry cook trained by the master chef, but paid at a lower salary level.

Preparing and freezing foods has had a revolutionary impact on the role of the menu maker. The menu maker is a person with considerable responsibility in whose hands lies the making or breaking of a hospital, hotel, restaurant, or cafeteria foodservice operation.

With on-premise preparation for freezing inventory, the production workload is evenly distributed, thus a wide variety of menu selections can be offered. The majority of complaints from chefs and cooks are due to being overworked on certain days and having too little work other days. By divorcing production from service, the menu planner can devote more time to planning garnishes and accompaniments, improving the appearance of food when served.

Menu planning becomes easy in a Ready Foods System as one is able to offer an a la carte style menu even in hospitals, nursing homes, and other institutional foodservice programs where this has not been possible previously.

With a Ready Foods System, a menu planner is able to overcome the following obstacles:

1. Operational handicaps in kitchen equipment and layout.
2. Uneven work flow and workload.
3. Loss of nutrients as items are prepared ahead and left heated in steam tables and ovens.
4. Waste and leftovers, and how to incorporate them within 48 hours.
5. Unappetizing, unattractive menu items resulting from haphazard "crisis" demand.
6. Very high labor costs.

Any decision to adopt a system for on-premise production of food for blast freezing requires an understanding of the many components of such a system. In the following chapters operation-tested data is presented on: the technology of cooking and packaging quantity foods for blast freezing; methods of holding, storing, tempering, and reheating; the kinds of quality control required to insure a desirable end product; and ways of testing systems performance. Much of the food preparation technology is also applicable in a pre-plate and chill system.

To complete this operating blueprint for on-premise blast freezing of food in quantity, a set of recipes with plating instructions has been prepared. It will appear as Volume 2, Blast Freezing Quantity Recipes.

PART 1

Cooking and Packaging Quantity Foods for Blast Freezing

1

The Blast Freezing Process

PRINCIPLES OF FREEZING

Changing liquid water to ice is called freezing. During this process, heat must be taken from the water. In principle, the liquid must first be cooled to its "freezing point"; at that temperature a great deal more heat must be released from the liquid before it changes to a solid.

The primary factor in the freezing of food is the crystallization rate. The rate is expressed in a property called specific heat, measured in BTUs. In the freezing process, the atoms and molecules of a liquid slow down and begin to form regular patterns as crystals. If freezing occurs slowly, large crystals develop. The process, called "heat of fusion," not only produces crystals, but also a change in volume of the frozen product. Since water is the major portion of all food substances, expansion by nearly one-tenth of original volume occurs during freezing.

Once we understand the physical changes that occur during freezing, we realize that improving the quality of frozen foods means controlling the water's heat of fusion and "expandability" effects on the cellular structures. Even though water may freeze at 32°F., it may also be supercooled or taken to a lower temperature before freezing begins.

The diagram below shows what happens to cells cooled at varying rates of speed.

Cooling Rate Effect in Determining Cell Viability— Percentage of Cells Surviving Assault of Low Temperature

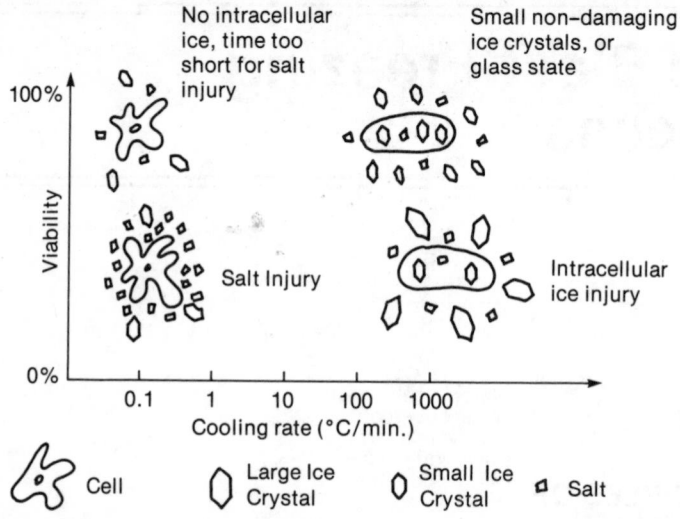

Physical, chemical and structural changes may be wrought by heat removal during any or all of these stages. The transient heat transfer relationship between the cell and its cold environment is illustrated in the diagram. Manipulating this relationship to achieve maximum advantage is the key to preservation of optimum time which directly affects the quality of frozen foods. In the following diagram, what can occur in the way of cell injury, salt concentration, and extra cellular ice, and the influence, or viability, of these factors on the cooling rate, is illustrated. Cells that are frozen slowly have been omitted because they cool too slowly for water to be lost by diffusion.

The following curve illustrating the elements of freeze preservation dynamics is based on factors cited by Dr. Ted Labuza, Professor of Food Science, University of Minnesota, in his lectures on freezing.

Another important factor to remember about freezing is that although pure water freezes at 32°F., foods contain dissolved particles in solution or colloidal suspension which will reduce freezing points to 30°F. to 25°F. Thus, common table salt and water may give a mixture that freezes many degrees below 32°F.

Successful "Freeze–Preservation" Dynamics Curve

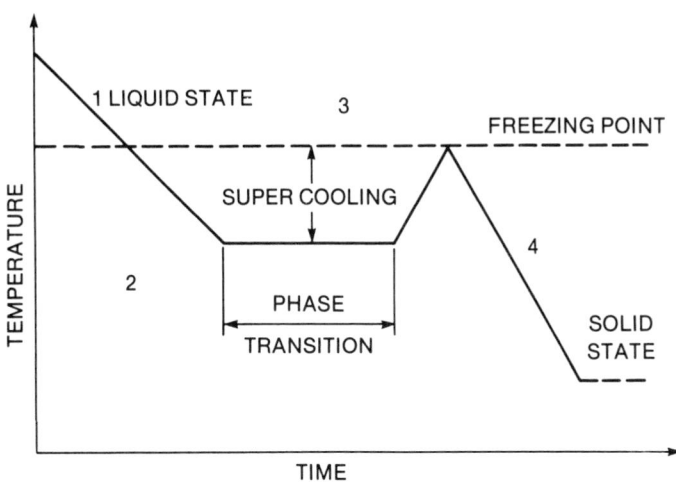

1. Water in cells cools to freezing point.
2. Water supercools.
3. Ice crystals form, usually abruptly, and phase transition goes to completion.
4. Further cooling occurs in solid state.

There are several other factors to bear in mind and/or determine before a successful freezing process can take place. It is essential to have a basic understanding of such properties of the foods involved as moisture content, specific heat, latent heat of fusion, weight, size and/or shape, and ingredient combinations. It is also important to determine the temperature of the product after it is cooked and the temperature when it enters the freezer after packaging.

Based on my experience, in developing a system of blast freezing for pre-plated meals, freezer manufacturers will be able to help you determine data on freezing time to arrive at a good quality frozen product. A majority of the recipes in the following chapters are tested and standardized, and so offer you a place to begin. It is advisable that the cooking time and temperature be followed.

The following table provides good data on the basic properties of food relative to freezing. Also, a sample form of product data is given to assist in the final determination of the freezing time of various foods.

Basic Properties of Food Relative to Freezing Food

Meat & Fish Products:

	% Water	Average Freezing Point, °F.	Specific Heat [Btu/lb. °F.] Above Freezing	Below Freezing	Latent Heat of Fusion Btu/lb.
Bacon	20	—	.50	.30	29
Beef (dried)	5–15	—	.22–.34	.19–.26	7–22
Beef (fresh–lean)	68	29	.77	.40	100
Beef (fresh–fat)	—	28	.60	.35	79
Brined Meats	—	—	.75	—	—
Cut Meats	65	29	.72	.40	95
Hams and Loins	60	27	.68	.38	86.5
Lamb	58	29	.67	.30	83.5
Livers	65.5	29	.72	.40	93.3
Pork (fresh)	60	28	.68	.38	86.5
Pork (smoked)	57	—	.60	.32	—
Poultry (fresh)	74	27	.79	.37	106
Poultry (frozen)	74	27	.79	.37	106
Sausage (casings)	—	—	.60	—	—
Sausage (drying)	65.5	26	.89	.56	93
Sausage (franks)	60	29	.86	.56	86
Sausage (fresh)	65	26	.89	.56	93
Sausage (smoked)	60	25	.86	.56	86
Veal	63	29	.71	.39	91

Fishery Products:

	% Water	Average Freezing Point, °F.	Specific Heat [Btu/lb. °F.] Above Freezing	Below Freezing	Latent Heat of Fusion Btu/lb.
Whole Fish					
Haddock, Cod	78	28	.82	.43	112
Halibut	75	28	.80	.43	108
Tuna	70	28	.76	.41	100
Herring (Kippered)	70	28	.76	.41	100
Herring (smoked)	64	28	.71	.39	92
Salmon	64	28	.71	.39	92
Menhaden	62	28	.70	.38	89

Fish Fillets or Steaks
Haddock, Cod,

Ocean Prch.	80	28	.84	.44	115
Hake, Whiting	82	28	.86	.45	118
Pollock	79	28	.83	.44	113
Mackerel	57	28	.66	.37	82

Shellfish

Scallop Meat	80	28	.84	.44	115
Shrimp	83	28	.86	.45	119
American Lobster	79	28	.83	.44	113
Oysters & Clams					
(meat & liquor)	87	28	.90	.46	125

Vegetables:

Artichokes	83.7	29.1	.87	.45	120
Asparagus	93	29.8	.94	.48	134
Beans (string)	88.9	29.7	.91	.47	128
Beans (lima)	66.5	30.1	.73	.40	94
Beans (dried)	12.5	—	.30	.24	18
Beets	90	31.1	.86	.47	129
Broccoli	89.9	29.2	.92	.47	130
Brussels Sprouts	84.9	31	.88	.46	122
Cabbage	92.4	31.2	.94	.47	132
Carrots	88.2	29.6	.86	.45	126
Cauliflower	91.7	30.1	.93	.47	132
Celery	93.7	29.7	.95	.48	135
Corn (green)	75.5	28.9	.80	.43	108
Corn (dried)	10.5	—	.28	.23	15
Cucumbers	96.1	30.5	.97	.49	137
Eggplant	92.7	30.4	.94	.47	132
Endive (escarole)	93.3	30.9	.94	.48	132
Lettuce	94.8	31.2	.96	.48	136
Mushrooms	91.1	30.2	.93	.47	130
Onions	87.5	30.1	.91	.46	124
Parsnips	78.6	28.9	.84	.46	112
Peas (green)	74.3	30	.79	.42	106
Peas (dried)	9.5	—	.28	.22	14
Peppers (sweet)	92.4	30.1	.94	.47	—
Potatoes (white)	77.8	28.9	.82	.43	111

	% Water	Average Freezing Point, °F.	Specific Heat [Btu/lb. °F.] Above Freezing	Below Freezing	Latent Heat of Fusion Btu/lb.
Potatoes (sweet)	68.5	28.5	.75	.40	97
Pumpkin	90.5	30.1	.92	.47	130
Radishes	93.6	—	.95	.48	134
Rhubarb	94.9	28.4	.96	.48	134
Sauerkraut	89	26	.92	.47	129
Spinach	92.7	30.3	.94	.48	132
Squash	90.5	30.1	.92	.47	130
Tomatoes (green)	94.7	30.4	.95	.48	134
Tomatoes (ripening)	94.1	30.4	.95	.48	134
Turnips	90.9	30.5	.93	.40	137
Vegetables (mixed)	90	30	.90	.45	130

Fruits & Miscellaneous:

	% Water	Average Freezing Point, °F.	Above Freezing	Below Freezing	Latent Heat of Fusion Btu/lb.
Apples	84.1	28.4	.86	.45	121
Apricots	85.4	28.1	.88	.46	122
Avocadoes	94	27.2	.91	.49	136
Bananas	74.8	28	.80	.42	108
Blackberries	85.3	28.9	.88	.46	122
Cantaloupes	92.7	29	.94	.48	132
Cherries	83	26	.87	.45	120
Cranberries	87.4	27.3	.90	.46	124
Currants	84.7	30.2	.88	.45	120
Dates (dry-cured)	20	−4.1	.36	.26	29
Dates (dry-noncured)	20	−4.1	.36	.26	29
Dates (fresh)	78	27.1	.82	.43	112
Figs (fresh)	78	27.1	.82	.43	112
Figs (dried)	24	—	.39	.27	34
Gooseberries	88.3	28.9	.90	.46	126
Grapefruit	88.8	28.4	.91	.46	126
Grapes	81.7	26.3	.86	.44	116
Honeydew Melon	92.6	20	.94	.48	132
Lemons	89.3	28.1	.92	.46	127
Limes	86	29	.89	.46	122
Mangoes	93	32	.90	.46	134
Oranges	87.2	28	.90	.46	124
Peaches	86.9	29.4	.90	.46	124

Pears	83.5	28.5	.86	.45	118
Persimmons	78.2	28.3	.84	.43	112
Pineapples	85.3	29.4	.88	.45	122
Plums	85.7	28	.88	.45	123
Pomegranates	77	28	.87	.48	112
Prunes (fresh)	85.7	28	.88	.45	123
Quinces	85.3	28.1	.88	.45	122
Raspberries	82	30.1	.85	.45	122
Strawberries	90	29.9	.92	.47	129
Watermelons	92.1	29.2	.97	.48	132

Miscellaneous

Beer (wood kegs)	90.2	28	1.0	—	—
Beer (steel kegs)	90.2	28	1.0	—	—
Bread	35.5	18–20	.74	.34	47
Butter	15	30.0	.64	.34	15
Cheese (American)	55	17	.64	.36	79
Cheese (Camembert)	60	18	.70	.40	86
Cheese (Limburger)	60	19	.70	.40	86
Cheese (Roquefort)	55	3	.65	.32	79
Cheese (Swiss)	55	15	.64	.36	79
Chocolate (Coating)	0.5	95–85	.30	.55	40
Cream (40%)	55	28	.85	.40	90
Eggs (crated)	73	27	.76	.40	100
Eggs (frozen)	—	27	—	.41	100
Honey	18	—	.35	.26	26
Ice Cream	67	27–0	.78	.45	96
Lard	—	—	.52	—	—
Maple Sugar	5	—	.24	.21	7
Maple Syrup	36	—	.49	.31	52
Milk	87.5	31	.93	.49	124
Nuts (dried)	3–10	—	.21–.29	.19–.24	4.3–14
Oleomargarine	—	—	.48	—	—
Candy	—	—	.93	—	—
Flour	13.5	—	.38	.28	—

Sample Form for Collecting Product Data
for Freezing

PRODUCT SPECIFICATIONS BEFORE AND AFTER COOKING

1. Dimensions _____ × _____ ; or _____ diameter
   × _____ height
2. Raw Product Weight _____ oz.
3. Water content—calculate from the recipe:

Basic Material	Percentage of Total	Cost Per Pound	Cost Factor	Water Content	Total Water Content
a. _____	_____ %	$ _____	$ _____	_____ %	_____ %
b. _____	_____ %	$ _____	$ _____	_____ %	_____ %
c. _____	_____ %	$ _____	$ _____	_____ %	_____ %
d. _____	_____ %	$ _____	$ _____	_____ %	_____ %
e. _____	_____ %	$ _____	$ _____	_____ %	_____ %
f. _____	_____ %	$ _____	$ _____	_____ %	_____ %
g. _____	_____ %	$ _____	$ _____	_____ %	_____ %

100%

$

Raw Product
Cost

%

Water Content
Raw Material

4. Final Product Temperature—Cooking
   a. Cook Method: _____ type of oil _____
   b. Cook Cycle: _____
   c. Weight Loss: _____
   d. Water loss, if known _____ %
   e. Cooking Temperature _____ °F.
   f. Product Temperature

   Equilibrated _____ °F.
   Internal   _____ °F. (Indicate Which)

With the basic product data at hand, one can easily calculate the amount of time required to freeze the food. According to Glew[1], Plank's equation can be used to determine this time. The example given is as follows:

Product Data—Creamed Potato

Density (p) of creamed potato $= 8.64 \times 10^3\,Kg/m^3$

Latent heat of water $(L_w) = 3.85 \times 10^{4\circ}\,C$

Proportion of water in creamed potato $= 80\%$.

Thermal conductivity (K) of frozen creamed potato is $1.06\ W/m^2$ ($^\circ C/M$) and for thawed creamed potato is $0.58\ W/m^2 (^\circ C/M)$

Heat transfer coefficient (h) of a lidded tray of creamed potato in air circulating at 5 m per sec $= 14.2\ W/M^{20}C$

Product temperature after cooking $= 80^\circ C$

Blast freezer air speed = 5 m per sec at $.25^\circ C$

Plank's Equation:

Step (1) $\dfrac{L_w \times p}{0_1 - 0_2} = \dfrac{3.85 \times 10^4 \times 0.80 \times 8.64 \times 10^3}{0 - (-25)} = 1.06 \times 10^7$

As the equation is concerned only with the heat involved in the freezing process 0_1 is taken as OC

Step (2) $\dfrac{a}{h} + \dfrac{a^2}{2}K = \dfrac{9 \times 10^{-3}}{14.2} \times \dfrac{81 \times 10^{-6}}{2 \times 1.06} = 6.72 \times 10^{-4}$

Step (3) $1 = 0.007\ (O_h - 0_1) = 1 + 0.007\ (80 - 0) = 1.56$

$T = (1.06 \times 10^7) \times (6.72 \times 10^{-4}) \times 1.56$

$T = 11,112$ sec or 185 minutes

From the above formula, it becomes clear that the time of freezing can be shortened if we change the following factors in the equation:

1. The density of the potato, since it affects the amount of water available in the potato, which relates to the specific latent heat. Therefore, in choosing the variety of potato for freezing and reheating it is best to select one that has a less compact cellular structure, or one with less water content, preferably one where density is almost within 80% of total composition.

2. Thermal conductivity of the creamed potato can be increased if the potatoes are either sliced or diced, yielding more surface area for heat transfer.

3. Blast freezer air speed can be changed according to the product entry temperature. If the food product after cooking goes through a blast chilling process prior to freeze processing, the initial heat flow is lower and the air speed can be reduced. This process controls the amount of dehydration in the food being frozen. The principle by which the blast freezer operates, using the air as a heat transfer media from the food to the coil tubes containing freon, affects the degree of moisture loss from the food.

Quick freezing equipment is a must to remove heat from foods after preparation effectively and rapidly. There are substantial advantages in quick freezing. These include: avoiding undesirable changes in palatability (texture and form); reduced flavor transferance; reduced nutrient loss; decreased bacterial count; and reduction in the "drip." Most meat products suffer from a "drip" caused by the movement of the water and salts or minerals in colloidal suspension from the inside to the outside of the cells. If freezing occurs at a slow rate, the water and solute freeze outside of the inner cellular structure instead of inside the cells, causing considerable damage. The speed of freezing, expressed in time as it relates to the development of the size of the ice crystals, has an important role in the final texture of the food.

BLAST FREEZING

Since heat must be removed at the fastest rate possible if frozen foods are to meet quality standards, blast freezing is the recommended process for quantity production. Understanding the elements of this process is essential. Blast freezing is defined by Rappole[2] as air freezing. It is one of the oldest and most economical systems to operate. A blast freezer is very easy to operate; food in individual plates or in bulk pans has only to be placed on wire shelving inside the interior of the cabinet for processing. The freezer cabinet is insulated and has a watercooled compressor. The freezing coil maintains an air temperature range from $-10°$ F. to $-40°$ F. when the temperatures of the product to be frozen are between 150°F. to 160°F. To maintain high product sanitation, the hot product must be reduced in temperature from 140°F. to 40°F. as rapidly as possible. Individual preplated meals should be frozen within a 60 to 90 minute period.

To maintain good quality in products being frozen, freezer manufacturers recommend that an ice front penetration rate of ½ in. per hour be accomplished. Based on the experiment performed at the Risley project,[3] it was discovered that in a Bally Still Air "Sharp" freezer, it required 2-½ to 3 hours to bring the multi-portion packs and 51 minutes to bring the single portion through the incubation danger zone (140° to 40°F.). It was concluded that the products, despite their long time in the danger zone, were safe based on the bacteriological studies performed, as long as the following operational criteria were followed:

1. Purchase of quality raw food with low microbial count.
2. Equipment for processing, plating, etc., selected to lend itself to good work flow, be easy to sanitize, and suitable for the operation. This processing equipment should not be shared anywhere else in the kitchen, especially with raw food preparation.
3. Preparation or processing techniques used by personnel need to be closely supervised and a minimum of direct handling of either the food or the equipment must be achieved.
4. Packaging prior to freezing has to be accomplished with maximum sanitation techniques. All utensils, equipment, or other supplies must be sanitized at all times. The sauces and gravies must be maintained at 180°F. to kill as many organisms as possible.

Also at the Risley project mentioned above, a regular Foster Holding Freezer was utilized to bring the product temperature down through the incubation danger zone. It too was declared satisfactory although it took 67.5 minutes to chill single portion packs. With the use of a blast freezer or blast freezer tunnel, it has been deduced that the ideal length of time that food can remain in the danger zone is 30 to 45 minutes for a preplate. As a general rule of thumb, frozen food, in 1 inch deep steam table foil pans, should be frozen to a temperature below 0°F. as quickly as possible, preferably in less than two hours, to minimize the formation of large ice crystals. If it takes longer than this, quality becomes a problem.

A majority of the recipes in Volume 2, Blast Freezing Quantity Recipes, call for a freezing time of two hours or less for bulk portioned items. Based on the panning criteria set up, no product more than 2 inches in depth or thickness is frozen. Since blast freezing is dependent upon the air velocity in cooling the products' temperature, it is a good rule not to exceed 2 to 2½ inches in depth.

Air circulation around each product should be adequate for maximum exposure to the cooling air in the freezer. For freezing, wire baskets are suggested for the preplates. Preplates can also be placed directly on wire shelves in the freezer cabinet.

A sample of specifications for an efficient blast freezer suitable for an operation producing 2500 to 5000 meals per day, with a product inventory of 10 to 14 days, appears in the appendix. These were the specifications for the freezer used for product testing and freezing that forms the basis of this book.

OPERATING AND MAINTAINING
A BLAST FREEZER

Satisfactory results from a blast freezer are assured only if proper operating and maintenance procedures are followed. Key points include:

1. Food to be frozen in a blast freezer should not have more than 75% to 80% moisture content. If moisture content is higher, the rate of freezing will not be adequate to bring the temperature of the center of the product down to −10°F. in less than an hour. If there is more than that amount of water in the product, the greater number of BTU's to be removed from the product requires a longer time in the danger zone.

2. Food to be frozen in a blast freezer should be formulated to a size, shape, weight, and configuration conducive to fast heat transfer. As an example, specs for chicken were changed from quarters to eighths. With eighths, there are no protrusions or irregular lumps that during the freezing would slow down the freezing rate. Such a slowdown would affect the rest of the components of the preplates.

3. Food to be frozen should have a higher ratio or percentage of solids. This will produce a good quality and stable product, especially after the storage and

A 3-door blast freezer for use in quantity production of frozen foods.

thawing processes. The increased use of evaporated milk instead of fresh milk, or meat stock instead of plain water will achieve the desired higher percentage of solids.

4. Food to be frozen in a blast freezer should be panned, plated and packaged based on the method of reheating to be used and the length of time the product will stay in freezer storage. The product depth should not exceed 2½ inches when using the half size pans that have been recommended in this book. The packaging design should be such that the shelf life of the product can be maintained for at least six months without undue damage to quality or microbial growth and contamination.

5. Food to be frozen in a blast freezer should be vacuum packaged or Cryovac processed and heat-sealed tightly, if economics warrant the extra expense for this packaging equipment. Since air is such a poor medium for heat transfer, any amount of air left inside causes a longer cooling down period and freezing time. For this reason almost full packing into a bulk pan to eliminate space for air is a recommended procedure. A tight heat sealing, together with suction vacuum packaging, will certainly insure a good quality precooked frozen product.

6. Food to be frozen should be placed in the blast freezer cabinet as soon as it has been prepared and packaged. There must not be any delay in the flow from processing to freezing.

7. Food to be frozen in a blast freezer that needs to be cut or sliced into serving portions coming from a large food mass, such as roast beef, turkey or pork, must be chilled quickly to 40°F. through a convected air chill refrigerator. In so doing, the meat drip from juices will be cut to a minimum. It will also prevent exposure of the roasts to the growth and development of bacteria which thrive in the mesophilic temperature range of 60°F. to 110°F. The meat slicer used for the roast must be sanitized after every three to four hours of slicing time as micro-organism build-up has been shown to be more than 10 to 4000 organisms per gram at the end of such a period.

8. Freezer preventive maintenance should be carried out as close to twice a month as possible. The blast freezer should be checked daily not only for temperature but for moisture condensation and freon levels. The freezer should have an alternate compressor for emergencies. It is practical and economical in the long run to have an alarm buzzer that rings if the freezer temperature rises to the danger zone.

9. To maintain adequate air circulation around the product, foods to be frozen in a blast freezer must be placed either in wire baskets or directly on the freezer shelving with no sheet pans, etc. under the product. Products should be placed at least two feet below light bulbs to prevent heat penetration.

The blast freezing process as clarified here is the foundation of the system described in subsequent chapters.

2

Equipment, Materials Used in On-Premise Blast Freezing System

Before considering the necessary basic equipment for successful on-premise freezing, you should evaluate the existing preparation and cooking areas. Is the kitchen adequately equipped with the tools and materials necessary for successful food production?

To learn the answer, first list the equipment available in the present kitchen. Indicate equipment you seldom use and that which needs repair or replacement. Many foodservice kitchens are either overequipped or under-utilized.

Why such widespread deficiencies in planning? Usually the lack of synchronization with the menu is the primary factor. For the menu dictates the efficiency of a kitchen as related to tool and equipment utilization. The importance of the menu plan, with its corresponding standardized recipes and portion control, can never be underestimated when it comes to equipping the kitchen. Various factors, such as the *type of menu, style,* and *the number of persons to be fed,* determine the type, size, and quantity of each piece of equipment needed in a kitchen.

Another important criteria is the degree or stage at which the food is purchased which, in turn, depends on cost economics and quality decisions. The Raw-to-Ready Scale, as shown in the accompanying chart, suggests which piece of equipment will be necessary to handle the various stages of pre-preparation that will be purchased.

A decision to buy a hamburger pattying machine might be cost effective if a production run of over 10,000 patties per day is projected. On the other hand, in that quantity it might be just as economical to purchase preportioned hamburger patties from the market.

An equally important consideration is the cost and availability of labor with the skills required for use of the equipment and tools. It is necessary to determine the cost of labor to evaluate the pros and cons of purchasing foods already prepared or precooked, or of starting from scratch, as shown in the Raw-to-Ready Scale.

A small institutional kitchen to be used for a cook and chill or freeze operation should be outfitted with the following basic equipment:

Shelving, dry storage

Refrigerator-Freezer combination (self-defrosting freezer preferable)

Freezer 12-16 cu.ft. (for storage)

Range, Electric or Gas, with four burners or two burners with a grill

Oven, single or double cavity

Deep Fat Fryer

Steam Cooker

Mixer, bench or portable

Blender

Work Table

Pot and Pan Sink with Garbage Disposal Unit

Dishwashing Machine

Service Carts

The tools necessary to produce a simple menu include:

A. *Basic Preparation*

Knives—French, paring, bread, butcher, and slicing

Spatulas—griddle, butter, and sandwich

Food scrapers

Ladles—dipper type, flat with slotted surface

RAW-TO-READY SCALE

COMPONENTS	1	2	3	4	5	6	7	8	9	10
FRUITS AND VEGETABLES	Raw Fruits Raw Greens		Frozen Fruits & vegetables		Pre-washed greens (ready to toss) Pre-washed, cleaned & cut fruits & veg.		Dehydrated fruits & veg. Canned fruits & vegetables	Frozen Juice concentrate	Freeze dried onions & parsley	Indv. portions Juices Fruits Vegetables Indv. Salads
POTATOES AND RICE				Processed Potatoes				Dehydrated potatoes Texturized Protein (bontrae)		Frozen/Canned Potatoes
SOUP ENTREES Beef Fish Poultry Eggs		Portion cut meats Stews Ground Beef Diced Chicken Pulled chicken pieces	Frozen fish Frozen eggs			Freeze Dried Eggs	Pre-fabricated portion cut pre-cut meats poultry	Frozen ready to bake or fry fish & poultry & beef entrees	Omelets, pancakes French toast, Waffles Freeze dried meats Freeze dried salads Canned or froz. sauces/gravy	Froz. Eggs Indv. Ready to serve: Soups Cereals Ready-to-serve potatoes

COMPONENTS	1	2	3	4	5	6	7	8	9	10
BAKERY COMPONENTS FOR BAKED GOODS & PUDD. FOR SPECIAL DIETS	Paygel flour Sugar Butter Milk				Ice Cream Mix			Pre-prepared mixes such as cakes and cookies	Pre-formed cookies Canned Pudding Froz. Bread, dinner rolls & sweet rolls	Indv. desserts Indv. Portion Spices Creamer Mustard Catsup Dressings Gelatine
DESSERTS PUDDINGS BREAD & ROLLS	LoNa Milk								Frozen pies	
BEVERAGES	Coffee								Freeze dried coffee Cocoa Mix Instant Tea Fruit Drink Mixes	Beverages

In the above graphic presentation, components are defined in the "raw to ready scale" as their use is visualized in the Ready Food System.

Large Spoons and Basting Spoon

French Whip made of heavy wire in two sizes and lengths (6″ and 12″)

Pastry Blender and Wheel, Pastry Cloth

Scoops—flour, sugar

Scales—1 gram, 10 lb. graduated in quarter ounces

Thermometers—meat, oven, candy, and deep fat fry

Chopping Boards, plastic (3)—for raw meat/poultry, for cooked items, for vegetables and fruits

Measuring Containers—1 cup, 2 cups, 1 quart, 1 gallon

Measuring Spoons—¼ teaspoon to 2 tablespoons

Mixing Bowls—round, straight-sided mixing bowls with following sizes: ¾ qt. and 1½ qts.

Scoops—No. 8 (8 oz.), No. 10 (4 oz.), No. 12 (2⅓ oz.)

Rolling Pins—2 sizes

Strainers, Sieves, and Colanders

Graters, Shredders, Dicers

Funnels and Sifters

Can Opener—electric, manual

Garlic Press

Nut Chopper

Apple Peeler/Corer and Slicer

Kitchen Scissors

Pepper Mill

B. *Cooking Area*

Pie Pans

Bun Pans 18″ × 26″

Cookie Sheets

Roasting Pans 18″ × 24″ × 4½″ deep

Baking Pans—full size (12″ × 20″ × 2½″ deep), half size, third size, quarter size, sixth size

Stock Pots—2 quart, 2 gallon

Paddle, stainless steel

Muffin Pans

Cake Pans

Ceramic Baking Dishes—round, square, and rectangular

Kitchen Timer

Kitchen Spoons and Tongs

Food Blanchers and Steamer

Double Boiler

C. *Freezing and Packaging Equipment and Materials*

Freezer Baskets made of aluminum with stainless steel wire

Plastic Dishpans for small items

Waterproof Felt–tip Pens

Aluminum Foil Sheets

Freezer Foil—polyethylene coated

Freezer Bags—polyethylene coated paper

Aluminum Foil Sheets for entree—disposable 5″ ×7″ with rounded corners

Freezer Food Wrap 14″ × 24″ 100 gauge perforated PVC (polyvinylidine chloride) treated for use in Anchor shrink wrap machine

Freezer Food Wrap 700 sheets/roll 18″ × 24″ 50 gauge perforated PVC treated for use in shrink wrap machine

Aluminum Foil Steam Table Pans half size 12-¾″ × 10-3/8″ × 2″

Portable heat sealer (electric iron on a warm setting is acceptable)

Shrink Wrap Machine—Model A5W (small unit, approximate cost $500) by Anchor Film Company in Webster Groves, Missouri, with dimensions: length 29″, width 22″, height 23″, tunnel opening of 20″ x 8″, belt speed 13 FPM, 20 amps 110 volts.

To determine the size, production capacity and quantity of equipment needed requires knowledge of the final menu and the type of ingredients to be purchased. The latter can be determined from the Raw–to–Ready Scale table.

As the volume of meals increases, it is necessary to evaluate each piece of preparation equipment to determine if it is adequate to produce the required number of meals. It has been argued that one of the disadvantages of a Ready Foods System is the large capital investment necessary. In an article, "Basic Planning Concepts for Ready Foods Systems," Michael Pinkert[1] of Gordon Friesen International contends that a ready foodservice concept does not necessarily require more capital and space than a conventional system. He cites four areas of possible savings:

1. Each piece of equipment is used at maximum efficiency during each shift. rather than just before specific meal periods.

2. Producing fewer items but larger batches on a given shift allows more efficient use of space, less frequent sanitizing of equipment, and fewer pieces of equipment.

3. Low and normal temperature storage areas are more efficient in space utilization, both vertically and horizontally, than production equipment such as fryers, ranges, and kettles that cannot be stacked.

4. Holding or serving equipment, such as steam tables, range tops or food warmers are unnecessary, thus reducing capital investment in these areas.

Along with the basic menu plan, six additional checks should be made before the kitchen layout and design is completed. The steps are as follows:

1. Determine labor requirements and automated equipment costs in relation to labor costs to see if an automated line is necessary and practical. Will ingredients be purchased in a raw, a semi-processed, a ready to combine, or a fully prepared stage? The cost of the automated equipment plus the labor cost in using it should not exceed the purchased cost of these food items at the desired pre-prepared state. The net savings from the purchase of automated equipment should be amortized in less than five years. (This is the rate of amortization used by most successful food corporations.)

2. Be sure production scheduling results in a sensible flow pattern of raw materials: from receiving to processing to packaging to the quick freeze units and, finally, to freezer storage. Handling should be kept to a minimum. Any delay in the flow pattern can affect not only the quality of the frozen products but their safety in terms of microbial growth and contamination.

3. Maximize the use of processing and packaging materials, such as oil, liquid nitrogen, freon, utilities—and even by-products of processing such as grease or meat drippings—that can be sold, or utilized in some other processing steps.

4. Stage and evaluate the plan through industrial engineering devices, such as time and motion studies, work simplification techniques, cross chart, ISO cost curves, and visual transformation of schedules into bar charts.

5. Next, allocate space for various production centers, depending on the product load schedule and turnover for each piece of equipment. Base co-location or proximity of equipment on the flow pattern, to prevent backtracking, crisscrossing, or bottleneck areas.

6. Be sure space dimensions are adequate for the needs of people, equipment, materials, aisle movement, and other factors necessary for the comfort and safety of the employees.

If the volume of meals does not justify the cost of automated equipment, it is practical to use smaller scale preparation equipment and produce continuous batches. Producing continuous batches with maximum utilization of equipment results in improved employee productivity.

A potential problem is that foodservice equipment is not of standard and uniform size. During our initial planning, I developed a cart to accommodate various sizes of steam table pans, bun pans, and baskets as shown in the following sketch:

Material Handling Cart

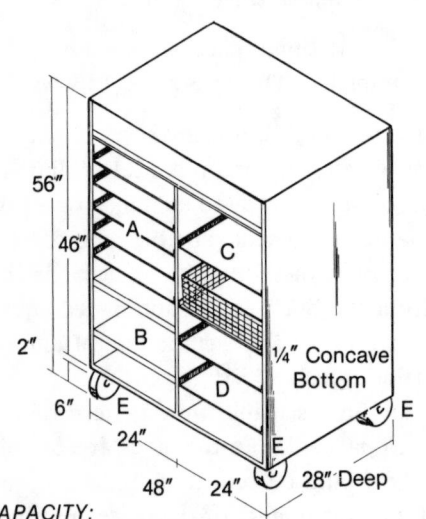

KEY:

A = 12"×21"×5" Patient Trays
B = 18"×26"   Bun Pan
C = 21"×28"   Wire Shelves
D = 21 (L) × 13 (W) × 10 (H)
    Nesting Wire S.T. Pan Basket
    (Angle extends in
    approximately 2")
E = Casters Metro Sealed Bearing
    "B" Series, 6" NSF
    or
    BL6 Series NSF
    or
    5" Swivel

CAPACITY:

Baskets	16 (12" centers)
Shelves	8 (12" centers)
Bun Pans	18 (5" centers)
Trays	45 Maximum

Equipment manufacturers, kitchen designers, and foodservice operators should resolve the problem of a uniform standard material handling module to offset ever-increasing labor costs. The impact of modular handling equipment is even greater in a Ready Foods System. Where food is prepared and frozen as soon as possible, the relationship of the size of the cart to the batch size is very important. There should be minimum time between the end of production and processing and freezing. A standard materials handling module could prevent the uneven, unpredictable delays that occur with resulting losses in time and motion economy.

Based on a 10,000 meals per day production schedule, as process procedures and workload schedules were finally defined by our design consultants, Kitchen & Cain,[2] we arrived at the following equipment schedule at Hennepin County Medical Center. A list of Group III equipment was later developed by the Central Food Facility Staff after some basic changes to make the kitchen flexible in production and capabilities.

Equipment Schedule[3]
Based On 3 Million Meals Per Year
(11,000 Meals Per Day)

Receiving/Storage/Pre-Preparation

Quantity	Description	Manufacturer	Model
1	Bench Scale	Berkel	1021/250
2	Portable Floor Scales 250#/cap.	Berkel	1121/250
2	Portable Floor Scales 500#/cap.	Berkel	1121/500
1	Recessed Scale 1000#/cap.	Berkel	5121/1000
1	Table, Rubber (meat cutting)	John Boos	Style M
1	Meat Saw	Berkel	V-14
13	Shelving (Meat Thaw Room)	Metropolitan Wire	
12	Shelving (fruit and veg.)	Metropolitan Wire	
5	Shelving (dairy cooler 18×60)	Metropolitan Wire	
35	Shelving (dry storage)	Metropolitan Wire	
9	Shelving (sanitation supplies)	Metropolitan Wire	
1	Vegetable Cutter	Qualheim	440
1	Vegetable Washer	Groen	GA1
1	Can Opener	Edlund	
1	Can Washer	Edlund	
5	Slop Sinks, 3-3 comp. 2-1 comp	Powell Co.	SS3-24726
1	Utility Washing Unit	Kewanee	
1	Knife Sharpener	Edlund	390
2	Hand Wash Sinks 1 stn.	Powell Co.	
1	Work Table 36×20	Powell Co.	

Ingredient Control Room

Quantity	Description	Manufacturer	Model
1	Desk Chair		
1	Spice Bins	Powell	SSBS8 SSBS10
5	Ingredient Bins	Rubbermaid	3649
2	Work Tables	Lincoln	1-6582

Receiving/Storage/Pre-Preparation [Cont'd]

Quantity	Description	Manufacturer	Model
1	Scales over & under (1 test kitchen)	Berkel	247
2	Scales over & under (pre-prep room)	Berkel	247
4	Scales over & under (2 pre-plate) (2 bulk-plate)	Berkel	247
1	Mixer (20 qt.)	Blakeslee	
1	Desk and Chair		
1	Under Counter Refrig.	Hobart	
1	Under Counter Dishwasher	Hobart	

Production

Quantity	Description	Manufacturer	Model
2	Revolving Rack Ovens	Despatch	BTF3–15T
4	Racks for Revolving Ovens	Despatch	DOB–B
1	80-qt. Mixer	Hobart	L800
1	Fryer	J. C. Pitman	18
1	Broiler	Sani–Serv	B–174
1	Exhaust Hood for Broiler	Duo–Aire	
2	Steamers	Market Forge	Jet D
2	Tilting Braising Pan	Groen	HFP/1–2
1	Work Table 30″ ×72″	Powell	SSTS310
1	Water Meter	Hatco	111
2	Jacketed Kettles—cook and cool (60 gal.)	Groen	DN60
2	Kettle 125 gal.	Groen	DN125
2	Jacketed Kettles—cook and cool (100 gal.)	Groen	DN100
2	Agitators	Groen	DN101
3	Basket Inserts	Groen	DN102
3	Insert Holder	Groen	DN103
1	Hoist	Wright	2101200
1	Trolley	Wright	1600010
1	S.S. monorail	Wright	NA
1	Heat Exchanger	S.T. Regis	F2
1	Pump	Haskon	300
	S/S Pipe Fittings		
4	Liquid Transfers	Cherry	

16	Self-levelling Dish Dispensers	Dyna	DL-20K
550	Bun Pans	Cres-Cor	
200	Bun Pans	Cres-Cor	
14	Racks for Heated Cabinets	Cres-Cor	
61	Racks for Heated Cabinets	Cres-Cor	201-1812
40	Plastic Tubs	Container Devlp. Corp.	SM3022-6

Pre-Plate Line

1	Conveyor Belt (denester)	Dake	
	Automatic Food Dispenser	Haskon	300 MC
	Film Wrapper	3M	211D
	Labeller/Coder	Avery	8
	T-Shelf for Discharge Loader	Raque	
2	Work Tables (30×72)	Powell	
5	Work Tables (30×60)	Powell	SSTS35
1	Pre-plate Freezer	Union Carbide	
	Bulk Line—Conveyor Belt (5′)	Conveyor Specialties	Custom
1	Bulk Line—Food Depositor	Haskon	
1	Bulk Line—Freezer	Teckton	
1	Bulk Line—Conveyor (5′)		Custom
1	Lidder	Ekco	123-B
1	Coders and Set of Characters		8
1	Conveyor	Metalers	ST2650-1
1	Taping Machine	Hamilton	100
5,000	Wire Baskets	Metropolitan Wire	

Pre-Plate Bulk

1	Fork Lift Truck	Yale	
1	Battery Charger	Yale	
1	Hand Transporter	Market Forge	
315	Pallets	Yancy Lumber Co.	

Salad, Sandwich, and Dessert Area

1	Booster Heater	Hobart	
1	Water Meter	Hatco	111
1	Work Table (96 × 30)		
1	Work Table (96 × 30)	Powell	
1	Juice Dispenser	Vitality	W-900A

Salad, Sandwich, and Dessert Area (cont'd.)

Quantity	Description	Manufacturer	Model
1	Soft Ice Cream Maker	Taylor	B–741–22
1	Sandwich Line Conveyor	Crimsco	AL50–24
14	Mobile Self–levelling dish carts	Dyna	DL–20C
1	Bread Buttering Mach.	Galapak	DL–22C
2	Work Tables (48×30)	Custom fabrication	
4	Work Tables	Powell	SSTS310
1	Sandwich Wrapper	Anchor	Q–P Tri–Sealer
1	Condiment Machine	Portion Pkg.	7104
2	Slicers	Hobart	1725RPM
1	Slicer	Berkel	818
1	Mobile Slicer Stand	Seco	3424
1	Mixer (60 qt.)	Hobart	L600
	Work Table (48×24)	Seco	

Test Kitchen

1	Broiler	General Electric	
1	Deep Fat Fryer	J.C. Pitman	18
1	Steam Cooker	Hobart	275A
1	Convention Oven	Montague	
1	Microwave Oven	Litton	550SB
1	Toaster (4 slice)	Savory	
1	Blender	Hobart	
1	Blast Freezer & Compressor	Hobart	
1	Mixer—12 qt.	Hobart	

Trayline

	Make-up Conveyor	Lincoln	
1	Tray Dispenser	Lincoln	Custom
1	Cart Support w/plate slides	Lincoln	
14	Self–Levelling dispensers, Condiment and Silverware Tables	Lincoln	
1	Sink	Lincoln	
4	Weigh Off Table	L–60108	
3	Stand for Drying 40 Trays	L PDC–40	

Sanitizing And Dishwashing

1	Kitchen Cooler	Custom	
1	Centralized Cleaning	Economics	
	System	Lab	Custom
1	50-ft. Dish Machine	Hobart	
1	Cart Washer, 2 to 3 Carts/min.	Champion	
1	Pot and Pan Washer	Metalwash	RS-30A
1	Pot and Pan Sink (18′)		
2	Pot and Pan Misc.		
	Utensils Racks	Seco	8974
	Pallet Washing	Metalwash	

Group III/Sub Group A
Equipment Schedule
Preparation & Cooking Equipment

Quantity	*Description*
1	Blender—1 gal.
13	Blenders—44 oz.
5	Can Openers, manual
1	Can Opener, electric
5	Can Opener Cleaning Brushes
10	Colanders
15	Knives—10″
12	Knives, grapefruit
6	Knife Holder
14	Hand Can Openers
2	Knives, roast beef slicers
48	Knives, paring
9	Knives, s/s blades
30	Knives, utility
25	Thermometers, 0–350°
6	Cook's Forks—14″
12	Cook's Forks—12″
4	Kitchen Forks—s/s
18	Cutting Boards—18″×24″×1″
4	Cutting Boards—12″×18″×1½″
15	Can Punch & Bottle Openers

Quantity	*Description*
12	Plastic Ice Scoops—2 oz.
2	Plastic Utility Scoops—2 qt.
36	Food Storage Boxes—18″×26″×9″
36	Lids, to fit above
12	Food Storage Boxes—12½″×24½″
12	Lids to fit above
30	Food Storage Boxes—18″×26″×15″
30	Lids to fit above
36	Food Storage Containers, round
36	Lids to fit above
4	Grater and Shredders
8	Mixing Bowls—¾ qt.
16	Mixing Bowls—1½ qt.
8	Mixing Bowls—4 qt.
4	Mixing Bowls—8 qt.
1	Mixer—Domestic
1	Meat Grinder Attachment for above
36	Oven Mitts—15″
2	Paddles—alum. 45″
2	Paddles—alum. 53″
66	Trays—18″×26″×1″
9	Bun Pans—18″×26″×1 1/8″
40	Bun Pans—18″×26″×1″
4	Food Container Pans—21¾″×6 1/8″ (24 qts.)
40	Meat Loaf Pans—16″×4″×4″
6	Roast Pans—alum. 18″×24″×4½″
6	Roast Pans—alum. with clips 18″×24″×4½″
12	Sauce Pans w/covers—1 ½ qts., alum.
8	Sauce Pans w/covers—2 ¾ qts., alum.
8	Sauce Pans w/covers—4 ½ qts., alum.
24	Steam Table Pans—perforated ¼″ holes
24	Perforated Handi-Pans—¼″ holes, 4″ deep
12	Perforated Handi-Pans—¼″ holes, 6″ deep
5	Apple Parers, s/s
4	Pitchers—4 1/8 qt.
30	Sandwich Spreaders, s/s
6	Egg Slicers
1	Lemon Sectioner

1	Onion Slicer—3/8″ slices
1	Tomato Slicer—¼″ slices
10	Skimmers, s/s
24	Spatulas
60	Spoons
36	Spoons, perforated—13¼″
6	China Cap Strainers, s/s
6	China Cap Strainers, fine mesh
6	Heavy Duty Wire Strainers—10 1/8″
12	Strawberry Hullers
18	Cake Turners—3″×8″ blade
8	Turners—offset pancake
8	French Whips—12″ long
8	French Whips—18″ long
8	French Whips—24″ long
6	Clean-up Brushes—5″×5½″

Group III/Sub Group B
Equipment Schedule
Quality Control Equipment

Quantity	Item	Description
1	OHAUS Moisture Balance Calculator	Moisture determination system OHAUS capacity, 610 grams; tare 200 gms., sensitivity 0.1 gram. Modified triple beam balance w/adjustable infra red heat lamp, designed for routine percent moisture analysis where a more expensive analysis is unnecessary. Percent moisture is obtained to 0.1% by use of a moisture calculator. Temperature range is 120%F. with 250 watt lamp. For 115 volt, 50/60 cycle A.C.
1	Fat Tester Direct Reading	Hobart Model F—101 Calibrated in grams. Capacity 5000 grams or 11.1 pounds. Accurate to 1 gram. Finished in corrosion-resistant white enamel. Stainless steel platform measures 9 × 9 ¾. Tare beam, poise and other external parts are chrome plated.

Quantity	Item	Description
1	pH Meter	Digital Readout, with Combination electrode, Orion, Model 601, Scientific Products, #H5792-1
1	Viscometer	Brookfield, Model LUT
1	Bacteria Kit	Portable, Swab Test Kit, PB 427 Millipore Corp. 20 units/kit

Group III/Sub Group C
Equipment Schedule
Sanitation, Warewashing, & Miscellaneous

Quantity	Description
6	Dishwashing Machine Brushes—nylon bristles, 3″
3	Dishwasher Spray Arm Brushes—36″
8	Floor Brushes—16″ sweep
4	Hi-Lo Scrub Brushes, plastic bristles
8	Kettle Drain Valve Brushes—26″ length, 1 3/8″ dia.
4	Long Handle Clean-up Brushes—20″ handle
2	Oven Brush/Scrapers
18	Pastry Brushes—nylon, 3″ width
12	Sanitary Bowl Mops
1	Swivel Head, Large Tank Brush—36″ plastic handle
6	Vegetable Brushes, oval
21	Utility Brushes—4″ handle, 10″ brush
10	Sweeping Brooms, upright
19	Dust Pans
6	Grip All Mop Holders—18″
5	Grip All Mop Holders—36″
2	Floor Buffer-Scrubbers—brush size 19″
2	Pad Holders—19″ brush size
1	Floor Scrubbing Pads
5	Floor Squeegees—24″
12	Squeegee Blades—24″
8	Floor Squeegees—18″
15	Squeegee Blades—18″
13	Floor Squeegee Handles

4	Window Squeegees—14"
8	Window Squeegee Blades—14"
4	Window Squeegees—12"
6	Mop Buckets—44 qt.
2	Mop Buckets—1 gallon
2	Twin Mopping Outfits—chassis w/two 11-gal. buckets
8	Mop Wringers—medium for 24 oz. mop heads
13	Mop Handles
3	Wet/Dry Vacuums—1.5 HP
3	Attachments for Wet/Dry Vacuum
1	Upright Vacuum Cleaner—½ hp motor
1	Attachment Caddy
21	Trash Containers—44 gal.
1	Trash Container—56 gal.
12	"Untouchable" Containers—23 gal.
19	Waste Baskets
24	Pistol Grip Spray Bottles—16 oz.
12	Deodorizing Screens for Urinals
29	Hand Towel Dispenser for C-fold towels
4	Sanitary Napkin Dispenser, coin-operated
29	Soap Dispensers
12	Toilet Paper Dispensers
4	Shower Curtains—6' × 6'
4	Litter Caddys
12	Plastic Aprons, heavy duty
6	Plastic Gloves, heavy duty

This equipment list is offered as a checklist for operators planning to introduce on-premise blast freezing systems.

3

Work Simplification

CONTINUOUS FLOW THROUGH KITCHEN DESIGN AND LAYOUT

Optimum efficiency in the preparation, storage, and serving of frozen food demands a continuous flow of ingredients from receiving to storage and service. To determine if a continuous flow is present, you must evaluate the schematic design and layout of the kitchen. Each piece of equipment should be positioned so the flow is continuous and smooth.

Dr. Lendal Kotschevar has concluded that every kitchen worker should be an island surrounded by the necessary equipment, materials, and ingredients. It is less costly to duplicate scales, scoops, ladles, measuring cups, and spoons, knives, and cutting boards, and, often, equipment, than to pay the price in decreased productivity. Moreover, with smooth and efficient product flow, quality control is more readily attained.

There is a dramatic way to determine if back-tracking, by-passing, or criss-crossing is occuring. During the preparation of a meal, have a production worker tie a continuous supply of string to his shoes; whenever he stops, tape the string to the floor. If you discover that the resulting lines are muddled, and/or the length of the string indicates considerable distance travelled, then the kitchen layout or the location of equipment and tools should be analyzed.

In most foodservice institutions, hiring an industrial engineering consultant to do a "cross chart" as a tool for analyzing the kitchen layout is a good investment. Often it is possible to reduce processing time, increase productivity, and reduce the fatigue and frustration of wasted efforts.

An efficiently designed kitchen is one that meets the needs of the institution. Providing this requires a menu plan, the "backbone" of every foodservice operation. There are several factors to consider in developing a basic menu plan where freezing of food is an important aspect of the flow chart. They include:

*Menu items that the potential customers like.

*Menu items that lend themselves well to freezing, thus insuring the same or better quality than freshly prepared foods.

*Menu items that can be prepared using available space and equipment (e.g., adequate freezer space and adequate batch cooking equipment).

*Menu items that meet the budget (freezing perishable items when they are in season allows buying at the lowest price).

*A menu that has the flexibility to turn leftovers into excellent frozen dishes.

*A menu that offers variety without too much labor expenditure in any one day. (In freezing foods, production need not have the ups and downs of daily meal-to-meal preparations.)

*A menu that can be prepared without a "demand and time crisis."

A flow chart illustrating the way to avoid a "demand and time" crisis appears at the top of the facing page. Menu planning is easier when this "demand and time crisis" is removed from the flow chart. If this was a conventional cooking to service chart, quality service could be achieved if the first four stages were accomplished as close to the service as possible. A sample of a good general work flow chart appears at the bottom of the facing page.

It is difficult to plan a menu when there is a poor layout and inadequate equipment and storage. How many of us are guilty of planning a meal which necessitates the use of the same oven from the entree down to the dessert? It is easy to do if one has not found the time to analyze the production schedule—to determine "where, when, and how" items should be prepared.

Once a decision is made as to the type of menu, efficient preparation scheduling must be planned. A Ready Foods System employs continuous preparation and processing time concentrated on a few menu items. It is recommended that large batches—25 or more portions—be processed. The preparation schedule depends on the inventory level needed. In developing efficient production scheduling, these steps should be followed:

1. Prepare standardized recipes with accurate portion control for all menu items. The estimated total number of portions to freeze is determined in terms

Typical Continuous Flow Chart for Freezing Food

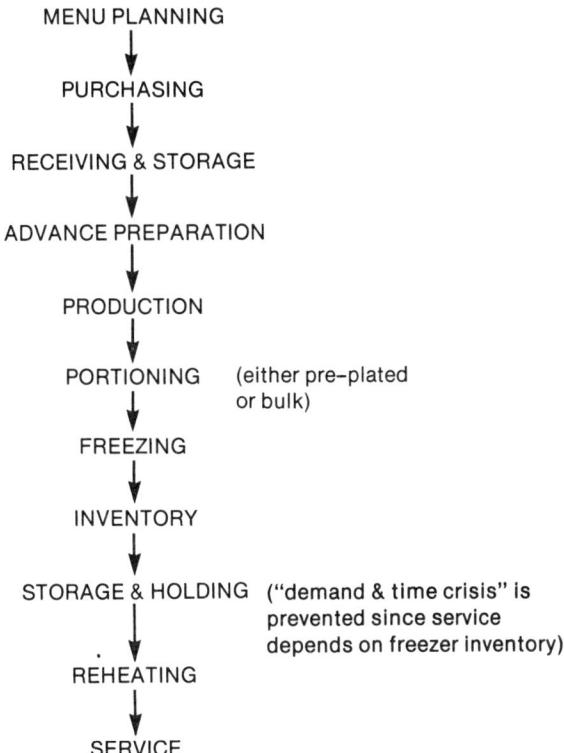

MENU PLANNING

↓

PURCHASING

↓

RECEIVING & STORAGE

↓

ADVANCE PREPARATION

↓

PRODUCTION

↓

PORTIONING   (either pre–plated or bulk)

↓

FREEZING

↓

INVENTORY

↓

STORAGE & HOLDING   ("demand & time crisis" is prevented since service depends on freezer inventory)

↓

REHEATING

↓

SERVICE

Central Food Facility
General Work Flow Chart

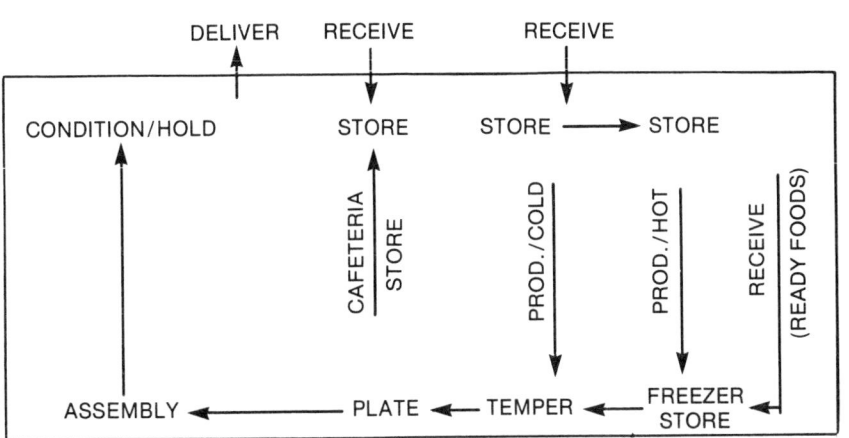

DELIVER   RECEIVE   RECEIVE

CONDITION/HOLD   STORE   STORE → STORE

CAFETERIA STORE   PROD./COLD   PROD./HOT   RECEIVE (READY FOODS)

ASSEMBLY ← PLATE ← TEMPER ← FREEZER STORE ←

of total poundage for ten days of product turnover, especially in an institution serving over 3000 meals per day.

2. For each product item information on dimensions, portion size and weight, moisture content, and initial and final product temperature should be collected, since all of these factors affect preparation, processing, and freezing time.

3. Establish a product flow diagram for each product to determine the necessary types and quantity of equipment needed. This diagram will also indicate the areas of the kitchen that each component or material goes through as it changes from raw to processed to frozen state.

4. Indicate for each product the various production procedures required, i.e. type of processing, total poundage of pre-plated and bulk packaged meals, portion control, specifications for raw materials, and projected time, temperature, and rate of freezing. This information should be based on research and previous experience. A tight inventory control is a necessity in managing on-premise preparation and freezing. (A detailed discussion of inventory is found at the end of this chapter.)

5. Develop a projected volume of production based on the unit portion control and the number of units to be produced. In an institution that uses both pre-plated and bulk packed meals, the projection will be different for each. To determine the number of units to be produced, it is recommended that the degree of acceptance for each item be estimated. This can be done through patient surveys or past history of these items.

6. Calculate production load in terms of eight hours continuous processing minus two hours for clean-up and down time. In determining batch size, make sure that each piece of equipment is utilized at its maximum and that raw materials processing is done in a continuous period and in as short a time as possible.

Here is an example of how a flow diagram and production procedure are coordinated. (One case used in the Flow Diagram refers to the ingredient control personnel.)

Production Procedure

Tuna Noodle Casserole	*Plated Entree*	*Bulk Pack*
Finished Components		
Tuna Noodle Casserole	7 oz.	77 oz.
Green Beans Almondine	3 oz.	
	10 oz.	77 oz.
Units to be produced	2500	228
Portions to be produced	2500	2500

Flow Diagram*

PRODUCT — TUNA NOODLE CASSEROLE

PRODUCTION LINES

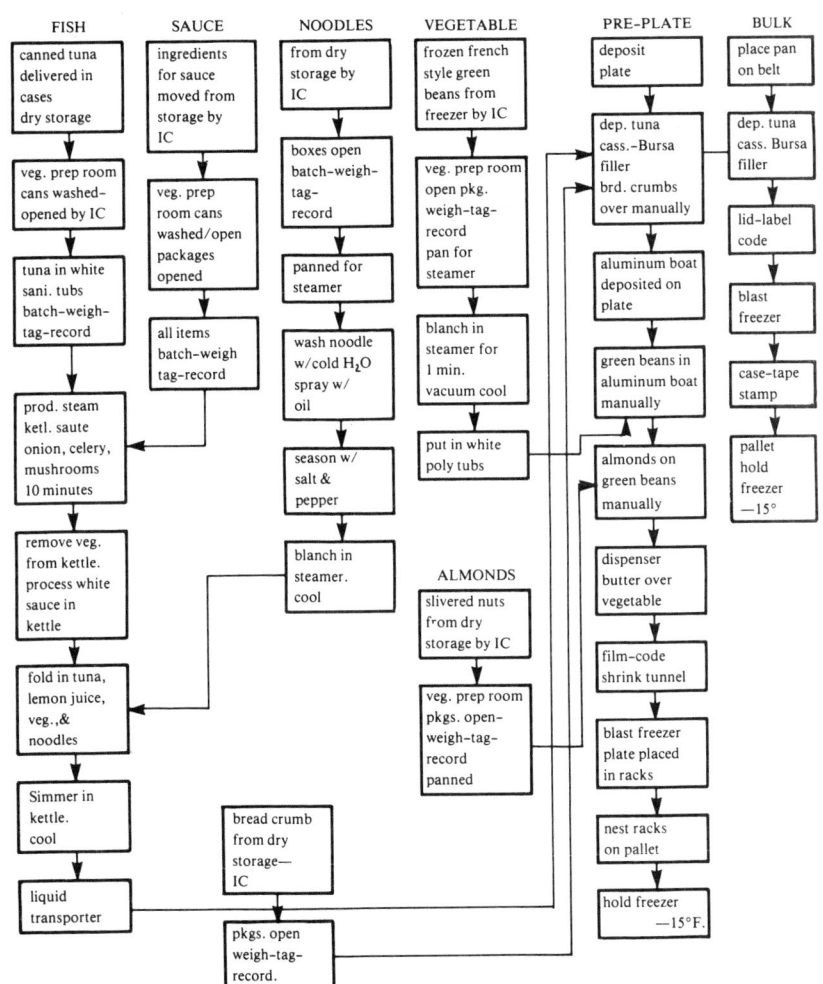

FISH	SAUCE	NOODLES	VEGETABLE	PRE-PLATE	BULK
canned tuna delivered in cases dry storage	ingredients for sauce moved from storage by IC	from dry storage by IC	frozen french style green beans from freezer by IC	deposit plate	place pan on belt
veg. prep room cans washed-opened by IC	veg. prep room cans washed/open packages opened	boxes open batch-weigh-tag-record	veg. prep room open pkg. weigh-tag-record pan for steamer	dep. tuna cass.-Bursa filler brd. crumbs over manually	dep. tuna cass. Bursa filler
tuna in white sani. tubs batch-weigh-tag-record	all items batch-weigh tag-record	panned for steamer	blanch in steamer for 1 min. vacuum cool	aluminum boat deposited on plate	lid-label code
prod. steam ketl. saute onion, celery, mushrooms 10 minutes		wash noodle w/cold H₂O spray w/ oil		green beans in aluminum boat manually	blast freezer
		season w/ salt & pepper	put in white poly tubs	almonds on green beans manually	case-tape stamp
remove veg. from kettle. process white sauce in kettle		blanch in steamer. cool	ALMONDS slivered nuts from dry storage by IC	dispenser butter over vegetable	pallet hold freezer —15°
fold in tuna, lemon juice, veg.,& noodles			veg. prep room pkgs. open-weigh-tag-record panned	film-code shrink tunnel	
Simmer in kettle. cool		bread crumb from dry storage— IC		blast freezer plate placed in racks	
liquid transporter				nest racks on pallet	
		pkgs. open weigh-tag-record.		hold freezer —15°F.	

---

*Hennepin County Medical Center, 5th and Portland, Minneapolis, MN.

TUNA CASSEROLE

Tuna fish (canned) is delivered in cases and stored in dry storage. As a first step in production it is moved to the vegetable preparation room by ingredient control personnel. Cans are washed, opened, and the oil drained from the tuna before it is put into white poly tubs. The tuna is batch weighed, tagged, and recorded, then moved to the production area.

Medium egg noodles are delivered in boxes and stored in dry storage. They are moved to the vegetable preparation room by ingredient control personnel. Boxes are opened, and the noodles are batch weighed, tagged, and recorded, panned for the steamer, and sent to the production area.

All remaining ingredients for the sauce and casserole are moved out of storage by ingredient control personnel. Cans are washed and opened, packages opened, and all ingredients are batch weighed, tagged and recorded. These items are placed in white poly tubs and moved to the production area.

In the production area, the noodles are washed with cold water, drained, sprayed with oil, seasoned with salt and pepper, and blanched in the steamer for five minutes. The noodles are rotary cooled, (a process whereby cold water is circulated with the agitating beaters through the steamers), then put in white poly tubs.

In the steam kettle, saute onions, celery, and mushrooms for ten minutes, then remove and set aside. Mix and process the white sauce in the same kettle. Simmer slowly for ten minutes. Fold in the tuna, lemon juice, vegetables, and noodles. Simmer slowly for ten minutes. Cool, then move by liquid transporter to the pre–plate and bulk production lines.

Bread crumbs for garnishing the pre–plated tuna casserole are moved from dry storage to the vegetable preparation area by ingredient control personnel. The packages are opened, the crumbs are weighed, tagged, recorded, put in a white poly tub and sent to the pre–plate production line.

Vegetable

Frozen French-style green beans are moved from the freezer to the vegetable preparation room by ingredient control personnel. The packages are opened, the beans are weighed, tagged, and recorded, then panned for the steamer. In the production area, the beans are processed in the steamer for one minute, rotary cooled, (see noodle prep above), then placed in white poly tubs and sent to the pre–plate production line.

Slivered almonds are moved from dry storage to the vegetable preparation room by ingredient control personnel. The packages are opened, the nuts are weighed, recorded, and tagged, panned, and then sent to the pre–plate production line.

Modifications Necessary for Special Diets

1. Tuna Noodle Casserole
   a) Categories 1, 2, 4 and 5—No Change.
   b) Categories 3, 6 and 7—The recipes for SF Tuna Noodle casserole and SF mushroom sauce will be used in place of the regular tuna noodle casserole.
2. Green Beans Almondine
   a) Categories 1, 2, 4 and 5—Almonds are to be omitted.
   b) Categories 3, 6 and 7—Almonds are to be omitted. Use SF margarine in place of liquid corn oil margarine over the beans on the pre-plate line.

MANAGING YOUR FREEZER INVENTORY AND STORAGE

Based on actual product turnover in the freezer, you will be able to determine the acceptance of a menu item. In a large institution using a cyclical menu, it is easy to find out which of the pre-prepared frozen products are not moving. The acceptance of frozen pre-prepared items in health care institutions is dependent on the census, type of patient, types of diets, and the seasonal changes affecting the moods of the patients. After history is recorded over a period of time, it becomes easier to project the volume of usage for each item.

It is best to store the items most often used at the most convenient level and space. Always use the top and bottom freezer shelves for items that have low popularity or are used less often, such as cranberries for turkey dinners, or appetizers used only for holidays or special functions. When a self-defrosting freezer is used, it is recommended that the newer products be placed on the center shelves; these can then be moved to the upper shelves as older products are used and rotated.

The stock level inventory of frozen pre-prepared foods is easier to manage if the following are kept in mind:

*Usage history of the menu item.
*Perishability factor (or shelf life) of the products.
*Space allowance for stock rotation.
*First in, first out rotation is followed.

At an inventory level of more than 3000 meals per day, it is recommended that 30-day usage history data be taken. If you discover there are products on the inactive list after a month, one of two decisions should be made: either product formulation should be changed (poor acceptance might be due to product quality), or these items should be deleted from the menu.

Quality loss during frozen storage results from time and temperature factors that produce physical and chemical changes. But remember that quality changes during delays between preparation and freezing are more catastrophic than the natural gradual changes that take place during freezer storage. I recommend that every step be taken to insure that products are stored in the freezer as soon after they are prepared as possible. The effects of delays between preparation and freezing are most apparent in items which contain pork, egg, and cream, and dishes where sauces and gravies may separate or curdle.

The changes during storage are usually gradual, depending on the following:

Size and shape which increases exposure to air, oxygen, and continuous cold air movement (the reason why ground beef items are more prone to loss of quality than whole roast beef).

Nature of the products and chemical behavioral changes in response to oxidation and dehydration and to physical changes due to fluctuating temperature in freezer storage causing freeze–thaw–refreeze cycles.

Type of packaging affects perishability (vacuum packaging improves shelf–life even of pork and pork products).

Storage temperature maintenance of the freezer at -5°F. to -10°F. For most processed products, storage at -10°F. is more than adequate to prevent qualitative changes during a period of six to eight months.

Moisture content inherent in the product and moisture absorption capability. The moisture content affects the rate and depth of ice crystals finally formed in the intercellular structure of the products. Where too much water is added to a sauce or gravy it is inevitable that breakdown or curdling will occur, especially after thawing. The absorption or migration of moisture from the sauce to other components with less moisture content will occur through osmosis. It is this process that leads to denaturation of protein gels or the further dehydration of the products.

One of the most important aids in managing a freezer is a perpetual inventory of the products in it. It is easier to maintain this file if the products are arranged in categories such as:

1. Appetizers

2. Entrees—casseroles, meats with sauces/gravies, roasts—plain

3. Starch/bread

4. Vegetables

5. Desserts—cake, pies, fruits, cookies, pastry

6. Salads—fruit, vegetable, and starch

7. Miscellaneous—relishes, jam, honey, sour cream, jellies

Perpetual inventory may be kept with a small recipe card file. It should have a record of each item in the freezer. The record should show the date of preparation and the balance on hand. Every withdrawal of any item must be recorded.

For a large institution, each product category should be palletized. Each pallet has the pre-plated and bulk pack meals packed in baskets or cartons. Pallet loads of baskets and cartons must have a mimimum clearance of six inches from freezer walls and adjacent pallets. This insures proper spacing for maximum air circulation.

Labelling products with product code number, color codings for general and special diets, batch size, and date of preparation or production run, will insure that stocks are rotated "first in, first out." For a very large foodservice operation, consider a "live pallet storage system" or even an electrically powered live pallet system. A live pallet storage system uses inclined roller conveyors as shelving so the baskets or cartons roll down to the discharge end as products are removed. The system is controlled by a series of mechanical brakes to prevent a fast descent of the pallets. Installing electronic counters at the end of each storage lane that are connected to a central computer bank will give instant information on each product both as to the inventory in the freezer and the incoming products from production runs. There are continuing opportunities for the application of work simplification methods in a blast freezing system.

4

Role of Thickening Agents in Recipe Formulation

The greatest damage that can occur during freezing of sauces and gravies has been attributed to certain chemical properties of the various starch molecules which cause some of them to go through a process of retrogradation. This process causes the gravies and sauces made with such starches to thin out or separate. This happens because these starches lose the ability to hold water and any frozen item made with them will not hold together. It is the amylose component of the starch molecules that causes this. The amylopectin component does not contribute to retrogradation.

Among the many changes which may occur in the thawed product there are some that are undesirable for sauces and gravies while others may be desirable for certain sauces. The resulting changes include increases in product opacity; liquid separation after thawing resulting in a coarse, granular texture; and development of a curdled appearance in the product.

The normal cereal starches such as corn, sorghum, wheat, and rice possess a high degree of the chemical property called amylose and, thus, are more prone to retrogradation and the development of a visually unappealing product. There are varieties of these cereal starches which have a larger amount of amylopectin and, therefore, do not lose visual appeal.

Various cereal companies have conducted studies and research which has led to the development of waxy starches and modified starches. The waxy maize (corn), waxy sorghum, and waxy rice starches are all cohesive in nature and considerably more stable when used in freezing than the common starches. During the reheating of sauces and gravies made with the waxy cereals, liquid separation does not occur. Although they have similar chemical properties, when tested these starches do not act in the same way as common starches.

There are several theories as to why waxy rice flour performs better than the rest of the waxy starches during freezing and refrigerated storage. One of the most obvious is the fact that waxy rice flour is 100 per cent amylopectin, a chemical property which does not cause separation. It is still starch, but its physical properties are completely different and pastes made up with it have a characteristic long, stringy quality. When waxy rice flour and ordinary cereal flour are mixed in a 1:1 ratio, the paste results in a better product than one made from either alone.

HOW TO USE VARIOUS THICKENING AGENTS FOR FREEZING SAUCES AND GRAVIES

1. Amylose–Amylopectin Ratio

If you are adjusting your own recipes for freezing one of the most important points to consider is the concentration of amylose–amylopectin in your total product formulation. Sauces thickened with 3/5 waxy rice flour and 2/5 ordinary wheat flour will show no liquid separation or curdled appearance for at least five months at 0°F. No matter where the source of the amylose is, either the potato in the stew or the noodles in the spaghetti, it is always practical to determine content of amylose and amylopectin so that there is a higher concentration of amylopectin. This can be done by adjusting the thickening agent so that it contains enough amylopectin. In this way you can provide the proper ratio for the final product. Manufacturers of rice flour and corn flour stabilizers can provide amylose–amylopectin ratios for their products.

2. Freezing Storage Conditions

It is critical to make sure that products which have thickening agents added will not suffer from a freeze–thaw–refreeze cycle during storage. Whatever thickening agent has been used, extreme fluctuations in temperatures ultimately result in syneresis in the thawed foods which gives it a highly objectionable, curdled, soggy appearance.

It is also important that the fast freezing process occurs at a rate that prevents the formation of large ice crystals. These cause the starch concentration to swell up and hydrate, thus increasing in concentration and resulting in an unsatisfactory product. The best temperature for the storage of these products to create the desired deep frozen state is -15 °F., and there should be little deviation in temperature.

3. Basic Preparation Temperature

In preparing sauces and gravies, it is best first to bring the mixture to a warm temperature of 100 °F. using either a melted fat or a portion of the liquid called for in the recipe. Experience shows the best method is to add a warm portion of the fat or liquid slowly to the thickening solution, heating it until it reaches a temperature of 140 °F. As soon as the ingredients are combined and a slurry is obtained, the mixture should be heated to 190°F. to 200°F. as rapidly as possible. The mixture should then be quickly cooled. (Where products can withstand vigorous mechanical agitation, use constant stirring and agitation.)

For recipes with delicate ingredients, such as beef stew, it is best to prepare the gravy mixture first in combination with the meat and then add the vegetables later.

4. Use of Additives, Stabilizers

Various additives and stabilizers, such as 1 percent citrus pectin, carrageenan gum, and algin derivatives, have been put to good use in some products, e. g. chicken a la king and roast meats with gravy. These additives have improved the stability of frozen products but only if the products have been kept at a temperature of -10 °F. to -15 °F.

5. Use of Freeze-Resistant Modified Starches

The use of modified cross-bonded starch has resulted in desirable consistency and stability in sauces and gravies. The cross-bonding starch with esters or ionized phosphate reduces the stringy cohesive nature of the waxy starches, increasing their ability to undergo mechanical agitation and also improving freeze-thaw stability.[1] The most commonly used freeze resistant modified starch is the waxy corn or maize. This is the starch used for the testing and standardization of the recipes developed for this system. (See Vol. 2)

6. Recipe Formulation

There is considerable difficulty in trying to arrive at a basic standard mixture of thickening agents as each variety differs. This affects the calculation of the ratio between amylose and amylopectin. Not only does the ratio vary in relation to the quantity being produced, but standards of consistency, viscosity, taste, and feel vary from one operation to another. There are people who feel that a thinner but a slightly grainy appearance is desirable in sauces. But there are those who contend that a thicker sauce with a very smooth appearance is ideal.

This may make it necessary for the individual developing a recipe for freezing to determine the inherent amylose content of the ingredients in the recipe without the gravy portion and adjust starch selection accordingly.

However, in Volume 2, Blast Freezing Quantity Recipes, there is a collection of tested recipes which can be used without any need for such calculations. If you choose to use your own recipes and substitute the waxy starch for the flour, cornstarch, or potato starch present in the original recipe, it is best to use a ratio of 60 percent waxy starch to 40 percent regular flour. If the consistency of the product after cooling is not what you intended, then it is easier to either reduce the wheat starch or the waxy starch, depending on the thickness desired.

When preparing an opaque sauce or product with a gravy that has to have an opaque (not translucent) look, it is best to use the formulation of 50 percent waxy starch to 50 percent regular wheat flour. If the sauce is to be used for a sweet–sour Cantonese sauce, or for chop suey, or chow mein, then we try to substitute waxy starch for 70 to 80 percent of the regular cornstarch that the recipe calls for.

It is also important to bear in mind if you plan to adjust your own recipes that the pH of the recipe has to be determined in order that the starch will not stay for too long a period in higher zones of pH3, as the acidity at that point substantially decreases the stability of waxy starches.

There are many available thickening agents on the market. A majority of them have been tested by various foodservice operations. Included below are some sample recipes for sauces and gravies in which each variety finds applications:

COMMERCIAL THICKENING AGENTS:

---

1. *Waxy Rice Flour (Nu-Flour)*
   Rice Products Company, Inc.

Laboratory Analysis[2]

Appearance .... Clean
Odor .... Normal
Color .... White
Crude Protein (1.11 percent Nitrogen x 6.25) 6.94%
Ash 0.35%
Moisture (1 hour at 130°C.) 11.9%
Calcium (Ca) 0.014%
Bulk Density (lb. per cu. ft.) 32.68
Screen Test: Remaining on 80 mesh screen 8.27%
Total Plate Count (per gram) 200
Salmonella (AOAC Supplement to 10th Ed.
1966, 1977 Method) .... Negative
Staphylococcus (Per 0.1 Gram Portion) .... Not Found

Distributors of Nu-Formula Flour

SAN FRANCISCO   RICE PRODUCTS COMPANY, INC.
                     260 California St. Ste. 501
                     San Francisco, CA. 94111
                     Phone (415) 392-0402

CHICAGO   CHICAGO COLD STORAGE DIV.
                     Beatrice Foods Company
                     1526 South State Street
                     Chicago, Illinois 60605
                     Phone (312) 842-2700

SAMPLE RECIPES FOR SAUCES

City College of San Francisco
Hotel and Restaurant Division

Recipe—Thin Cream Sauce

Ingredients		*Quantities*	*Cost*	
	Amount	8—4-oz. Servings		
	Servings	16—2-oz. Servings	Unit	Total
Milk		1 qt.	.17	.17
Nu-Formula Flour		¼ cup or 1½ oz.	.16	.015
Margarine		1/16 lb.	.25	.015
		Total Cost		.20
		Per 4 oz.		.025
		Per Portion 16 oz.		.0125

Method: Bring milk to boil, add margarine, and then Nu-Formula Flour which has been mixed with water to form a paste. Cook for 2 minutes and sauce is ready for use.

Related Information: Makes a thin cream sauce which may be used for creamed vegetables.

This cream sauce was frozen and thawed gradually at a temperature of 40°F. in a refrigerator and then re-heated. The sauce did not break down from freezing and re-heating.

For Quantities of 100 Servings:

Milk .... 3 gal.

Nu-Formula Flour .... 1 1/8 lb.

Margarine .... ½ lb.

Salt and white pepper to taste.

City College of San Francisco
Hotel and Restaurant Division

Recipe—Medium Cream Sauce

Ingredients		*Quantities*	*Cost*	
	Amount	8—4-oz. Servings		
	Servings	16—2-oz. Servings	Unit	Total
Milk		1 qt.	.17	.17
Nu-Formula Flour		2 cup or 3 oz.	.16	.03
Margarine		1/16 lb.	.25	.015
		Total Cost		.215
		Per 4 oz.		.027
		Per Portion 16 oz.		.013

Method: Bring milk to boil, add margarine, and then add Nu-Formula Flour which has been mixed with water to form a paste. Cook for two minutes and sauce is ready for use.

Related Information: Makes a medium cream sauce which may be used for chicken, seafood, or turkey.

This cream sauce was frozen and thawed gradually at a temperature of 40°F. in a refrigerator, and then re-heated. The sauce did not break down from freezing and re-heating.

For Quantities of 100 Servings:

Milk .... 3 gal.

Nu–Formula Flour .... 2–¼ lb.

Margarine .... ¾ lb.

Salt and white pepper to taste.

City College of San Francisco
Hotel and Restaurant Division

Recipe—Thick Cream Sauce

Ingredients		*Quantities*	*Cost*	
	Amount	8—4-oz. Servings		
	Servings	16—2-oz. Servings	Unit	Total
Milk		1 qt.	.17	.17
Nu–Formula Flour		¾ cup or 4 ½ oz.	.16	.045
Margarine		1/8 lb.	.25	.03
		Total Cost		.245
		Per 4 oz.		.03
		Per Portion 16 oz.		.015

Method: Bring milk to boil, add margarine, and then add Nu–Formula Flour which has been mixed with water to form a paste. Cook for two minutes and sauce is ready for use.

Related Information: Makes a thick cream sauce which may be used for Cheese souffle.

This cream sauce was frozen and thawed gradually at a temperature of 40°F. in a refrigerator, and then re-heated. The sauce did not break down from freezing and re-heating.

For Quantities of 100 Servings:

Milk .... 3 gal.

Nu-Formula Flour .... 3½ lb.

Margarine .... 1 lb.

Salt and white pepper to taste.

City College of San Francisco
Hotel and Restaurant Division

Recipe—Very Thick Cream Sauce

Ingredients		*Quantities*	*Cost*	
	Amount	8—4-oz. Servings		
	Servings	16—2-oz. Servings	Unit	Total
Milk		1 qt.	.17	.17
Nu-Formula Flour		1 cup or 6 oz.	.16	.06
Margarine		1/8 lb.	.25	.03
		Total Cost		.26
		Per 4 oz.		.03
		Per Portion 16 oz.		.016

Method: Bring milk to boil, add margarine, and then add Nu-Formula Flour which has been mixed with water to form a paste. Cook for two minutes and sauce is ready for use.

Related Information: Makes a very thick cream sauce which may be used for croquettes.

   This cream sauce frozen, thawed gradually at a temperature of 40°F. in a refrigerator, and then re-heated did not break down from freezing and re-heating.

For Quantities of 100 Servings:

Milk ....3 gal.

Nu-Formula Flour ....4½ lb.

Margarine ....1½ lb.

Salt and white pepper to taste.

2. Modified Tapioca Starch (Purity 69)
National Starch & Chemical Corporation

Laboratory Analysis [2]

Physical:
    Color   -white
    Form   -Powder
    Moisture -approx. 12 percent
    pH   -approx. 5.5 percent

Cooked Starch:
Aqueous preparations are clear, smooth, and short textured, exceptionally stable and do not set to a gel. Highly resistant to breakdown under high temperatures and low pH conditions.

Taste:
    Quick release of natural flavors
    No mushing or dulling effects
    No cereal or starchy taste
    Excellent taste

Freeze-thaw and shelf-life stability:
    25 or more freeze-thaw cycles
      are possible
    Texture remains unchanged
    No evidence of syneresis
    Increased tolerance to varying
      storage conditions.

RECIPE RATIO

A ratio of 1:1 Purity 69 and all purpose flour was found to be desirable in all of the testing and research done for the Masters Thesis of Paul Deignan at the Cornell Hotel and Restaurant School.

Distributors of Purity 69

Available in all locations.

3. Waxy Maize (W-13)
American Maize Products Company

Laboratory Analysis

Description:

A modified waxy maize starch which exhibits increased resistance toward hydrolysis in low pH media, overcooking, and mechanical shear.

3. Waxy Maize (W-13) [Cont'd]

Typical Analysis:

Moisture, percent 12

pH (1:3) 5.5

Screen: percent through 200 mesh 94.5

	Nutrients Per 100 Gram Portion *Dry Solids Basis*
Calories	408
Protein (gm)	0.4
Fat (gm)	0.2
Carbohydrate (gm)	99.0
Calcium (mg)	5
Phosphorus (mg)	6
Iron (mg)	0.5
Sodium (mg)	110
Potassium (mg)	4
Magnesium (mg)	1
Zinc (mg)	0.05
Copper (mg)	0.05

This product does not contain significant amounts of vitamins, fat, cholesterol, or fatty acids.

Characteristics:

W-13 STARCH is designed for use in a broad line of food preparations. These products will exhibit excellent clarity and brilliance; a semi-fluid body; and long-term storage stability.

Application:

W-13 produces extremely stable fruit pie fillings of excellent clarity and when used as a blend with other starches, W-13 produces a smoother, more stable cream and chiffon-type filling.

W-13 is also applicable to canned and frozen gravies, soups, spaghetti sauces, and other food preparations which benefit from its unique gel character and clarity.

Distributors of W-13

Available in all locations.

SAMPLE RECIPE

American Maize Products Company
Technical Service Department
Representative Formula

Name of Product—Beef Gravy

Method of Mixing and Comments	Ingredients Used in Order of Mixing	Weight of Ingredients	
		Lb.	Oz.
1. Slurry starch in portion of water.	Water	200 gal.	
	W–13	53	8
	Salt	32	
2. Bring remaining water and seasoning agents to a boil	Onion Powder	9	5
	Tomato Paste	2 No. 10 cans	
3. Add starch slurry to above. Heat with agitation to 190°F.	Caramel Coloring	5	10
	Monosodium Glutamate		13
	Peppertone		10 ½

As a result of experiences with various thickening agents at Hennepin County Hospital, we developed a starch conversion formula which one may use in the event that the starch called for in the recipe is not available.

Thickening Agent	Grams/Oz.
Purity 69 (freeze resistant)	9 oz./15 grams
W–13 starch (freeze resistant)	2 oz./30 grams
Clear jel* (freeze resistant)	8 oz. (reduce liquid portion of recipe by 4 oz.)
All Purpose flour	7 oz./15 grams
Cake flour	6 oz./15 grams

*Available in 6–oz. bottle at retail grocery stores.

If you have recipes that call for all purpose flour as thickening agent, you may reduce 60 percent of its total weight and substitute for that weight a corresponding weight of the freeze resistant starch. For example:

Recipe calls for 16 lb. of all purpose flour

$$\frac{.60\%}{9.60\ \text{lb.}} \quad \begin{array}{r} 16.0 \\ -9.6 \\ \hline 6.4 \end{array}$$

The ratio to use: $\dfrac{4.15}{7.15} = \dfrac{X}{145}$

$$7X = 580$$

$$X = 83\ \text{oz.} = 5\ \text{lb. 2 oz.}$$

The changes in the recipe then call for

All Purpose flour   6.4 lb.
Purity 69 starch $\underline{5.2\ \text{lb.}}$
                              11.6

You may wonder why the total weight of thickener has been reduced. It is because the freeze resistant thickening agents are more potent since their gel capacity permits them to tighten up the liquids at a faster rate at a lower temperature.

The importance of thickening agents in many blast frozen products underscores the need for thorough understanding of the various types and how they may best be used.

5

Freezing Sauces
and Gravies

Achieving a sauce or gravy that is smooth, consistant, viscous, and free–flowing after freezing and thawing involves the use of principles and preparation techniques similar to those involved in the making of ice cream.

The basic ingredients necessary for a good sauce or gravy are fat, flour, liquid, and spices in proper combination. The time and temperature these ingredients are subjected to will be determined by the type of sauce desired.

There are two methods of making a basic white sauce, according to Richards and Treat.[1] Method I: (The conventional method) Melt the fat and flour, and blend. Scald milk, add blended fat and flour stirring vigorously. Cook five to seven minutes. Add seasoning.

Method II: Make a smooth flour paste with some of the cold liquid and add it to the remainder of the boiling liquid stirring rapidly. Add fat and seasoning. Use Method II for making very thick sauces.

The variations of ingredients and their amounts are determined by the use to which the sauce is to be put, whether as a glaze, pie filling, as part of a stew, or as sauce for croquettes. Whatever combinations and proportions of ingredients are used to control the thickness of the sauces and gravies, it is important that they produce a completely homogenous mix. The same kind of homogenous mix is also necessary in the making of a good ice cream. To produce such a mix for ice cream, the fat and flour mixture has to be stirred vigorously to break up and disperse the fat molecules and to prevent the separation of the ingredients during freezing.

A well-mixed, smoother roux may be achieved by the slow addition of a cool roux to a hot liquid. Roux is formed as a result of the browning process that occurs in combining flour and fat, usually in a 1:1 ratio, over heat. After it is combined, the roux can be chilled. As the cold roux and the hot liquid equalize in temperature after they have been combined, a vigorous agitation with a wire whip is necessary before the combination is brought to its final temperature of 190°F. to 200°F. It is not good to undercook the mixture for a sauce or gravy as the necessary additional reheating will result in an undesirable, thick product.

The sauce mixture must be cooled as rapidly as possible during the freezing process. If this is not accomplished, large ice crystal formations will cause liquid separation from the solid portion after thawing and reheating. Large ice crystals also produce a curdled appearance and granular texture. It has been recommended by Rogers[2] that every sauce and gravy recipe should maintain a high percentage of soluble solids to improve stability and melt-out properties. A sauce made from a brown stock with wine added to it is far better than a sauce made with plain water.

In foodservice operations where large batches of sauces and gravies are prepared, there are several methods of preparation. The first and most efficient method is used for the product made when the fat of the meat is rendered or the meat itself is rendered of its fat and juices. This method consists of the addition of the thickening agent to the rendered fat and liquid after the meat has been removed. A cold mixture is prepared first from the thickening agent and the liquid. It is then slowly stirred into the hot liquid.

In the recipes developed for Vol. 2, at least two cups of the hot liquid were added to the cold mixture since modified waxy maize starch was used in the preparation. It is important that as soon as all of the cold mixture is added to the hot liquid in a steam-jacketed kettle, the agitating mechanism be started at high speed before the temperature of the combination reaches 190°F. A temperature of 190°F. to 200°F. has to be maintained during this process so the effects of the thickening agent are not diminished.

The second method of sauce preparation was used with success in preparing sauce or gravy for chicken a la king or chicken pot pies. For this purpose the fat is melted first. Next, the flour and other thickening agents are sifted together. The melted fat is added to the flour mixture and blended to a smooth paste with just enough cooking to remove the taste of the raw starch.

The preparation of the sauce or gravy for swiss steak differs from the above method since the margarine and flour mixture is allowed to reach a golden brown color. A slow addition of the hot liquid to this roux is necessary to equalize the temperature and to give the roux adequate time to absorb the liquids, especially when using a waxy maize or cornstarch mixture as a thickening agent. If one part of the roux becomes set and thick and the rest becomes watery, there is no way of changing the result.

There are basic sauces and gravies that are important to a successful freezing program. Variations of these basic sauces are often called Veloute, Espagnole, Bechamel, or Mornay. In the sauce recipes that follow certain modifications of the ingredients have been made. The basic tomato recipe may also be used to provide the base for creole sauce or spaghetti sauce.

Sauces for Use in Frozen Products

| **Title** MEAT GLAZE | **No.** |
| **Yield** 25 (1 qt.) | **Portion Size** 1 oz. |

Ingredients	*Amount*
Meat or Poultry Broth (or juice from roast meat or poultry)	1 qt.
W–13 Starch	19 gm. (2 Tbsp.)

Procedure:

1. Mix the W–13 starch with some of the cold stock.
2. Heat the meat or poultry broth to boiling. Add the W–13 starch mixture and cook 2 minutes, stirring constantly with a wire whip.
3. Remove from heat and cool.

| **Title** BASIC WHITE SAUCE (MEDIUM) | **No.** |
| **Yield** 100 | **Portion Size** 2 oz. |

Ingredients	*Amount*
* Margarine	1 lb.
Flour	12 oz.
W–13 Starch	4 oz.
Milk, hot	2 gal.
* Salt	50 gm. (4 Tbsp.)
Pepper, White	6 gm. (1 Tbsp.)

* For low sodium diets, omit salt and use salt free margarine.

Procedure:

1. Sift the flour and W–13 starch together.
2. Melt the margarine. Add the flour and starch mixture and blend to a smooth paste.
3. Heat the milk, and add this slowly to the white roux, stirring continuously until thick and smooth.
4. Add the salt and pepper and mix well.

Title BROWN GRAVY (THICK)	**No.**
Yield 100	**Portion Size** 2 oz.

Ingredients	*Amount*
Clear Fat, from drippings	1 lb., 4 oz.
Flour, Wheat, Hard	14 oz.
W–13 Starch	6 oz.
Garlic Clove, crushed (optional)	1
***Stock or Water, hot	2 gal.
**Salt	40 gm. (3½ Tbsp.)
*Pepper, White	6 gm. (1 Tbsp.)

*Omit for bland diets.
**Omit for low sodium diets.
***If it is stock, use salt free for low sodium diet.

Procedure:

1. Pour drippings from roasting or frying pan into a separate container, allowing brown particles to remain in pan.
2. Let the clear fat rise to the top of drippings. Skim off all fat. Put 1 lb. 4 oz. back into the pan.
3. Sprinkle flour evenly over fat in meat pan.
4. Cook over low heat, stirring constantly, until flour is rich brown.
5. Add garlic.
6. Add stock or water gradually, stirring constantly, and cook until thickened, about 5 minutes.
7. Check seasoning; add more as needed.

Title COUNTRY GRAVY (THICK)	No.
Yield 100	Portion Size 2 oz.

Ingredients	Amount
* Chicken fat or shortening	1-¼ lb.
* Chicken stock	1 gal.
Milk, hot	1 gal.
Flour	14 oz.
W-13 Starch	6 oz.
* Salt	40 gm. (3½ Tbsp.)
Sage	6 gm. (2 tsp.)
Paprika	6 gm. (2 tsp.)
Pepper, White	7 gm. (1 Tbsp.)

* For low sodium diets, omit salt. Use salt free chicken fat or salt free shortening and salt free chicken stock.

Procedure:

1. Melt fat.
2. Stir flour into the melted fat. Cook until light golden brown.
3. Add chicken stock to the fat-flour mixture, stirring constantly until thick and smooth.
4. Heat the milk. Add the heated milk to the sauce, stirring well to blend thoroughly.
5. Mix the salt, sage, paprika, and pepper together and add to the gravy. Blend well. Simmer *slowly—DO NOT BOIL*. Long, *slow* cooking develops the flavor of this gravy.

| **Title** TOMATO SAUCE | **No.** |
| **Yield** 100 | **Portion Size** ½ oz. |

Ingredients	*Amount*
Flour	4 oz.
W–13 Starch	15 gm.
* Margarine	6 oz.
* Tomato Juice	2 qt.
* Onions, chopped dehydrated	10 gm.
* Salt	1 tsp.
Pepper, White	2 gm. (1 tsp.)
* Worcestershire Sauce	tsp.
Basil	1 ¼ tsp.
Garlic Powder	15 gm. (2 Tbsp.)
Thyme	3 gm. (1 tsp.)
Bay Leaf	3 gm. (1 med. leaf)

* For low sodium diets, omit salt and worcestershire sauce. Use salt free margarine, salt free tomato juice, and use 6 oz. fresh chopped onions in place of dried.

Procedure:

1. Rehydrate onions using ice water.
2. Melt margarine. Add chopped onions and saute for 5 to 10 minutes.
3. Sift flour and starch together with salt and ground pepper. Add to the margarine and onion mixture. Mix to a paste.
4. Add tomato juice and mix until smooth. Add the Worcestershire sauce, basil, and garlic powder. Mix well.

Variations

1. Chop 10 green peppers into ½ in. squares and blanch. Add to above sauce and simmer until peppers are done.
2. Chop celery, okra and add to above sauce for creole.
3. Add 2 No.10 cans crushed tomatoes, 1 No. 10 can tomato puree, and 2 tsp. oregano leaves for spaghetti sauce.

Title SOUR CREAM GRAVY	**No.**
Yield 100	**Portion Size** 3 oz.

Ingredients	*Amount*
Margarine	2 lb.
Flour	10 oz.
W–13 Starch	6 oz.
Beef Stock (made from beef consomme)	1 gal.
Garlic Powder	8 gm. (1 Tbsp.)
Salt	1 oz.
Pepper, White	6 gm. (1 Tbsp.)
Cream of Mushroom Soup	3 50-oz. cans
Sour Cream	3 qt.

Procedure:

1. Blend melted margarine with flour and W–13 Starch mixture and cook it to make a light, honey brown roux.
2. Add stock, stirring constantly until smooth and thick.
3. Add garlic powder, salt, and pepper and mix well.
4. Add cream of mushroom soup gradually. Use a wire whip to mix smooth.
5. Stir 1 quart of hot gravy into sour cream slowly—*DO NOT BOIL.*
6. Add this sour cream–gravy mixture to the rest of the gravy. *DO NOT BOIL.*

Other sauce and gravy recipes will be found in Volume 2, Blast Freezing Quantity Recipes.

6

Preparing Entrees
for Blast Freezing

To have a successful freezing program, it is important to strive to retain the quality that was inherent in the product before it was frozen. The greatest challenge in freezing is in the areas of product formulation and preparation techniques for entrees which will be frozen. As stated earlier, physical and chemical changes take place in pre-prepared foods during the freezing, thawing, and reheating cycles. However, based on our experience and that of other foodservice operators in the industry, we find it is not too difficult to achieve quality in frozen, pre-prepared entrees if the following principles are kept in mind:

1. Select entree items that are popular and have a rapid product turnover. Entree items should not be stored for more than 30 to 60 days, especially if the total volume of meals required does not exceed 5,000 meals per day. For a larger volume operation, it is possible to have a longer storage inventory level, but one must be selective in the entrees chosen for preparation.

2. Avoid a higher percentage content of protein in entrees, such as eggs (particularly egg whites), shrimp, lobster, crab, and other shellfish, since it

produces an increased tendency toward protein denaturation, thus resulting in toughening of the tissues. With loss in quality, prolonged storage becomes very impractical.

3. Note that oxidation, resulting in a fast rate of rancidity, occurs in certain foods with a high percentage of fat, such as pork, bacon, fatty fish, sausages, turkey and chicken fat, and creamed poultry dishes. During frozen storage, not only oxidation affects cooked pork, but also color and flavor changes can occur in cured ham, pre-cooked ham, Canadian bacon, frankfurters, etc. They can develop a gray, greenish color with an off odor and a rancid flavor if storage is prolonged.

4. To arrive at good quality pre-prepared frozen entrees, a standard product formulation for sauces and gravies is most important. Sauces and gravies are additional protection to the other meat components of entree dishes.

5. Assure a uniform, consistent temperature for entrees in frozen storage. Any temperature fluctuation affects the ice crystallization that will occur not only in the entrees with sauces and gravies but also in items such as creamed dishes, salad dressing, ice cream, sherbets and ices, and other dairy products which have a high percentage of soluble solids in their recipes.

6. Give vegetables and fish extra careful cooking and preparation. Quick blanching and short interval steaming of vegetables and fish are the only preparation necessary before the actual freezing of these products.

7. Maintain a product formulation that results in a range of pH3 to pH4.5. This range offers good stability in sauces and gravies and also assures product safety as an added guarantee against microbial growth and contamination.

8. Select entree items that assure maximum productivity, good purchasing volume, and high dollar value in return for the investment. It is not practical to spend money freezing water. Instead, freeze concentrates of au jus, consommes, glaze, thick sauces, and gravies. These items can be produced at an economical rate with fewer cooks and later rehydrated and reconstituted by lower salaried employees.

9. Purchase raw ingredients or materials of high quality to begin with. Freezing does not improve the quality of the components. Make sure that a low microbial count is part of the specifications for purchasing. Some foodservice operators who freeze food have specified certain types and varieties of vegetables that have a specific moisture content as part of their detailed specifications. Portion size, shape, depth, and density have to be controlled in order to meet the requirements of most of the reconstitution ovens available at the present time. There is no magical oven that thinks for itself; if one pork chop is bigger and denser than another, the oven cannot determine when additional heat input should or should not be applied. Until such a computerized oven exists, it is a must that standard, uniform portion control specifica-

tions and procedures become an integral part of purchasing for a freezing program.

PURCHASING BY SPECIFICATIONS

As stated previously, good quality materials for use in the freezing of pre-prepared foods is one of the most important aspects in the entire system. A tight, but flexible, set of standard specifications is important in any foodservice operation, although its importance is magnified even more in a Ready Foods System.

Such a system will involve large batches and production runs which mean thousands of dollars in investments. An error in receiving materials that do not meet standard specifications can mean a loss in productivity and a great waste of management time. Surveys have shown that the majority of orders in both commercial and non-commercial operations have been placed without the use of specifications or written ordering procedures. Many foodservice operations rely on brand, label, or on the suppliers' high degree of salesmanship. In a Ready Foods System, substituting other ingredients or manipulating the amount of materials in the recipes will not work at all. Once you have established certain specific product formulations, it is essential to follow every step in order to maintain quality in the final product.

Freezing entrees has been a commercial practice since the 1950s when large scale production of casserole-type entrees was undertaken by Stouffers, of Cleveland, Ohio. I was fortunate enough to visit this plant in 1970. This is one of several food processors that emphasizes and implements good quality in purchasing ingredients. Unfortunately, the reason several of these large food corporations have not made a successful dent in such mass feeding areas as hospitals, schools, large restaurant chains, and airline feeding, is because standardization of recipe formulation for so diverse a market was difficult. A hospital patient will require different seasonings, fat content, and protein specifications than a customer in a restaurant. However, sooner or later, someone will realize that dialogue and a mutual commitment is necessary between foodservice operators and frozen food processors. If there is no standardization of frozen precooked products, all operators may eventually be convinced that they should freeze their own formulas. This system gives them the flexibility of establishing their own controls and standards.

The following standards for specifications will give the reader some insight as to how to develop purchasing standards. It is crucial that these standards are known, implemented, and used by the receiving clerks, purchasing agents, preparation and production crew, and all of the supervisory and management personnel.

MEAT SPECIFICATIONS

For a large operation producing at least 10,000 meals per day, the United States Department of Agriculture makes a meat acceptance service available which is designed to assure management that meats they purchase comply with detailed specifications approved by USDA.

As shown in the meat specifications used at Hennepin County, it is always best to state the item number, name and desired standards, such as grade or selection, weight range, formula (fat content, additive content, fillers, etc.), and a statement of refrigeration or freezing temperature for each of the meat products. Usually, a foodservice operation spends more than 30 percent of its total food cost for meats alone.

Beef and Veal

To determine a basic standard for quality in beef, it is best to look not only at the grade but also the fat marbling of each piece of meat. The amount, color, size, and shape of the marbling shows the quality of the meat. Wenzel[1] has summarized this as follows:

	Prime Grade	*Canner Grade*
Amount of Fat	Abundant (¾ inch over ribs and loin)	Deficient
Color of Fat	Creamy White	Yellow
Character of Fat	Firm, brittle	Rough, soft, oily
Distribution of fat		
(a) exterior	smooth, even cover	rough, poor cover
(b) interior	abundant	deficient
(c) between chine	abundant	deficient
(d) rib overflow	abundant	deficient
(e) between ribs	extensive	lacking

Unfortunately, due to the inadequate grain supply for cattlefeed, it is inevitable that the standards for marbling will change, especially if the cattle feed on grass.

MINIMUM STANDARDS OF QUALITY FOR MEAT COMPONENTS OF FROZEN ENTREES

Meats (Raw and Processed)

In general, raw meats (beef and veal) are to be USDA choice, and processed meats should be of top packer's brand.

Beef and Veal

Ground Chuck: USDA choice, lean, fresh–chilled, all beef, no trimmings, 14 to 16 percent maximum fat

Ground Beef (lean):	USDA choice, fresh–chilled, lean, all beef, no trimmings or additives, 17 to 18 percent maximum fat, NAMP No. 137
Beef Patties:	USDA choice, lean, fresh–chilled, 4/lb. all beef, approximately ½ inch thick, 10 lb. pack, NAMP No. 136, 18 percent maximum fat, no additives
Corned Beef:	USDA choice, ½ inch fat cover, deckle off, brine cured, from round, 8 to 12 lb. average
Fresh Beef Brisket:	USDA choice, fresh deckle off, ¾ inch maximum fat, 10 lb. average, NAMP No. 120
Beef Stew Meat:	USDA choice, uniform cut, 1 inch cubes, no excess fat or gristle, 10 lb. pack., NAMP No. 1195
Chuck Roast:	USDA choice, boneless, clod out, needled and tied, 11 to 13 lb. average
Top Sirloin Butt:	USDA choice, fresh–chilled, boneless, trimmed, 11 to 13 lb. average, NAMP No. 1184R
Cubed Steak:	USDA choice, fresh–chilled, 4/lb. tenderized, 5 oz. 3½ × 3½ inch or thicker, minimum fat, processed meat not acceptable, NAMP No. 1100
Boneless Top Round (Inside):	USDA choice, fresh–chilled, shank off, 20 lb. average, vacuum packaged, NAMP No. 168
Rib Eye Roll:	USDA choice, fresh–chilled, 7 to 9 lb. average, NAMP No. 1109AR
Tenderloin Steak:	USDA choice, fresh–chilled, 4 oz, closely trimmed with no ragged or thin edges, 1 inch thickness, no variance permitted, NAMP No. 1189
Top Sirloin Butt Steak:	USDA choice, boneless, portion cut to 6 oz., ¾ inch thick, or variance, fat in excess of ½ inch to be trimmed
Brochette Meat:	USDA choice, fresh–chilled, tenderloin cubes approximately 1 inch × 1 inch, ½ inch variance permitted, packed 10 lb. to a carton
Strip Loin:	USDA choice, fresh–chilled, New York Cut, maximum strip, denuded, no tail, no side, approximately 8 to 12 lb. in weight, not more than 7 in. width. NAMP No. 1180 Boneless
Prime Rib (Oven Prepared):	USDA choice, 10 to 11 lb. deckle gristle off, NAMP No. 104
Brochette (Sirloin Tips):	USDA choice, sirloin (loin end) cubes, approximately 1 inch × 1 inch × ½ inch. NAMP No. 181
Baby Beef Liver:	USDA choice, peeled, deveined, and sliced 4/lb portion controlled

Corned Beef: USDA choice, fresh–chilled, precooked from bottom round, fine layer of ½ inch fat at bottom, deckle off, brine cured, 35 percent maximum shrinkage

Boneless Top Round: USDA choice, shank off, without any addition such as sodium or potassium, bone in, tied roast ready

Veal Cutlets: USDA choice, fresh–chilled, chopped, no breading, 4 oz. portions, 10 lb. pack

Veal Leg: USDA choice, boneless, shank off, chilled (BRT.)

Veal Stew Meat: USDA choice, uniform cut, 1 inch cubes, no gristle or fat

Veal, Ground: USDA choice, fresh–chilled, 17 to 18 percent maximum fat, all veal

Pork

The same factors are used as in specifying beef in relation to confirmation, finish, and quality, with the exception of grading, which for pork is indicated as U.S. No. 1, U.S. No. 2 and U.S. No. 3.

Finish (Fat)	*U.S. No. 1*	*U.S. No. 2*	*U.S. No. 3*
Color of Fat	white	white	white to cream
Texture of Fat	firm	firm	soft
Amount of Fat	moderate thick	excessive	very thin
Distribution	even	not so even	uneven

Portion controlled pork cuts are a basic requisite in a freezing program. Quality control is necessary to maintain a tight receiving procedure so weight deviation will not be more than 5 percent for each portion cut.

Pork Loin: USDA No. 1, fresh–chilled, boneless, fat cover trimmed to ¼ inch, all bones, cartilage, lumbar vertebrae, butt bones and intercostal meat removed, 10 to 12 lb. average, NAMP No. 413

Pork Cutlet: USDA No. 1, fresh–chilled, needled twice, 4 oz. portion, no breading, packed 10 lb. per box in plastic bag, no preservatives or additives

Pork Chops: USDA No. 1, fresh–chilled, center cut, trimmed to ¼ inch fat cover, cut 3 or 4 per lb., NAMP No. 1412

Boston Butt: USDA No. 1, fresh–chilled, boneless, trimmed to ¼ inch fat, blade bone intact, 6 to 8 lb. average

Salt Pork: USDA No. 1, fresh frozen, slab, 8 to 10 lb. average

Bacon:	USDA Grade 1, fresh-chilled, smoked, cured, sliced 18 to 20 slices per pound, packed 12 lb. per box with waxed paper between each layer of slices, preferably Cryo-vac packaging for bacon
Ham:	Pullman Style, pre-cooked with 10 percent or less gelatine packed in 9 lb. tin with key opening lid, 6 to 9 tins per case, packer's top brand domestic
Ham:	Packers top brand, fresh-chilled, boneless, fully cooked, smoked and cured, no water added, 8 to 10 lb. average
Pork Sausage:	Roll, cured, fresh, not more than 3½ percent extenders, mildly spiced, packed in 10 lb. rolls
Pork Sausage:	Links, cured, fresh, mildly spiced, not more than 3-½ percent extenders, 12 links per lb., packed 10 lb. per case

Poultry

The highest quality is USDA Grade A. Grade A birds are fully fleshed and neat, well-finished, and attractive in appearance. This grade applies to chickens, turkeys, ducks, geese, and guinea. Poultry must first be federally inspected for wholesomeness before being graded for quality. Often, the inspection mark and the grade shield are displayed together on the package.

In developing specifications for poultry, it is advisable to include the following:

• Type—Indicate whether fresh, chilled, or frozen is desired.

• Class—Grade of the poultry does not indicate how tender the bird is. It is practical to state young, mature, or old (stewing chicken, yearling turkey, or mature duck).

• Size or weight—If you want a turkey to weigh 20 to 22 lb. dressed, then it must be specified.

• Style—This indicates the stage of pre-preparation (ready to cook, eviscerated, cut-up as halves, quartered, or in parts). Some birds are also available in boneless or pressed rolls.

The poultry specifications used in the development of the recipes in Volume 2, Blast Freezing Quantity Recipes, were:

Chicken, fryers:	USDA Grade A, fresh-chilled, 2½ lb. average, cut in 1/8s.
Chicken, baking:	USDA Grade A, fresh-chilled, eviscerated fowl, 5 to 7 lb. frozen.

Turkey (young toms and hens):	USDA Grade A, fresh–chilled, 22 lb. average, frozen.
Turkey, breasts:	USDA Inspected, fresh–chilled, 8 to 10 lb. average, breastbone in, shin cover intact, frozen.
Turkey, thighs:	USDA Grade A, fresh–chilled, boneless, cut from 22 lb. average young tom turkey.
Chicken:	USDA cooked, diced, Grade A, no skin, no turkey, frozen, no sodium preservative. Product must be diced in 1 inch cubes not extruded. Packed in plastic bags in 10 lb. boxes.
Turkey, rolled:	USDA Grade A, 60 percent white, 40 percent dark meat, fully cooked, frozen to contain less than 10 percent gelatin.
Turkey, ground:	USDA Grade A, fresh–chilled, from young turkey without bone or additives.

Fish and Other Seafood

The most common forms in which fish and shellfish are purchased are steaks, fillets or sticks, pieces (crabmeat), or in the round. There are no definite USDA standards, but we have developed a set of specifications based on Federal standards. Most fish used in institutions is in some frozen form. Fish should be delivered still frozen and show no signs of having been thawed.

Among the shellfish that might be used for freezing, the oyster, clam, scallop, crab, and shrimp need some detailed description.

Oysters—in purchasing SHUCKED oysters, they are often marketed as
Straights (ungraded)
Counts (large size, perfect in shape and color, and unbruised)
Selects (perfect condition, smaller than counts)
Standards (what is left over after counts and selects are graded)

Clams—those most commonly used are shucked, either in chilled or frozen form, or are canned. The same standards of quality and units of purchase are used as for oysters.

Crabs—the meat from the soft shell crab is sorted in lump form (white muscles of back fin), flake meat (edible meat from the rest of the body), and claw meat (from the claws but brownish–red in color). Personally, I have preferred either the lump or the claw meat in salads, au gratin sauces, and appetizers. It is important that crabmeat is only partially cooked as crabmeat toughens very fast and loses its delicate flavor.

Shrimp—fresh shrimp, known as "green shrimp," is the most delicate form to handle, because it tends to toughen with even a little cooking. Fresh shrimp are graded according to the number per pound. Jumbo shrimp (Prawns) come under 24 per pound, U–10's are under ten to a pound, and small provide 42 or more per pound. For use in shrimp creole, we have been purchasing frozen shrimp, either in pieces or in small size. These shrimp come packaged in polyethylene bags or in No. 2½ or No. 10 cans.

Lobster—the most practical size to purchase is less than two pounds in weight. We have been purchasing lobsters without shells, either raw or pre-cooked. We prefer using the raw form, especially in lobster cantonese or in salads, appetizers, or newburg.

Specifications for fish and other seafood follow:

Fillets—boneless sides cut from small fish, no breading, frozen.

> Cod, Icelandic, skinless
> Halibut Steak 4–5 oz.
> Haddock Fillets, skin on 6–8 oz.
> Perch, Ocean, skinless 4–6 oz.
> Walleye Pike 6–8 oz.

Portions—cut from frozen formed blocks of fish.

> Cod, 3 oz.
> Pollock, 3 oz.
> Haddock, 4 oz.
> Haddock, breaded (square 4 oz. portion not more than 1 oz. breading)
> Pre-cooked breaded Icelandic Cod, Grade A, not minced 1 oz. portion with ½ oz. breading

Fish Sticks

Shellfish:	Shrimp, raw IQF pieces, packed 12/3 lb. per case
	Shrimp, breaded IQF, 16–19 count, round
	Shrimp, breaded IQF
	Scallops, Raw sea, IQF, 6/5 lb. per case
	Crabmeat, Alaska King, 6/5 lb. per case

Prepared Meats

Bologna	pre-cooked, cured, not more than 3½ percent extenders, approximately 10-lb. sticks
Salami	pre-cooked, cured, mildly seasoned, regular style (not Italian), not more than 3½ percent extenders, approximately 10-lb. sticks
Liverwurst	pre-cooked, cured, firm pack, not more than 3½ percent extenders, approximately 6-lb. sticks

Pepperoni	pre-cooked, cured, not more than 3½ percent extenders, firm, does not require refrigeration for normal storage, approximately 4-lb. sticks
Wieners	all beef, skinless, mildly seasoned 10 wieners to the pound, packed in 10-lb. boxes
Pork Sausage Patty	pre-cooked, cured, not more than 3½ percent fillers or extenders
Pork Sausage Roll	pre-cooked, cured, not more than 3½ percent fillers or extenders

Minimum Standards of Quality
for Eggs

Grade—The grading of eggs is one of the most scientific grading feats developed by the USDA. The grade refers to the interior quality which is indicated by how the yolk stands up against the white, and to the condition and appearance of the shell. There are three grades used:

USDA Grade AA—the yolk is firm and high, the white is thick, stands high when viewed from the side and envelops the yolk firmly, while the amount of thin white is small and makes an almost uniform circle around the egg yolk.

USDA Grade A—the yolk is firm and high, the white is reasonably thick, stands fairly high when viewed from the side and envelops the yolk somewhat loosely while the thin white is medium in amount and encircles the egg yolk somewhat irregularly.

USDA Grade B—the yolk is somewhat flattened, the white is medium in amount and flatter than Grade A, while the thin white comes in a medium or large amount and very unevenly encircles the yolk.

The use to which the eggs are to be put determines which grade to purchase. If they are to be used only for hollandaise sauce or for baking or as an emulsifying agent in dressings, it is practical to use Grade A or Grade B, rather than spend the extra cost on Grade AA. We found in developing recipes for freezing an advantage in using frozen eggs prepared from Grade A or B eggs rather than using Grade AA eggs that crack easily when handled.

If an entree contains any egg products, they must meet these standards:

Eggs—Fresh USDA white, fancy, heavy weight. At least 30 percent of each 30 dozen cases shall be quality Grade AA. Candling certificate to be enclosed in each case.

Minimum Standards of Quality
for Dairy Products

Dairy—Since fresh dairy products are one of the most delicate ingredients, they need detailed specifications and careful handling, and it is important that the product temperature be checked upon delivery. The temperature of dairy products must be between 35°F. and 40°F. An exception is frozen cream toppings and frozen dairy desserts which, of course, must be at a lower temperature. The different varieties of milk used in cooking have "Grade A—pasteurized Milk" as the sole standard of quality.

Cream—Pasteurized cream is highly desirable for use in recipes that are to be frozen. A light whipping cream contains 30 percent to 36 percent butterfat, while a heavy cream contains at least 36 percent butterfat. Since cream is perishable, it is best to use fresh cream for cooking.

For entrees that require sour cream, it is advisable that the sour cream be added last and that it be whipped with a small amount of stabilizer, such as one teaspoon of gelatin which has been dissolved in ¼ cup of water before adding. To prevent curdling, a small amount of hot liquid from the gravy should be combined with the whipped sour cream before the cream is slowly mixed with the rest of the hot liquids. After a stabilizer is added, sour half-and-half becomes stable during cooking, freezing, and thawing, so you can substitute it for regular heavy sour cream. In the hospital, because of the various low cholesterol diets, we use sour half-and-half, instead of regular sour cream.

Milk or milk products—must meet these standards:

1. Milk—3.25 percent butterfat, not less than 8.25 percent non-fat solids.
2. 2% Milk—2 percent butterfat; 8.25 percent non-fat milk solids.
3. Chocolate Skim Milk—3.25 percent butterfat; less than ½ of 1 percent butterfat.
4. Cream, half-and-half—10.5 percent butterfat; 19 percent total solids (protein, milk, sugar, and minerals).
5. Cream—32 percent butterfat.
6. Sour Cream—not less than 0.5 percent butterfat; not less than 8.25 percent total solids.
7. Yogurt—1.75 percent butterfat; 12 percent non-fat milk solids, 14 percent cane or beet sugar, 4 ½ percent Yogurt culture, 1.35 percent citric acid, and 3.5 percent fresh frozen fruit solids.
8. Buttermilk—not less than 0.5 percent butterfat; not less than 18.25 percent total solids.
9. Skim Milk—not less than 0.5 percent butterfat; 10.9 percent total solids.

Minimum Standards of Quality
for Cheese

Cheese made from cow's whole milk contains about 20 percent to 36 percent protein, 27 percent to 33 percent fat and moisture content, depending on the softness or hardness of the cheese. Soft cheeses contain 40 percent to 75 percent moisture and hard cheese has 30 percent to 40 percent.

Processed cheeses, which include American, Swiss, and Old English, are often used for sandwiches and luncheon cuts. Varieties that are often used in recipes developed for this system of food production and blast freezing are listed below:

American Cheddar—is used for cheese sauce, macaroni and cheese, cheese in tuna noodle casserole, and au gratin potatoes. A standard of quality to be used is U. S. Grade AA: firm, smooth, waxy, with tiny white specks, although U. S. Grade A may be substituted on occasion if it is to be used in a cooked item only.

Cottage Cheese—is the natural soft curd formed when milk sours. Then it is drained, salted, and packaged into pints and half-gallon plastic covered containers. Cottage cheese comes in either the cultured large-soft, or the small, hard, curd.

Mozzarella Cheese—is often used with pizza dishes, lasagna, Veal Parmesan, and with noodles. This cheese is firm and creamy white.

Parmesan Cheese—is ripened from 12 to 18 months, usually resulting in a very granular, light yellow cheese with a sharp flavor, then grated and packaged in plastic bags or plastic covered containers.

Roquefort Cheese—is made of sheep's milk, usually in the caves of Roquefort, France. There are American versions of this cheese, sometimes called Blue Cheese, and they can, on occasion, be satisfactory substitutes.

When entrees to be used in a blast freezing system contain any cheese and cheese by-products, the following minimum standards need to be met:

1. Cottage Cheese—creamed with not less than 4 percent butterfat.
2. Salt Free Cottage Cheese—creamed with not less than 4 percent butterfat; no salt or sodium preservative added.
3. Low Sodium American Cheese—pasteurized process USDA Grade A; not more than 3 percent emulsifiers; no salt or sodium preservatives added.
4. Mozzarella—USDA Grade AA; bulk; sliced; firm, creamy, white cheese.
5. American Cheese—USDA Grade AA; bulk; smooth texture; hard; yellow to reddish.
6. Cream Cheese—USDA Grade AA; made from sour cream; soft curds made into a homogenous mixture.
7. Swiss Cheese—USDA Grade AA; au naturel; domestic; firm; ripened; creamy color with large holes.

8. Sharp Cheddar—USDA Grade AA; bulk; firm; smooth; waxy; strong flavor; of 32° sharp cured.

9. Blue Cheese—USDA Grade AA; crumbles; domestic.

Butter and Margarine

There are no definite compulsory federal gradings for butter or margarine. If the butter maker wishes to use the USDA grade stamp, the following grades are given:

USDA Grade AA or U.S. 93 score—fine, highly pleasing flavor

USDA Grade A or U.S. 92 score—pleasing and desirable flavor

USDA Grade B or U.S. 90 score—may possess mustiness; taste scorched or woody; may possess bitter taste; be coarse, acid, and aged

USDA Grade D or U.S. 89 score—may be barny, cheesy, fruity, metallic, oily, sour, garlic, yeasty

Margarine is a combination of fats and oils with cultured milk. The oils can be soybean, cottonseed, corn, peanut, or a combination of two oils. Margarine usually has 3 percent salt added.

Butter and margarine are delicate in flavor and have a tendency to absorb flavors readily from the surrounding medium. Packaging is an important part of the specifications. It is all right to freeze butter and margarine, but both must be packaged and wrapped very well.

Specifications for butter and margarine used in recipes developed for blast freezing are the following:

Butter:

Grade A, 92 Score, 1-lb. prints, wax paper wrapped 32 lb. cases

Pre-Sliced, Grade A, 92 Score, 72 squares per lb., each on a cardboard chip, 24 lb. per case

Grade AA, 92 Score Salt-Free, wax paper wrapped, 1-lb. prints

Pre-Sliced, Grade AA, 92 Score, Salt-Free, 72 squares per lb., each on cardboard chip, 10 lb. per case

TYPES OF COOKERY FOR ENTREES TO BE FROZEN

Defined here are the general cooking methods that may be used on entrees as well as other components of the menu which is part of a blast freezing system:

Boiling—is the basic method used in successful freezing programs to cook the most important ingredients, i.e. the sauces and gravies for various entrees. It is important to keep in mind that the thickening agent for sauces and gravies is most effective if the liquid is heated to 200°F. before the roux is combined with it. An alternate thickening method is to make a smooth paste out of the flour, the starch mixture, and the cold liquid. Slowly bring mixture to the boiling point with vigorous and constant stirring. This procedure is not so practical in large scale operations because large batches are difficult to mix thoroughly. I have also discussed a good method where a part of the hot liquid is slowly added to the cold paste or roux and then this warm mixture is combined with the rest of the hot liquid and brought to a boiling point while stirring constantly.

Boiling—is also the method used to reduce stock (meat stock, a wine stock, or cream stock). This results in a creamier, more freeze-resistant sauce or gravy, because there are more concentrated solid particles in the liquid.

Poaching—is often associated with fish or vegetables. In preparing entrees for freezing, poaching has an advantage over blanching or steaming, in that a good cream or butter sauce can be made using the poaching liquid. This sauce used over the fish when freezing adds flavor and also provides protection against freezer burn.

Steaming—finds its best application in vegetable cookery for items like cauliflower, peas, brussels sprouts, cabbage, green beans, and other vegetables with delicate flavor.

Searing and sauteeing—are two cooking terms commonly interchanged, although the main difference is in the stage of doneness. Searing is done very quickly and at high temperatures, just to seal in the juices of the meat. It is very practical to sear meats for freezing, as it gives the meat an additional moisture and oxygen barrier, thus preventing dehydration and oxidative rancidity. The seared effect toughens the outer cellular part of the meat which, in turn, reduces the "drip" loss of the juices.

Sauteeing is a process that actually cooks the meats, fish, and vegetables in a small amount of combined butter and oil. It is desirable to mix butter and oil for sauteeing as the smoke point of butter is very low and the oil raises the smoke point. However, when searing meat at a high temperature, oil should be used.

Broiling—is not a commonly used method of preparation for meats to be frozen because this method extracts juices from the meats, resulting in a dried piece of meat. It is difficult to produce perfectly broiled meat even in a conventional system, because of the lapse of time between preparation and serving. (The best techique, if foods must be broiled, is to have the broiler hot enough to brown the meat to preserve the juices, and then to cook the meat at a moderate heat for a very short time, just enough to cook through the center part.) However, since it is difficult to reheat broiled meat without having it taste like a steamed meat, broiling is not recommended for items to be blast frozen.

Roasting—involves searing meat in the oven at a temperature of 425°F. for 15 to 30 minutes, then turning the heat down to 300°F. to complete the cooking. The thermometer should indicate 145°F. to 155°F. internal temperature for rare, 160°F. to 170°F. internal temperature for medium, and 170°F. to 175°F. internal temperature for well done.

One of the important points to remember in roasting meats for freezing is that you will have to apply additional heat after the roast is thawed. So if you wish to have a medium done roast at the serving point, it is best to get a medium rare doneness at the freezing stage. For tougher cuts of meat, pot roasting is a good method of tenderizing, adding moisture and flavor to meat. A recipe has been developed (see Volume 2, Blast Freezing Quantity Recipes) for a glaze that should be poured over any pot roast before freezing to add flavor and to prevent further dehydration.

Frying—is not the most practical method of cooking for inexperienced cooks preparing entrees for a cook–freeze system. One has to master the techniques of adapting each component to the time and temperature that the fried product needs for reconstitution. Some foodservice experts think that deep fat frying is easy as you just immerse the food in very hot fat or oil. However, using too high a temperature causes fat to smoke, break down, and have an unpleasant burned taste. Changing the oil is a complicated task that must be performed each time the oil gets overheated. If the temperature of the oil is too low, the product absorbs more oil, thus making it greasy. At too low a temperature, the moisture loss from meat is increased through osmosis.

Frying in oil or shortening within a temperature range of 335°F. to 370°F. is a popular method. It includes pan-frying, oven-frying, and deep-frying. For breaded or battered products, the oven-frying method has been successfully used. Although deep fat frying compares favorably in producing quality results, there is a difference in the degree of fat absorption. Deep fat frying results in a greater absorption. Increased fat absorption makes the products soggy after thawing and during reconstitution. The frozen food industry has achieved a breakthrough with the use of a special hydrogenated oil, the use of methyl ethyl cellulose (especially for potatoes), and by pre-blanching the product to reduce moisture loss.

It is important to make sure that the temperature of every batch of food to be deep fat fried is checked with a thermometer. There is a drop in temperature every time a basket full of cold or frozen food is lowered into the fat. Therefore, the temperature should be brought back up to 350°F. before a new batch is placed in the fat. In the United States, J. C. Pitman & Sons, Inc. has a deep fat fryer with baskets that are automatically lowered, and then raised when the batch is finished, and the fat temperature is automatically controlled for each batch. The task of changing oil is also minimized as the fryer has its own self-cleaning filter. In this way, the oil can be reused over and over again.

BASIC PREPARATION TECHNIQUES FOR ENTREES

The art of successfully preparing entrees for freezing depends on basic knowledge of the physical, chemical, and textural changes that take place during freezing. As discussed in the earlier chapters, the kind, size, shape, and amount of each ingredient plays an important role in the method and time necessary for the preparation of each product. It must be kept in mind during planning that these physical and chemical changes occur at various stages on the flow chart, from the time the raw material is received up to the time the food is thawed and reconstituted. The role of management lies in the control and manipulation of the materials to be frozen, taking into consideration the rate of oxidation, time, temperature, moisture content, degree of doneness, and bacterial growth. Each of these factors if improperly controlled, can affect the final quality of the precooked, frozen products.

In terms of preparation techniques, we have found that recipes with lower moisture content are more satisfactory in product formulation, and in preparation for sauces and gravies, as has been noted previously. Certain meats, fish, and vegetables have to be cooked partially or just enough to inactivate various enzymes, e.g., peroxidase in vegetables. The degree of doneness is also dependent on the type of reconstitution or reheating oven that one is planning to use. Plating techniques have been tested and proven to be another important factor in determining what preparation methods have to be utilized. For microwave oven reconstitution, mashed potatoes have to be plated with a large dimpled space in the middle for even heat distribution.

There are no major modifications in the basic preparation methods for entrees with one important exception: bear in mind that cooking occurs not only before the products are frozen, but also during the reconstitution of these items. Due to the differences in the final product temperature desirable for each entree, it is best to calculate the cooking time and temperature for each production run. The entree recipes in Volume 2, Blast Freezing Quantity Recipes, were pre-tested, produced, and frozen for several years at Hennepin County Medical Center. It took several modifications and trial runs before the right product combinations, rate of heat penetration, and degree of doneness in preparation desirable for freezing were determined.

Soups for Freezing

We decided not to prepare soups for freezing for the following reasons: (1) A good variety of soup concentrates and freeze dehydrated soups is available at economical cost. (2) The additional cost of freezing water is not justifiable. Water presents freezing, packaging, and storage problems. However, food-service directors Chuck Beyer[2] and Paul Doyon[3] have found that those soups made of pureed vegetables are usually better quality when frozen than soups made from plain beef stock. Soups with a high soluble solid content result in a better quality soup. Cream soups should be made either out of canned cream or out of the freshest supply of cream that has been heated in a double boiler.

A basic cream soup used in various foodservice institutions is made with a thin white sauce, as sometimes pure cream is too rich and too delicate to keep hot as required in soup making. In order to arrive at a good quality frozen cream soup, you must have a good cream sauce base. For best results remember the following points:

1. Since curdling is a problem, it is always good to aerate at a very fast rate and to mix the ingredients while they are in the low temperature range of 140°F. to 160°F. This means that ingredients like fat, flour (in a combination which is 70 percent waxy maize starch), seasonings and garnishes such as mushrooms, potatoes, and onions are brought to the boiling point. You should prepare the flour-fat mixture with the hot cream-milk using the same method as required in preparing a sauce. Saute or cook the garnishes separately and combine these with the flour-fat and hot milk mixture as the very last step prior to freezing.

2. In preparing cream soups with vegetables such as tomatoes that have a pH range less than three, add these acidic vegetables last. It is also best not to have these ingredients constitute more than 8 percent to 10 percent of the total volume of solids present in the soups. When the fat-flour mixture has come to a boiling point, add the milk or cream. Stir and cook. The acidic vegetables are combined with the soup just prior to freezing.

3. It is important when using stock as part of the hot liquid for cream soups that you skim off the *fat* that rises to the top of the stock. This is easily done by refrigerating the stock until the fat hardens.

Entrees

We have avoided broiling and frying meats for freezing and reconstituting in microwave ovens. As pointed out previously, dry heat methods of cooking, such as broiling, increase the tendency for protein denaturation which results in toughening of the connective tissues and also extraction of salts from the meat. There is a technique to overcome this often used by food processors.

They use a special glaze with a small amount of oil that prevents good quality meats from losing their juices. It also helps to start with high heat in the broiler or griddle and sear the meat before turning the temperature down. As for frying, especially chicken or fish in a batter, oxidative rancidity occurs at a rapid rate in storage. These products also lose their crispness during storage, thawing, and reconstitution. There is a need for a reconstitution oven which will "crisp" fried products while heating the food to 170°F.

Food processors in the United States have been using glucose or honey in their batter for fried chicken which helps preserve the "crispness" of the product. In England, they have used additives such as glyceryl monostearate to prevent oiliness in fried products, and to increase crispness in the batter.

Most of the meat entrees planned for preparation in our central food preparation facility were based on roast meats, such as chicken, turkey, pork, and beef. O'Brien, Spotorno, and Mitchell, food processors in San Francisco, Ca. use a large, covered, steam–jacketed kettle for pot roasting. They have devised a special packaging technique to reduce meat shrinkage due to excessive drip loss. Meat roasts are seared or pan braised at very high temperatures, then immersed in a large kettle containing seasoned stock for a few minutes to absorb flavor. After immersion, the meat is immediately removed, wrapped, and sealed tightly in a boilable bag for additional cooking in the steam–jacketed kettles.

To retain meat quality during recipe preparation for freeze processing, the following guidelines are recommended:

Time and Temperature Guide for Preparation of Meat

Type of Meat	Recommended Method of Preparation	Fresh/ Thawed	Frozen	Internal Temperature (with Use of Meat Therm.) When done
Beef				
Boned rolled & tied Rib Rare	Roast in Oven or in Steam- Jacketed Kettle wrapped in high density poly bags at 300°F.	25 min./lb.	50 min./lb.	140°F.
Medium		30 min./lb.	75 min./lb.	160°F.
Well Done		45 min./lb.	2 hr.10 min./lb	170°F

Chuck Roast	Same as above	30 min./lb.	75 min./lb.	160°F.
Rump Roast	Same as above or braise in Tilting Braising Pan at 300°F.	30 min./lb.	75 min./lb.	160°F.
Porterhouse Steak 1 inch thick	Grill	20 min. (total)	25 min. (total)	150°F.
NY Strip Sirloin	Grill	15 min. (total)	25 min. (total)	150°F.
Round Steak	Grill	20 min. (total)	30 min. (total)	150°F.
Hamburger Patty	Grill	15 min.	20 min.	175°F.
Beef Stew	Pan-braise Steam-Jacketed Kettle or Tilting Braising Pan	2 ½ hr. (total)	3-3 ½ hr. (total)	175°F.

Pork

Rib/Shoulder or Loin Roast	Roast in oven at 300°F. or in Steam-Jacketed Kettle wrapped in poly bag	60 min./lb.		185°F.
Fresh Ham	Roast at 300°F.	35 min./lb.		185°F.
Center Cut Chops ½ inch thick	Grill at 350°F.	30 min. (total)	1 hr. 10 min. (total)	185°F.
Loin cut chops	Grill at 350°F.	35 min.	60 min. (total)	185°F
Sausage (1 lb.)	Grill at 375°F.	10-15 min. (total)	20-25 min. (total)	185°F.

Lamb

Leg Should. (Boned, rolled & tied)	Roast at 300°F. or braise in SJK wrapped in poly bags	30 min./lb. 40 min./lb.	50 min./lb. 1 hr. 10 min./lb.	180°F. 180°F.

Time and Temperature Guide (cont'd.)

Type of Meat	Recommended Method of Preparation	Fresh/ Thawed	Frozen	Internal Temperature [with Use of Meat Therm.] When Done
Chops	Grill at 350°F.	10–15 min. (total)	25–35 min. (total)	180°F.
Patties	Grill at 350°F.	10 min.	20 min. (total)	180°F.
Veal				
Leg	Roast at 300°F. or braise in Steam Jacketed Kettle wrapped in poly bags	25 min./lb.	35–40 min./lb.	170°F
Loin	(same)	30 min./lb.	50–60 min./lb.	170°F.
Chops ½ inch thick	Grill at 350°F.			

The preparation of fish and other seafood entrees for freezing offers a unique challenge. Most of the fish prepared and served in large foodservice operations, such as hospitals, restaurants, and colleges, is either baked, broiled, or deep fat fried. Fish is a very perishable and delicate product to handle, because of its fat and collagen content. Enzymatic changes due to improper refrigeration result in an unpleasant taste and poor texture. Although spoilage is not always detectable right away, a slimy feeling indicates the quality of the fish has already deteriorated to a point where it should not be used. The large amount of collagen in fish makes it too soft and mushy if even slightly overcooked.

If fish is being prepared for freezing, either by grilling, pan-braising, steaming, or poaching, it is always well to remember that undercooking or not cooking at all is best. There are two basic rules to follow: first, that fish with high fat content such as salmon, trout, bullhead, catfish, herring, northern pike, smelt, and tuna are best prepared either baked, grilled, or pan-braised. Normally, these types of fish are broiled, but as explained earlier, broiling extracts inherent natural fat from the fish, thereby making it drier during reheating. Second, keep in mind that lean fish, such as haddock, halibut, flounder, perch, sea bass, sunfish, and white fish are better poached or steamed with herbs, spices, and wine. It is recommended that fish be basted with a sauce during poaching or baking.

Much of the fish on the market now is breaded fish for use in deep-fat frying or baking in a high speed convection oven. The basic batter recipe to follow in breading fish or other seafood is:

Title BASIC BATTER RECIPE	No.
Yield 100 Batter Portions	Portion 2 oz. per fish

Ingredients	Amount
Cake Flour	6 lb.
Waxy Rice Flour	2 lb.
Waxy Maize Cornstarch	1 lb.
*Baking Powder	4 oz.
Egg Yolk	2½ lb.
Non-Fat Milk Powder	1 lb.
*Salt	2 oz.
Pepper	1 oz.
*Monosodium Glutamate	4 oz.
Iced Water	1 qt.

*For low sodium diets, omit salt and Monosodium Glutamate and substitute a low sodium baking powder.

Procedure:

1. Sift together the cake flour, starch, and baking powder, salt and pepper to produce a seasoned flour.

2. Beat egg yolks slightly and add non-fat milk powder, and the monosodium glutamate.

3. Just before dipping pieces of fish in the egg yolk mixture, add iced water to it and mix slightly.

4. Dip pieces of fish in the egg mixture, then dip the fish lightly in the flour mixture.

5. Assure a continuous product flow by having one person assigned to the egg-milk mixture and another one to the seasoned flour. If the products are not going to be fried immediately, then the breading process should not be started. There must not be a gap in the process flow.

In order to achieve a successful frying operation for battered products, whether it be of fish, poultry, or beef pies, follow these procedures:

1. In Japan, batter frying, or "tempura" cooking, is done with pure sesame oil in order to produce the best quality end product. The best kind of oil for

frying in the United States, since sesame oil is too expensive, is a combination of corn oil and cottonseed or soybean oil.

2. It is necessary that the size of the frying equipment used is correct for the batch being fried. This permits a continuous process and minimizes delays between the time the products are fried and the time they are fed to the freezing tunnel or put on the blast freezer shelves.

3. In order to insure clean oil for frying, it is best to purchase a self-cleaning filter. If this is not economically feasible, it is recommended that the oil be changed as often as the product turnover requires it to be. After oil has been used for frying fish, it is not good to use it to fry other foods.

4. In frying, do not let the temperatures exceed 400°F. (204°C.).

5. Have the amount of oil in the fryer required by the volume of the product being fried. If bubbling occurs to the point that the fat overflows, then there is either too much product being fried or there is too much oil in the fryer.

6. Try to prevent the oil from stagnating or having idling time as this just burns oil. This is why a continuous flow process is necessary once the fryer is turned on.

7. Maintain the fryer in a clean, sanitary condition and if any coils or elements are not in good condition have them replaced immediately. The fryer must be completely cleaned of dirt and grease and burned food accumulations, inside and out. It is also wise to see that a thorough rinsing takes place.

8. The exhaust hoods over the fryers must be cleaned after each frying period. It is possible if there is an accumulation of grease in the hood for a prolonged period to have a fire start spontaneously.

The recommendations listed above are very important because the shelf life of fried foods is completely dependent on how well oxidative rancidity due to the development of fatty acid formation is prevented.

There is frozen, breaded, uncooked fish available in the market which has several advantages over the pre-fried, battered kinds. Unfortunately, when it comes to microwave oven reconstitution, there is no browning or crisping that can take place. Therefore, prior to freezing, it is practical to fry the battered fish for half the required time and then place the pre-fried battered fish in an oven, set at 400°F., for 10 minutes, or to deep fat fry the fish at 400°F. for less than 15 minutes, to brown the fish enough to assure eye appeal.

Our basic recipe for beef stew has no potatoes, as we can usually add them if desired at the stage of reconstitution. Frozen potatoes have a tendency to absorb moisture and become mushy after thawing. Beef stew-type entrees are the most difficult to control because the quality depends so much on the ratio of the sauce to the meat and vegetable mixture. The quality of the stew is also affected by the final moisture content of the vegetables which is established by the cooking time set for the product mix. Undercooked or overcooked vegetables have a tendency to upset the ratio between the hot liquid and the thickening agent. It is also not good to produce a finished batch of stew that is larger than an amount equal to what the tilting braising pan or steam-jacketed kettles held at the start of the stew preparation when the beef cubes were seared. It is difficult to recover the amount of browned flour from the meat cubes if they are seared in too large a quantity.

Recipes that call for cooked chicken, such as chicken a la king, chicken chow mein, or chicken pot pie, need to have the hens prepared by *simmering*, rather than roasting. It is best to remove the skin of the hen so it will not get mixed with the cooked pieces. In order to remove all the possible chicken fat, take the hens out of the stock after simmering and place the stock in the refrigerator. After the fat becomes cold, it is visible and easy to separate. Chicken and turkey fats are unstable, thus oxidative rancidity occurs at a rapid rate. The unpleasant flavor that is associated with rancidity becomes pronounced if a delay occurs between preparation and freezing. Turkey fat, as compared to chicken fat, undergoes oxidative rancidity to a greater degree during freezer storage. This is due to the fact that chicken fat contains higher levels of tocopherol, which is a natural antioxidant.

Work out food preparation procedures to retain product quality and safety. The quality of a product is at stake if the time between handling and freezing is not kept to a minimum. The safety of a product is reduced, especially in creamed poultry products, if the product remains in the bacteria danger zone between 140°F. to 40°F. Within minutes in this zone, bacteria counts increase until product temperatures are finally lowered to 0°F.

Out of the numerous products cited in Rappole's[4] Risley Project thesis, it was discovered that only two production runs had high coliform counts and one product had a high Staphylococcus aureus count. The positive tests appeared on the single portion pouches. The production run contamination is not difficult to envision, because of the excessive handling involved, especially during the preparation of a la king. In the tests showing positive Staphylococcus aureus, it was not determined whether the organisms present were or were not of the actual food poisoning type. It has been thought that the possible point of contamination was the step where the funnel and the human hand touched, i.e. during the transfer of the product into the individual pouches.

The additional preparation before freezing of plain, whole, roast meats or sliced meats, ground beef patties, and other ground beef, pork, and veal mixtures in casserole-type entrees can be summarized as follows:

1. We concluded that the addition of texturized vegetable protein to beef patties and ground beef recipes in amounts equal to at least 5 percent to 8 percent of the total weight of the raw beef has several advantages in freezing pre-cooked entrees; they are:

a)   Texturized vegetable protein, if properly combined with ground beef of 17 percent to 18 percent fat content, will absorb some of the excess fat. The absorption of fat during cooking decreases the potential for oxidative rancidity because the fat molecules are not as free when they are bound tightly with these texturized vegetable molecules.

b)   The addition of texturized vegetable protein improves the moisture retention rate for the meat, thus there is less dehydration during freezer storage.

c)   Texturized vegetable protein also binds the various herbs, spices, wine, milk, cream, sour cream, Worcestershire sauce, and other flavorings, so that flavor transference and flavor potency reactions are reduced. During the preparation of hamburger patties, salt should be reduced to a minimum, so that the withdrawal of fat molecules from the rest of the meat does not occur. In this way, the rate of oxidative rancidity arising from the fat at the surface of the meat is somewhat delayed.

2. We have discovered and proven during several years of usage that putting a salt-free, low-calorie glaze on roast meats before freezing and then plating sliced meats with this glaze protects the meat itself from dehydration and flavor transference and somewhat reduces the amount of natural meat juice loss during the reconstitution process. During reheating, the meat glaze is the first liquid to dehydrate, leaving the natural moisture in the meat intact.

3. Another technique that has been used is to brush the roasts and the sliced or portioned beef patties with a small amount of cold cooking oil before reconstitution. The oil not only acts as a barrier to seal the internal juices inside the meat, but also during microwave reconstitution serves to reactivate the fat molecules on the outer surface instead of the internal ones. In this last application, the microwaves penetrate fat molecules at a faster rate, thereby decreasing the tendency for the moisture inside to migrate outward.

4. Cook meat quickly and try to skim off the fat as soon as it solidifies. Wait until the roast has reached an internal temperature of 40°F. before slicing. In a large institution, it is safer, since one is dealing with larger batches, to use a blast chill refrigerator in bringing the temperature down as fast as possible to a temperature below 40°F.

Sandwiches

There are inherent problems in freezing sandwiches, because of some basic chemical and physical changes that take place when fillings are made for sandwiches and also when the contact between the filling and the bread takes place.

In preparing grilled cheese sandwiches, especially for microwave oven reconstitution, there are several helpful techniques to remember. They are:

1. Use day-old bread made with a high egg content. The majority of the bakeries produce "egg bread" but the Federal agencies refuse to allow labelling it as such, based on inadequate ingredient percentages.

2. To produce toasted sandwiches, grill the bread at 425°F. which requires the use of an oil with a high smoke point. A reduction of the temperature to 350°F. will insure a certain degree of melting of the cheese. It is important that the two bread slices be fused by the cheese. This fusion provides a fatty barrier for the bread. When the bread slices are fused there is less space for moisture migration and less opportunity for oxidative rancidity to occur during freezer storage and thawing.

3. Use a vented, moisture-vapor proof bag or wrap made of cello-polyethylene or plio film. Wrap the sandwich after it has cooled completely to prevent moisture condensation.

4. Use a swiss-cheddar cheese as there is less tendency for it to be tough and stringy after reconstitution in the microwave oven.

5. Do not use aluminum foil for wrapping cheese sandwiches, as the acids in the cheese will corrode the foil. These holes will cause a complete loss of protection from oxidation and moisture migration.

6. When thawing a toasted or grilled cheese sandwich, it is best to remove it from the bag to prevent the loss of crispness. Immediately reheat the sandwich in a microwave oven, regrill it in a medium hot pan, or reheat it on a grill without additional butter or oil. This type of sandwich must be thawed rapidly, as the bread becomes stale very fast.

Cold Sandwiches with Fillings—Bread staling stops as soon as 0°F. is reached during freezer storage. The bread slices must be buttered on each side with at least one-half to three-fourths ounce of butter or margarine.

Experience demonstrates that excellent sandwich fillings are made with cream cheese in combination with shrimp, turkey pieces, nuts, olives, tuna, crab, lobster, clams, salmon, dried beef, liver pate or braunschweiger, sardines, and with blue cheese. However a filling made of cream cheese combined with any of the cured meats, such as ham, bologna, corned beef, Canadian bacon, loses its flavor and becomes rancid after four or five months.

Loaf sandwiches filled with cream cheese, egg salad, and beef salad or turkey salad have been prepared and frozen. These frozen loaf sandwiches have excellent flavor, color, and quality. Unfortunately, the loaf sandwich loses all its good quality by the end of three months. Included in the sample recipes in Volume 2, Blast Freezing Quantity Recipes, is a modified mayonnaise recipe that has a good shelf life for freezer storage.

Frozen sandwiches of excellent quality are made with the following fillings: roast beef, turkey, and chicken; flaked fish or deep fried fishwich, including tuna, salmon, and sardines; processed meats including salami, pepperoni, summer sausage, pepper loaf, and liverwurst; cheese including cheddar cheese, swiss–cheddar, and Camembert; and peanut butter.

There are no problems when it comes to the freezing of sandwiches, as long as the two slices of bread are spread generously and evenly with either butter, cream cheese, modified sour cream, or margarine softened to room temperature. Sour cream can be used instead of butter by adding (per 100 portions of cream) one teaspoon of gelatin dissolved in one ounce of warm water. Whip this gelatin into the sour cream with a vigorous motion, using a wire whip or aerate in a blender.

Hot Sandwiches with Meat Fillings—Hot sandwiches commonly used for freezing are hamburgers, sloppy joes, steak filets, fishwiches, roast beef, turkey, and pork cutlet sandwiches. The basic techniques in the preparation have been given. The most important technique to remember is in the handling of the bread or buns, so they will not become soggy or tough when reconstituted. The same principles apply to these buns that apply to the bread for grilled sandwiches. It is preferable to have egg in the bread for a good "caramelizing," i.e. browning or toasting effect. The egg also has a tenderizing effect when the bun is reconstituted in a microwave oven. If they are to be frozen with the sliced meats or the meat fillings in place, the buns or bread must first be toasted or grilled well at high temperature using a half margarine half cottonseed oil mixture.

Operation tested recipes for entrees have been included in Volume 2, Blast Freezing Quantity Recipes.

7

Preparing Fruit
for Blast Freezing

Fruit has been provided by nature with an outer protective coating to prevent the entrance of micro-organisms which ultimately cause spoilage and decay. Unfortunately, fruit during the various stages of growth is subject to insect bites, wind bruises, and other mechanical actions that penetrate the skin. When the skin has been invaded by micro-organisms, the fruit loses its high germicidal strength. Micro-organisms which cause deterioration of fruit include various bacteria, yeasts, and molds.

It is important to wash all fruit thoroughly before blanching. Washing and blanching will reduce the microbiological count of the raw fruit. The destruction of these organisms during the freezing process is also dependent on the type of molds or yeasts present, as there are mold spores resistant to freezing. The type of freezing method used and the time required to freeze fruit will affect the level of microbial contamination. Fast freezing done intermittently is considered the best not only for microbiological control but quality control as well. In addition, immersion of fruit in suspensions of sugar or salt will affect contamination levels.

Blanching of fruit consists of immersing the products in steam, hot water, or hot syrup. It seems to me that steam blanching results in better tasting products, with a minimum loss of flavor and soluble solids. Steam blanching keeps the fibrous tissues more intact, thus making the fruit aesthetically better.

The raw fruit should be washed in ice cold water and prepared according to the desired final size, shape, and dimensions of the products. Washing and preparation procedures for fruit should be accomplished quickly, to avoid excessive water absorption into fruit tissues.

A continuous flow has to be maintained from the time the fruit is picked through to the time it is frozen. The packing syrup should be prepared ahead of time and cooled down. There are two fruits—apples and cranberries—which do not need syrup or sugar added prior to freezing. Because of their firm outer pericarp, they need only be blanched or treated with antioxidant to retain color. We have used a citric, malic, and ascorbic acid formula which has been very successful in preserving quality.

We have been successful in preserving quality in frozen fruit and vegetables by adding ascorbic acid, malic, and citric acid, not only for fruit, but for vegetables and salads as well. Ascorbic acid added to sugar syrup when packing avocados, apricots, sweet cherries, plums, peaches, and figs, eliminates darkening when frozen. The simplest method is to add ascorbic acid to the syrup or sugar pack prior to packaging and freezing. Use one teaspoon pure ascorbic acid, ¼ teaspoon citric acid, ¼ teaspoon malic acid for each two quarts of water used or ½ teaspoon of each mixed with each pound of dry sugar. Pure ascorbic, citric, and malic acids are available from drugstores and distributors of supplies for food processors.

When preparing fruit for freezing, select a high quality product from a variety that can withstand freezing. Freezing does not improve the quality of fruit; it only preserves the original fresh quality of the product.

It has been emphasized in various pamphlets distributed by the Extension Service of the University of Minnesota that various kinds of fruit selected for freezing should be slightly riper than those selected for canning, but they should not be soft or mushy. Fruit must be picked at the optimum stage of maturity, as tree-ripened fruit contains higher levels of vitamins and richer flavors.

It is recommended in this bulletin that fruit be packed with sugar as losses of Vitamin C are greater when fruit is packed without sugar. Of course, it is also a good idea to add citric and ascorbic acid to the fruit prior to freezing. Unsweetened fruit will naturally lose quality faster than those packed in sugar or syrup.

There are three ways to pack fresh fruit for freezing, depending on the degree of sweetness desired and the inherent tendency of the fruit to discolor upon exposure to air. *Dry Pack* is often used for strawberries, apples, raspberries, blueberries, peaches, and apricots. When dry packing, fruit has to be sorted, washed, and prepared for the table, i.e., peaches or strawberries would need to be sliced. *Sugar Pack* is a method where dry sugar is sprinkled over the' fruit in a shallow dish, tray, or bun pan, and the fruit is tossed gently so that each piece is coated with sugar. Then the fruit is packed lightly into packaging containers suitable for the type of fruit being frozen. *Syrup Pack* has to be prepared in advance by dissolving the sugar required in cold water. The syrup pack formula is as follows:

Syrup Percent	*Amt. of Sugar Per 1 qt. Water*
20	1 cup
30	2 cups
40	3 cups
50	4–½ cups

The sugar has to be stirred occasionally. Let the syrup stand in the refrigerator until needed, but never more than two days. Put the fruit in a packaging container and cover with syrup leaving enough space at the top for the expansion of fruit that occurs during freezing.

Described below are preparation techniques and proportions of sugar to water for freezer packaging of selected varieties of fruit.

Apples

Selection: Use a good cooking variety ripened to crisp eating stages.

Preparation: Peel and cut into slices by one of the two methods described here:

Sliced Apples:

Method 1—To prevent darkening, soak 15 minutes in solution of one level tablespoon of sodium bisulfite to one gallon of water. Drain and pack without water, or mix 5 to 7 pounds of fruit with one pound of sugar.

Method 2—Soak slices for 15 minutes in brine (½ cup salt per gallon of water), drain, pack in 30 percent syrup with ascorbic acid added.

Whole Apples—Do not peel or slice. Wash in ice cold water and pack into plastic bags to be used for pie, sauce, or other baked or cooked desserts. Do not thaw before peeling after being frozen. Use immediately.

Applesauce—It is not as good as canned applesauce, but can be prepared in the usual method.

Baked Apples—Prepare as usual, cool by floating pan in iced water.

Apricots

Selection: Select well–ripened fruits of a uniform, golden yellow color.

Preparation: Peel if desired, cut into halves, remove pits. Unpeeled apricots are not good for baked desserts as the skin toughens.

Syrup Pack—40 percent syrup with ascorbic acid. Use one pound sugar for 4 to 5 pounds of fruit.

Avocados

Selection: Use soft, ripe fruit free from dark blemishes.

Preparation: Wash, peel, remove pits, cut into strips, immerse quickly for 5 minutes in ascorbic citric, and malic acid solution, and drain.

Syrup Pack—in 20 percent syrup with ascorbic acid.

For making puree: add 1 ½ tablespoon of sugar and 2 teaspoons of lemon juice to one cup of avocado puree.

Berries

(Blackberries, blueberries, boysenberries, youngberries, huckleberries, loganberries, raspberries):

Selection: Use firm berries with a bright color and appearance, good flavor, and no blemishes.

Preparation: Wash, sort, and discard berries that are blemished or bruised, under–ripe, poorly colored, or formed.

Dessert:

Syrup Pack—in 40 percent to 50 percent syrup.

Sugar Pack—use one pound of sugar for 4 to 5 pounds of berries.

Cooked or Baked:

Dry Pack fruit.

Cherries, Sweet

Selection: Use any good quality cherry.

Preparation: Steam, wash, pit, and drain.

Syrup Pack—in 30 percent syrup with ascorbic acid.

Sugar Pack—use one pound sugar for 5 pounds fruit with ascorbic acid.

Cooked as in topping—Use same formula.

Cherries, Sour

Preparation: Same as above.

Sugar Pack—use one pound of dry sugar to 4 pounds fruit with ascorbic acid.

Citrus Fruits

Preparation: Sprinkle sugar over each layer of fruit and refrigerate. Let stand overnight until the juice covers as much fruit as possible. Add ¼ teaspoon ascorbic acid to 4 pounds of fruit if it is going to be stored long.

Cranberries

Selection: Use any available variety that has firm plump berries with good colored, glossy skins.

Preparation: Sort and discard blemished and bruised fruit. Wash in cold water and drain.

Dry pack.

Currants

Selection: Use Red Labe and similar large-fruited varieties.

Preparation: Wash in cold water, remove stems, lift out fruit, and drain.

Sugar Pack—with one pound sugar to 4 pounds currants.
Dry Pack.

Figs

Selection: Use any good variety.

Preparation: Wash, stem, peel if desired. Halve, slice or leave whole.

Syrup Pack—in 40 percent syrup.

Gooseberries

Selection: Use any good cooking variety.

Preparation: Remove blossom ends and stems. Wash, lift from water and drain.

Pies and Preserves—Dry pack.

Grapes

Selection: Use Thompson Seedless and Tokay that are ripe and firm.

Preparation: Sort, stem, and wash grapes. Lift from water and drain. Thompson Seedless can be packed whole or halved; remove seeds from Tokays.

Syrup Pack—with 40 percent syrup.

Grapefruit

Selection: Any good variety available.

Preparation: Pack and freeze alone or in combination with oranges, peaches, pineapple, cherries, and seedless grapes.

Syrup Pack—in 40 percent syrup with ascorbic acid.

Melons, Musk

Selection: Use Honeydew, Burpee Hybrid.

Preparation: Wash, halve, and remove seeds. Cut flesh into ½ to ¾ inch cubes or balls.

Syrup Pack—using 2 cups sugar to one quart water.

Melons (Cantaloupe, Casaba, Honeydew, Persian)

Selection: Use any good variety with firm flesh, extra good flavor.

Preparation: Cut into uniform slices, cubes, or balls.

Syrup Pack—with 30 percent syrup; serve partially frozen.

Peaches and Nectarines

Selection: Use Alberta, July (Early), Fireglow, J. H. Hale, and Hale-Haven. Cling Stone variety not good for freezing. Choose well-ripened fruits, especially ripened and held at 75°F.

Preparation: Peel, pit, and slice fruit directly into syrup or sugar with ascorbic acid.

Syrup Pack—40 percent sugar with ascorbic acid.

Sugar Pack—use one pound of sugar to four pounds of fruit.
Make sure the fruits are completely covered to prevent browning.

Pears and Plums

Selection: It does not matter, as these fruits do not freeze well.

Preparation: Wash, peel, halve, core, and slice and immerse in *boiling* 40 percent syrup for one to two minutes. Chill rapidly in refrigerator.

Syrup Pack—in 40 percent syrup with ascorbic acid.

Pineapple

Selection: Use fruit of dark orange-yellow color, bright appearance, unblemished, with fragrant odor. If the top leaves pull out easily, then it is ready and ripe enough to freeze.

Preparation: Wash, peel, remove eyes and core, and cut into desired shapes.

Syrup Pack—use 40 percent syrup.

Sugar Pack—use one pound of sugar to five pounds pineapple.

Prunes

Selection: Use Italian and Stenley.

Preparation: Wash, halve, and pit.

Syrup Pack—use 40 percent syrup with ascorbic acid.

Sugar Pack—use one pound of sugar to four pounds of fruit.

Rhubarb

Selection: Use Valentine, Chiprano, Canada Red, and McDonald.

Preparation: Wash thoroughly, trim, and chain. Cut in 1 inch pieces. Rhubarb sauce is very good frozen.

Dry Pack.

Syrup Pack—with 40 percent syrup.

Strawberries

Selection: Earlimore, Trumpeter, Sparkle, Dunlap, Gem and Superfection. Choose firm, ripe, bright red color, with rich aromatic flavor, and free from rot.

Preparation: Sort and discard blemished, bruised, and discolored berries. Hull and sort. Wash each berry separately.

Sugar Pack—slice, using one pound sugar to four pounds fruit.

Syrup Pack—only for whole peaches using 40 percent syrup.

Serve before completely thawed.

Frozen Fruit Salads, Fruits for Mixes

Selection: Select well-ripened fruit from the various kinds of fruit to be used. Combine acidic fruit with non-acidic fruit to prevent browning. There are two or three fruits not good for freezing: raw apples, raw grapes, and nuts. Dressings that may be used are French, vinegar and oil, sweet Russian, modified mayonnaise, and sour cream.

Nuts

The storage life of nuts, whether shelled or unshelled, is greatest at freezing temperature, but an asurance of top quality and utmost freshness are essential. It is best to pack nuts in metal or glass containers with tight-fitting lids.

Quantity recipes which incorporate the fruits which have been discussed in this chapter appear in Volume 2, Blast Freezing Quantity Recipes.

8

Preparing Vegetables for Blast Freezing

Raw vegetables that are to be blast frozen must first either be blanched or steamed to inactivate the enzymes, especially peroxidase which causes bad odors, flavors, and off-colors during freezer storage.

A simple test can be performed, as mentioned by Glew,[1] to determine whether the time and temperature the vegetables have been exposed to are adequate to completely inactivate the enzymes. In this test first a drop of one percent solution of guraiacol is dispersed on the cut surface of a cooked vegetable. Next a drop of one percent hydrogen peroxide is smeared on the same surface. If a brown color develops immediately, the enzyme peroxidase is still present, as Glew points out.

Reducing the cooking and preparation time for vegetables also maximizes the vitamin C and vitamin B retention of the frozen products. In Oriental cookery vegetables are prepared so as to be crisp, crunchy, and partially cooked.

The availability of good quality frozen vegetables during the last quarter of the century has resulted in maximum usage of these vegetables. To obtain the best quality frozen vegetables, the time required for processing vegetables from the garden to the freezer should not exceed two hours.

In general, raw vegetables have to be prepared the same way as they would be when served raw. After picking or cutting, wash the vegetables thoroughly in cold, running water. Trim off excess leaves or brown spots and discard imperfect items. Prepare the vegetables in the form desired; krinkle cut, sliced, diced, etc., and place these vegetables in a wire basket that fits a large aluminum or stainless steel kettle when the water is in a rolling boil. It is a common practice to use one gallon of water per pound of vegetable and for leafy greens to use two gallons of water. Cover immediately and keep the heat high. It is best to use a timer, as too long blanching period results in mushy vegetables and increased loss in color, vitamins, and other nutrients. Under-blanching results in poor inactivation of the enzymes, producing changes in odors and flavors and causing product discoloration.

The procedures in basic preparation and blanching for various vegetables are as follows:

Techniques for Preparing Vegetables for Freezing

Vegetable	*Preparation*
Asparagus Martha Washington Mary Washington F_1 Hybrid varieties	Remove woody and blemished stalks. Wash in cold running water. Cut tips into lengths desired, cut off fibrous end to be used for soup and purees. Process rapidly, very perishable. Water scald small stalks 3 min.; steam scald 4 min. Water scald med. stalks 3½ min.; steam scald 4½ min.; Water scald large stalks 4 min.; steam scald 5 to 5½ min.
Beans **Lima**	Wash and remove beans from pods. Discard blemished beans. Don't wash after shelling. Large Fordhook beans require maximum time. Water scald small and medium size 3 min.; steam scald 3½ to 5½ min.
Green and Waxed Beans	Use Blue Lakes and Tendercrop varieties. Discard blemished, small, immature beans. Wash in cold running water. Avoid iron utensils (discoloration). Water scald 3 min.; steam scald 4 min.

Soy Beans	Use Giant Green Bansei varieties. Pick well-developed pods that have green beans. Wash in cold running or ice water. Shell. Discard blemished beans. Water scald 3 min.; steam scald 4 min.
Beets	Use Ruby Queen. Select small, tender beets. Discard blemished beets, remove tops and wash. Cook beets until tender, then remove skins, and cut to desired sizes.
Broccoli	Use Waltham 29 and Spartan Early. Discard off-colored heads or any blossoms. Remove tough leaves and ends. Cut stalks to fit kettle. Immerse stalks ½ hour in brine (¼ cup salt to one quart water) to remove small insects. Rinse in fresh water. Split lengthwise, leaving heads about one inch in diameter. Water scald 4 min.; steam scald 5 min. (pref.)
Brussels Sprouts	Use Jade Cross or Catskill. Pick firm, compact heads of good green color. Discard discolored heads. Wash and trim. Soak for ½ hour in salt brine (¼ cup salt to one quart water). Water scald small and medium heads 4 min.; large 5 min. Steam scald small and medium heads 5 min.; large 6 min.
Carrots	Use Nantes and Chantenay varieties. Pick smooth, tender, small carrots before roots become woody. Try to harvest in cool weather, as small, immature roots harvested during hot weather contain less carotene and do not freeze well. Remove tops, wash, and scrape. Dice or slice. Water scald 3 min.; steam scald 4 min.
Cauliflower	Use Snowball strains. Select well-formed, compact, white heads. Trim off leaves and break heads into cauliflowerettes about one inch in diameter. Soak for ½ hour in brine (¼ cup salt to one quart water). Rinse in cold water immediately. Work rapidly to prevent browning. Water scald 3 min.; steam scald 4 min.
Corn	Use Golden Beauty, Sugar King, Sugar and Gold. Harvest in early morning. To test for maturity, press kernel. If milky juice comes out, then it's mature. After corn is picked, it must be processed immediately. Fresh

Vegetable	*Preparation*

corn: take kernels from cob after scalding, cutting close to cob: take kernels from cob after scalding, cutting close to cob. Water scald 4½ min.; steam scald 5½ min. To freeze whole corn on the cob, follow the timetable: Midget 1¼ inch diameters, water scald 7 min.; steam scald 9 min. Small to medium 1¼ to 1½ inch diameter, water scald 8 min.; steam scald 9 min. Medium to large, over 1½ inch diameter, water scald 11 min.; steam scald 12 to 13 min. Cool for 15 min. in cold water after scalding.

Eggplant

Blanching raw eggplant is not recommended for freeze processing. It is best to deep-fat fry, grill, or include in casseroles. But you may still freeze and try to prevent discoloration by immersing in ¼ cup salt per one gallon of cold water. For easy separation, package slices with two pieces of freezer paper between slices. Water scald 4½ min.; steam scald 5 min.

Greens

Wash thoroughly, discard thick stems. Scald, drain thoroughly to remove as much water from leaves as possible.
Water scald 2 min. (spinach, kale, beet and mustard greens, celery, and cabbage); water scald 3 min. (chard and collards).

Kohlrabi

Choose young, tender, early white or purple Vienna. Cut off tops, wash, peel, and dice in ½ inch cubes. Water scald for 2½ min. Steam scald 3 min.

Mushrooms

Pick young firm mushrooms. Prepare as quickly as possible. Leave button-sized mushrooms whole and slice large ones. After cutting, immerse in lemon juice and water (3 teaspoons juice to two cups water). Scald 4 min. for small whole or medium; scald 3 min. for cut pieces. Mushrooms sauteed in butter or other fat and frozen have good quality when thawed.

Okra

Choose young, tender pods about 2 inch to 4 inches in length. Remove stem by cutting carefully without touching the seed pod, thus juice will come out. Water scald small or medium pods 3 min.; large pods 4 min. Steam scald small and medium pods 4 min.; large pods 5 min.

Onions   Freezing is not recommended for raw onions, but deep-fried, battered onion rings can be frozen on cookie sheets then placed in bags for storage.

Parsnips   Choose smooth, firm roots free from woodiness. Wash, peel, and slice lengthwise, into ¼ inch strips, or crosswise. If parsnips seem woody, do not bother to prepare for freezing. Water scald 3 min.; steam scald 4 min.

Peas (Green)   Use Frosty, Laxton's Progress, Little Marvel, and Dark Seeded Perfection. Do not pick overmature or Alaska peas or other starchy peas. If the pea pods are hard to shell, then blanch them for one minute in boiling water and then dip in cold water for one minute. Do not wash after shelling. Discard tiny peas. Handle peas as quickly as possible, as any delay causes toughening of the skins. Shelled—water scald 2 min.; steam scald 3 min. Edible Peapods (Oriental cookery)—water scald 3 min.; steam scald 4 min.

Peppers (Hot)   Remove core from green pepper. No scalding is necessary if to be used in uncooked foods as salads.

Peppers (Pimiento)   Wash thoroughly. Cut out stem ends and remove seeds. Peel pimiento by roasting in oven at 400°F. for 3 to 4 min. until skin is cut open and charred. Cool; can be packed dry without heating. It is easier to pack if scalded. Water scald 3 min.; steam scald 4 min.

Potatoes   Wash, peel, remove eyes, any bruises or spots. Cut as desired. Water scald 5 min.; steam scald 4 min.

Pumpkin   Pick at optimum maturity as determined by trying to remove stem. If it comes loose right away, then pumpkin is mature. Wash thoroughly, cut as desired. Bake or steam until tender. Cook, scoop pulp from rind, and mash through blender or ricer. Water scald 3 min.; steam scald 4 min.

Vegetable	*Preparation*
Rhubarb	Use McDonald Crimson or Chipman's Canada Red. Select crisp, tender, good, red colored stalks in early spring. Remove leaves and woody ends, discard blemished and tough stalks. Wash and cut into one-inch lengths. Do not blanch. Instead, cover with syrup or pack with sugar—one cup to one quart rhubarb (especially suitable for making pies as no added sugar is necessary).
Sauerkraut	No additional preparation is necessary.
Squash	Same preparation as for pumpkin.
Turnips and Rutabagas	Use Laurentian variety for rutabagas and purple top and white Globe for turnips. Remove tops, and wash and peel. Cut as desired. Water scald for 2½ to 3 min.; steam scald 3½ min.
Sweet Potatoes	Use Puerto Rico types, Georgia Red, and All Gold and Jersey types. Pick medium to large, mature sweet potatoes that are smooth and bright. Wash thoroughly. Cook either by steaming, boiling, broiling (with skin on) in pressure cooker, or in the oven (with skin on) until *almost* tender. (Raw sweet potatoes darken during freezing storage.) Cool, peel, and cut up into desired pieces or mash. To preserve bright red color, immerse in four tablespoons of lemon juice to two cups cold water. Add ¼ cup orange juice and one cup brown sugar with one teaspoon lemon juice to 1 quart of mashed or cut-up, cooked sweet potatoes as it adds flavor and preserves the color. This may be added as a glaze to the potatoes before freezing.
Tomatoes	Do not use fancy grade tomatoes for freezing. Whole tomatoes may be washed, wrapped, and frozen to be served as salad. If fully cooked until pulpy, extra juice may be strained off. Add one teaspoon of salt per quart. May also be frozen as stewed tomatoes except omit crackers or bread crumbs until after tomatoes are thawed or reheated.

THE IMPORTANT ROLE OF BLANCHING IN THE FINAL QUALITY OF FROZEN VEGETABLES

Blanching is the method most often used to prevent undesirable discoloration and deterioration during prolonged storage of fresh vegetables. This process enhances the quality of vegetables because it inactivates various enzymes which play a role in the deterioration of products during storage.

Blanching not only prevents deterioration but it also destroys large numbers of micro-organisms. This process removes various mucilage-like substances, dirt, and other extraneous materials from the outer surfaces of the vegetables. With a reduction in microflora and surface contamination, product shelf life is improved.

Blanching prior to freezing improves the penetration of cold temperature through the intercellular structure of the fibrous vegetable tissues. With a small degree of partial cooking and softening of these tissues, an advantage is gained in making these vegetables easier to package for freezing.

Chilling Vegetables After Blanching

After vegetables have been blanched, it is recommended that a fast chill be obtained. Chilling stops further cooking, which toughens tissues causing a loss of tender texture and fine flavor. Rapid chilling of hot vegetables prevents the leaching of water soluble nutrients. If product is allowed to cool slowly at room temperature, several vitamin and mineral losses are incurred. Prolonged holding of vegetables at high temperatures has resulted in large losses in vitamin B and vitamin C levels. Rapid cooling of blanched vegetables also controls bacterial growth and contamination.

Hot blanched vegetables should be chilled immediately in cold running water, immersed in iced water, or placed in a chilling refrigerator or blast freezer to quickly reduce product temperature down to 40°F. or below. The use of ice, in a ratio of 1 lb. of ice to 1 lb. of vegetable, is also recommended to quick chill vegetables. There are several advantages in the use of a blast freezer for cooling. Vegetables can be quickly reduced in temperature from 170°F. to 40°F. Blanched vegetables can be spread out individually in thin layers on cookie sheets or freezer baskets to promote uniform cooling.

Once the product is properly chilled, it may be packaged. Drain the vegetables prior to packaging to remove all water. Excess water will interfere with the freezing process. Draining of water is also important in the control of microbiological contamination and growth.

I believe it is best to freeze vegetables in small, loosely packaged batches. Packing vegetables in bulk slows the rate of freezing. The outer surfaces of the food mass will freeze faster than the center areas. Consequently, the center sections remain for longer periods of time in the 100°F. to 60°F. danger zone, where rapid bacterial growth occurs. It is also at these temperatures where spoilage enzymes react, producing slimy, mushy textures and unpleasant flavors. It is best that no more than 15 to 25 lb. of vegetables in bulk be frozen at one time. To accommodate vegetable freezing, the upper shelves of a 24 to 36 cubic foot freezer can be utilized instead of using this space for frozen food storage.

Correct packaging plays an important role in preserving the color, texture, and flavor of frozen vegetables. It is best to wrap product in air-tight, moisture- and vapor-proof containers, sealable plastic pouches, or pouches in which foods can be reheated prior to serving. An example of a reheat pouch is "Scotchpak", manufactured by 3M Company in St. Paul, Minn. Pouches can be filled with blanched vegetable, sealed with a heat sealer or iron, and then frozen. It is preferable that vegetables be combined with white sauces or its variations. The addition of monosodium glutamate to sauces will preserve color and enhance the flavor of frozen packaged vegetables.

9

Preparing Starchy Vegetables and Pasta for Blast Freezing

To assure the best quality for foods in these categories when frozen, each must be prepared according to its own specific guidelines.

Potatoes

Potatoes may be prepared as french fried, stuffed baked, patties, puffs, or hash browns. There are several important factors to remember when choosing and preparing potatoes for freezing.

In the selection of potatoes, choose product on the basis of composition and quality. As a rule of thumb, the specific gravity (percentage of solid content) and the reducing sugar content are dependable guides. Characteristics of a top quality potato termed *Fancy* indicate that the potatoes are hard, firm, shallow-eyed, smooth shouldered, free from bruises, cuts, scabs, dark corky spots, slightly green colors, and are not leathery or spongy. The specific gravity of potatoes ranges between 1.05 and 1.11. Product used for baking and deep fat frying should have a specific gravity higher than 1.11. Potatoes with higher specific gravity have less tendency to absorb fat and produce a higher yield.

The storage temperature that potatoes are subjected to affects the starch-sugar ratio. It has been found by various researchers from Ohio State University under Gould[1] that after being subjected to storage below 50°F. for a prolonged period, the potato starch is converted to sugar, resulting in sprouting. A sugar concentration higher than 1 percent usually results in darker and browner potatoes when cooked and frozen.

French Fried Potatoes

If cost economy indicates that the purchase of ready french fries for frying is more expensive than preparing your own, I would advise that pre-blanching of the potatoes be done prior to deep fat frying. Potatoes should be fried to the point where they are half brown so that reheating in a good fat or oil will produce a crisp fried product without dehydration. The type of oil used in frying affects the shelf-life of french fried potatoes. A discussion of the principles of good deep fat frying of products for freezing has been presented in more detail in Chapter 6. The french fries must be drained completely of excess fat. Product should be spread uniformly on a cookie sheet for rapid freezing.

Mashed Potatoes

In the preparation of the popular mashed potato, mix the fresh cooked potato with non-fat milk solids, butter or margarine, and salt. Add hot water until desired results are achieved. Use a blender or a mixer with a wire whip to aerate the product and to prevent lumps.

Mixing the milk solids and fat prior to mashing gives the butter or margarine a chance to melt and blend well with the potatoes. This process prevents the glossy, heavy, and sticky effects of overmixing the gluten starch in the potatoes. For microwave cookery, use the back of a No. 10 scoop to form a large dimple in the potato. This is done to achieve a uniform penetration of microwaves and to eliminate the formation of cold spots. A basic mashed instant potato formula for reconstitution in a microwave oven is presented in Volume 2, Blast Freezing Quantity Recipes.

Stuffed Baked Potatoes

You may use the same procedure in preparing stuffed baked potatoes as is used in the preparation of mashed potatoes. Spoon the potato filling lightly back into the shell. For best results in microwave cookery, loose pack the filling for even heat penetration. Mashed potato spooned into a baked potato shell produces an excellent, high quality product when reheated. The tendency to compact the potato is less when spooning potato into a shell than when using a scoop. The scoop, because of its ladling mechanism, double folds the potato, compacting it, and yielding a lower quality product when reheated. Also during reheating, the potato shell produces steam, which makes the filling puffier.

Baked, Braised, or Steamed Potatoes

Potato preparations including hash browns, potato cakes, potato balls, should be grilled at high temperature until product is slightly brown. An allowance for additional cooking time should be made during reconstitution.

Oven-browned potatoes have been produced and frozen and have been very good products. As in the case of mashed potatoes, it is important to have the right specific gravity. The raw potatoes are first steamed or parboiled and finished off by baking in an oven at a high temperature of 400°F. to 425°F. It is also important that the bun pans be sprayed with a corn-cottonseed oil mixture before the potatoes are placed in single layers.

The plain, buttered, diced potato that has been steamed produces a fair product if reconstituted in a microwave oven. It has been our experience that for low calorie-diabetic diets, we have had to add the diet's fat allowance. The addition of fat protects the outer skin of the potato from becoming tough and damp during reconstitution. The fat molecules also activate the microwaves at a faster rate so that heat penetration is almost immediate.

Rice

Plain rice should be prepared for freezing by the addition of butter during the boiling process. The Indian and Middle East style of cooking rice is by far the best method for freezing in that the rice is browned in butter or margarine, seasonings and spices, such as garlic, onions, pepper, and saffron. Chicken or beef broth instead of plain boiling water is added, which makes the rice more flavorful. The Spanish or Mexican method adds tomato juice, tomato, and green pepper pieces to the rice, thereby imparting not only flavor but attractive color as well.

Our experience showed the best rice for freezing to be that prepared from recipes such as rice confetti, rice pilaf, scalloped rice O'Brien, and fried rice. The type of fried rice where chopped bacon or diced beef, pork, chicken, or shrimp is added produces an excellent combination of flavors. These additions assist in improving the heat penetration of the microwaves without toughening and dehydrating the rice grains. The best method of cooking rice is in small batches, sauteed, or fried in margarine until golden brown. A tilting braising pan or small steam-jacketed kettle is ideal for rice preparation. One must never attempt to cook five pounds of rice in a large 100 gallon steam-jacketed kettle.

Spaghetti, Macaroni, and Other Pastas

This type of starch is one of the most difficult to control during preparation for freezing. There have been several controversies over the way noodles should be handled. The best method that I have observed is to prepare small batches of pasta, not exceeding 18 to 20 pounds uncooked noodles (250 portions) per 100 gallon capacity steam-jacketed kettle. The kettle should not be filled to more than half its capacity to allow for the expansion of the noodles during cooking. Before uncooked noodles are added to the water in the kettle, make sure it is rapidly boiling. Stir the pasta frequently after adding it to the water until the water returns to a boil. The length of time that the noodles are boiled is a major concern. It the noodles are overcooked and become mushy, then a sticky and slimy product results after freezing and thawing. Once cooked, do not let stand in hot water or the noodles will stick together. Drain off hot water and rinse immediately with cold water. After draining cold water, the noodles must be stirred gently with melted margarine.

Another secret in the preparation of noodles and other pasta is to make sure that the noodle-water ratio is adhered to very strictly. The amount of water available for absorption must be adequate to allow expansion of the noodles and to maintain separation of noodles after expansion. Scissors may be used to cut noodles to obtain accurate portion weight and length.

The use of meat stock for boiling noodles is limited because of the expense incurred in meat stock that is not totally absorbed by the noodles and, therefore, wasted. The availability of inexpensive chicken bouillion or consomme has made it easier for institutional operators to utilize the extra advantage of these flavors.

Sweet Potatoes, Hot Potato Salad, Baked Beans

Sweet potatoes glazed with a brown sugar, orange juice, and margarine sauce yield an excellent product after freezing. The quality upon reheating is comparable to a freshly prepared product. It is advantageous to freeze sweet potatoes in single layers covered with the glaze.

Hot German potato salad is by far one of the best frozen salads if prepared correctly. The potatoes for the salad should be slightly overcooked, in order that when potato salad is reconstituted after thawing, the sweet-sour sauce will not break down from the extra moisture content of potatoes. Since we have started making the potato salad with dehydrated potatoes, dehydrated onions, dehydrated celery and parsley, the consistency of the sauce has been better controlled during the reconstitution process.

Baked beans are an excellent product to freeze. The addition of salt pork and pork steak to our recipe has not only added flavor, but improved the consistency and reconstitution of this product.

Quantity recipes for many of the dishes mentioned in this chapter appear in Volume 2, Blast Freezing Quantity Recipes.

10

Preparing
Baked Goods
for Blast Freezing

Baked goods are an important aid to pleasing patrons, making an essential element in the blast freezing system. Following the recommendations in this chapter will insure the production of baked good that will have a just made taste whenever they are served.

FREEZING FROZEN BATTERS AND DOUGHS

The discussion of whether the freezing of batters and doughs can be successful is often controversial. However, most cake batter recipes or product formulations will freeze well. In order to obtain a quality frozen batter, it has been reported by Tressler, Van Arsdel and Copley[1] that there should be slight modifications in formulation and mixing procedures.

The most critical ingredient to be considered in making a change is the type of leavening agent. The use of stabilized dicalcium phosphate baking powder and sodium acid pyrophosphate varieties produces good cake batters. The baking powder should be increased by 0.20 percent to 0.25 percent of the amount required for a similar batter that would normally be baked off right away. The shortening should be a hydrogenated vegetable shortening or an emulsified liquid shortening (emulsifier such as sobitan monostearate with polyoxyethylene sobitan monostearate). It is important that extra effort be taken in whipping and mixing so that larger air inclusion occurs.

For cake batters that require liquid, egg whites may be substituted for dried egg whites, as they show better results in volume and freezer storage tolerance.

The role of temperature maintenance is one of the most important factors to consider when freezing cake batters. To retain good quality, the product must be stored at $-10°F$. or below. If the frozen batter is stored above $-10°F$., it tends to lose air inclusion. There is a tendency toward redistribution and relocation of the packed air bubbles within the fat molecules, producing water separation from the batter. These changes affect the texture, volume, and overall quality of the cake. When finally baked, the cake has a coarse texture, reduced volume, and irregular form.

The preparation of frozen, unbaked, yeast dough presents many problems. According to Tressler there is one method of achieving stability in frozen bread dough; double the concentration of yeast normally used in the recipe and minimize fermentation time using the straight–dough method. They have discovered that the sponge method does not produce a good quality product. Further research and development might pave the way toward the use of this method, as it does offer better flavor and oven aroma as compared to the straight–dough method.

In order to achieve a successful program in freezing unbaked yeast dough, certain ingredients must be used.

1. Yeast—the use of either compressed or dry yeasts yields a good quality frozen unbaked dough. It has been recommended by Tressler that the amount of compressed yeast used in a recipe should equal 6 percent to 10 percent of the flour weight. The amount of active dry yeast used should equal 3 percent to 5 percent of the total flour weight. The yeast substitution factor is one regular sized cake of compressed yeast (⅔ oz.) to one package of dry yeast.

Both the compressed yeast and the dry yeast may be dissolved in liquids such as water or milk. The temperature of the liquid should range between 85°F. and 100°F. for compressed yeast and between 105°F. and 115°F. for granulated dry yeast. In any yeast–raised dough, the activity of the cells can be destroyed with too warm a liquid. If some or all of the yeast cells die, then the dough will not rise.

2. Flour—the use of a high protein quality, medium strength, winter or

spring wheat flour is recommended. High protein quality indicates a high gluten concentration within the dough. Gluten engulfs the carbon dioxide that yeasts produce causing the dough to rise.

3. Salt—should be added in quantities equal to 1.5 percent to 2.0 percent of total flour weight.

4. Sugar—the amount of sugar added should equal 5 percent to 10 percent of the total flour weight. A higher sugar content makes it possible to increase proofing time without considerable yeast activity.

5. Fat—lard should be added in amounts equal to 5 percent of the total flour weight in order to produce uniform texture and grain.

6. Whey—the use of powdered, dried, sweet dairy whey gives the dough a good crust color due to its high lactose content. There are some experts who prefer to add egg yolks, as it makes the dough richer, more tender, and produces a golden color.

Various mixing, kneading, and fermentation techniques assist in producing high quality, frozen yeast dough. The authors, Tressler, Van Arsdel and Copley, recommend the use of a high speed dough mixer with a refrigerating jacket to maintain ingredient temperatures between 65°F. to 70°F. Low temperatures during mixing inhibit fermentation.

Dough mixing is accomplished when the product mass starts to separate from the mixing hook. According to Mr. Rudy Harder,[2] a former instructor of baking at Dunwoody Institute, one is able to tell when dough is properly mixed by the smooth, silky feel of the dough. It also has a tendency to "ball up" into a large conglomerate mass. Some bubbles will also be noticed just at the surface of the dough.

Fermenting the dough before freezing is another controversial issue, as there are diverse opinions on this matter. What I recommend is based on the experience of Mr. Harder, who contends that the ultimate use of the dough determines when and for how long the fermentation process should take place.

Large institutions, desiring to please clientele by serving freshly prepared rolls and bread, should eliminate fermentation. The shelf life of frozen, unbaked doughs decreases in proportion to the amount of fermentation allowed. Tressler summarizes that the best procedure is to mix all ingredients in a minimum amount of time at 70°F. (21°C.), allow the dough to relax for five minutes, divide, knead, round, mold, and freeze as rapidly as possible.

The principles applicable to freezing sauces and gravies also apply to freezing batters and dough. A very rapid freeze is the ultimate goal in order to reduce large ice crystal formations. The freezing efficiency of a blast freezer yields cost savings based on labor-saving, energy utilization, and production of high quality products. The techniques discussed in earlier chapters on continuous work and product flow also have a great impact on final quality of these products. An organized, continuous product flow including ingredient mixing, punching, molding, forming, freezing, and packaging results in excellent baked products. The handling of the most delicate ingredient, the yeast with its living cells, will determine the ultimate texture, grain, and form of the frozen product after baking.

FREEZING BAKED BREAD AND ROLLS

When freezing baked goods, the delicate nature of these products has to be considered. "Staling" is a process which causes baked bread and rolls to lose their resilience because of moisture migration from the inner core of the bread crumb towards the outer surface of the crumb. Staling can be prevented if the baked product is cooled, packaged, and frozen quickly after baking. It is also important that there is continuous product flow from the time the product leaves the oven until it is inside the freezer. For a fairly large, semi-automated, bakery plant, the whole baking-freezing process occurs almost simultaneously on a continuous automated conveyorized belt. There is a central commissary for a public school system in Pennsylvania where the belt is continuous from the oven into a freezer tunnel. In this method, the product is not handled outside of the oven, so it is exposed to the air for less time and will not become stale.

As previously stated, time and temperature are important factors contributing to staling which can be controlled if there is a fast processing rate during freezing. The use of a wrapper for bread insulates it, and thus slows the rate of freezing. This is also true when other baked products such as sweet rolls and other bread-type rolls such as Parkerhouse, croissant, sesame, etc., are being frozen. The common practice of wrapping before freezing is difficult to alter, but for speedier freezing, products should be left unwrapped.

FREEZING PIES AND PASTRY

When freezing unbaked fruit pies, follow the same procedures presented earlier for preparing fresh fruits for freezing. The enzymatic changes of fruits must be controlled to achieve a quality product.

Thickening agents used to prepare pie filling are the same as those recommended for frozen sauce and gravy preparations. The use of tapioca, waxy maize starch, or instant Clearjel, available from most baking suppliers, has been found to produce good quality fruit fillings. The proper cooking of filling helps prevent undesirable physical changes that take place in the gelatinized stages of starch cookery. Undercooking the starch in pie fillings results in a "pulpy," coarse texture and loss of water holding capacity, thus causing deterioration of the fruits in the filling.

A rapid freeze is essential if the formation and growth of large ice crystals is to be minimized. Fast freezing prevents separation of the liquid from the solid portion.

The most common problem in baking frozen, unbaked pies is formation of moist soggy bottom crusts. What most baking experts suggest is separate handling of the bottom crust. It is advantageous to partially brown the bottom crust or brush it with an egg yolk-oil mixture prior to filling it with fruit. The use of a high grade, fairly strong, soft wheat flour, containing 8.0 percent to 8.5 percent protein, mixed with a high percentage of shortening has been found by Tressler to be of immense help in alleviating soggy crust. Another technique mentioned by Tressler is to cool fruit pie filling to 40°F. or below before filling the crust. The cold filling will not readily soak into the pastry.

The role of shortening is very important in making a good flaky crust as shown by Mr. Harder in his experimental baking course. He contends that pure lard is by far the best shortening to use in making pie crusts.

When I was involved in college feeding at Ohio State, we prepared unbaked pie crusts at a rate of 500 to 1000 per day. The pie crusts froze so well that we literally stacked one crust on top of the other. We packed them with shrink wrap between each crust. By doing so, we were able to store many crusts in a small space. Leaving the crusts in pans when possible makes handling easier and protects against breakage.

It is recommended by Tressler that the preparation of pie crusts be done in an air-conditioned room, so that the pliability of the dough may be controlled. The ingredients used in making pie crust should be mixed with a minimum amount of handling.

Pie crusts should be frozen before they are packaged. Frozen crusts are easier to handle and there is no possibility of the shortening being reabsorbed from the frozen crust. Since most pie fillings are made with sugar, there is an increased possibility of softening at higher temperature which makes packaging difficult. The freezer storage for these pies should be lower than $-10°F$. and must never be allowed to rise above $0°F$.

The preparation and freezing of custard, chiffon, and cream type pies should follow the same techniques that were discussed earlier in the section on the basic preparation of cream sauces and custards. When the recipe calls for whipped cream, one may either use a commercial, non-dairy whipped topping or stabilize the whipped cream with one teaspoon of gelatin dissolved in two tablespoons of warm water, heated and incorporated during the whipping stage. The addition of gelatin helps achieve final stability in the whipped cream after thawing.

For custard, chiffon, and cream pies, a single pie crust is used. These pies should be thawed in a refrigerator before serving. Many foodservice operators prefer to freeze the pie crusts separately and fill them at serving time with freshly prepared fillings.

The quality of custard, chiffon, and cream filled pies is excellent after freezing, especially when a stabilizer has been used and when tapioca, instant Clearjel, or waxy maize starch has been used instead of cornstarch or flour.

Due to the additional dehydration occurring during freezer storage, the formulation of crumb crusts has to have added shortening if the final product is to be a tender, easy-to-cut crust. Depending on the type of filling to be used, the pie crusts may or may not be baked before freezing. For fresh strawberry pie, the crumb crusts can be baked before freezing, as the strawberry filling does not have to be cooked, and it will be cold when placed in the crust.

FREEZING CAKES, COOKIES, MUFFINS, SHORTCAKES, AND WAFFLES

Of all items to be frozen, I have found cakes, cookies, muffins, shortcakes, and waffles to be of highest quality after thawing. This group also has the longest shelf life among baked products. There are few changes necessary in recipe formulation and freezing produces no change in quality. Chocolate or chocolate-flavored cakes may present the only freezing problem as there may be textural changes in the crumb or in the chocolate icing.

The basic principles suggested for the baking of cakes should be adhered to closely. The quality of these products depends on the baking time and temperature. Underbaking or overbaking creates problems. Complete reliance on an oven thermometer and a timer is not enough. One should also test for doneness with a toothpick to make sure adequate baking has occurred.

Packaging is one of the most important factors in preserving the quality of frozen cakes. The packaging protects cakes from dehydration, hardening of the icing, and condensation of moisture on product surfaces during thawing. The cake must be rapidly cooled before freezing so that moisture migration will not occur. All cakes should be frozen prior to packaging, especially those with icing or frosting.

Cookies are the most foolproof desserts to prepare and freeze. A regular recipe formulation will produce quality frozen baked cookies. Frozen cookies have an extremely long freezer shelf life. Therefore, to reduce the heavy workload during the holiday season, this product can be prepared several months in advance. To freeze cookies, place the product on the top shelf of a blast freezer or a self-defrosting storage freezer, prior to packaging. Leave product on cookie sheets during freeze processing. When solidly frozen, transfer cookies into individual moisture-, vapor-proof, plastic bags or plastic containers.

Muffins, waffles, and pancakes are not difficult to prepare for freezing. The only change necessary in the preparation of waffles and pancakes for freezing is that a very hot griddle is used in order to brown the product quickly and, at the same time, to retain desirable moisture.

Frozen pastries, such as eclairs and cream puffs, retain high quality up to a year without deleterious changes in form, flavor, appearance, and texture. Quickly freeze such products as soon as they are filled, so the shells do not have time to absorb moisture from the filling. Temperature maintenance for freezer storage must be at $-10°F$. or below. This is critical, for any temperature fluctuation increases the possibility of moisture migration which results in a soggy, tough texture in the filling and crust.

It is possible to make maximum use of the menu appeal of fresh baked breads and desserts when their production is properly coordinated in the blast freezing system.

11

Controlling Microbial Contamination During Preparation and Freezing

Commercially prepared frozen and dehydrated products have introduced new health problems for those foodservice operators who believe that because food is frozen, it is safe. Fortunately most foodservice operators realize that cooking and freezing food does not make it free from pathogenic micro-organisms. The growth of yeasts, molds, and bacteria in frozen foods occurs at temperatures as low as 14°F. Some bacteria remain alive, even after prolonged freezer storage and will cause spoilage when the food product thaws.

Low temperature is not an effective means of destroying micro-organisms in foods. According to Weiser, Mountney, and Gould,[1] low temperature simply slows up their multiplication and reduces their metabolic activities. These authors are not firm in their opinions as to the mechanism causing bacteria death at low temperatures. It is probably due to mechanical crushing of the bacterial cells by crystallized water. Most reseach on mechanical crushing of bacteria concludes that *slow* freezing, producing large ice crystals, causes a greater degree of mechanical disruption to bacteria than rapid freezing that produces small ice crystals. It has been postulated that perhaps "salt death" or excessive concentration of crystalloids causing the separation of the solvent from the solution causes cellular death.

Several factors influence the destruction of micro-organisms in frozen foods. They have been cited by Weiser, Mountney, and Gould[1] to be:

1. Kind of organism and whether or not it sporulates; for example, mold spores are very resistant to freezing.
2. Fast, as opposed to slow freezing; fast freezing seems less deadly than slow.
3. Kind of food that bacteria thrives on, such as sugar, salt, proteins, colloids, and fat which serve as preservatives for these micro-organisms. Conversely, high moisture or high acidity can increase the chances for destruction of these organisms.

A majority of the food poisoning outbreaks traced to frozen foods have been caused by pre-cooked meat products and ready-to-serve dishes, especially those which contain milk, cream, and eggs. Frozen items containing dairy and egg products are known to be more prone to growth of micro-organisms because some of the bacteria in these products exhibit heat resistance tendencies and are able to withstand pasteurization. Based on previous studies done by Rappole,[2] serious contamination often occurs during preparation prior to freezing and is traceable to improper handling by personnel.

There are several cold-loving bacteria known as psychrophilic organisms that thrive in foods under refrigeration and freezing. The positive role of the psychrophilic organisms is not known. Several experts believe these micro-organisms help eliminate or reduce food poisoning outbreaks. If allowed to grow, these micro-organisms cause undesirable biochemical changes which alter the taste, color, aroma, and texture of certain products. Due to these changes, the product becomes unacceptable to eat although growth of food poisoning organisms is hindered. During the thawing period, higher temperatures favor the growth of these micro-organisms. Once an increase in the bacterial cells' growth occurs, the food product either should be cooked almost immediately or discarded. The authors, Weiser, Mountney, and Gould recommend that thawed frozen food never be refrozen.

Frozen food manufacturers conclude that cooking and freezing does not produce a sterile product. The preparation, cooking and handling of food prior to freezing destroys the natural spoilage flora found originally in the food, but at the same time, increases the chance for microbal contamination. As Glew[3] emphasizes in his book, if the preparation, cooking, freezing, and packaging processes proceed in an efficient and expedient manner, microbial contamination is minimized.

Bacterial growth in pre-cooked frozen foods is a function of time and temperature. Anyone attempting to prepare, process, and freeze foods should be aware of the role of the following basic factors:

1. The design and layout of the equipment in the food processing area. A good work flow is insurance against high bacterial contamination.

2. The purchase of excellent quality ingredients with low microbial counts.

3. Correct food preparation and handling procedures as related to efficient production scheduling and techniques, personnel handling practices and procedures, cooking and processing times and temperatures, and sanitary usage of tools and equipment.

4. The effects of additional handling in portioning, packaging, and sealing prior to freezing.

5. The speed of freezing as it controls the amount of time a product is in the danger zone for bacterial growth and contamination.

6. The method of handling frozen product, storage, inventory, and turnover as it relates to the physical design and layout of freezer storage.

7. Whether to thaw the product prior to reheating. The method used will influence this decision.

Even with the various good handling controls that can be established, followed, and implemented, there remain several viable pathogenic organisms that food operators planning to freeze food should be alert to.

The most serious micro-organism that survives freezing is *staphylococcus aureus*. Food products that are highly susceptible to staphylococci growth include fish; shrimp; poultry products, such as turkey and chicken; and products containing cream and other fresh milk components.

What needs to be emphasized to food processors is the use of *salmonella-free* ingredients, especially eggs, poultry and other meat products. Meeting this objective is insurance against possible growth of these organisms during storage and thawing periods. Such researchers as Litsky, Fagerson, and Tellers[4] have proved as a result of studying prepared frozen meat pies and pre-cooked foods that viable salmonella is hard to discover.

There are microbacterial competitors which help control the development of toxins from various pathogenic organisms. This is especially true in the case of clostridium organisms existing with natural saprophytic flora in frozen precooked foods. These organisms assist in reducing clostridium botulinum spore growth. It was also demonstrated by Saleh and Ordal[5] that the introduction of lactic acid bacteria into chicken a la king prevented the development of clostridium botulinum toxin. It is good to know that the growth of these pathogens is hampered by storing and maintaining product at 0°F. The introduction of oxygen, moisture vapor-proof films for packaging precooked frozen foods enhances the growth of clostridium, due to the anaerobic environment produced. If contaminated product is allowed to thaw and remains in a refrigerated state for a considerable length of time, considerable growth can occur.

Vacuum packaging of precooked frozen food almost totally eliminates the possibility of oxidative rancidity during storage. This is due to the elimination of oxygen in contact with food surfaces. The removal of oxygen could possibly limit the activities of natural saphrophytic organisms, permitting the growth of anaerobes. Some of these anaerobes will include certain strains of clostridium.

It has been pointed out that precooked frozen food has built-in safety insurance against food poisoning. This is because the growth of natural saprophytic bacteria causes unacceptable organoleptic changes. The precooked frozen food undergoes detectable spoilage and quality deterioration, making these products unacceptable to the consumer long before they become unsafe to eat. Therefore, large scale mass food poisoning should be avoidable.

MICROBIAL CONTROL AS A FACTOR IN PLANNING AND DESIGNING KITCHEN EQUIPMENT AND LAYOUT

There are several basic considerations in planning or selecting a design for a sanitary foodservice facility.[6] Tressler[7] emphasizes that production of prepared frozen food should be maximum sanitation operation. It cannot be effectively implemented in proximity to a dirty operation. It is even important to have controlled ventilation so that the air from the highly contaminated areas cannot be circulated to maximum sanitation areas.

Overall considerations in designing a facility should incorporate these principles:

• The flow of production from food receiving to serving should avoid criss-crossing or backtracking between areas.

• Production and service should be smooth, rapid, and require a minimum expenditure of workers' time and energy.

• Materials should have minimum handling and be stored at the point of first usage.

• Quality control should be established and checked at every point in the production flow.

• Work areas should be compact to reduce distances travelled by workers. Maximum allowances for aisle space should be provided. Time and distances traveled by materials and personnel must be set to account for the perishability of products and that take into account frequency of the trips required from the storage areas.

• The ideal temperature for a work area is 65°F. to 75°F. Fatigue increases when the temperature goes above 75°F. Air-conditioning and proper ventilation are necessary to achieve the desired temperature in the kitchen. Acoustical ceiling materials may be used if ventilation is adequate to minimize grease and moisture absorption. Mechanical ventilation should be provided for food production, dining, warehouse, locker, and toilet facilities. A minimum of 10 room volumes of outdoor air per hour is recommended.

• Equipment should be designed and placed to meet the standards of the National Sanitation Foundation and the Underwriters Laboratories, Inc. A seal of approval bears the initials NSF and UL on equipment that meets these standards. Equipment must be nonabsorbent, continuous and smooth, free from open seams, cracks, exposed junctions, and sharp corners. It should be easily cleaned and there should be access around and under it for cleaning and inspection. Moving parts on mobile equipment should be equipped with guards or casings. Floor-mounted equipment, unless readily movable, should be sealed at the base or elevated a minimum of 6 inches above the mounting surface.

• The adequacy and safety of water, steam, and heat must be carefully evaluated. Pipes and electrical wiring must be concealed because steam and water pipes with temperatures higher than 120°F. – 140°F. are dangerous.

• Floor drains must be located so that water is quickly removed from dishwashing, warewashing, and pre-preparation areas. All floors should be water mopped and sloped gradually toward the drains with approximately a ½ inch drop at the drain plate.

• Floors must be smooth, non-skid, easily cleanable, and rapidly drained after hosing and washing. All crevices and cracks must be sealed. Floor must be impervious to stains and grease accumulations. Joints in tile or similar material should be resistant to food acids. Corners between the floor and walls should be coved and sealed. Several seamless tile floors meet these criteria.

• Adequate toilet facilities, including washrooms and hand sinks, should be located to prevent criss-crossing between clean and dirty areas. Lavatories should be equipped with wrist, knee, or foot action valves.

• The design of the facility must include rat-proofing and elimination of areas where roaches and other insects might enter. Flat surfaces that rest directly on the floor should be sealed to the surface with a mastic or cement that will prevent the entrance of vermin. Pipe hoses should be attached to all vertical lines for gas, steam, electricity, and plumbing to prevent harboring vermin. Openings for pipes should be sealed to prevent the entry of vermin. Screens and electrocuting panels should be at all receiving and distributing docks to eliminate flies and other insects. Boxes, crates, cartons, and other leftovers from storage areas should not enter preparation or assembly areas. All residuals from receiving and storage should be taken care of outside the building.

• Bell alarms and light signals should be used to provide fire and extinguishing system alarms as well as malfunction alarms for low temperature storage. These alarms should be centrally located either in a supervisory area or an area with 24-hour staffing.

CHECKLIST FOR IMPLEMENTING AN EFFECTIVE FOOD SANITATION PROGRAM

Refrigerated and Chilled Vestibules: Proper temperature maintenance; insect and pest control; proper floor design and construction; garbage and compactor area with sanitizing and hosing equipment.

Frozen Storage: Temperature maintenance with alarm buzzer in danger zone; adequate shelving for continuous air circulation; cartons stored 24 inches below light bulbs to prevent heat penetration; blower fan and condensation coil guards to prevent dust accumulation; adequate aisle space for air circulation and product movement; alarm bell to signal dangerous temperature; waste line connected indirectly to building drain.

Production Areas: splash guards and hoods for open cooking equipment; proper pressure guages and thermostats for steam equipment; proper insulation and venting for ovens.

Tray Conveyor Assembly: Self-cleaning; refrigerated holding units for perishable products.

Transporting: NSF approved carts or modules; proper ventilation to prevent air movement from corridors or other soiled areas.

Patient's Serving Areas or Galleys for Reheating: proper air pressures; air filter with 90 percent efficiency; hand sink; refrigerated storage and holding areas for temperature maintenance.

Warewashing: area must be separated in a room or alcove; space allocated for receiving, scraping, sorting, stacking, washing, and sanitizing soiled and clean materials; mobile conveyors or carts; effective bacteriological count and removal of food particles; dishmachines approved by NSF and UL; area for storage of detergents; service sink; easy-to-clean wall finish; horizontal exhaust; leakproof joints and condensation drip lines; clean openings every 20 feet; mechanical ventilation.

Waste and Garbage Disposal: direct pickup of waste accessible to outside; space allocated for either mechanical destruction or compaction.

Sanitation Supplies: adequate storage for housekeeping equipment and detergent supplies; easy to clean, smooth wall finish; mechanical ventilation with 10 room volumes of outdoor air per hour.

Handwashing: lavatories in food preparation, warewashing, and toilet facilities equipped with waist, knee, or foot action valves.

The food industry has not kept up with the excellent dialogue between design engineers, food sanitarians, and operators in the dairy industry. That is why Tressler[7] points out that there is too much equipment that is often neither suitable, sanitizable, nor really economical. He cites pieces of equipment designed with parts that are so difficult and laborious to disassemble that the only expedient method for cleaning is water flushing. He suggests that equipment used in precooked frozen food operations not be shared with other areas of preparation, particularly raw food preparation. It is also important, according to his past experiences, that equipment used in the preparation of precooked foods be washed and sanitized in a separate area from that used for other operations.

Glew[3] summarizes the role of the design and layout of equipment in relation to the degree of microbacterial growth. The degree of subsequent contamination and number of micro-organisms will depend upon the plan of the production unit and the production method used. The arrangement of equipment should prevent cross contamination and completely separate cooked and raw materials in time and place. The design of equipment should be such that cleaning operations are easy and effective.

MICROBIAL CONTROL DURING THE PREPARATION, COOKING, AND FREEZING PROCESSES

Ingredients

One of the most important components in the bacteriological control of frozen foods has been that of purchasing raw materials and ingredients with low bacterial counts and high quality standards. Previous chapters tell why freezing will not improve quality or reduce the bacterial count of those ingredients that have high counts to begin with.

It is vital that management purchase ingredients with tight quality specifications and stringent microbial standards. These standards must be followed and implemented so that state and federal regulations will be met and protection against contamination will be accomplished. Bacteriological requirements must be specified in terms of standard plate, coliform, staphylococcus, yeast and mold count.

In the operation where the blast freezing system outlined here was developed, these vital bacteriological standards were evolved, established, and implemented:

1. All meat components to be used for processing prepared foods shall have been passed and inspected by the Meat Inspection Division of USDA.

2. A certificate from an outside laboratory hired by the food vendor shall be provided. These test results will be confirmed by our own Hospital Laboratory to conform to the following standards:

    a. Viable aerobic bacterial plate count not to exceed more than 50,000 colonies per gram.

    b. Coliform plate count—5 coliforms or less.

    c. Coagulase positive type staphylococci—negative.

   d. E. coli—negative.

   e. Perfringens—negative.

It is a good practice to inspect the processing facilities of prospective vendors. Tours of their facilities will give one a direct insight into their standards of sanitation and hygiene in the plant itself. One can also observe the method of handling product by food handlers and processors in each location.

Various controls must be established for the receiving, handling, and storage of materials and equipment. Refrigerators and freezers must be kept sanitary, and proper temperatures consistently maintained. Bacteriological counts must be done on random sampling of all meats, dairy, and other perishable products. Fat content, because of its effect on oxidative rancidity and spoilage, must be analyzed to insure that specifications are met. There must be knowledge of the preservatives and additives used to insure that the products meet the Food and Drug Administration regulations.

Temperature controlled storage of perishable, non-perishable, and precooked products, such as roasts for slicing, remains very critical. Tressler[7] holds that meats, in particular, should be refrigerated during the lunch break, and that any unused food materials should be properly dated, tagged, and refrigerated at the end of each shift.

I have observed in food processing companies that the storage areas for raw meats, fish, poultry, and dairy products are separated from the refrigerated areas containing the cooked products. Dairy products such as cottage cheese, sour cream, and whipped cream are not only easily contaminated, but also absorb odor and flavor rapidly from raw vegetables and raw meats.

Product rotation and turnover should be fast and geared toward tight production scheduling. In a cook/freeze system, according to Glew, the ordering of raw materials in the correct amounts is simplified and there should be no "leftovers" as all the incoming raw materials can be cooked and frozen as scheduled. Various stock items in a kitchen must be rotated and inventory managed so that perishable products received first are used first to prevent food contamination and spoilage. Date labelling has helped here. Canned goods and other perishable products also need proper inventory management. Rodent, insect, and pest control is maximized as long as semiperishables such as noodles, rice, and flour products are not stored for a long period or at a humid, hot temperature.

Preparation Methods

According to Tressler, the most serious source of microbial contamination for precooked and prepared frozen foods has been in the processing and fabricating procedures. Production scheduling and programming should be expressed in time elapsed from a zero starting hour or in terms of the set hour of the day.[8] The most complicated part of the production process is when two separate operations need to be done almost concurrently, but completion time is different. An example cited by Glew[3] is the production of meat pies with pastry tops. The pastry and the meat filling may come from different parts of the production unit, and some delay can occur in combining the pastry top and the meat filling. Such delay could make the temperature of the meat filling ideal for bacterial growth and contamination.

Meat slicing, dicing, and other forms of extra handling after the meat is cooked is a critical area in preparation for bacterial growth. Tressler mentions that boning cooked meats required contact with worker's hands and this with the prolonged holding at room temperature resulted in rapid increases in bacterial count in the boned meats. Glew reiterates this concern for bacterial growth and contamination during meat slicing by discussing the effect of slicing over a two-hour period. He observed that the total of living organisms per gram rose from between 10 to 200 organisms on the first slice to between 4000 to 6000 organisms on the last slice. Thorough cleaning and sanitizing after each production shift is recommended so that the equipment used will not serve as a source of bacterial contamination. It is a good rule to require that all utensils, equipment, and work surfaces in contact with food be sanitized every two hours during processing runs.

"The time during which product remains in the room temperature range during processing and freezing should be as short as possible; therefore, lengthy holding of ingredients and products on the production line during line breakdowns, and long freezing times are to be avoided."[2] Certainly, these statements could also apply to a regular conventional system but due to the volume of meals being prepared in a cook-freeze system, the impact of the time-temperature relationship becomes magnified.

Production scheduling must be tight so that the quantity of food prepared will not exceed the load capacity of the chill refrigerators and the freezers. Each production run must be done as efficiently as possible. Foods that are perishable should be refrigerated at 40°F. or lower. Preparation of foods should be done at temperatures higher than 140°F. The amount of time the product remains in danger zone or the bacterial incubation temperature range of 140°F. to 40°F. should either be avoided or minimized. The internal temperatures of large volume products, such as roasts, should be cooked higher than 160°F. to 165°F. and then chilled down to 40°F. as rapidly as possible. A rapid cooling method sufficient to reduce bacterial growth and to inactivate food enzymes will guarantee against product deterioration during storage.

Personnel Handling

In an article published in *Hospitals,* Harder[6] stated, "Although a fully automated foolproof system can be established in food service, the human element involved in the design and implementation of a system is still the most important factor and cannot be taken for granted.''

A sanitation checklist covering personal hygiene and appearance should include the following: clean hair, hands, nails, and uniform; a hair net or cap worn at all times; good posture; non-offensive breath and body odors; and overall good health. There are several recommendations for maintaining good sanitary work habits. These include:

1. Wear a clean uniform daily with a hair net or cap.

2. Wash hands thoroughly with soap (iodine content) and hot water before work, after each production run, and after using the restrooms.

3. Do not wear rings or any form of jewelry, pins, beads, or anything that could come apart and fall in the food.

4. Personnel involved in the handling of raw materials should not go into production, plating, or assembly areas. The use of color coded caps and uniforms will insure that only authorized personnel are at each respective station.

5. Equipment used for raw materials processing must not be intermingled with equipment for production or assembly. In fact, the sanitation and disposal methods for each area must be physically separated. Chopping boards, slicers, scales and other utensils such as scoops, ladles, and knives must be supplied in sufficient numbers to prevent sharing of these pieces.

6. Touching and scratching eyes, hair, scalp, face, hands, ears, or other parts of the body should be avoided.

7. Smoking should be allowed only during break and lunch times, and only in the areas set aside for that purpose.

8. Each employee should report any cuts, burns, or skin infections so that proper medication can be recommended by the nurse in charge.

9. Every employee should try to avoid coughing or sneezing, especially near exposed food.

10. Production personnel should test and sample food in the test kitchen, never in the processing areas. A clean spoon or fork for every sample of each batch must be used.

11. The use of sterilized plastic gloves whenever handling food products is mandatory. With few exceptions, personnel must use tongs, scoops, ladles, or other equipment for stirring, mixing, portioning, or transferring food.

12. Equipment such as pallets, loadsters, and transfer carts from receiving areas should not be used to transfer prepared foods to the freezer or chill areas.

13. Packaging containers of raw materials or semi-processed goods from outside vendors should never be placed on work counters or surfaces used for the preparation, assembly, and serving of food.

14. Food preparation equipment, especially slicers, should be taken apart and sanitized after each production batch.

15. Preventive maintenance of all refrigerators, freezers, preparation, portioning, and assembly equipment should be done in a regular manner.

16. Each employee should immediately remove any spills or excess food from work area surfaces to prevent bacterial growth and contamination.

Management and employees must be taught to include various bactericidal products in cleaning and sanitizing all equipment. Deignan[9] cites the previous experience of Adamczyk in utilizing iodine or chlorine compounds. He recommends the use of these products for sterilizing utensils before, during, and after production and packaging at the end of each run.

Employee commitment in the sanitation program is important so that a basis of understanding and dialogue is established between management and employees. "When food service personnel are made aware of the source of micro-organisms, their effect on food, and how the growth of microbes can be prevented, only then can quality be maintained. Knowledge is not enough; it must be practiced."[9]

Harder emphasizes the role of in-service training where each employee is indoctrinated about the "why" of the program as well as "how to do it." Team meetings should be held, and employees given a chance to develop ideas they think are important. A monthly report on the bacteriological level will indicate where they could have failed.

A continuing education program should include daily on-the-job training to orient each worker and supervisor to the philosophy of why and how to work in a sanitary way. Instructions on accomplishing each part of the program need to be discussed frequently. Tools and equipment with safety devices and alarm systems for both equipment and operations are necessary. A final quality assurance check on time and temperature of food at each step—from the time it is received to the time it is served to the patients—insures that the program is being implemented, and gives employees and supervisors a sense of satisfaction in their accomplishments. A daily follow-up is required to prevent carelessness and make certain that procedures are implemented correctly. Use rating sheets to grade standards of performance as excellent, acceptable, or unacceptable. With these methods, each employee will be able to determine how and where he can improve his ratings.

MICROBIAL CONTROL FOR THE COOKING-TO-FREEZING STAGES

Food products which do not undergo any heat treatment or cooking process during production have been described by Glew[3] to have minimal microbiological problems so long as they are not contaminated before they enter the production areas or during the portioning or assembly periods.

Cooking destroys many, if not all, of the pathogenic micro-organisms that may be naturally present in these ingredients. The baking process is not as effective as boiling in destroying micro-organisms in food. The limitation of heat penetration when frying foods, especially any product with a depth greater than 1 to 2 in., means this method may not destroy all of the spore-forming, thermophilic, and heat-resistant bacteria.

Blanching, water scalding, and precooking will usually decrease the microbial content of raw fruits, vegetables, and starches. The most common contamination comes in the handling after blanching which can increase the bacterial contamination. If there are serious delays between blanching and pre-cooking, the possibility of the growth of some heat-resistant spores becomes greater. Glew[3] has mentioned that the optimum temperatures 30°C. to 40°C. (86°F. to 104°F.) are most conducive to heat resistant spores. If conditions become favorable for food poisoning organisms to multiply, then the meat and poultry products can produce the most dangerous hazard. Glew also emphasized that any delay between portioning and freezing must be avoided by a tight scheduling of production, portioning, and freeze processing. Tressler[7] pointed out that experiments done by Straha and Combes (1952), Obold and Hutchings (1947), Angelotti (1959, 1960), all proved that precooked foods should not be held at room temperature, illustrating that the danger zone is between 40°F. and 120°F. Considering these findings, precooked foods must not be held more than 2 hours before freezing.

The next process to be accomplished as expediently as possible is the packaging of the precooked foods. Each food product should be packaged in sanitary, moistureproof, laminated plastic containers or pouches, and covered with heat sealed or tight fitting lids. What is most important is that food portioned into packages not exceed a 2 inch depth.

The time the food spends on the packaging line must not exceed the over-all limitation of two hours from preparation and processing to freezing. To control microbial growth it is best to portion hot products into individual containers prior to quick freezing at 0°F. It was mentioned by Tressler that hot filling prior to quick freezing produced a nearly sterile product, based on studies by Logan, Harp, and Dove. In his dissertation, Deignan[9] recommended that packaging products cold prior to freezing in a slow freezer should be done for sandwiches, soups, sauces, and gravies.

To summarize, the packaging process must not exceed its share of a maximum of two hours between preparation and freezing to reduce the length of time the food product dwells in the danger zone between 40°F. and 140°F. The scheduling of production should include the time of portioning and packaging prior to freezing. During the experiment conducted by the University of Leeds Hospitals in Leeds, England, Glew[10] emphasized that the portioning of food be done at temperatures below or higher than the danger zone. "Bacteriologically, the main hazards occur in the preparation and cooking before freezing and hence are common to both conventional systems and small scale precooked frozen food systems. If the production of precooked frozen food in a kitchen, originally intended for feeding by conventional methods, is increased, thought must be given to the suitability of equipment, existing organizational problems, and education. Bacteriological hazards may be increased because there will be longer delays due to larger quantities of food being prepared giving any bacteria that are present more time to multiply."

Freezing reduces the microbial activity of micro-organisms. It has been proven in several experiments by Raj and Liston[11] that freezing, thawing, and refreezing causes some decrease in the total numbers of bacteria in seafoods.

During the freezing process, it is important to bring the food product from 140°F. down to 0°F. in no more than 45 minutes. Since the growth activity of most micro-organisms varies with different temperatures, it is obvious that the slower the rate of freezing, the faster the growth of micro-organisms. Is it possible, then, to use a regular conventional storage freezer to freeze large quantities of food? The answer to this question is yes, as there are many food-service operators who have attempted to do so and have found out that it is safe to freeze in a conventional freezer. The major drawback, though, is that the size of production load is limited. The rate of freezing is affected by a rise in the internal air temperature in the freezer when a large amount of product is placed into it. There are also limitations on the type of food that may be frozen and placed in a conventional freezer. The single portion packs or a 2-in. deep bulk pan may be frozen quite satisfactorily. But any amount exceeding a five pound pan load should not be attempted. With a slower rate of crystallization, the formation of large ice crystals destroys the cell membranes, thus ruining the quality of the products.

Blast freezing offers several advantages in microbial control of precooked foods. It has been shown by Glew[3] that most pathogenic organisms grow and multiply best between 20°C. and 45°C. (68°F. and 113°F.), but psychrophilic spoilage organisms can grow at lower temperatures. He cited the advantage of the blast freezer as producing a rapid freeze that hinders the growth of spoilage organisms.

Blast freezing has the ability to destroy between 20 percent and 80 percent of bacteria present if they are in the vegetative state. Unfortunately, food poisoning organisms are not in the vegetative state. The most toxic is the clostridium botulinum, a spore-bearing, anaerobic organism. Freezing has little or no effect on bacterial spores, viruses, and toxins which are very stable at freezer temperatures. The work of Fitzgerald as summarized by Gould[1] showed clearly the ability of many bacteria to survive and multiply on meat at freezer temperatures. The spoilage of fresh meat and meat products is dependent on the rate of saprophytic micro-organism destruction, including the pathogenic and toxigenic bacteria.

It has never been proved why blast freezing has advantages over liquid nitrogen in the efficient reduction of micro-organisms. My basic hypothesis is the fact that a slower rate of freezing produces micro-organism destruction that is similar to a "slow death," thus causing more destruction in the viability of the bacterial cells.

Once the food products being frozen reach the internal temperature of 0°F., the freezer should be maintained at −10°F. so that the product will not suffer from temperature fluctuations when the freezer is opened or closed. It has been discussed by Glew that the cycling of the temperature during storage (frequent fluctuations in temperature) not only causes changes in the ice distribution in food but also causes increased destruction of micro-organisms during storage. Since quality changes due to temperature fluctuations far outweigh the advantages incurred from decreased bacterial numbers, the method is not highly recommended.

Gould has confirmed the old concept that the faster food is thawed, the greater the quality retention. Experimentation at Victory proves this statement true. In this case, he recommended a faster rate of defrosting as long as the liquids have time to be reabsorbed quickly into the tissues.

Several experiences of Rogers[8] have led him to conclude that there are advantages in the application of microwave heat as a form of reheating if done through an intermittent series of short bursts of waves. Contemporary microwave ovens have an equilibrating cycle allowing time for cold molecules of food to catch up with the super hot molecules. A more detailed discussion of reconstitution methods occurs in a later chapter.

Thawing is best done at a refrigerated temperature, preferably in a tempering refrigerator. The tempering area should be closely monitored as to time and temperature to make sure the products are not stored longer than necessary.

Frozen prepared food should be stored and maintained constantly at a freezer temperature of -10°F. I have seen disastrous changes in frozen foods if such a temperature is not maintained. Such changes include mushy texture, meat drip, loss of flavor, spoilage, and rancidity resulting in poor quality upon thawing.

As previously discussed, there are several viable micro-organisms that are present in food during freezer storage. Foods that need to be reconstituted should achive a temperature higher than 165°F. to 175°F. Glew[3] has mentioned that micro-organisms are destroyed when food is reheated for 25 to 40 minutes to 176°F. (80°C.) in a forced air convection oven. Even though the reconstitution process is assumed to have killed all of the micro-organisms, it is still recommended that food be consumed almost immediately.

Thawing of frozen foods is a very delicate process. The quality of some products is changed drastically when thawing is not adequately and properly controlled.

RECOMMENDATIONS FOR EQUIPMENT AND UTENSIL SANITIZING

Sanitation is commonly misinterpreted to mean plain cleaning. Sanitation means that the area in consideration has had its microbial content reduced. Sanitation differs from cleaning in that it goes beyond scrubbing, loosening the soil, or mechanically removing soil particles through vacuuming, water suction, or high-powered water pressure. Sanitation is accomplished either by heat or chemical processing. One of the equipment service bulletins[12] described sanitation as a decontamination process where objects or surfaces are already physically clean. Sanitation is only effective when caked-on soils are completely removed.

Heat Sanitizing: Exposing a clean object to high heat for a long enough period of time to sanitize. The higher the heat, the shorter the time required to kill harmful organisms. Immersion of dishes and utensils in water at 170°F. (about 82°C.) for no less than 30 seconds is generally recommended by most regulatory authorities.

Chemical Sanitizing: Exposing a clean object to a chemical compound that will sanitize. Factors affecting the sanitizing action of these chemicals are concentration of the substance and the time the substance is allowed to remain in contact with the surface. Chemical sanitizers are used on surfaces that cannot be sanitized through the use of heat. The three most common sanitizing compounds are chlorine, iodine, and quaternary ammonium. When choosing a sanitizing compound or chemical, make sure it is non-toxic and can be utilized on surfaces which will be in contact with food.

I would like to cite from the same bulletin a good sanitizing method for steamtable pans, food storage containers, and cooking-serving utensils.

Steamtable Pan, Food Storage Container, Cooking and Serving Utensil Sanitizing

1. Scrape off all excess soil prior to placing into sink.
2. Place scraped utensils into a wash solution as quickly as possible to prevent food soil from drying on surfaces. The longer the soak, the easier and

faster the utensil can be cleaned. Note: Hot water removes grease while cold water softens potato, egg, rice, and cereal residues.

Preliminary Set-Up for Hand Washing and Sanitizing

1. Measure the amount of water required to fill the wash sink. (To calculate gallons, multiply in inches the length times width times depth of the sink tank and divide by 231.)

2. Make a mark at this level on the side of the sink so you will know the water quantity each time.

3. Measure the amount of detergent necessary for the number of gallons of water, following directions on the package. Soak utensils for a short time before washing.

Washing

1. Maintain wash water at 110°F., or above. Hot water helps to remove micro-organisms.

2. Wash utensils thoroughly inside and out. Scrub with a clean fiber brush. Use a wire brush to remove burned-on food. Do not use steel wool!

3. Rinse utensils in clean hot water (120°F. to 140°F.). If a utensil feels greasy, it is not clean. Rinse water should be free of suds.

Sanitizing

1. Fill sink with clean hot water (170°F.) unless a sanitizing agent is used.

2. If a sanitizing agent is used, water temperature between 75°F. and 120°F. is sufficient. Add the sanitizing agent to the water.

3. Completely cover all utensils with hot water (170°F.) for at least 30 seconds. If a sanitizing chemical is used, soak for the recommended amount of time.

4. Remove, drain, and air dry on a clean surface or rack. Do not use a towel to dry!

5. Store clean utensils on shelves or racks. If pans are stored, place them upside-down and cover.

Slicer Sanitizing

1. Disconnect the electrical cord before starting to clean a slicer. Set the blade control at zero to reduce the possibility of accidental cuts. Leave the knife guard in place until ready to clean the knife.

2. Remove all loose food particles from metal surfaces. Dismantle. Remove parts into sink. Wash parts in a hot (110°F.) solution of detergent. Rinse with clean water.

3. Clean the stationary parts in place. Be careful of the blade. Use detergent solution (110°F.) and scrub with a long-handled brush or thick cloth.

4. To sanitize removable parts, dip into a sanitizing solution and warm water for recommended period of time. To sanitize stationary parts, wipe with a sanitizing solution.

5. Allow all sanitized parts to air dry. Replace the guard as soon as the blade and guard are dry.

To illustrate the details involved in the sanitation and housekeeping of a large food commissary, here are performance standards for these areas from Hennepin County Hospital.

Sanitation and Housekeeping Standards and Checklist for Direct Food Production Areas in a Central Commissary

1. CLEANING TASK PERFORMANCE DESCRIPTION: The following definitions of performance standards are established at Hennepin County:

A. The following standards of performance shall be considered unacceptable.

1. *Dust and Dirt*—The presence of dust and dirt or related material on vertical and horizontal surfaces to the degree that it is noticeable and will mark clothing or skin.

2. *Stains/Marks*—Their presence to the degree that it is noticeable and alters the appearance of vertical and horizontal surfaces or items of furnishing.

3. *Litter/Refuse*—The presence of litter or refuse on top of, underneath, or behind vertical and horizontal surfaces or items of furnishing.

4. *Sanitation*—The condition of sanitation that will cause odor or create a possible health hazard.

5. *Microbial Requirements*—Standards for bacterial count.

a. *Direct Food Contact Surfaces:* Monthly sampling with swab techniques shall provide bacterial counts not to exceed 100 coliforms/gm (agar plate count) and no coliforms present on direct food contact surfaces.

b. *Indirect Food Contact Surfaces:* Quarterly sampling with Rodac plates shall provide bacterial counts not to exceed 10,000 colonies per gram, and zero coliforms present.

2. CLEANING AREA DESCRIPTION:

A. *Dry Storage, Refrigerated and Freezer Storage (including tray line, plating, tempering, cart parking and staging, and dispatching refrigerators and freezers), Janitorial and Storage Closets, and Soap Storage Room.*
Daily

1) Sweep and/or vacuum floors in dry storage.

2) Damp wipe and sanitize waste receptacles and re-line with bags.

3) Wash and sanitize floors in all walk-in refrigerators.

4) Clean and damp mop janitorial closets and soap storage room.

5) Wash and clean refrigerator and freezer doors and casings.

Weekly

1) Wash and sanitize mobile shelving in storage and walk-in refrigerators.

2) Wash and sanitize inside of refrigerators (walls, ceilings, doors, and floors) as needed. Refer to manufacturer's manuals and check with CFF Sanitation Supervisor.

3) Walk-in freezers to be defrosted, cleaned, and sanitized according to manufacturer manuals, every six months to a year, or as requested by CFF Sanitation Supervisor.

B. *Sculleries, Pots & Pans, Cart Wash Rooms, Tray Wash.*

Daily:

1) Hose down floors, walls, and ceiling with pressure wash system and sanitize.

2) Clean and sanitize pot and pan and hand sinks.

3) Check for and replace burned-out bulbs.

4) Use pressure wash system on empty storage carts, self-levelling dispensers, tray receivers, mobile units, and any other equipment pertaining to this area. Dispensers must be dried to prevent rusting.

Weekly

1) Scrub and sanitize walls, ceilings, floor, and plumbing fixtures in scullery areas.

2) Clean pressure wash system.

3) Clean floor drains.

Monthly

1) Clean both sides of windows in scullery areas.

2) Clean lighting by removing shields and tubes to clean reflectors.

Annually

1) Mechanically scrub and reseal floor areas (do not seal quarry tile floors).

C. *Cold Food Production, Tempering and Plating, Tray Line Assembly, Home Delivered Meals, and Nourishment and Nourishment Cart Assembly Areas.*

Daily

1) Spot wash and sanitize lower half of tile walls in all units (up to 5 ft. high).

2) Clean and sanitize both sides of doors and casings.

3) Clean door windows in these areas.

4) Replace burned-out light bulbs.

5) Damp wipe and sanitize cabinet fronts (upper and lower cabinets).

6) Clean and sanitize all production equipment, such as can openers.

7) Clean and sanitize empty mobile platforms, dish carts, tray receivers, and dispensers.

8) Clean and sanitize all floor areas.

9) Clean and sanitize the plating conveyor table and auxiliary fixtures.

10) Clean and sanitize tray assembly conveyor belt and its auxiliary fixtures.

11) Clean and sanitize the cold food assembly conveyor and its auxiliary fixtures.

12) Clean automatic wrapping machine.

Weekly

1) Clean and sanitize cold food slides used in the tray assembly area.

2) Mechanically scrub all floor area and reseal (not quarry tile) as requested by CFF Sanitation Supervisor.

3) Scrub and sanitize all garbage disposal units.

4) Clean and sanitize shelving in upper and lower cabinets using the pressure wash system.

D. *Hot Food Production, Ingredient Control.*

Daily

1) Clean and sanitize floor areas.

2) Spot wash and sanitize lower half of tile walls (up to 5 ft. high).

3) Scrub and clean thoroughly drains and troughs in this area.

4) Replace burned out bulbs.

5) Clean and sanitize all sinks.

6) Damp wipe and sanitize cabinet fronts (upper and lower cabinets).

7) Clean and sanitize production equipment such as trunnion kettles, steam cookers, steamers, etc. inside and out.

Weekly

1) Completely clean and sanitize walls and ceilings using pressure wash system.

2) Clean and sanitize cabinets, work tables, and counter tops.

3) Clean and sanitize empty mobile bins, platforms, and shelving.

4) Scrub, degrease, and sanitize hoods, filters, and air vents.

5) Clean and sanitize exterior of the tilting fry pan.

6) Degrease, clean, and sanitize ovens, ranges, broilers, and deep fat fryers according to manufacturers' specifications.

7) De-scale, de-lime, and sanitize kettle assembly.

8) Clean and sanitize mixers, can openers, and the outside of ovens.

9) Replace burned-out bulbs.

Monthly

1) Clean lighting by removing shields and tubes to clean reflectors.

2) Clean interior of ovens according to manufacturers' recommendations.

6 Months to Year

1) Scrub and sanitize walls, ceilings, and floors. Use pressure wash system where applicable. Mechanically scrub and seal floors as necessary (not quarry tile) as requested by CFF Sanitation Supervisor.

2) Clean and degrease grills, ovens. Clean self–cleaning ovens, according to manufacturers' manuals.

To achieve maximum performance in kitchen sanitation and house-keeping, performance standards need to be established. Here are recommendations:

A. Night Cleaning requirements as per cleaning task performance description.

1) All production areas shall meet minimum standards for litter/refuse and dust and dirt.

2) All production equipment shall meet minimum standards for sanitation, stains/marks, and dust and dirt.

3) Window glass, exterior and interior (areas that can be reached from floors or step ladder) shall meet minimum standards for stains/marks and dust and dirt.

4) Completed work shall appear as original finish or surface unless changed for ease of maintenance.

5) Adequate supervision to perform above requirements.

6) All storage areas (including refrigerator and freezer) shall meet minimum standards for sanitation, litter/refuse, stains/marks, and dust and dirt.

7) Scullery and cart wash rooms shall meet minimum standards for sanitation, litter/refuse, stains/marks, and dust and dirt.

8) Janitorial, storage closets, and soap storage rooms shall meet minimum standards for sanitation, litter/refuse, stains/marks, and dust and dirt.

9) All other areas listed in Exhibit A shall meet minimum standards for sanitation, litter/refuse, stains/marks, and dust and dirt.

10) Completed work shall appear as original finish or surface unless changed for ease of maintenance.

11) Adequate supervision to perform above requirements.

Personal Hygiene Standards

Certain hygiene standards should be met by every foodservice worker. Hair nets for women and caps for men are a protective measure to be observed by all personnel. Clean aprons and uniforms, and comfortable, well-fitted shoes are essential; elimination of jewelry, except a watch and/or wedding rings, and the avoidance of excessive makeup and nail polish are further requirements.

Correct work habits must be stressed. Sanitary food handling procedures include:

1. A complete medical checkup at least once a year, including a chest X-ray.

2. Report every injury at once, regardless of the severity, to the supervisor for first aid. *AVOID DELAY!*

3. Hands washed frequently throughout the day, certainly before work, after using the toilet, after coughing and sneezing, after meals and coffee breaks, after smoking, and after handling soiled objects and unclean surfaces.

Handwashing is a simple procedure. But to be effective the finger nails and the areas between the fingers require special attention. The hands should be washed under running water at a temperature of 110°F. to 120°F. with sufficient soap to form an abundant lather. The type of soap used is not significant since studies have shown that bar soaps do not transfer bacteria among individuals nor do they support bacterial growth.

Washing should proceed by cupping the finger tips within the palms of the hands and rubbing vigorously. This procedure will clean the nails and finger tips. The areas between the fingers are cleaned by interlocking the fingers and working them back and forth, and from side to side. After completing this procedure, hands should be rinsed thoroughly and dried with single service paper towels. Careful attention to this method of washing will assure that hands have been thoroughly cleaned.

The hands of those who prepare and serve food must be clean at all times to safeguard the health of those who are dependent on this service.

4. When working on the line, with food, in the tray room, or in the cafeteria, wear plastic disposable gloves.

5. Keep hands out of food as much as possible. Use spoons, forks, tongs, or other appropriate utensils. If you do handle food, you're only increasing the chances of contamination.

6. Do not handle food when sore throat or upset stomach symptoms are present.

7. Use only clean utensils in preparing, cooking, and serving food. Use a clean spoon each time you taste-test food.

8. Grasp such utensils as spoons, forks, tongs, knives, etc., by their handles. *That's what they're made for!*

Pick up, and carry glasses by their bases, cups by their handles, and plates by their rims, being careful to avoid contamination of the serving surfaces.

9. Keep work surfaces clean, and work area organized and orderly.

10. Refrigerate unused food, and clean up any spillage promptly.

11. Keep floor clean and dry. Pick up any loose objects from the floor *immediately* to prevent injury.

12. Aisles, passageways, and stairways must be kept clean and free from obstructions.

Do not permit brooms, pails, mops, cans, boxes, etc., to remain where someone might fall over them. Wipe any grease spills immediately from stairs, floors, or ramps. This holds for *ANYTHING THAT FALLS ON THE FLOOR!* These are serious hazards.

13. Do not place clothing, boxes, shoes, etc., on, or sit on, food preparation surfaces.

14. Observe the "NO SMOKING AND NO EATING RULE" in the preparation areas.

INTRODUCTION TO SANITATION PROCEDURE MANUAL

On the following pages are cleaning and sanitizing procedures for all of the equipment that was listed earlier.

I. AREA OR ITEMS: Small Electrical Equipment.

II. PRODUCT:
   A. As provided
   B. DILUTION: As indicated

III. SUPPLIES AND EQUIPMENT:
   1. Cellulose Sponge
   2. Double-Compartment Pail
   3. Small, Stiff Brush

IV. PROCEDURE:

1. Immediately after use, take bowls, beaters, and all removable parts to automatic pot and pan washer for washing and sanitizing.

2. Fill one side of double-compartment pail with warm solution. Use separate sponges for wash and rinse compartments.

3. Use sponge and detergent solution to thoroughly scrub all stationary parts of equipment. Pay particular attention to underside of heads, corners, handles, and underneath rolled rims.

4. Rinse thoroughly with sponge and squeeze nearly to dry.

5. Replace removable parts.

6. Return cleaning equipment to proper storage after cleaning.

7. Wash hands thoroughly, following procedure outlined in "Personal Hygiene" section of manual before proceeding to another task.

I. AREA OR ITEMS: Food Waste Disposer

II. PRODUCT:
A. As provided
B. DILUTION: As indicated

III. SUPPLIES AND EQUIPMENT: None.

IV. PROCEDURE:

1. Always allow the water to run for at least three minutes after last food waste has been put through the disposer. (This will allow unit to remain clean and will flush all waste material through the drain.)
2. If unused food falls into disposer or sink, throw it away. It is contaminated.
3. Always wash your hands thoroughly according to the "Personal Hygiene" section before moving on to another task.

NOTE: To avoid jamming the disposer, never put silverware or cooking utensils into it.

Should food preparation utensils happen to come into contact with the disposer, consider them contaminated, and wash them accordingly.

I. AREA OR ITEMS: Chopping Boards

II. PRODUCT:
A. As Provided
B. DILUTION: As indicated

III. SUPPLIES AND EQUIPMENT:
1. Nylon Brush
2. Clean Cloths

IV. PROCEDURE:

1. Scrape block free of grease.
2. Wet block with warm water.
3. Sprinkle with crystals of specified dishwashing detergent.
4. Brush thoroughly, using a hard bristle brush.
5. Let stand 20 minutes.
6. Rinse. Wipe dry.
7. Return cleaning equipment to proper storage after cleaning.
8. Wash hands thoroughly, following procedures in "Personal Hygiene" section of manual, before moving on to another task.

I. AREA OR ITEMS: Can Openers and Food Choppers

II. PRODUCT:

   A. As provided
   B. DILUTION: As indicated

III. SUPPLIES AND EQUIPMENT:

   1. Stiff–Bristled Brush
   2. Long–Handled Brush

IV. PROCEDURE:

1. *CAUTION:* Disconnect the electric power and clean blades with great care to avoid accidents and injuries. Remove guard only long enough to clean.
2. Disassembled parts should be taken to pot sink and flushed with cold water spray to remove loose soil.
3. Put all parts through dishmachine, run full cycle, and let air dry.
4. Scrub base of equipment with stiff brush and hot chemical solution. Rinse thoroughly.
5. Give special attention to can opener blades. Scrub all parts with a stiff-bristled brush.
6. Rinse with clear water and sanitize with recommended chemical.
7. Lubricate regularly as recommended by the manufacturer.

I. AREA OR ITEMS: Sandwich Boards

II. PRODUCT:

   A. As provided
   B. DILUTION: As indicated

III. SUPPLIES AND EQUIPMENT:

   1. Double Compartment Pail
   2. Suitable Brush
   3. Sponges

IV. PROCEDURE:

1. Fill both compartments of pail with warm water. To the wash compartment, add specified dishwashing detergent in the ratio of 2 ounces per gallon of water.
2. Apply solution to surface and wash thoroughly using brush.
3. Rinse with clear water.
4. Allow to air dry.
5. Return cleaning equipment to proper storage after cleaning properly.

6. Wash hands thoroughly, following procedures in "Personal Hygiene" section of manual, before moving on to another task.

I. AREA OR ITEMS: Trunnion Kettles, Steam Cookers, Deck Steamer, Kettle Assembly, Tilting Braising Pan and Trough, etc.

II. PRODUCT:
   A. As provided
   B. DILUTION: As indicated

III. SUPPLIES AND EQUIPMENT:
   1. Stiff Brush
   2. Drain Brush

IV. PROCEDURE:
   1. Flush kettle with warm water immediately after use and allow to drain.
   2. Close valve, fill kettle to ¼ mark with hot water. Add chemical. Brush-wash all surfaces inside and out. Use proper brush to clean the draw-off pipes and outlet valves while the solution is draining. Scrub the adjacent piping, braces, and valves.
   3. Rinse all surfaces with hot water.
   4. If any scale or film remains on kettle after daily cleanup, it must be given special de-scaling treatment.

APPROXIMATELY ONCE A WEEK:

1. Fill kettle with warm water to just above the normal liquid level. Turn on steam.
2. While water is heating, add specified de-limer.
3. Bring water to near boil for one hour, brushing above the liquid level occasionally during this soak period.
4. Open drain valve and brush off loosened scale as the kettle empties.
5. Rinse all surfaces with hot water.
6. Return cleaning equipment to proper storage.
7. Wash hands thoroughly before proceeding to another task.

I. AREA OR ITEMS: Hoods, Filters, Air Vents, Ovens, Broilers

II. PRODUCT:
   A. As provided
   B. DILUTION: As indicated

III. SUPPLIES AND EQUIPMENT:

1. Nylon Brush
2. Cellulose Brush
3. Metal Scraper
4. Pressure Washer
5. Dish Machine
6. Double Compartment Plastic Pail

IV. PROCEDURE:

1. Range, ovens, and broilers must be cool enough to touch the top. Scrape off all loose particles.
2. Remove filters.
3. Lay each filter flat in a dish rack. Do not stack them. Put each through a full wash cycle in the dish machine. Examine each filter as it comes from the machine. If not thoroughly clean, run it through again. Stack filters and let air dry. Once a week, filters should be soaked in hot solution of degreaser. Flush with hot water and follow process above.
4. When ranges and broilers are cool enough to touch, take removable parts to pot and pan sink for washing. (Sanitize according to pot washing instructions in manual.)
5. Spray all surfaces inside and outside including hood surface with pressure washer.
6. Remove hard soil from stationary parts with dull metal scraper or stiff brush. Pay special attention to corners and other hard to reach areas.
7. Dial "rinse" on pressure washer and rinse thoroughly and wipe dry.
8. Wipe ovens with chemical solution using cellulose sponge and let air dry. Once a week use oven cleaner according to cleaning section in manual.
9. Return cleaning equipment to proper storage after cleaning thoroughly.
10. Wash hands properly, following procedures in "Personal Hygiene" section of manual.

NOTE: Be sure the entire exterior and area underneath and behind equipment is cleaned. Failure to do so can cause odor development.

I. AREA OR ITEMS: Dispensers, Juice Machine

II. PRODUCT:

A. As provided
B. DILUTION: As indicated

III. SUPPLIES AND EQUIPMENT:

1. Cellulose Sponge
2. Clean Cloth
3. Tub and Jet Brush

IV. PROCEDURE:

1. Remove cabinet cover to expose the concentrate reservoir, lid, and the valve assembly body.

2. Remove the reservoir, lid, and valve assembly according to manufacturer's directions. Place remaining concentrate in another container and refrigerate.

3. Wash all removable parts in chemical solution. Clean the insides of all tubes and jets with a brush.

4. Sanitize by allowing all parts to soak for a minimum of two minutes in chemical solution.

5. Rinse the parts in clear water and reassemble.

6. To clean outside, wipe with sponge dipped in the same solution. Polish dry with clean cloth.

7. Return cleaning equipment to proper storage after cleaning thoroughly.

8. Wash hands thoroughly, following procedures in "Personal Hygiene" section of manual, before proceeding on to another task.

I. AREA OR ITEMS: Self-Levelling Dispensers, Tray Receivers, Mobile Units, Pressure Washer, Cabinets, Stationary and Mobile Shelving

II. PRODUCT:

    A. As provided

    B. DILUTION: As indicated

III. SUPPLIES AND EQUIPMENT:

    1. Clean Cloths

    2. Double Compartment Pails

    3. Stiff Brush

    4. Pressure Washer

IV. PROCEDURE:

1. Take mobile units to cart wash room. Spray wash holding nozzle about six inches from surface paying close attention to rims and under sides. Use stiff brush if necessary. Dial pressure washer to "rinse" and rinse thoroughly.

2. Use double compartment pail to clean stationary shelving, etc., using one compartment for wash and one for rinse. Use stiff brush, if necessary, to remove any stuck-on material.

3. Rinse thoroughly and allow to air dry.

4. Clean equipment thoroughly and return to proper storage.

5. Wash hands thoroughly, following procedures in "Personal Hygiene" section of manual, before proceeding on to another task.

I. AREA OR ITEMS: Walk-In Refrigerators

II. PRODUCT

A. As provided
B. DILUTION: As indicated

III. SUPPLIES AND EQUIPMENT:

1. Double Bucket with Mop Press
2. Two Stage Dolly
3. Two Clean Mops

IV. PROCEDURE:

1. Wipe up spilled liquids or foods immediately so they do not complicate cleaning or create unnecessary hazards.
2. Mop floor daily according to the wet-mopping instructions in floor maintenance section.
3. Clean equipment properly after use before putting into storage.
4. Wash hands thoroughly, following procedures in "Personal Hygiene" section of this manual.

I. AREA OR ITEMS: Roll-In Refrigerator

II. PRODUCT:

A. As provided
B. DILUTION: As indicated

III. SUPPLIES AND EQUIPMENT:

1. Double Compartment Plastic Pail
2. Cellulose Sponges
3. Nylon Brush

IV. PROCEDURE:

1. Fill both compartments of pail with warm water. To the wash compartment, add specified dishwashing detergent in the ratio of 2 ounces per gallon of water. To the rinse-sanitizing compartment, add specified sanitizing agent in the ratio of 2 ounces per gallon of water.
2. Remove food to protected temporary storage.
3. Apply detergent solution with sponge; for persistent soils, use brush.
4. Squeeze sponge as dry as possible and wipe solution off surfaces.
5. Using remaining clean sponge, apply specified sanitizing agent solution making sure to rinse and squeeze sponge thoroughly several times to be sure sanitizer touches all surfaces.
6. Let air dry.

7. When refrigerator has obtained safe storage temperatures, return food.

8. Wash hands thoroughly, following procedures in "Personal Hygiene" section of manual, before moving onto another task.

I. AREA OR ITEMS: Nourishment Refrigerators

II. PRODUCT:

    A. As provided

    B. DILUTION: As indicated

III. SUPPLIES AND EQUIPMENT:

    1. Double Compartment Plastic Pail

    2. Nylon Brush

    3. Clean Cellulose Sponges

IV. PROCEDURE:

1. Fill double compartment plastic pail with warm water. Add specified dishwashing detergent to wash compartment in the rate of 1 ounce per gallon of water. Add specified sanitizing agent to rinse compartment in the ratio of 2 ounces per gallon of water.

2. Remove contents to protected temporary storage. There should be no delay in procedure once the cleaning process has been started.

3. Carry shelving to sink for thorough cleaning and sanitizing. Use detergent solution and thoroughly scrub using clean cellulose sponge. Use nylon brush for difficult-to-remove spots.

4. Rinse well with clear tap water, then sanitize with second sponge from sanitizer solution.

5. Scrub inside of box thoroughly using clean sponge, or nylon brush where needed, with detergent solution. Special attention should be given to corners, doors, openings, gaskets, hinges, catches, and floor of box.

6. Will cellulose sponge, rinse down interior with clear tap water to remove all traces of cleaning solution.

7. Using second cellulose sponge from sanitizer solution, wipe down entire interior area to sanitize and prevent mold.

8. Return shelving and contents.

9. Wash exterior of refrigerator, using damp sponge from detergent solution. Rinse with sponge and clear tap water. Dry with clean cloth.

10. Return cleaning equipment to proper storage after cleaning thoroughly.

11. Wash hands thoroughly, following procedures in "Personal Hygiene" section of manual before moving on to another task.

    Once each week, substitute specified silver dip at the ratio of 2 ounces per gallon for regular detergent in Step 1. This will remove and control alkaline and mineral deposits.

I. AREA OR ITEMS: All Refrigeration

II. PRODUCT:

A. As provided

B. DILUTION: As indicated

III. SUPPLIES AND EQUIPMENT:

1. Squeeze Mop
2. Pressure Washer When Applicable
3. Long–Handle Brush

IV. PROCEDURE

1. Wipe up spilled liquids or food.
2. Move all food and equipment to one side or remove completely.
3. Spray down walls and ceilings with pressure washer, holding nozzle valve about 6 inches from surface.
4. Scrub any hard–to–remove soil with long–handle brush.
5. Spray floor liberally with pressure washer, then agitate vigorously with brush or mop.
6. Turn pressure washer to "rinse" and rinse flooring liberally.
7. Squeeze residue toward and into floor drain.
8. If time permits, let air dry. Otherwise pick up water with mop.
9. Return cleaning equipment to proper storage after cleaning thoroughly.
10. Wash hands thoroughly, following procedures in "Personal Hygiene" section of manual, before proceeding to another task.

I. AREA OR ITEMS: Counters, Shelves, Work Tables (stainless steel)

II. PRODUCT:

A. As provided

B. DILUTION: As indicated

III. SUPPLIES AND EQUIPMENT:

1. Double Compartment Plastic Pail
2. Nylon Brush
3. Cellulose Sponges

IV. PROCEDURE

1. Prepare a solution using 2 ounces of specified dishwashing detergent in wash compartment filled with mildly hot water (120°F.).
2. Remove all items from shelves, tables, and counters.
3. Wipe down all surfaces with sponge dipped in solution. Wash small areas

at a time to prevent streaking. Scrub where necessary with a non-metallic scouring pad or scraper.

4. Wipe clean with sponge squeezed nearly dry.

5. Apply specified sanitizing agent solution mixed in other compartment. Leave surface damp but not soaking wet.

6. Let air dry.

7. Return utensils to proper storage after cleaning properly.

8. Wash hands thoroughly, following procedures in "Personal Hygiene" section of manual.

I. AREA OR ITEMS: Sinks and Drainboards

II. PRODUCT:
   A. As provided
   B. DILUTION: As indicated

III. SUPPLIES AND EQUIPMENT:
   1. Plastic Pail
   2. Nylon Brush
   3. Cellulose Sponge
   4. Clean Cloths

IV. PROCEDURE:

1. Fill bucket with warm water. Add specified pot and pan soaking agent in the ratio of 2 oz. per gallon of water.

2. Wash a small area of the surface at a time with sponge dipped in detergent solution. Use brush for stubborn soils and hard to reach places. For heavy contamination, spray specified stainless steel scratch remover in 1:20 concentration. Wipe with clean damp cloth.

3. Squeeze sponge as dry as possible and wipe off solution, leaving surface damp.

4. Let air dry.

5. Return cleaning equipment to proper storage after cleaning pail, sponge, brush, and dispose properly of cloths.

6. Wash hands properly, following procedures in "Personal Hygiene" section.

One day each week, substitute specified silver dip, at 2 oz. per gallon of water for regular detergent in wash solution. This will remove and control alkaline and mineral deposits.

I. AREA OR ITEMS: Hand Sinks (stainless steel), Sinks, and Lavatories

II. PRODUCT:
   A. As provided
   B. DILUTION: As indicated

III. SUPPLIES AND EQUIPMENT:
   1. Plastic Pail
   2. Clean Cellulose Sponges
   3. Hand–Sink Brush
   4. Clean Cloths

IV. PROCEDURE:
   1. Drain and flush surfaces thoroughly with clear water to remove soil residues. (When more than one sink is involved, follow each procedure for all rather than starting and completing all procedures for one sink and then going onto the next.)
   2. Mix cleaning solution of specified pot and pan soaking agent with 2 oz. per gallon water. Sponge down thoroughly (including faucets) entire sink, inside and out, until thoroughly clean. Clean faucets, soap dishes, and plumbing pipes prior to cleaning the interior.
   3. Clean overflow vent with hand–sink brush.
   4. Cleaned surfaces should be rinsed with warm water.
   5. Moisten sponge in solution to wash all other surfaces and plumbing underneath.
   6. With clean sponge wash all surfaces (wall) near sink likely to have been soiled through the use of hand–sinks, with specified pot and pan washing solutions.
   7. Rinse surfaces of solution and reapply on a sponge that has been dampened.
   8. Let air dry.
   9. Return cleaning equipment to proper storage after cleaning pail, sponges, brush, and disposing of cloths properly.
   10. Wash hands following procedures in the "Personal Hygiene" section.

   One day each week, substitute specified silver dip, at 2 oz. per gallon water for regular detergent in wash solution.

I. AREA OR ITEMS: Halls, Entrance, Stairwells, Railings, Elevators
                 (& controls), Dock, and Hallways

II. PRODUCT:
   A. As provided
   B. DILUTION: As indicated

III. SUPPLIES AND EQUIPMENT:

    1. Double Compartment Pails
    2. Cellulose Sponges
    3. Clean Cloths
    4. Mop and Mop Heads

IV. PROCEDURE:

    1. Wipe clean with warm solution, with particular attention to areas subject to contact with hands (such as around light switches, and areas soiled by splashing solutions or waste materials).
    2. Rinse with clear water and allow to air dry.
    3. Return cleaning equipment to proper storage after cleaning thoroughly.
    4. Wash hands thoroughly, following procedures in "Personal Hygiene" section of manual, before proceeding to another task.

    I. AREA OR ITEMS: Floors, Walls, Ceilings, Doors, Moldings, Horizontal Surfaces, Ledges, and Partitions

II. PRODUCT:

    A. As provided
    B. DILUTION: As indicated

III. SUPPLIES AND EQUIPMENT:

    1. Double Compartment Pails
    2. Mop and Mop Heads
    3. Cellulose Sponges
    4. Clean Cloths
    5. Stiff Brush

IV. PROCEDURE:

    1. First empty floors of as much movable equipment as possible. Sweep entire floor to remove loose soil.
    2. Put cleaning solution in one side of compartment pail, rinse solution in other compartment.
    3. Divide floor area into thirds or quarters.
    4. Go over surface thoroughly with mop or stiff brush and rinse with hot water.
    5. Squeeze to floor drains. If time permits, let air dry.
    6. Damp wipe all walls, doors, moldings, horizontal surfaces, and partitions with solution, then rinse sponge in solution and squeeze dry. Rinse with clean hot water, let air dry.

7. Return cleaning equipment to proper storage after cleaning thoroughly.

8. Wash hands thoroughly, following procedures in "Personal Hygiene" section of manual, before proceeding to another task.

I. AREA OR ITEMS: Dish Machines—De-scaling

II. PRODUCT:

    A. As provided

    B. DILUTION: As indicated

III. SUPPLIES AND EQUIPMENT:

    1. Suitable Brush

IV: PROCEDURES:

    1. Spray or brush specified silver dip on hard-to-reach places.

    2. Fill rinse tank ¾ full with hot water.

    3. Add ¾ can specified silver dip to rinse tank.

    4. Turn on pump and circulate rinse until lime film is removed.

    5. Drain tank and flush with clean hot water.

    6. Return cleaning equipment to proper storage after cleaning thoroughly.

7. Wash hands thoroughly, following procedures in "Personal Hygiene" section of manual, before moving on to another task.

I. AREA OR ITEMS: Dish Machine

II. PRODUCT:

    A. As provided

    B. DILUTION: As indicated

III. EQUIPMENT AND SUPPLIES:

    1. Double Compartment Plastic Pail

    2. Nylon Brush

    3. Clean Cloths

    4. Pressure Washer

IV. PROCEDURE:

    1. Turn off conveyor.

    2. Turn off steam valves.

    3. Turn off pump motors.

    4. Open drain valves.

    5. Open machine doors and remove curtains—leave doors open. Scrub curtains with specified dishwashing detergent solution in the ratio of 2 ounces per gallon, using a nylon bristled brush. Rinse curtains thoroughly with clear water and hang outside machine to dry.

It is important to wash and dry curtains each day to prevent the growth of mold and prolong the life of the curtains.

6. Remove and rinse the wash arms. Poke out any particles from the spray nozzles.

7. Remove and wash strainers. Do not strike strainers against hard surfaces to remove debris. This will bend edges and allow debris to enter tanks and pumps.

8. Hose down interior of machine; use a nylon brush, if necessary, to dislodge any particles or soil.

9. Wash exterior of machine with specified dishwashing detergent solution, 2 ounces per gallon of warm water, and wipe dry with clean dry cloth.

10. Return cleaning equipment to proper storage after cleaning thoroughly.

11. Wash hands thoroughly, following procedures in "Personal Hygiene" section of manual, before moving on to another task.

NOTE: Twice weekly, substitute specified silver dip for the regular detergent, in the ratio of 2 ounces per gallon warm water used to prevent alkaline film build-up.

I. AREA OR ITEMS: Serving Ware

II. PRODUCT

    A. As provided

    B. DILUTION: As indicated

III. SUPPLIES AND EQUIPMENT

    1. Dish Washing Machine

    2. Garbage Disposal

    3. Soiled-dish and Clean-dish Tables

    4. Soak-tank

    5. Suitable Brushes

    6. Dish Racks

IV. PROCEDURE:

    NOTE: Wear plastic gloves at all times when working near machine for your own protection.

    1. a. Arrange racks to receive soiled cups, glasses, and trays in scraping area.

    b. Arrange clean carts, dollies, etc., to receive clean dishes at discharge end of machine.

    c. Start disposal unit. (Do not put any garbage into unit when it is not running or when water is not flowing.)

    d. Fill detergent dispenser to begin and during use as indicated by red light. Make sure rinse injector is filled to proper level with specified water spot remover. Turn tank heater, water pump, and water heater on.

2. Scrape dishes as follows:

   a. Remove milk cartons, straws, paper, etc., and place in garbage cans.

   b. Place cups and glasses in racks upside down, inspecting inside cups and glasses to remove any debris, napkins, etc., which may have been overlooked.

   c. Remove food, debris, and gross soil from dishes by scraping and flushing into disposal. Keep a nylon brush handy for stubborn and congealed foods, egg, etc.

   d. Stack trays and dishes according to size and shape.

3. Remove dishes from scraping area and place in machine, placing all of one kind together and in line.

NOTE: Start conveyor and let run briefly before loading machine. Leave enough space between dishes to allow wash–sprays to reach both sides.

Do not mix small dishes with large plates. It is impossible for sprays to reach the small dishes and proper washing will not take place. Glasses and cups must be racked upside down, otherwise proper washing action will not take place. (If dishes turn over while in the machine, this indicates improper spray pressure. NOTIFY YOUR SUPERVISOR IMMEDIATELY.)

4. Place dishes in dish machine, and let go through the complete washing cycle.

5. Unload dishes as they emerge. Allow the dishes to travel as far as possible toward the end of the machine for better drying.

  I. AREA OR ITEMS: Refuse Receptacles

 II. PRODUCT:

   A. As provided
   B. DILUTION: As specified

III. EQUIPMENT AND SUPPLIES:

   1. Pressure Washer
   2. Nylon Hand Brush

IV. PROCEDURE:

1. Check to be certain there is enough detergent–sanitizer in the pressure washer reservoir.

2. Turn on water. Water temperature whould be a minimum of 160°F.

3. Place can in position on garbage disposal drain table.

4. Spray wash interior of can to dislodge all soil residues. Allow detergent chemical action to cut soil deposits. Use nylon hand brush to scrub heavy soils.

5. Spray again aiming spray directly against all surfaces.

6. Flush and drain into disposal unit.

7. While can is on draintable, spray wash outside of can.

8. Flush and drain.

9. Store cans in inverted position on racks to air dry.

10. Hose down surrounding walls and floors. Squeegee to floor drain.

11. Return cleaning equipment to proper storage after cleaning thoroughly.

12. Wash hands thoroughly, following procedures in "Personal Hygiene" section of manual, before moving on to another task.

I. AREA OR ITEMS: Storage Cabinets

II. PRODUCT:

A. As provided

B. DILUTION: As specified

III. EQUIPMENT AND SUPPLIES:

1. Plastic Pail

2. Cellulose Sponges

3. Clean Cloths

IV. PROCEDURE:

1. Fill pail with warm water. Add specified pot and pan soaking agent in the ratio of 2 oz. per gallon of water.

2. Remove all items from the shelves.

3. Scrub all exposed surfaces with detergent solution, using cellulose sponge.

4. Wring sponge and wipe up solution, making sure to leave surface a little damp.

5. Let air dry.

6. Return all items to proper storage.

7. Return cleaning equipment to proper storage after cleaning pail and sponge and disposing of cloth properly.

8. Wash hands thoroughly, following procedures in "Personal Hygiene" section.

Each third cleaning, substitute specified silver dip, at the ratio of 2 oz. per gallon of water, for regular detergent in the wash solution to remove and control alkaline or mineral deposits.

I. AREA OR ITEMS: Mirrors and Shelves

II. PRODUCT:

A. As provided

B. DILUTION: As specified

III. EQUIPMENT AND SUPPLIES:

1. Double Compartment Plastic Pail
2. Clean Cellulose Sponges
3. Clean Cloths

IV. PROCEDURE:

1. With clean cloth or moist sponge using specified dishwashing detergent in the ratio of 2 ounces per gallon of water, wipe down mirrors and shelving. Avoid use of wet sponge on light fixture.
2. Rinse with damp sponge.
3. Dry with clean cloth.
4. Return cleaning equipment to proper storage after cleaning thoroughly.
5. Wash hands thoroughly, following procedures in "Personal Hygiene" section of manual, before moving on to another task.

I. AREA OR ITEMS: Stainless Steel

II. PRODUCT:

A. As provided
B. DILUTION: As specified

III. EQUIPMENT AND SUPPLIES:

1. Plastic Pail
2. Cellulose Sponge
3. Nylon Brush
4. Clean Cloths

IV. PROCEDURE:

1. Fill plastic pail with warm water. Add specified pot and pan soaking agent in the ratio of 2 oz. per gallon of water.
2. Wash a small area of the surface at a time, using sponge dipped in detergent solution. Use brush for stubborn soils and hard-to-reach places. For heavy contamination: Take specified stainless steel scratch remover. Spray, wipe clean with damp cloth.
3. Squeeze sponge as dry as possible and wipe off wash solution.
4. Spray specified sanitizing agent at 1 oz. per gallon concentration for disinfectant.
5. Return cleaning equipment to proper storage after cleaning pail, sponge, brush, and dispose properly of cloths.
6. Let air dry.
7. Wash hands properly, following procedures in "Personal Hygiene" section.

One day each week, substitute specified silver dip at 2 oz./gallon of water for regular detergent in wash solution. This will remove and control alkaline and mineral deposits.

I. AREA OR ITEMS: Cart Washing (spray method)

II. PRODUCT:

A. As provided
B. DILUTION: As specified

III. EQUIPMENT OR SUPPLIES:

1. Pressure Washer
2. Nylon Hand Brush
3. Clean Cloths

IV. PROCEDURE

1. Check to be certain there is detergent sanitizer in the dispenser bottle.

2. Place cart in position for spray cleaning. It is advisable to raise the back of the cart so the solution will drain.

3. Turn on water supply. Water temperature should be minimum of 160°F.

4. Use brush and detergent solution to scrub all parts where soil is visible. Pay particular attention to casters, corners, crevices, etc.

5. Thoroughly hose down entire cart, including casters.

6. Allow cart to drain. Excess solution or water droplets may be wiped dry with a clean cloth.

7. Hose down surrounding walls and floors. Squeegee to floor drain.

8. Return cleaning equipment to proper storage after cleaning thoroughly.

9. Wash hands thoroughly, following procedures in "Personal Hygiene" section of manual, before moving on to another task.

Microbial contamination can be controlled in blast frozen foods if foods are: (1) prepared in a well-designed kitchen; (2) produced, held, and reconstituted under conditions of maximum sanitation; and (3) programmed so personnel know what is required and take the necessary steps to assure safe food items. Monitoring of these programs should be continuous.

12

Packaging for Blast Frozen Foods

PACKAGING AND FROZEN FOOD QUALITY

Food packaging is a term denoting the use of containers, or component systems, with labeling or product identification, for purposes of protecting, containing, identifying, merchandising, and facilitating distribution of food items. From this standpoint, it is inevitable that it plays a major role in the progress of pre-prepared convenience foods in the United States. Because of the keen competition among U.S. food processors, food packaging has become more and more an integral part of continuous research and development. Food packaging, in general, has not only met its goals of protecting foods, and providing related services, but it has also met the goal of merchandising the product to motivate the consumer to buy again. As consumers have gotten into the habit of purchasing food prepared commercially, they have become accustomed to new kinds of packaging, such as boil-in-the-bag, ready-to-bake casseroles in aluminum foil pans, or ready-to-serve pies and desserts in foil pie pans.

The factors affecting the quality of precooked foods after they have been prepared should determine the functions the packaging system plays during freezer storage, handling, food reheating, assembly, and distribution to satellite areas outside of the kitchen. There are two methods of packaging foods prior to freezing. The first method is hot packaging of food products maintained at temperatures above 140°F. In this method, food items are filled, packaged, and frozen. The second method is cold packaging, whereby the food items are first chilled to 40°F. and then packaged cold prior to freezing. Since these two methods may be utilized, the packaging materials to be used in a freezing system must withstand a thermal resistance range of 200° to −30°F. (blast freezer). If the end service aspect of reheating precooked foods is taken into consideration, then the thermal resistance range will increase to 400° to 500°F. The type of packaging material chosen also depends on the reheating method employed and on the end use of that product.

As the operation becomes larger, perhaps even producing and freezing over 10,000 meals per day for freezer inventory, it becomes a necessity to have an automated system of production, filling, portioning, and packaging. With an automated system, it is possible to feel safe and secure that microbial contamination is minimized. A safe system also requires the use of high quality ingredients with low microbial counts for the menu items to be frozen and packaged.

Maintaining the quality of the precooked foods prior to packaging is also of critical nature. Prime quality must be maintained throughout the freezing, packaging, storage, and reheating processes. The palatability of the precooked foods must also be retained. With well prepared foods packaged at peak palatability, there is only one further point of concern, i. e., the method of reconstituting and assembly of the food items adopted by the end user.

The elements in freezer storage that affect packaging need to be analyzed to determine the packaging needs of precooked foods.

Moisture loss during freezer storage has to be reduced or prevented, in order to avoid dehydration or freezer burn. The longer prepared products are stored in the freezer, the more important it is to find a packaging material with a low moisture–vapor transmission rate. It is essential to put emphasis on packaging material that prevents dehydration when such material is to be used in a blast freezer. The principle behind the blast freezer is its capability to reduce food temperature instantaneously, using high velocity of air flow through the coils of the evaporator. The air velocity, together with its low moisture level, increases the dehydrating effect on the food being frozen. The effect of moisture loss can be detected more in high protein foods, such as eggs, meat, fish, and poultry. Since water molecules are an intrinsic part of amino acids, the removal or reduction of water causes protein denaturation. A change in the structure of the protein also causes a change in the texture of the protein upon reheating.

Oxidative rancidity in precooked foods occurs on very short contact with atmospheric oxygen. Foods contain not only oxidizable compounds, such as enzymes, but also fats and oils which are readily hydrolyzed. Some food processors add a group of chemicals called "anti-oxidants," which inhibit the oxidative rancidity. The anti-oxidants combine with the free radical produced by the unstable compound called "hydroperoxide." Rancidity produces undesirable flavors and odors. It sometimes also produces product discoloration and vitamin A and C destruction. Oxidative rancidity may be eliminated by vacuum packaging, Cry-o-vac processing, or by displacing all oxygen in contact with food surfaces with nitrogen or carbon dioxide.[1]

Chemical acidity caused by interaction between the packaging material and the precooked foods needs to be prevented. There are certain food groups, such as fruits and vegetables, that interact with packaging materials, causing discoloration not only in the food but also in the container. If it is left inside an aluminum foil pan after reheating, any acidic items such as tomato sauce will pit and discolor the lid. This is why it is important that food not be left in these pans after prolonged heating and refrigeration.

The packaging materials directly in contact with the food surfaces have to be durable enough so that extra handling during the thawing and reheating processes will not cause the package to lose its shape or to break, allowing loss of liquid contents. Another aspect of packaging to consider is the outer shipping or distribution container. These containers must be resistant to both internal and external mechanical damages. The final appearance and quality of products, such as stuffed peppers, chocolate eclairs, lasagna, and chicken pot pies, are dependent on how strong and durable these external packing materials are in resisting stress and damage.

The *end use* of the product is another important factor that affects the ultimate function of packaging. It is quite difficult to transfer products such as chicken pot pies, lasagna, strawberry shortcakes, and fruit pies with trimmed crusts from the containers in which they are cooked. Therefore, it is less costly and makes handling easier to be able to use the same container for freezing, reheating, and serving functions. For individual pre-plated meals, the delicate and fragile nature of the smaller products makes it even more important to use the same packaging container for the freezing, reheating, and serving functions. The extra step required in transferring the products, if the same container is not used, will incur additional exposure to oxidative rancidity and moisture loss, thus affecting quality. This is one of the reasons why the most ideal system is the use of pre-portioned, individually plated meals. The only disadvantage to this system would be the increased capital investment for a large freezer storage area, to keep a minimum of 10 days product stock level.

The intended use of the product determines whether the packaging material should be soft, pliable, rigid, or firm.

It has been emphasized by Pinkert and Hysen[2] that the type of reheating energy affects the type and size of packaging materials used. Cafeteria foods are often packaged in half- and full-size foil pans as they are reheated in convection, infrared, quartz, or electronic ovens, and in pressure steam cookers. For patient meals, food is often plated individually in high-density plastics to fit the most commonly used reconstitution oven, the microwave oven. There are pre-plates which are packaged in "pop-out" containers. These containers are made of aluminum foil or high-density plastic. In both, the sauce or gravy is placed at the bottom. The entire plastic dish is inverted during tempering and reheating.

Since the same dish is to be used for reheating, there are certain standards to be met in order to produce quality products acceptable to consumers. These standards are as follows:

1. The packaging container used for service must provide for venting, especially for deep fried foods that have been dipped in batter.

2. The packaging container must provide good heat transfer and heat retention qualities and be able to withstand a temperature range between $-30°$ and $400°F$.

3. The packaging container must be air-tight, water and greaseproof, and must possess a low moisture-vapor transmission rate.

4. The packaging container must not taint or stain the product or produce off-flavors during reconstitution.

5. The packaging container must be easy to handle in terms of opening, sealing, resealing, and closing.

6. The packaging container must be safe and durable so as to prevent cracks, sharp edges, and crumpled look, thus making it difficult to use in serving.

7. The packaging container must be economical and also available at all times.

8. The packaging container either must be recyclable or must be economical to wash for re-use. The containers should fit and conform to the standard dishwashing or pot washing machines without expensive modifications.

9. The packaging container must be one which can be labeled.

It is essential that labeling becomes an integral part of the packaging, identifying the type of frozen product contained. One of the surveys conducted by the Research and Development Committee of the American Society for Hospital Food Service Administrators for the American Hospital Association[3] found that several of the complaints from foodservice operators concerned labeling of frozen precooked packages. Labels are often lost or fall off during the reconstitution process. Packaging should emphasize labeling and identification of products. Harder[4] cited that labeling should include nutrient and ingredient content, method of reconstitution, and handling warnings on frozen food products, such as "Keep Frozen," "Fragile," "Do Not Thaw Before Reheating," or "Keep Refrigerated." There has been considerable concern expressed about date labeling as well as warning signals to indicate if the products defrosted at any time during transportation. I often emphasize the fact that even if the most efficient date labeling system is used, improper handling of products is more detrimental to quality and more of an invitation to microbial contamination than prolonged or overextended storage of frozen precooked foods.

The control of quality and microbial contamination during packaging is dependent upon the *time* and *temperature* factors that affect the food being processed. Packaging is important. Damage during freezer storage can be prevented only if the packaging materials effectively protect the quality, size, shape, and aesthetic appeal of the packaged products.

PACKAGING SYSTEMS

History of Packaging for Frozen Meals

Before a detailed discussion is presented on recommended frozen precooked food packaging materials, it is well to review the history of frozen food packaging.

The beginning of packaging paralleled the start of quick freezing research. The progressive and rapid development of frozen fruits and vegetables led to the advent of new packaging methods for these products. In the initial stages of packaging frozen meals, Tressler[5] developed a cellophane-lined carton with a top-opening, Peters-type lock end suited for the Birdseye method of freezing, which was later followed by the Marathon Corporation's carton. This rectangular paperboard container did not require an inner bag as the liner material was laminated with a wet-strength, waterproof, and moisture-vapor proof paper.

The development of laminated cartons was followed by the use of foil containers. Reynolds Metals Company developed a leakproof, moisture-vapor proof container that could go through automatic closing machines. This type of container became widely used because of its good heat transfer ability.

Discussion of the use of heavy guage permanent aluminum or stainless steel pans will be limited in this book because of the high initial capital investment and the high cost of washing the reusable stainless pans. The use of rigid aluminum foil containers for freezing, chilling, and reheating food has been recommended by several foodservice operators who have had experience in the cook-freeze system. Tressler shared this recommendation when he showed that the rigid aluminum foil container comes closest to satisfying all of the criteria required for a package to be used for precooked frozen foods. At Hennepin County Medical Center, an aluminum gauge of .0035 inch for individual foil preplates and a gauge between .007 to .009 inch for bulk containers, either in half or full steam table pan sizes, was selected.

A cook-freeze system requires at least three basic containers: individual portion containers, pre-plate combination platters, and bulk portion containers. For the individual portion, a majority of foodservice operators prefer to use *boil-in-the-bag* or *individual pouches*. The "boil-in-the-bag" pouches, commonly made of high-density, polyethylene materials, are excellent packaging containers for single servings of special diets that are too difficult to forecast and produce. The preferred construction for boil-in-the-bags is the lamination of high-density polyethylene with mylar or polyester plastic.

Glew[1] has enumerated the various physical characteristics of plastic materials as they affect the packaging criteria for a cook-freeze system. I have found that, in terms of cost, durability, strength, and thermal resistance, the best combinations for a laminate plastic used for bags or pouches are the following:

Medium density polyethylene/foil/polyester
High density polyethylene/foil/cellophane
Low density polyethylene/cellophane
Polyethylene coated oriented polypropylene/polyester foil

Of the above three-layer laminates, the most efficient and economical combinations are the last two. The type of lamination necessary is determined by the heat treatment, the mechanical abuse that bag or pouch will be subjected to, and the type of freezing for which it is intended. Polyethylene is a good material as it withstands temperatures as low as $-60°F$., making it especially applicable for liquid nitrogen freezing. Polyethylene is heat sealable and provides an excellent material for shrink wrapping applications. Oriented polypropylene has excellent moisture-vapor properties and offers heat sealability as well. Glew has recommended the use of a Saran coating that produces a good oxygen barrier which polyethylene does not. He also notes that research on the usage of Nylon 11 (Relsan) with polyethylene will result in economical alternatives over the use of polyesters.

Because of the physical abuse that "boil-in-the-bag" pouches undergo, these bags have been constructed of double ply materials. Sufficient bag length is provided to accommodate the product and allow several inches of extra material to seal the pouch. This extra flap of material provides an area to grip while the bag is being immersed in boiling water, or being placed in steamers, and for ripping open the bag to empty the contents after reheating. The main disadvantage of this bag is that a very limited variety of products can be placed in it. In Sweden, I observed that pouched products were limited to cut up meats, fish, and poultry items, and sliced meats and poultry to which sauces or gravies were added.

The filling machine for these bags consisted of several cylindrical dispensers. Individual plastic bags made of mylar were attached to each cylinder through which sauces were dispensed into the bag from a sauce machine. The sauces or gravies were passed through a chill tunnel similar to an ice cream making machine prior to pouch filling. The meat components are manually placed in the bags before they are attached to the filling machine. The boil-in-bag containers are not suitable for products that have irregular contours or pointed edges such as chicken legs and pork chops.

Individual meals plated in rigid aluminum foil containers have become popular. Their most recent gain in popularity has been in public and private school feeding programs. TV dinners, where portioned food is frozen, stored, and reheated in the same rigid foil container, have been widely accepted in the domestic market due to the ease of handling and reheating. This type of packaged pre-plated meal can be reheated in a conventional oven, convection oven, or quartz oven. Continuing tests may result in products that can be reheated in a microwave oven. The aluminum foil is coated with a polyvinyl plastic which protects the foil from the arcing of the electromagnetic waves. The arcing causes the waves to reflect back into the megatron, burning out this component of the oven. These coatings also prevent foil pitting caused by strong acids and alkaline salts produced in the food during the tempering and reheating stages.

One of the most important reasons for using boil-in-the-bag and rigid aluminum foil packaging materials is the technique used by the industry in vacuum packaging foods in these containers. In vacuum packaging, oxygen is removed as the vacuum is created, thus permitting an airtight, leakproof seal. With rigid aluminum foil containers, new hermetic sealing machines produced by Ecko and Raque assist in obtaining an almost complete airtight seal. The semi-automated and completely automatic conveyorized filling, packaging, sealing, and freezing lines that I have seen make one marvel at the rate of productivity that could be achieved in normal hospital operations. Any foodservice operation that exceeds 3000 meals per day should try to analyze the pros and cons of a cook-freeze system with the use of semi-automated production, portioning, filling, packaging, and sealing machines. The cost savings obtained from a uniform portion control program, due to exact and precise measuring equipment, should speak for itself when capital expense for this equipment is amortized. The principle of automatic portioning of 100 macaroni and cheese plates will certainly have more advantages than the system in which food is portioned either hot or cold from bulk pans into individual plates manually. The advantages of an automated portioned filling of one product run at a time over the conventional method of portioning one plate at a time is obvious and needs no further discussion.

Usually, it is also advantageous to use semi-automatic sealing equipment as it offers increased efficiency over tight overwrapping or lid sealing with vacuum or air suction pumps. A semi-automatic sealing machine also increases speed and productivity, thus decreasing labor hours for cutting and sealing. Sanitation and maintenance of safe conditions are other convincing factors for selection of semi-automatic portioning, packaging, and sealing equipment. Rappole, in this feasibility study, showed that bacterial contamination of the chicken a la king that was being studied may have possibly occurred during filling through a funnel. However, it must also be kept in mind that a well-developed and implemented sanitation program for equipment and utensils used in portioning is also needed to safeguard against additional microbial contamination.

Unfortunately, there are limitations on the usage of semi-automated portioning equipment, e.g. it has been found that product dimensions must not exceed 1-in. cubes. We experienced no pumping problems when products mixed with sauces or gravies had correct densities and flowability characteristics. Menu items such as pork chops, steaks, veal cutlets have to be portioned manually, but these are items that I do not recommend for freezing in bulk. These products should be used in limited freezing applications for individual pre-plated meals for selected special diets. They should be chilled prior to plating and stored no longer than 72 hours.

Bulk aluminum foil containers should be constructed with a full curl flange rim which assists in making the container more rigid. Based on our experience, the product level should be right up to the top of the foil container, except for products which expand during reheating, such as noodles and macaroni.

Specific Applications of Packaging Materials for Sandwiches, Canapes, and Appetizers

For hamburgers, hot dogs, or individual sliced meats, such as salami, pepperoni and braunschweiger, the use of moisture-vapor proof cellophane and polyethylene is excellent. The application of a perforated foil paper-polyethylene, foil laminate has been used for hamburgers to be reconstituted in infrared ovens or forced air convection ovens. The perforations help in preventing the buns and the beef from being steamed. Hors, d'oeuvres or appetizer-type sandwiches should be stacked in paper corrugated cartons. Regular cold sandwiches should be shrink wrapped with a cellopolyethylene laminate film to prevent dehydration and oxidative rancidity. Delicate canapes and cocktail hors d'oeuvres should be packaged in a plastic tray with thermo-formed indented pockets of the right size and shape to hold each snack. There are several food processors that package canapes on corrugated cardboard flats and overwrap the unit with shrink film so the canapes will stay in position until they are thawed.

Packaging for Outside Container for Distribution and Transportation

If precooked foods, such as pre-plated meals, are to be stored, distributed, and transported, it is important that they are enclosed by a rigid corrugated cardboard container. These containers are a standard shipping container for all frozen foods.[6] In the University of Kunicum in West Berlin, Germany, the pre-plated meals were stored in a heavy duty plastic box that has dimensions similar to the standard corrugated cardboard box. Although plastic boxes are expensive, the amount of reuse in an on-premise cook-freeze system has been such that amortization of the investment has been rapid. There was no need for printing labels as each box has a computerized code, indicating the production run date and intended area of use, whether it be for patients or cafeteria patrons.

Corrugated cardboard containers are made of 3 plies of paperboard from Natural Kraft, the two outer boards of which are always flat and are called "liners" or "facings," and the third ply, the one that is corrugated, is glued in between. For delicate products, such as pies, a six-sided corrugated insert fits snugly around each of the pies, which are packed with another straight corrugated board separating one layer of pies from another.[5]

FACTORS AFFECTING THE FINAL DECISION ON A PACKAGING SYSTEM

During the initial planning for Hennepin County Medical Center, we decided that there would be two packaging systems: individual pre-plated meals and bulk-plated entrees, incorporating starch and vegetables. Consideration was given later to introducing boil-in-the-bag packaging for small volume entrees, such as renal beef stew. Judging from a cost and quality standpoint, it will not be advantageous to portion a 1-oz. serving of meat and 2-oz. serving of starch and vegetables onto a regular size plate.

There are several basic factors which influence management's final decision on a packaging system. These factors are as follows:

1. *Modularity of the containers* to be used is a first and foremost factor to take into consideration when management has decided to pursue a pre-plated program or even a bulk-plated system. It is difficult to handle portioned precooked frozen foods that have to be tempered and thawed before they are reheated. There is no heating system in the United States that reheats pre-plated food from a frozen state to serving temperature in the same oven and produces quality results. Several companies have taken some innovative approaches that were close to developing an oven to be used both as a module for thawing and then for reheating. These various types of reconstitution are discussed in Chapter 15, "Alternate Methods of Frozen Food Reconstitution."

The choice between permanentware or disposables is based on the cost of labor in washing the permanentware and the cost of a continuous supply of disposables. The present trend of increasing labor costs is balanced by the increasing cost of plastic caused by the petroleum shortage. In weighing the use of disposable aluminum foil pans against reusable heavy gauge aluminum or stainless steel pans, one has to face the burden of increasing steel prices, the large capital investment tied up in freezer storage inventories, and the increasing cost of labor for pot and pan washing. Dorney[7] mentioned in his article that the reason why they chose to use reusable aluminum pans over disposable pans was because of the low wage scale for foodservice employees in Britain.

2. *Type of reheating method* somewhat determines the composition, size, and shape of the containers to be used. A majority of foodservice operators utilize convection ovens or conventional ovens, thus giving the edge to aluminum foil instead of plastics which have a tendency to melt. Harder[4] has recommended that packaging used by food processing companies be geared in design to the new reconstitution equipment being developed. Newer packaging of frozen products must be developed to be compatible with microwave oven cookery or the new version of microwave oven called Chemetron Votator, which has a sensor in the tray that controls the degree of microwave interaction with the food molecules.

3. *Availability of supplies* is critical, especially when plastic material availability fluctuates with petroleum supplies. During periods of limited supply of plastics there seems to be no problem in securing aluminum foil and in purchasing it at an economical cost.

4. *Aesthetic appeal to the customer* is important as any container that gets warped or buckled during transport or reconstitution will certainly affect aesthetic appeal for the customer who has to eat from such a dish. Because of warping or denting which produces pinholes, there are possibilities of loss in quality due to dehydration or oxidative rancidity. Another problem that has been cited by a survey[3] is the degree of condensation in the overwrap film in both the pre-plated and the bulk-portioned meals. The amount of condensation contributes to the "watering" of the sauces or gravies in the dish. It not only looks unappealing, but also tastes bad, since it dilutes flavor.

5. *Types of storage space* available in the refrigeration and freezer areas will influence the size, shape, and configuration of the dishes and pans, as will the transport module used in food distribution, food receiving, and food reconstitution. There are three types of storage systems available, including fixed shelves, mobile shelves, and live pallet shelves. The most economical, but not the most efficient, is the fixed shelf type of storage. Mobile shelves can be moved from one area to another. These shelves maximize space utilization although it is only a one-aisle space. The type I prefer is live pallet storage. Even though it is more expensive than mobile shelves, it increases the productivity of storeroom clerks and minimizes accidents and falls. This system has a series of inclined roller conveyors. Each length of the inclined roller conveyor carries a single product per opening. The biggest advantage to live storage is

that it insures the quality of products, especially the more perishable ones, as it promotes a first-in, first-out (FIFO) stock rotation.

6. *Cost of capital investment* should not be ignored. Semi-automated packaging equipment is just as expensive as reusable aluminum and stainless steel pans.

7. *Type of menu, product selections, and volume of clientele* are the last but not the least important factors to consider. The range of products suitable for boil-in-the-bag or pouch packaging has been discussed earlier in this chapter. Aluminum foil pans in the commonly used 12-by 10-by 2-in. size carry 25 meat, fish, or poultry portions with a total pan weight of five to six pounds and a 12-by 20-by 2-in. size carries 50 or more meat, fish, or poultry portions with a total pan weight of ten to twelve pounds. The type and volume of service certainly affects the packaging system. For a restaurant with an ala carte menu, you would normally select boil-in-the-bag or pouch containers, while most hospitals and other large institutions use bulk aluminum foil pans.

Final Recommendation

What every foodservice operator would most like to see at the present time is standardization of packaging. It has been found by Livingston and Mario[8] that there are 19 different sizes of containers with foods packaged in mylar/poly, nylon, high-density polyethylene, tempware trays, and aluminum trays. The most commonly used and well-liked bulk container is the half-size, disposable, aluminum foil pan. This size pan seems a lot easier to fill, thaw, and reconstitute. The pan weighing five pounds is also easier to handle than the full size pan. The use of full size pans may result in warping, denting, severe spilling, and in burns during the reheating of entrees.

The type of material used in any packaging system seems to be more critical than the other factors presented. The physical, chemical, and aesthetic properties of the various types of material seem to lead to the conclusion that either aluminum foil will remain "king pin" in the packaging world or some chemist will develop a high-density, durable, will-not-taint or discolor plastic. This to-be-developed durable plastic can be thermoform-molded into a configuration similar to a half size pan and will also be heat resistant to withstand the temperature range of $-60°$ to $500°F$. We are getting close to seeing this a reality. While dreaming of this new super miracle plastic pan, we must also think of the ecology problems that this plastic pan will bring, so I have decided that we should have a reusable, super miracle, plastic pan to solve ecology questions. I would even suggest that the filling and lidding of this pan occur through a vacuum packaging machine, a machine that will try to evacuate all of the air out of the pan, thus leaving no possibility for oxidative rancidity to take place. Should we go this far? We might develop a bacteria-free environment in doing so. Unfortunately, it has been proven by Solberg[9] that there might be hazardous conditions due to the increased rate and growth of certain micro-organisms because of the anaerobic conditions that result from vacuum packaging.

Whatever we do in modern packaging techniques, we should strive toward combining our talents and resources toward the packaging of the convenience foods of tomorrow—not only meeting the present needs for protection, merchandising, and stability, but also making great strides and advances in the areas of nutritional and ecological aspects of packaging.

Labelling and Packaging System at
Hennepin County Medical Center

These pre-plated meals are lidded with 3M film made of a new, bi-axially-oriented, polyvinylidine chloride and this film is heat sealed to the disposable container made of polystyrene. Due to our past experiences in reconstitution with the microwave oven, 3M oven and Trexo oven, we have selected a permanent, 5-by 7-in. rectangular shaped dish. The heat dissipation and transfer becomes more uniform when the product surface contact is at maximum and when the depth and density of the material being heated is not more than 1 in. high, or more than 10 to 12 oz. in weight. A large plate looks more appealing than an overcrowded small plate such as airlines use. Work has been done with various plastic manufacturers in the research and development of a disposable pre-plate which can also become the cover during the process of reconstitution. This will reduce the packaging/lidding cost for the microwave oven (Chemetron Votator) that was chosen as the reconstitution module.

Packaging of frozen foods is one of the other important components in freezing. Innovative packaging materials, such as moisture, vapor, and oxygen resistant films which can be vacuum sealed to the container, are available. Without proper packaging, there is a loss of moisture from the product in the form of water vapor resulting in freezer burn, general deterioration in quality, and decreased shelf life.

Each pre-plate and bulk portion pan will be properly labeled with:

1. Name and number of the product, color coded for general or special diets.
2. Date of production.
3. Ingredients.
4. Net weight per portion.
5. Color coded label.
6. Reconstitution method from frozen state.
7. Nutritional content.
8. Handling precautions.

Bulk portion aluminum foil pans are transferred into cartons for palletizing. These cartons are closed with gummed tape that has been reinforced with strong threading for added strength.

PART 2

Holding, Storing, Tempering, and Reconstituting Frozen Foods

13

Freezer Holding and Storage for Precooked Foods

PREVENTING CHANGES IN FROZEN FOOD

There are many chemical, physical, and qualitative changes that occur in foods during freezing, storage, and reheating. These changes can be prevented if the necessary steps are taken.

Oxidative rancidity may occur during frozen storage, depending on storage time and temperature. Oxidative rancidity is caused not only by exposure to oxygen, but also by hydrolytic cleavage of fats. The fats present in food are often catalyzed by enzymes. Specific food categories are catalyzed by specific enzymes which explains the use of peroxidase for oxidative rancidity in fats, phenolase for fruits or vegetables, and ascorbic acid oxidase for ascorbic acid.

There are other enzymes, such as lipase, which react to the breakdown of fats. Chlorophylase catalyzes the breakdown of chlorophyll and proteinase catalyzes protein foods. Slowing the rate of oxidation and hydrolysis is dependent upon adequate inactivation of the enzymes mentioned.

Blanching and steam scalding are cooking processes that inactivate the enzymes found in fruits and vegetables. According to Glew,[1] it is generally assumed that if foods are prepared using normal cooking times and temperatures, a majority of the enzymes will be inactivated.

Oxidative rancidity is often caused by the oxidation of fats. This is affected by temperature, light, use of peroxides, use of metal catalysts, and the presence or absence of lipoxidase enzymes, metals or minerals.

The moisture content of frozen, precooked foods changes when the products are subjected to a wide range of temperature fluctuations. When moisture increases, mold growth may occur.

Let's examine the several factors to consider if successful frozen storage is to be assured.

Type of Product

The type of product that enters the freezer influences the possible oxidative and hydrolytic changes that may occur. Deterioration in quality of the following products occurs because of the nature of the product:

1. Ham, cured picnic ham, frankfurters, Canadian bacon, bologna, and other cured products, such as corned beef and creamed chipped beef, will lose their red pigmentation and turn a brownish–gray first, then completely gray later. After 6 weeks, detectable flavor changes are observed due to oxidative rancidity.

2. Batters and unbaked goods containing baking powder have a very short storage life since the acid and soda in the baking powder slowly interact with the dough resulting in CO_2 developing. As the gas diffuses, the batter loses its leavening power.

3. Many spices change in flavor after several months of storage. Pepper, onion, sage, thyme, and garlic lose flavor. In consequence, highly spiced dishes lose quality faster than dishes more bland in flavor.

4. Sponge cakes made with egg yolks cannot be kept for long periods because possible oxidation may result in negative flavor changes in the yolk.

5. Products, such as fruits and vegetables, which have not been blanched or scalded may lose color. There also may be Vitamin C destruction. Vegetables and fruits which are high in Vitamin C contain pectin which, if exposed to oxidation, creates a mushy texture, caused by cellular breakdown.

6. The whites of hard–cooked eggs become tough and inedible due to protein denaturation as their moisture content diminishes.

7. In products containing sauces and gravies prepared from wheat flour or cornstarch, retrogradation of gelling during storage causes the free water to separate from the gelled parts.

8. Seafood items will toughen somewhat during freezer storage due to protein damage arising from the loss of water. This occurs as the water withdraws

to become ice around the product. This process results in an increase in salt concentration in the seafood as the moisture diminishes, thus causing the texture of the product to be chewy and gummy.

9. Oxidative rancidity is dependent on the fat content of the product. Adequate fat content affects flavor and overall appearance of the product. The following foods are listed according to their rate of oxidative rancidity which is based, in turn, on their fat content:

1. fatty fish
2. turkey, chicken with skin on
3. fried foods
4. pork
5. dairy products
6. shellfish and fish
7. beef, veal, lamb
8. meat pies, casseroles, and some fish
9. fruits and vegetables
10. juice concentrates
11. poultry pies
12. fruit pies

Fried foods are expecially subject to oxidative rancidity because most of the fat absorbed during frying remains on the surface areas of the food in direct contact with air.

Low Temperature Maintenance

Freezer storage time and temperature are the two most important factors in maximizing the retention of quality in precooked frozen foods. Quality loss is minimized in most products if they are stored at a temperature of $-10°F$. or below. Only if there is to be product turnover on a monthly basis or oftener, would I recommend that freezer storage temperature be maintained at $0°F$.

Because the freezers are usually used during the entire operating period, it is possible that freezer doors will be opened a minimum of 20 times during that period. For an operation preparing less than 500 meals per day, the potential for opening and closing of the doors will be even greater.

If there is inadequate freezer capacity in a small operation, the need for more frequent delivery of frozen food, and consequent opening of the freezer, will cause the temperatures of stored frozen products to fluctuate. In a small freezer where product rotation is seldom practiced, where doors are opened frequently, and products placed in somewhat tight quarters, the probability of temperatures fluctuating over a wide range is great. Products at the front on top shelves can reach a temperature of 25°F. and products in the center of the top shelves can reach an even higher temperature. The item which should be most carefully stored is the individually-plated meal, as a drop or increase in ambient temperatures more readily affects its temperature producing faster quality loss than happens in larger packages of bulk food.

Tressler[2] says that, generally speaking, the speed of chemical reactions in frozen food is increased 2½ times when the temperature is raised 18°F. (10°C.) He has a rule-of-thumb formula for storage of precooked frozen foods: if a food retains its fresh quality for 3 years at −18° to −20°F., it can be held in good condition for 1 year at 0°F., but only for 6 months at 10°F. Note: These rules may be applied only if the items are frozen solid and temperature fluctuations are nonexistent.

Most persons engaged in freezing food for foodservice operations believe that foods containing sugar or other water soluble solids will have a longer storage life than other products. However, Tressler observed that fruit pies containing a high percentage of sugar soften at 10°F. to 15°F. and the rate of deterioration is very rapid. Temperature fluctuations affect products containing sugar since the separation of liquid increases as the range of temperature fluctuation increases.

It has also been found that temperature fluctuation affects any item that has the potential for starch retrogradation since the accelerated thawing and reforming of ice solids causes the starch to separate into free liquids and gel formations.

Quality of Food

Purchasing top quality raw foods and other ingredients for freezing is necessary to ensure quality during storage. Adopting quality product standards, such as those meeting the fat content and microbial count for USDA choice meats, assures that these items will be in good condition when they are stored in the freezer.

One of the products for which freezer storage is most critical is seafood. Older seafood, already rancid, stale, and dehydrated, is not going to taste better after freezing. In fact, freezing will even add to the deterioration of these items if they are not properly packaged.

The variety and type of raw fruits and vegetables selected will affect the storage life of frozen fruits and vegetables. Some varieties deteriorate faster than others.

The rate of freezing also affects the size of the ice crystals. If freezing is so slow that large crystals are formed, the products can easily develop hydrolysis and rancidity. After thawing, these products become mushy and watery and develop off flavors.

Quality of Products Prior to Freezer Storage

Quality not only includes the "freshness" component of the raw materials but also the palatability of the precooked frozen foods. This factor is determined by appearance, flavor, color, texture, consistency, odor, degree of doneness, and the moisture content standard for that particular product.

If there is a noticeable difference between a freshly prepared high quality entree and a frozen precooked high quality entree, it is an indication that the food was not properly frozen. Frozen food of the proper quality can compete in standards of acceptability with its freshly prepared counterpart.

The major problem lies in the fact that many people are prejudiced against frozen foods. However, these mental barriers are slowly being overcome as the volume of sales of precooked frozen foods increases steadily. The range and variety of acceptable frozen products now on the market are the result of the intensive product research and development undertaken by the frozen food industry.

The level of quality in precooked frozen food is quantifiable and measurable to some extent. In the equipment discussed in Part 2, Chapter 1, a list of quality control equipment has been included. To determine whether frozen precooked foods can pass the minimum standards established by management, there have to be well-developed tests of quality. Basic characteristics of food products that offer a definite basis for judgment are of two types: measurable quality standards (objective) and unmeasurable quality standards (subjective).

Among the various instruments that may be used for measuring the quality of precooked frozen food are the following:

1. A microbial count based on a standard plate count. The absence of staphylococci is a good sign of clean, wholesome food.

2. A pH meter measuring the acidity or alkalinity of the foods. The acidity indicates whether the item has been subjected to poor preparation techniques causing the pH to go higher. Any abrupt change in pH, whether a decrease or an increase from the normal for the item, indicates organoleptic unacceptability.

3. A spectrophotometer to measure the intensity of color. Using this machine, a partial substitution of food coloring for the expensive egg yolk may be made to produce the right color intensity. This instrument is most com-

monly used by food processors in product research and development to find color combinations in food that increase acceptability.

4. A viscosmeter, a machine that determines the flowability and viscosity of the product.

5. Texture is an attribute of quality that relates to the "shearing" or cutting property of food. Instruments which measure texture include a piece of equipment that uses compression to determine the feel (and texture) of fresh or stale bread. Meats are measured by cutting or shearing; tenderness is a measure of the amount of gristle and connective tissues encountered.

6. A fat tester for meats is a simple instrument that separates the fat from the rest of the meat by heating the test patty until all of the oil and fats are extracted. Tressler recommends that meats for freezing be aged from 7 to 10 days.

Type of Cookery and Stage of Doneness

The optimum degree of cooking to be done to food for freezing varies with the end product desired and the type of reheating to be used. Generally speaking, a majority of the food products, except for baked breads, rolls, and other yeast products, should be cooked to 80 percent of doneness.

Frying, broiling, and grilling are methods of cookery that withdraw moisture from meats if not done properly. Even when executed in a manner to avoid this, they are not usually the best methods of cookery for freezing.

Frying as a method usually adds fats and oils to the product. Fat absorption increases in lower temperature frying, while a crisper product comes with higher temperature frying. The latter has less fat absorption, because it seals the outer layer with a crisp crust. A deep-fried, battered product has about the shortest shelf life and poorest quality upon reheating. However, in time a reheating oven and innovative packaging will be developed that will produce high quality, deep-fried food.

The longest shelf life for precooked frozen food products is in items that have a well-stabilized sauce or gravy and in casserole-type entrees. The next group of products that has a long shelf life include IQF fruits, baked goods, such as breads, cakes with fruit, cookies, cookie dough, pancakes and waffles, and certain vegetables with sauces or gravies. There are also certain precooked roasts that have longer shelf lives, especially when vacuum packaged in polyurethane pouches.

Degree of Doneness

Food, as a rule, should be cooked to a medium done stage. Fruits and vegetables are an exception as they need only scalding or blanching, and so are baked products which need to be completely done.

Types of Spices and Flavorings Used

Spices noted for losing potency during freezer storage are onion, pepper, sage, thyme, garlic, ginger, cardamon, and nutmeg. For some reason, the use of greater amounts of spices actually contributes to faster deterioration of product quality. The practical way to preserve the potency of spices is to make sure they are exposed to air as little as possible. Experiments have demonstrated that if spice companies would portion and package basic spices in the regularly used weights, such as ½ oz. or 1 oz. amounts, we could retain the necessary flavor in foods during freezer storage. An additional step that would seem to be desirable would be for spice companies to also package spices in edible films that would add to the protein or carbohydrate content of the dishes they were used in.

Method of Packaging

Next to quality ingredients, the most important factor affecting freezer storage shelf life is the efficiency of the packaging method and the filling of the packages. The amount of surface exposed, the amount of oxygen left inside the package, the percentage of fill weight, and the impermeability of the film to moisture, gases, punctures, acidity, and thermal stress variances are factors that affect the shelf life of precooked frozen products.

Additionally *time and temperature* are two variables affecting product quality. The less time the product remains in the package, the less deterioration there will be. The need for a continuous product flow from preparation to packaging to freezer storage is mandatory. For larger operations able to afford them, semi-automatic packaging fillers and portioning machines increase the stability of the frozen product during storage.

Use of Antioxidants and Preservatives

Antioxidants are groups of chemicals that slow down or reduce oxidative rancidity. Their effectiveness is based on their combining the chemical selected with free radicals (resulting from the hydrolytic cleavage of fat) to prevent them from developing into chain reactions that produce more free radicals. Antioxidants also act as deactivators for trace metals, the precipitating factor in the reaction between the fatty acid part of the liquid and the oxygen in the air.

Natural preservatives, such as vinegar, ascorbic acid, lemon juice, sugar, salt, and soy sauce are very effective in improving the stability of meats, fresh fruits, and vegetables. Chemical preservatives such as acetic acid, malic, citric, lactic and barbaric, calcium or sodium salts of propionic acid, sodium propionate, and sodium diacetate have been widely used for breads and rolls. Meats have been preserved by smoking and curing, with formaldehyde, salt, and sodium nitrite.

RECOMMENDATIONS AND SUMMARY

Here are basic recommendations for establishing a well-maintained, efficient freezer storage program.

TEMPERATURE MAINTENANCE—Every storage freezer must be kept at − 10°F. at all times, and the setting must be such that, in spite of the rate of opening and closing doors, the internal cabinet temperature of − 10°F. is maintained. As demonstrated in experiments described by Tressler, most foods deteriorate drastically at temperatures above 0°F. Fluctuating temperatures must also be avoided to prevent thawing and re-freezing in any part of the product.

SHELVES AND MOBILE RACKS OR SLIDES FOR STORAGE—The type of equipment used, e. g., mobile racks or tray slides, will affect the design and layout of the freezer storage area. A freezer, properly designed and laid out for frozen food storage, provides adequate and uniform air circulation around the product so there is equal heat penetration at the top, sides, and bottom of the products.

An efficient physical layout also reduces the time that personnel spend looking for products. When using mobile racks or tray slides, it is best to identify and place products in the same location at all times. Freezer baskets are recommended for storing small items that may get lost if stored at random on racks or trays.

The use of the principle FIFO (first in—first out) for day-to-day product turnover and inventory control is highly recommended. With this system, the problem of a product exceeding its shelf life is prevented, or reduced to a minimum. Inventory control contributes to accurate purchasing and production forecasting. For an operation serving 3000 meals per day, product turnover should be set at a monthly rate if at all possible.

So that personnel assigned to the freezer storage area are able to work efficiently, it is best to provide them with snowmobile suits and nylon gloves to insure them against frostbite, which is progressive in nature. A warm hat that covers the ears, especially vulnerable to frostbite, is essential since the heat loss rate from the head is greater than from any other part of the body. Most storage freezers have air circulating fans that need to be turned off while personnel are working inside. No person should work in a freezer for more than an hour to an hour-and-a-half without a rest period in a warm area.

The following list summarizes freezer storage time for both raw and cooked products and categorizes them by length of storage life.

Short Storage Life
Maximum 2 weeks to 2 months

Product	Maximum Storage Life at 0°F.
Appetizers	3–4 weeks
Bacon, Canadian	2 weeks
Batter, Muffin	2 weeks
Batter, Spicecake	1–2 months
Biscuits, Baking Powder	1–2 months
Bologna, sliced	2 weeks
Cake, Sponge	1–2 months
Cake, Spice	1–2 months
Cream Puffs, Filled Eclairs	1 month
Dough, Roll	1–2 months
Frankfurters	2 weeks
Gravy (wheat flour base)	2 weeks
Ham, slices	2 weeks
Ice Cream and Sherbets	1 month
Oysters, shucked	3 weeks
Poultry Giblets	1–2 months
Poultry Livers	1–2 months
Sandwiches and Canapes	
cheese	3 weeks
bologna	3 weeks
Sauce, White (wheat flour base)	2 weeks
Sausage	1–2 months
Yeast Dough, unbaked	2 weeks
Baked goods from bakery	2–3 months
Batter, Devil's Food	4–6 months
Batter, Gingerbread	3–4 months
Batter, White Cake	4–6 months
Breads, Rolls, Coffee Cakes	4–6 months
Brownies and Bars	4–6 months
Cakes, various kinds	4–12 months
Chicken, fried	4–6 months
Cookies, baked	6–9 months

Short Storage Life (cont'd.)

Product	*Maximum Storage Life at 0°F.*
Cookies, unbaked	4–6 months
Crab	6–8 months
Cream Puffs, Eclairs, unfilled	3–4 months
Fish, fatty	6–8 months
Fruit, purees	6–8 months
Ham, baked, whole	4–6 months
Liver	6 months
Lobster	6–8 months
Meatballs	6–8 months
Meat Loaf	6–8 months
Pies, Chicken	6–8 months
Pies, Fruit, unbaked	4–6 months
Pies, baked	3–4 months
Pies, Meat	6–8 months
Pie Shells	6–8 months
Pork Roast	6–8 months
Potatoes, French fried	8–10 months
Sandwiches	
roast beef	6–8 months
various spreads	6–8 months
turkey	6–8 months
liverwurst	6–8 months
Soups	4–12 months
Shrimp	6–8 months
Turkey	4–6 months

Long Storage Life
Frozen convenience foods in this group will remain
in good condition for one year at 0°F., if properly packaged.

Products

Fruits	*Starch Products*	*Miscellaneous*
applesauce	breads	gravies (modified starch)
apples, baked	cake, fruit	rice pilaf

blackberries
blueberries
cherries
plums
raspberries
strawberries
peaches

cookies, baked
cookie dough
pancakes
rolls
waffles

vegetables in butter,
cream, au gratin sauce
white cream sauce
(modified starch)
egg whites

Pre-cooked Entrees—Bulk Packed*

baked beans
beans and sausage
beef burgundy
beef goulash with macaroni
beef stew
braised sirloin tips
braised short ribs with gravy
chicken fricassee
chili with beans
egg omelets—plain, cheese, bacon
gravy with sliced beef
stuffed green peppers
Swedish meatballs
Swiss steak
tuna and noodles
turkey a la king
turkey with dressing

lasagna
macaroni, beef, and tomato
macaroni and cheese
meatballs, polynesian
meatballs, stroganoff
noodles and chicken
salisbury steak
seafood newburg
spaghetti sauce with meat
spaghetti sauce with meatballs
stuffed cabbage rolls
turkey with gravy
veal parmigiana
veal stew

Pre-cooked Meats

corned beef
broiled beef patties
broiled beef and peppers
broiled Italian beef
peppered beef
roast beef
breakfast pork patties
broiled veal patties

---

*For frozen individual pre-plated meals, reduce shelf life by 6 months.

The safeguarding of food quality during freezer storage is one of the most important elements in a successful blast freezing program. Only quality ingredients should be used in foods for freezing but their quality must be protected with proper temperature maintenance and use within the designated storage interval. Constant monitoring is justified to protect the investment in quantities of stored blast frozen foods.

14

Tempering Precooked Foods Before Reconstitution

WHEN AND HOW TO TEMPER

The most controversial issue in microwave cookery is whether frozen precooked products should be tempered or thawed before reconstitution. Tempering has usually been considered desirable for four reasons:

1. To reduce reconstitution time and prevent dehydration or moisture migration;
2. To produce equal, even, heat penetration and distribution to prevent cold spots;
3. To reduce reconstitution time, thus expediting serving time;
4. To reduce reconstitution time to limit product breakdown and drip loss.

Tempering frozen precooked products prior to reconstitution, i.e., cooking food from a thawed state, does not seem necessary to maintain the quality of the product, an argument I feel is reinforced by the operating conditions described as follows.

Conventional thawing practices have always meant keeping the product in a 40°F. refrigerator for several days prior to reheating. A technique used at

Manning's, Inc. in Portland, Ore. some years ago was to place frozen products packaged in polyethylene pouches in a large bain-marie or water bath to thaw. This method has not gained popularity even though products thawed this way have better quality than products reconstituted in regular, convection, or microwave ovens.

The length of reconstitution time required for frozen precooked food products depends largely on the degree and stage of thawing of the frozen product. Clearly, products should be thawed uniformly so that even heat penetration and distribution may be accomplished. If thawed at room temperature, the time the product spends in the danger zone for microbial growth and development is longer. Another undesirable effect of prolonged thawing is that the outside of the product usually thaws first, leaving the inner core still frozen. Ultimately, the drip or juice loss is so significant that there is cellular damage in the tissues whether the raw ingredients are animal or vegetable.

The frozen products that require the most delicate handling during thawing are precooked items that will not undergo any heating prior to serving. Thawing these precooked foods and holding them at room temperature for more than 6 to 8 hours will produce staphylococci, organisms that grow at temperatures about 45°F. and are responsible for foodborne illnesses and food poisoning. Staphylococcus aureus causes the majority of food poisoning. Staphylococcus produces a soluble toxin called enterotoxin, the presence of which is not easily detectable as it is odorless and tasteless. This toxin may produce symptoms such as nausea, vomiting, abdominal cramps, severe diarrhea, and prostration. Even though the symptoms of the illness are short-lived and the mortality rate is very low, its development will have serious consequences for a foodservice operation.

If frozen precooked products are thawed inside a refrigerator, there is no guarantee that the internal core temperature will reach the range between 40°F. to 140°F. at a fast enough rate so that the period of time in the danger zone is minimized. It is also true that for frozen products that are kept too long in the danger zone, there is a corresponding decrease in product quality.

Normally, thawing is done in a storage refrigerator, whether door-type, walk-in, or pass-thru. When a bulk load of frozen product (0°F.) is placed into a refrigerator at 40°F., the internal temperature will be pulled down causing the compressor to shut off. Because refrigerators are insulated, the internal temperature will remain below normal until the doors are opened allowing warm air to enter the unit. Thawing will start when large amounts of warm air have entered the refrigerator. With the type of product load described above, the thawing time for frozen products in a refrigerator is unnecessarily increased.

To allow for the thawing time required by this method, production must be scheduled 3 days in advance of service. Production scheduling for an operation producing 3000 meals per day or less will suffer from the effects of the necessary tight schedule unless an unusually large walk-in thawing refrigerator is built into the system with a correspondingly large freezer storage facility.

A thawing refrigerator is a unit that permits the rapid and uniform thawing of frozen foods in a controlled environment. When the cabinet is not required for thawing operations, it can operate as a regular 38°F. holding refrigerator.

This type of refrigerator can completely thaw a frozen product in approximately half the time required by conventional methods. A frozen bulk load of 400 lb. is generally defrosted in 10 to 16 hours, although irregularly-shaped and/or dense products, such as roasts or turkeys would take more time. Using a thawing refrigerator prevents developments like the uncontrolled and inadequate thawing prior to reheating in a fast heating oven, such as a microwave oven, that result in waste and spoilage, flavor and texture changes, discoloration (because of incomplete inactivation of enzymatic activity in fruits and vegetables), and increased "drip" from moisture loss.

In a small foodservice operation, the thawing refrigerator may be used as a storage refrigerator during daily hours of operation and for thawing during the night. With this system, when the operation begins preparation in the morning, the frozen foods are properly thawed and ready for service.

For a medium-sized operation, preparing less than 3000 meals per day, and relying largely on the use of bulk frozen foods, a thawing refrigerator can be used continuously. When large amounts of frozen foods are required, products should be labeled with the date and time when they are initially placed in the refrigerator for thawing. As products are withdrawn for thawing, shelves should be replenished with fresh frozen stock.

The location of the thawing refrigerator is an important factor in its being used to the maximum. At Hennepin County Hospital, the thawing refrigerators are walk-ins, about 25 by 20 ft. rectangular-shaped, insulated boxes. These refrigerators are located beside the walk-in freezers and adjacent to the main production areas. They are reached through the same pass-thru doors that lead to the walk-in freezer which minimizes temperature loss.

Other steps will assure maximum use of thawing refrigerators.

1. The packaging system should insure moisture and gas impermeability, and provide an air-tight, leakproof, durable, and impenetrable package for the product. With increased circulation during thawing, improperly packaged foods will suffer from a fast rate of dehydration and loss of moisture.

2. Packaging must follow the recommended product configuration for effective and fast thawing. Research has established that a 2-in. deep frozen

product will thaw more uniformly and have better quality since deeper pans require proportionately more time to thaw.

3. Plastic film materials, and aluminum foil or metal pans, because of their high heat conductivity rate, are the best media for thawing food.

4. Corrugated boxes should be removed before the individual products are placed in thawing refrigerators because cardboard acts as an insulator.

THAWING TEMPERATURE

Effect on Bacterial Growth and Development

When frozen products are defrosted, the rise in internal temperature is a major concern; therefore, the heat that is applied should not increase that temperature. According to Maclinn,[1] the coefficient of heat transfer is influenced by the air temperature, the number of units of frozen product stacked together, the degree of air circulation between units, the type of casing material, the number of individual packages within the case, and the density of the product itself. A majority of the frozen fruits, vegetables, fruit juice concentrates, and fruit and meat pies in institutional cases have appoximately the same coefficient of heat transfer when exposed to elevated temperatures.

Freezing prevents food from spoiling because spoilage agents are almost non-functioning at + 15°F. Micro-organisms that cause food illnesses cease activity at 40°F. but from 40°F. to 60°F. certain psychrophilic bacteria thrive and grow.

Staphylococcus and several species of flavobacterium can withstand freezer temperatures better than other micro-organisms. Thus thawing temperatures between 0°F. and 100°F. can create favorable zones for potential bacterial multiplication. Fortunately, Maclinn demonstrated that the fears of many people that thawed frozen foods cause food-borne illnesses are not substantiated in fact. He explained that when a frozen food is brought to a temperature of 15°F., where psychrophilic organisms can grow, these organisms do not immediately spring into full-scale growth and development. First, they must go through a period of adjustment to the new environment. Even after the food is actually thawed, there is no growth for a considerable period of time.

There are four phases in the growth of bacteria after food is thawed. The first is the lag phase, the initial period during which the bacteria are getting used to these new conditions. There is no reproduction. Many of the micro-organisms may not even survive. Consequently, the total number of bacteria may fall.

In the second phase, called the logarithmic phase, micro-organisms begin to multiply and their numbers increase logarithmically.

As the waste products of their living process accumulate in the third, or resting phase, reproduction slows until the increase stops. In the fourth phase, the bacteria begin to die because of these waste products and the colony enters the death phase.

Considering these four phases of micro-organism growth, after the product increases in temperature above 15°F., the role that the lag phase plays becomes clear when evaluating the potential for spoilage of frozen foods.

Maclinn cited a study performed by Hucher and David of the New York Agricultural Experiment station which showed that chicken pies thawed and held at 34°F. had no bacterial growth for 70 hours. Maclinn ultimately demonstrated that if the bacteria are allowed to grow in the natural phases outlined above, there is built-in protection in frozen foods: 1) in the partial destruction of bacteria by the freezing itself; 2) in the lag phase during which growth is delayed; and 3) in the logarithmic phase where growth slows because of low temperatures. Fears about the safety of thawed foods for public consumption may be eliminated *as long as every step or precaution is taken to keep the temperature from going above 40°F. and the time the thawed product spends in the danger zone is not more than 48 hours.*

Effect on Quality Standards

Deterioration in quality during thawing is a function of time and temperature. Based on the study initiated at the USDA Western Regional Research Laboratories, Albany, Ca. in cooperation with the Refrigeration Research Foundation, it was established that various types of frozen food have different stabilities during frozen storage and thawing, depending on their discoloration rate and/or the oxidative rancidity inherent in the product or added to the product.

The study used various qualitative methods such as chemical and physical tests, and organoleptic evaluations by a trained panel of flavor evaluators, to determine the level of quality for each product. When 75 percent of the panel could detect a difference between the test samples and the control, the time was noted as the point at which the first signs of quality loss were detectable. This established that holding temperatures above 0°F. speed up the qualitative changes in frozen foods. For example, an internal product temperature of 25°F., in sensitive fruits and vegetables such as peaches and cauliflower shortened the time required for the first detectable sign of quality loss to appear from 1 year at 0°F. to 2 days at 25°F. This clearly shows the effects that storage temperatures above 25°F. have on quality loss.

Peterson[2] has dissected the role that thawing plays in the total organoleptic quality of the frozen food. He stressed the point, also made in these pages, that during the thawing process there is loss of acceptability. He was surprised to discover that for chicken pies, incipient unacceptability began after 48 hours of storage at 41°F., at 16 hours at 68°F., and at 6 hours at 99°F. For chicken pies with a higher inherent bacteria count, organoleptic unacceptability was reached even earlier, after 30 hours at 68°F.

During the defrosting of the chicken pies, Peterson also found that the degree of intensification or blending of flavors reached its peak during the initial phases of thawing. There was then a progressive lessening of the degree of strong, desirable flavor until a rapid onset of undesirable defrost flavors made the product inedible. He studied the effect of thawing on the quality of frozen, prepared macaroni and cheese, and turkey dinners and concluded that the vegetables defrosted first, followed by the sauces and gravies, and then the remainder of the entrees.

The rate of organoleptic quality was associated not only with the corresponding growth and multiplication of micro-organisms but also related to the pH level of the food. Any rapid decreases in pH or increase in acidity coincided with organoleptic unacceptability.

RECOMMENDATIONS AND SUMMARY

Product thawing or tempering before reconstitution is still a major unresolved issue in the cook–freeze system in foodservices, especially in institutions where large volume production is required. At the initial stages of planning for the Hennepin County Medical Center Central Food Preparation Facility, a search was started for an oven that would not only rethermalize food but cook it as well, with this process starting with the food in the frozen state, omitting any need for thawing or tempering. Unfortunately, we found no oven capable of reconstituting foods from a frozen state that proved successful in meeting the quality standards set for large scale production.

Uncle Ben's, Inc., Food Services Division,[3] strongly recommends that thawing be accomplished in a refrigerator at a temperature between 36°F. and 40°F., with the product held no longer than 48 hours. These same conditions were recommended by both Maclinn and Peterson, et al, based on their studies and experimentation.

The methods of determining whether a product is uniformly tempered, and what stages of thawing the inner and outer layers of the product have gone through, still need to be researched in relation to volume foodservice operations.

There are several *temperature indicators* on the market that note if thawing has occurred. One of them, used by poultry and turkey processors, changes color permanently if the product reaches a pre-established temperature.

Another practical and inexpensive technique would be to use a eutectic ice, a concentrated solution of salt in water which has a freezing point lower than water alone. When it melts, eutectic ice indicates that a predetermined temperature has been reached. Various food processors have considered the use of a strip of paper soaked in a chemical with the same physical properties as eutectic ice.

A program for loading thawing refrigerators with new loads of bulk frozen foods, and for collecting thaw times should be established. Efficient purchasing and production forecasting can be established if such a program is workable and realistic.

Each foodservice operation will have a different scheduling program. Because of the variety of products, container sizes, and packaging materials available, manufacturers of thawing cabinets are not able to supply specific statements on thaw time. In developing your own thawing timetables consider these points:

1. Load quantity and product weight in pounds;
2. Product size, shape, density, and depth;
3. Load type—whether the load is made up of fruits, vegetables, casseroles, or roasts has an effect on the rate of heat to thaw in different quantities;
4. Containerization or packaging materials used—metal containers conduct heat faster than plastic or cardboard; and
5. Load spacing—products too near each other reduce air circulation around product surfaces.

The selection of an effective, rapid thaw refrigerator system is important. In selecting a rapid thaw refrigerator, look for the construction features recommended for a regular freezer in Chapter 2.

The only difference between them is that the thawing refrigerator has a system of alternating heating and cooling cycles to maintain air temperature below 45°F. during the thawing phase. When the product load is completely thawed the cabinet will automatically operate in the cooling cycle, preventing product temperatures from exceeding 45°F.

One of the thawing refrigerators available from Victory Manufacturing, Div. of McGraw-Edison Corp., Plymouth Meeting, Pa. offers increased air circulation uniformly distributed throughout the product zone. This paves the way toward even thawing and is accomplished through four auxiliary mullion fans which are automatically activated during the thaw cycle. The fans are positioned to homogenize the cabinet air to avoid cold and hot spots within the product zone. Upon completion of the thawing cycle, the cabinet operates as a regular storage refrigerator with temperature maintained at 38°F.

Available microwave tempering equipment made by the Raytheon Company is described as having a 25 kw, 915 MHz multi-mode conveyorized microwave tempering unit. For a bulk load of 1000 lb. of frozen meats, this equipment requires about 5 kw for lamb and over 11 kw for beef to bring the temperature to 29°F. from a frozen state of 0°F. For a product 6 in. or more thick, it is possible to control tempering to within 0.5°F.

There are several advantages cited for this type of tempering as compared to thawing refrigerators: 1) the use of this microwave tempering tunnel unit requires less space and less labor in loading and unloading products; 2) the time required is shorter (typically 15 minutes) in contrast with several hours for a thawing refrigerator. With these advantages, the length of time the product spends in the danger zone is minimized; product inventory is more easily accomplished, and production runs can be separated. In addition, the cost effectiveness of large production runs is realized.

When tempering frozen foods in a microwave oven, make sure they are frozen solid. If not, the product will suffer from unequal microwave penetration and the colder spots will reach a thawed temperature faster. The thawed portion will absorb most of the energy. Various product formulations are also necessary if the use of a microwave oven for thawing is to be effective. Experience has shown that these formulations must be similar to those that apply to reconstitution in a microwave oven.

The various techniques for microwave thawing tested and adopted at Hennepin County Medical Center included:

1. Large, irregular food masses, such as turkeys, beef roasts, pork roasts, should be prepared and packaged so that the cross sectional thickness is not too great. To assure this, 8-to 10-lb. roasts of beef have to be cut into halves or quarters, and turkeys have to be sectioned into legs, thighs, and breasts. If roast beef slices are to be reconstituted in a microwave oven, the slices should be arranged either like shingles on the roof of a house or like bacon in a package.

2. Portion controlled meats, such as steaks, chops, cutlets, etc. thaw best if a 3/1 cut or 4/1 cut layered and separated with wax paper is specified. The size of these portions is not too important in thawing in a microwave, although size does become a problem where these meats have been frozen together and need to be separated.

3. The desired size, shape, and fat content of beef has been formulated for microwave oven tempering and reconstitution. Cubes of beef for products should not exceed 1-in. squares. For ground beef patties, a fat content

between 18 and 20 percent produces a quality product. Patties with less than 18 percent fat, e. g. ground chuck, quickly dehydrate, while patties with more than 20 percent fat splatter grease on the internal cavity of the microwave oven.

4. Casseroles and combined dishes thaw best when they are wrapped in high-density polyethylene to protect them from dehydration. For items that are high in fat content, occasional splattering and explosions inside the cavity occur, especially if sequential cycling reconstitution is not followed. To thaw casseroles and combined dishes, it is best to use two 5-minute, short interval cycles with a pause between the intervals. This method is only applicable for a casserole contained in a dish or a polyethylene pouch with a depth of not more than 2 in.

5. Fatty materials, such as bacon, require almost half again as much energy.

6. Individually plated frozen meals can be thawed and reconstituted by the differential heating container which offers controlled reconstitution for frozen dinners. The principle behind this container is to limit the energy provided to certain components of the dinner, which tend to heat too rapidly, and to allow unlimited energy to be absorbed by the components that heat more slowly.

Dr. Decareau[4,5] believes that greater use of microwave ovens will dictate the development of a type of packaging that has built-in shielding. Such packaging will allow items like complete dinners and casseroles to be reconstituted in the same package in which they were frozen.

7. Bulk plated frozen meals may be tempered in a thawing refrigerator at 36° to 40°F. Meals of this type should not be thawed at room temperature. In attempts to thaw the bulk plated meals in an infra-red/microwave combination oven, the quality of the reconstituted products was not good; the edges were burned along the sides and the center had cold spots. This condition resulted because microwave ovens designed to hold a 12 in. by 10 in. by 2 in. pan have only 1 megatron. Microwave ovens with 2 megatrons make it possible to have even, uniform energy penetration to all areas, including the center of the pan of food.

THE APPLICATION OF ELECTRONIC OR DIELECTRIC HEAT IN DEFROSTING FOODS

The principle behind the dielectric oven, as described by Gould, Weiser, and Mountney,[6] is the application of alternating currents of a few megacycles frequency through condenser plates or electrodes between which food is placed in containers made of insulating materials, such as glass. The food defrosts rapidly as the dielectric currents in the capacitor are strong and quickly penetrate to all parts of the food.

This method raises the temperature more quickly as the heat comes from the inside. Since the heat is coming from the food itself, it becomes a very efficient and economical method. However, there are still a few control problems which need more research and development.

Another electronic device which has the potential to thaw and reconstitute individually plated frozen meals through electrodes inside the dish that holds them is called the 3M Integral Heating System. A more detailed discussion of this is presented in Chapter 15.

15

Reconstituting Frozen Foods in Microwave Ovens

SYSTEMS EFFICIENCY

The heat required for frozen food products is determined by the number of BTU's per pound needed to raise the temperature of the food from -10°F. to a serving temperature of 160°F. to 180°F. (A British Thermal Unit is the amount of heat which will raise the temperature of one pound of water one degree Fahrenheit.)

The factors cited in the chapter on freezing foods—moisture content, internal temperature, portion weight, size and configuration, depth and density, fat content and type of packaging—are the same factors that affect the efficiency of reconstitution systems.

There are several basic objectives in choosing the right type of reconstitution equipment. They are:

1. The adaptability of the oven determines whether menu selection variety can be increased, or an improvement in the quality of reconstituted products can be achieved.

2. Food quality must be maintained or improved by accelerating the release of flavor and aroma, retention of moisture or juiciness, and the enhancement of product appearance.

3. The rate of reheating should occur with minimum delay to reduce the dwell time of the food through the danger zone from 40°F. to 140°F.

4. Equipment should place minimum demand on labor.[1]

5. The output should be geared not only to peak loads but to off-peak loads as well.

6. The rate of heat penetration must be uniform so that the more dense materials will be heated almost simultaneously with the less dense products.

7. It must be designed so that less skilled help are able to operate it.

8. It should be easy to clean and sanitize so that good microbial control is possible.

9. It should require minimal labor and training time to operate. Possible reduction in staffing can be important.

10. It should be easy to maintain without requiring special skilled engineers to repair and maintain it.

11. It should meet the operating performance standards established by the various regulatory agencies.

There are three basic methods of heat application used for reconstituting frozen foods: conduction, convection, and radiation.

Heat transfer by conduction is caused by the temperature differential between the surface and the center of the product being heated. The rate of heat transfer can be increased by increasing the surface temperature. Some examples of equipment that heat by conduction are grills, deck ovens, deep fat fryers, steam jacketed kettles, and tilting braising pans. One caution: if the temperature is set too high, the product will suffer from product dehydration, increased meat drip, and charred flavors.

Convection heating is accomplished through a fluid medium by movement of this medium. The introduction of circulation fans increases the rate of heat transfer, provides more uniform heat penetration, and allows a lower temperature to be used. According to Decareau, at present convection heating is used primarily to reconstitute precooked frozen foods. New large roll-in convection ovens will reconstitute 200 to 300 individually preplated meals.

Insofar as conduction and convection ovens do not keep pace with increasing demands made by foodservice operators for a faster oven, the use of radiation methods of heat transfer will become widespread. Reconstituted in a convection oven, a preplated meal takes 35 to 40 minutes to reach serving temperature from a frozen state, or 20 to 25 minutes from a refrigerated state. But in a microwave oven, it takes only one to one-and-a-half minutes from a frozen state, or 30 to 45 seconds from a refrigerated state.

The infrared method is a function of the difference between the fourth power of the absolute temperatures of the energy source and the object to be heated. Decareau notes that if the source temperature is doubled, the heat flow is increased by a factor of 16. What is important is the extent to which the item being heated will absorb the radiant heat energy.

Microwave heating uses radar frequency radiation to stir or agitate the water molecules throughout the food. Microwave energy is the fastest available method of reconstitution. Radiation is the process of emitting radiant energy in the form of waves or particles. These waves radiate outward from the center, like waves on the surface of a pond, travel at the speed of light, and carry small bundles of energy, called photons, which vibrate at various frequencies. There are two basic kinds of radiation: ionizing and non–ionizing. Microwaves are the non–ionizing type.

Microwave energy possesses three basic properties: absorption, transmission, and reflection. Like light waves, microwave energy can be reflected. Metals prevent this and so do not permit heat to reach food. Many other materials, including glass, transmit microwaves and again, since there is no absorption, there is no heating.

PRINCIPLES OF MICROWAVE OVEN COOKERY

Microwave ovens operate at room temperature as only the presence of food generates any heat in the oven. The basic parts of a microwave oven are: 1) door, 2) magnetron, 3) waveguide, 4) mode stirrer, 5) power supply, 6) power cord. The function of the power supply is to convert low voltage line power to the high voltage required by the microwave generator—the *magnetron*. You will encounter this word, magnetron, several times in this book, so it is important to understand its role.

When the magnetron is energized, it generates high frequency energy, which passes down the waveguide to the cavity. The mode stirrer helps control the flow of energy and cause it to be distributed more uniformly. Without the stirrer, there would be severe hot and cold spots during reconstitution. Microwaves that miss the food are reflected from the metal surface lining the cavity and bounce back and forth until they hit the food. If there is no food in the cavity, the microwaves will be reflected back to the magnetron, which process burns out the magnetron valve. This can also occur if a metal container is placed inside the cavity, though there are some modified ovens where the magnetron valve is protected against this.[2]

Microwaves are absorbed better by water molecules than by ice crystals. The amount of moisture in a food has a direct bearing on its heating rate in a microwave oven. The same principle applies to freezing food, especially through liquid N_2 where food with 80 percent moisture will take more time to freeze to a specific temperature than food with 50 percent moisture. Consequently, if both types of food are placed in a microwave oven, then hot and cold spots will occur.

Various types of food affect the amount of microwave energy required to heat them to serving temperature. A pound of water will heat only half as fast as a pound of fat. Specific Heat is a measure of the product's ability to hold heat compared to water. Water has a specific heat of one (1.0), while fats are 0.5.

The type of container or packaging materials that could come in contact with microwaves are classified into two groups: metallic and dielectric. Metallic material reflects the microwaves, which means the waves will heat the surface and not penetrate it.

Dielectric materials can be divided into good and bad dielectrics. The good dielectrics absorb little energy from the microwaves. The bad dielectrics absorb microwaves readily; water is an example. There are some materials which fall between good and bad dielectrics, such as glass, china, plastic, and paper.

Absorption depends on the composition of a substance and its depth. Microwaves are capable of penetrating instantaneously to a depth of one to one–and–a–half inches. Thus, microwaves penetrate only the outer layer of the food mass, so the center portion must rely on heat conducted from the hot outer regions. The surface layers also radiate some of the excess heat to the surrounding air. Even after removing food from the cavity, heat conduction continues at a rate dependent upon the thermal conductivity of the food.

Microbiology and Microwaves

There has been much controversy regarding the use of microwave heat in killing food micro–organisms. Controlled experiments have demonstrated that short microwave heating cycles are as destructive to bacteria in the vegetative state as the longer thermal methods. Olsen[3] has experimented with aspergillus, rhizopus, and penicillin on unwrapped bread and concluded that the use of microwaves for two minutes reduced their growth.

Organisms in the spore stage, however, require higher temperatures in many cases than can be obtained when heating by microwaves or other methods unless this is done under pressure, where higher temperatures can be reached.

Lasey,[4] et al, concluded from experiments that a minimum exposure for three minutes was an unreliable method of reducing bacterial counts in mashed potatoes.

Compared to other methods of reconstitution, a microwave oven heats food faster so the length of time the food is in the danger zone is minimized. One of the most undesirable, unsanitary practices in foodservice is allowing food to stand for lengthy periods of time. This practice is frequently encounttered because (1) food takes several hours to cook in a conventional oven. Then (2) after it has been cooked, it is allowed to stand in a lukewarm condition on steam tables. When food is being heated for immediate service it should be kept at 140°F. or higher and must not be kept longer than two hours. The quality deteriorates if food is held for too long above 140°F. but a lower temperature will cause bacterial growth and contamination.

Factors Affecting Microwave Cookery

1. Standard Product Specifications

The importance of a standard product specification is critical when we discover that the time of microwave heat cycles varies greatly from one product to another, depending on size, weight, shape, density, and type of packaging. Product formulation depends on how tightly the specifications for the ingredients are followed, implemented, and evaluated. As for microwave oven application, the reconstitution times are critical in terms of seconds. A timing error of 10 seconds in reconstitution time could result in a dehydrated, burned look.

2. Starting Temperatures

One of the reasons frozen food is difficult to reconstitute in a microwave oven is the rate of thawing differential between the warmer food (partially thawed) and the colder food (unthawed, with some ice crystals). Since microwaves are absorbed more readily by water than the ice crystals, it is difficult when water and ice crystals are both present in the product being reconstituted.

When frozen bulk food is reconstituted in a microwave oven, the rise in temperature to bring the product to serving tempeature is dependent on the amount of ice crystals and the specific heat of the food. (The specific heat is a measure of the product's ability to hold heat compared to water, which has a specific heat value of one (1.0).)

The formation of ice crystals inside the food molecules cannot be totally homogeneous, even when the food is subjected to sharp freezing through liquid nitrogen. The nature of the cellular composition even varies within the same group of foods.

To alleviate the problem, the microwave cycle has to be accomplished in sequential timing with a "rest" period between the "on" cycles. It is important that the frozen food be heated for a short time to warm the surface layers of the product. Then the product should be removed immediately, and allowed to rest for 5 to 6 minutes so that heat will flow from the surface to the center portion of the product. The food may then be returned to the microwave oven and reconstituted for the same amount of time as you would a thawed refrigerated product.

3. Plating is affected by density and depth, moisture content, size, shape, and weight of the portions, cellular composition, and stage of doneness.

Density is an important consideration in food plating. The denser the food, the longer it will take to heat. Remembering microwave energy characteristics, we should place the denser materials on the outer rim of the plate. This configuration assists in developing even heat distribution as the denser materials will absorb more microwaves coming from the megatron tube. When microwaves are applied to products with a dense but loose texture, the heat generated is easily conducted, paving the way toward the uniform distribution of water or fat molecules in that product. Because of the muscular composition of red meat, it is difficult to cook these meats from the raw state. A few ovens combine microwaves with forced convection to compensate for this problem.

Moisture content also affects the way food should be arranged for microwave heating. Moist products should not be placed in the center portion of the plate, since the lower the moisture content, the shorter the reconstitution time. Thus, sliced meats with low moisture have a tendency to overcook and dry out. Sauces and gravies may be used to reduce the dehydration of sliced meats during reconstitution.

As I explained, water takes twice as much heat as fat to increase its temperature by one degree. The simple formula to calculate the heating time in microwave ovens is as follows:

$$\text{Heat required} = \text{Weight (lbs.)} \times \text{specific heat} \times \text{temperature}$$
$$\text{BTU's} \qquad\qquad\qquad\qquad \text{Difference (°F.)}$$

Since most ovens (1KW) provide 57 BTU's per minute, the heat required, divided by 57 BTU's per minute, will give the heating time.

When two foods at different starting temperatures are heated simultaneously in a microwave oven, the colder food takes longer to reach a given temperature.

The size and shape of the portions on a plate affect the heating time in a microwave oven. The most difficult heating problems encountered were in products such as quartered chicken, hot dogs, Polish sausage, prime rib, baked potatoes, cabbage wedges, and other irregularly shaped foods. We were able to solve our problems by changing the size or processing of the meat, or by cutting potatoes in half, or stuffing them instead of using a plain potato.

Another technique we use is to avoid irregularly shaped, dense food. Regular shapes heat more uniformly; irregular shapes have thin and thicker parts and, the thinner parts overcook and dry out by the time the thicker parts are done. We have specified deboned, rolled, and tied roasts, chicken legs, thighs, and breasts instead of quarters, and smaller or halved baked potatoes. There are plating techniques we use, such as placing beef slices or cabbage leaves like shingles, or shielding the thin, narrow parts of the chicken or turkey with foil.

The weight of the portion also affects the plating technique. Pinkert[5] recommended that after determining the specific timing for a single standard portion weighing a certain number of ounces or grams, one then can estimate the timing for a larger portion by adding five seconds for each additional ounce. For one-ounce meats as in renal diets, five seconds should be deducted.

To determine the reconstitution time for a pre-plated dinner, a total of all standard desired times for each item on the plate—meat, starch, and vegetable—should be calculated. Once this total is arrived at, five seconds should be deducted from the time required for the sample plate.[5]

One of the most important plating techniques for microwave oven reconstitution is to keep the food within the inner well of the plate and prevent overlapping on the rim. Recalling how microwaves bounce back and forth between the metal surfaces inside the oven cavity, it is simple to conclude that a more uniform reflection and absorption will occur if the portions are placed in an orderly, compact mass.

One of the most thorough studies evaluating the preparation and plating of frozen dinners was done by Fenton and Gleim.[6] They emphasized the importance of plating combinations of food that are satisfactory not only in nutritive value, color, shape, texture, and flavor, but possess uniform temperatures. They also mentioned that the rate of heat penetration depends mainly on the nature of the food, the amount, and the shape. They found that loose textured vegetables, such as broccoli, require a much shorter time than compact vegetables, such as mashed squash. This observation contradicts the principle that the lower the moisture content, the shorter the reconstitution time, since broccoli is about 90 percent moisture. Finally, if possible, the combinations of food on a plate should have almost equal shelf life.

A more detailed discussion of plating techniques is presented in the latter part of this chapter.

4. Role of Packaging and Packaging Containers

One of the advantages of microwave cooking is that often it can be accomplished in the serving dish or package in which the food was purchased. In theory, all materials, with the exception of metallic surfaces, are transparent to microwave energy.

We have discovered, though, that some china dishes absorb microwave energy. Some plastic containers melt above certain temperatures. Melamine plasticware, due to its porosity, absorbs enough energy to cause charring in places, and can become too hot to handle. Some ceramic dinnerware may absorb several watts of power for each ounce of weight. We consider this to be an advantage as the heat retention helps keep the food hot longer during the service period.

Plastic containers are well suited for microwaves ovens providing the thickness is not less than 0.015 and 0.0175. In the initial period of development, the high density polyethylene and polypropylene were widely used. The disadvantage with polypropylene is that it is not able to withstand freezing temperatures of $-10°F$. or lower. High density polypropylene is most often used for cook-freeze systems as it is able to be heated above 290°F. The most frequently used plastic containers have been polystyrene laminated with cellophane or polyethylene. These containers have proved successful also in cook-freeze applications since polyethylene can withstand a temperature as low as $-60°F$. The combination of these two materials helps lower costs because polystyrene is cheaper.

Preplated meals need to be covered with a lid to prevent dehydration. The lid should be made of the same plastic materials as the container, although a thinner density may be used.

"Boil-in-the-bag," or plastic pouches made of polyester laminated with polyethylene, are frozen food containers in which the foods are reconstituted by immersion in boiling water. This is one of the simplest and most economical methods of reconstitution. The practicality of this type of packaging in large sizes, containing five to ten pounds, will depend on the surface exposure of the pouch and the rate of heat penetration to the center of the food. The rate of heat penetration is increased by vacuum packaging so the insulating effect of air around the food is minimized. The pouches and bags need to be enclosed in a coated, lithographed, paper carton to prevent any mechanical damage. The pouches and bags are delicate to handle and have an unattractive, wrinkled appearance as they come from air vacuuming. The pouches and bags are excellent packages for precooked frozen foods for microwave reconstitution, though a few punctures or holes must be made to relieve steam pressure inside the package.

Paper ware has good practical application for microwave oven reconstitution. A variety of excellent paper products is available. Some operators have found that paper does not have adequate rigidity and the aesthetic appeal necessary for frozen food containers. Paper manufacturers are improving their products through excellent color and designs which somewhat alleviates some of these complaints. With paper containers, bulging and wrinkling occurs from the microwave absorption. To solve this problem, several manufacturers have developed polyethylene laminated paper. Beyond laminating paper with plastic, manufacturers should be testing the use of metallic strips or aluminum foil in varying thicknesses, sizes, and shapes to help eliminate uneven microwave penetration due to the composition, density, and geometry variations is food.

SPECIAL TECHNIQUES IN MICROWAVE RECONSTITUTION

EGGS AND EGG PRODUCTS

We have found eggs to be one of the most difficult foods to heat in a microwave oven unless you know what must be overcome. First of all, we tried to prepare soft-cooked eggs. They exploded like hand grenades.

An egg is actually an airtight container with a very porous shell. The thin membrane of the egg white encloses the egg yolk and can build up pressure and expand so rapidly inside the air chamber that it immediately explodes. The technique to follow is to place the egg inside a container. Add a small amount of hot water and provide as little microwave exposure as possible. The egg must be at room temperature and the water must be boiling so there is no imbalance causing the egg to explode.

There are no problems when it comes to the reconstitution of fried, poached, and scrambled eggs or omelets as long as the proper preparation, plating, and reconstitution times are followed.

MEATS, FISH, AND POULTRY

Roast meats have to be prepared and cooked to a less than rare doneness, until the internal temperature is around 125°F. The only exception, of course, is pork, which has to be cooked as high as 140°F. The cooking of raw red meats in a microwave oven, especially raw meat joints, is not always successful. Some microwave ovens have been combined with a charcoal grill and rotating spit as mentioned by Napleton[7] in his book.

The application of microwave ovens to precooked roast meats is quite successful as long as the meats are not cooked beyond a medium rare doneness. The roast should be trimmed of all visible fat. It is best that the roast be chilled down as fast as possible to reduce time in the danger zone. There are new blast-chill ovens or new heat exchangers that are placed in special kettles to chill meats. If roasts are to be placed in kettles, then it is best to wrap the roasts in high density polyethylene bags. The top part of the bag should be punctured so that the warmer air will be able to escape. The roast beef slices should be either very thin and rolled like crepes or sliced about ⅓-inch thick. Each slice should be brushed with our sauce recipe called meat glaze. (See page

59.) This meat glaze can be used for low calorie, diabetic, and for salt-free diets.

Portion controlled meats should not be cooked in microwave ovens as it is faster to use conventional grills, tilting braise pans, deep fat fryers, or forced convection ovens. Steaks should be seared or grilled (not broiled, as this method dehydrates the steak). The steaks should be brushed with a meat glaze that has gravy coloring combined with it. These portion meats can be reheated in a microwave oven with good results. The meats should be reheated without a cover or lid and should be cooked in minimum time to achieve the desired doneness. Steaks, pork chops, and lamb chops should be plated so that the gristle with the fat should face towards the center of the plate, as this fat cooks much faster than the protein in the food.

Spareribs without sauce must be reconstituted covered to prevent dehydration.

Plain fish fillets must be seared lightly for a few minutes and must not be totally cooked. If fish has to be served without a sauce or butter, then a small amount of poaching sauce may be used to marinate the raw fish before it is cooked. There are excellent cooking results for fish in a microwave oven. Seafood and shellfish can also be cooked in a microwave with good moisture and flavor retention. With conventional cooking, it is often easy to have lobster or crab overcooked to a point where it becomes tough. A lobster does not toughen when cooked in a microwave oven. The microwaves activate every water or fat molecule in the raw lobster without undue dehydration, whereas, in regular steaming or boiling, the loss of moisture and rapid heat penetration affects the muscular composition of the shellfish.

POTATOES, NOODLES, MACARONI, AND OTHER PASTA

Mashed potatoes should be made from instant flakes or granules. Mashed potatoes made from scratch should be whipped with milk, water, and butter so that the starch granules are not too compact when reheating. Mashed potatoes should be scooped and then depressed in the middle. I call this putting in a "dimple." The recipe for mashed potatoes is given in Volume 2, Blast Freezing Quantity Recipes.

Baked potatoes should not be reconstituted in a microwave oven unless the rest of the preplate is covered or shielded from the microwaves. However, if stuffed baked potatoes are used, the product comes out hot, moist, and flavorful. No one has explained why baked potatoes do not heat well. From my own knowledge of the cellular composition of potatoes, the starch granules are too dense and compact, so that microwave absorption is not efficient. Besides, the penetration of microwaves is only effective beyond a 1½ inch depth. We have cut baked potatoes in half and have found the halves to be a fair quality product.

Heating tiny whole potatoes is not a problem because there is maximum surface exposure in and around the potatoes. As long as the diameter is not over 1 to 1¼ inches, with uniform rapid heating, the potatoes will heat evenly. Cubed potatoes should have a cream sauce or butter to prevent dehydration. The cubes should be ⅓ to ½ inches in size.

Rice should be cooked with butter, consomme, or broth instead of plain water. Pastas may be reconstituted properly if the starch has not been cooked to complete doneness. (See recipes in Volume 2, Recipes for Quantity Blast Freezing.)

VEGETABLES

We find some unresolved problems in reconstituting vegetables in the microwave oven. The legume-pod type of vegetables such as peas, lima beans, black-eyed peas, and baked beans explode and then shrivel as the skins puncture and the gas trapped under the skins escapes. We have plated these vegetables submerged in butter sauce and a quality product is achieved. The best method is to protect these vegetables with a shield, like aluminum foil, or place them in a container that reflects microwaves or in a container laminated with a material that reflects the microwaves.

Vegetables such as raw cabbage, cauliflower, sprouts, peas, and Chinese cabbage may be cooked from a raw state in a container with a little water. If a little more doneness is desired, these vegetables should be steam scalded for 5 to 7 minutes prior to plating. Frozen vegetables, such as peas and corn of uniform size and with maximum surface exposure do not require cooking; they should be plated in a semi-thawed state just enough to separate and weigh into individual portions.

Vegetables such as broccoli and cauliflower with stems that are somewhat dense and compact while their flower parts have loose cellular composition are difficult to reconstitute from the raw state. The differential in mass causes uneven heat penetration. The best method is to scald these vegetables for 5 to 7 minutes and have the final cooking done in the microwave oven. The scalding is necessary to inactivate the enzymes in order to increase the shelf life of these vegetables.

Beets, spinach, and stewed tomatoes are vegetables that are difficult to reconstitute as they splatter over the interior of the microwave cavity. These vegetables should be plated separately in a dish with a cover. Plain, whole, cherry tomatoes should not be frozen and reconstituted in a microwave oven, as they behave like peas and baked beans.

BAKED PRODUCTS

Products requiring pie pastry or puff pastry offer the biggest challenge for product formulation and reconstitution procedures in a microwave oven. The microwave energy produces a "topple-over" effect due to the steam rising from the fruit filling to the pastry shell. The product has a "steamed look" because of the sogginess of the top and bottom crusts. Puff pastries without fillings may be reconstituted as long as you puncture the skin so steam may escape.

Other baked products reconstitute successfully in the microwave oven as it revives every water and fat molecule being hidden among the encapsulated starch or flour granules. However, reconstituted baked products have to be eaten immediately as they will dehydrate faster than the original product.

MICROWAVE OVEN—AS IT RELATES TO NUTRIENT STABILITY

Several research and experimental projects have led to the conclusion that destruction of vitamins or loss of vitamins is minimal when foods are cooked or reconstituted in a microwave oven. If compared to a conventional food system where hot foods are kept warm in a steam table or in food warmers, the losses in the microwave oven have been proven to be much less. Kahn and Livingston, at the 28th Annual Meeting of the Institute of Food Technologists, showed that the thiamine retention of precooked frozen food that has been reconstituted in a microwave oven was 15 percent higher than a freshly prepared meal held on steam table for one hour.

Vegetables that have been cooked without water or just scalded for a few minutes prior to reconstitution should retain more of their natural vitamins and minerals. Vegetables cooked in water lose their vitamins and minerals as the liquid comes out of their cells.

Applying a faster reconstitution time to tempered or frozen products through microwaves should have considerably less destructive effect on nutrient content. There should be more specific research to determine and compare the effects of cook-chill, cook-freeze, and the various reconstitution methods in comparison with the conventional system of preparing and holding at warm temperatures during service.

We had three years of experience with microwave oven reconstitution. When using these ovens, a definite time schedule, pre-plating combinations, and food arrangements have to be planned. In spite of all our planning, those food items that were of a denser medium became overheated or dried out during reconstitution. These facts should be kept in mind when planning to use microwave ovens for reconstitution in a blast freezing system.

16

Alternate Methods of Frozen Food Reconstitution

Frozen food requires fast heat transfer if it is to retain the highest quality and spend the least time in the danger zone between 40°F. and 160°F. The oven temperatures that we have used in reconstituting precooked frozen food in our operation range from 400°F. to 425°F. We discovered that puff pastries, battered fried products, or pizza crust were of better quality when reconstituted at a higher temperature of 450°F. Processors of most commercially prepared pizza recommend that it be reheated only for 10 to 15 minutes at 450°F.

The special characteristics of the types of equipment—other than microwave—that will provide the necessary fast heat transfer for frozen foods are noted in the following pages.

FORCED AIR CONVECTION OVENS

The use of forced air convection ovens for reconstitution of frozen foods has several advantages. Since a stream of hot air is forced on the top and around the top of the frozen food product, uniform heat circulation is accomplished. Because of the good air circulation with the cold air being continuously replaced by warm air, there is no air (hot or cold) stagnating inside the cabinet. Since this is so, the reconstitution of frozen food takes much less time in a forced air convection oven than in a standard conventional oven. One of the advantages is the increased rate of heat transfer, making the time food is in the danger zone shorter.

There are disadvantages to the forced air convection ovens, although many foodservice operators use them to reconstitute frozen food. This oven has a tendency to dehydrate products, especially if the covers on the foil pans are removed. Unless crispness is desired, it is always best to have frozen food well covered or with the lid left on while reconstituting. It is recommended that the products that do not need crisping be reconstituted first. After a few minutes, the area in which the fried or batter-coated foods are located should be uncovered and subjected to a high temperature of 425°F. Uneven heating, which produces cold spots in foods that are more than 2 inches in depth is also a factor to be considered when forced air convection ovens are being used. However, the best dry heat method of reconstituting precooked frozen foods remains the forced air convection oven.

BOIL-IN-THE-BAG

This method is one of the best methods for reheating frozen prepared foods, especially vegetables, sauces and gravies, potatoes, entrees with sauces, and small precooked roasts that have been vacuum packaged. Roasts will reheat well in a plastic pouch as long as there is a direct surface contact between the meat and the steam or hot water.

Experiments at Cornell have shown that food in boil-in-the-bag packaging or in pouches should not be held in a thawed state even when refrigerated. Further, once the food in these pouches has been heated, it should be used. Any leftovers should be discarded. Rappole[1] stated that there is danger in using such leftovers because of the possible growth and toxin production of Type E Clostridium Botulinum. Clostridium Botulinum will multiply at 38°F. and in four to six weeks produce enough toxin to be lethal.

PRESSURE STEAMERS, DOUBLE BOILERS, FLEXSEAL SPEED COOKER

Pressure steamers can also be used for reheating frozen prepared foods. When using the recipes in Volume 2, Blast Freezing Quantity Recipes, the length of time for cooking frozen pre-prepared foods must be closely watched or the foods will get overdone. Also in reheating be sure that the products are not compact so there can be even steam circulation around the food.

For a small foodservice operation, the use of double boilers has practical application for frozen pre-prepared dishes such as chicken a la king, beef stew, casseroles, shrimp, lobster, gravies and sauces, and other delicate products which cannot be reconstituted with direct heat.

Flex seal speed cookers have been widely used for cooking frozen vegetables, sauces, gravies, potatoes, and for reconstituting frozen puddings or casseroles.

RANGE TOP, GRILL AND DEEP FAT FRYERS

The use of the top of the range is good for food items such as precooked chicken a la king, casseroles, stews, chili, goulash, soups, sauces, and gravies.

A grill may be used to reheat or sear portion controlled meats such as chops, cutlets, and steaks if they are to be served and eaten immediately.

Products that have been precooked, such as precooked egg rolls, and battered products, such as fried chicken, chicken cordon bleu, fried fish, and fried turnovers, may be reheated in a regular deep fat fryer. Remember that fryers have limitations due to slower heat recovery. It is not practical to overload the fryer or to fry for prolonged periods.

ELECTRONIC OVEN

According to Tressler[2] this type of cooking is dependent on the application of heat to the surface of the food. Once the surface attains a certain temperature, the heat is absorbed by conduction through the food until it is finally cooked to the stage of doneness desired. Electronic cooking is done through the use of high frequency radio waves to produce heat throughout the food mass. The activated molecular action caused by the radio waves ultimately generates the heat used for cooking. The only difference between this and microwaves is that microwaves travel at a higher frequency of 2450 megacycles.

Because of the various advantages and disadvantages noted above for each of the types of reconstitution equipment available in the market, there have been several new innovative approaches to reconstitution equipment designs. These new equipment designs for reconstitution have been referred to by Livingston and Chang in their article in the *Cornell Hotel and Restaurant Administration Quarterly,* as "Second Generation Reconstitution Equipment." Information about Second Generation Equipment as presented by Livingston and Chang follows:

Second Generation Reconstitution Equipment

Method	Manufacturer & Model*	Equipment					Gas Requirements
		Electrical Characteristics					
		Input (KW)	Output (KW)	Volts	Amp	Freq. (MHz)	
Steam + Radiant Heat	General Electric CC 40	9.65		208/230			
Convection + Steam	Crown X CJO–35–E–4935 with CJSI–42	51–75		208 220–240			
	Crown X CJO–34–E–4934 with CJSI–43	25.5– 37.5		208 220–240			Natural Gas 1,000 BTU ft @ 6–8"
	Despatch Revers A Flow BTC 2–83 & BTC 3–15			115 230 or 460	35 18		
	Adams Equip. Corp. Adamatic Roto Revent (gas, oil or electric)	35		208–220			
Infrared + Refrigeration	Foster Refrig. Corp. Recon + Plus K–C	21.5		115 230	18 54		

Infrared + Convection	Foster Refrig. Corp. Recon + Plus K–O	2.2		115	19	
	Foster Refrig. Corp. Recon + Plus K–1	7.5		208 / 230	36 / 33	
	Foster Refrig. Corp. Recon + Plus K–3	15		208 / 230	43 / 40	
	Foster Refrig. Corp. FT–T & K–7–2–FT–T	31		208 / 230	87 / 78	
	Foster Refrig. Corp. Recon + Plus K–10–FT–T	40		208 / 230	115 / 100	
Microwave + Convection	Micro–Aire Corp. Micro–Aire	7	0.5–2	190–240	41	2450
	Genesys Systems, Inc. 4033		0.5–2	240	50	2450
Microwave + Radiant Heat	Magic Chef MC–100		0.5/1	240	17	2450

More detailed information on second generation reconstitution equipment is based on experience in an actual operation.

MICROWAVE OVEN

Although the microwave oven has been the prototype of all reconstitution systems, it too has disadvantages. One of them is the need for matching the hot foods with the cold foods and the time and staff it takes to make sure this is done.

However the problem of cold spots has been solved by the "pause cycle" in one newer version of the microwave oven. In this Litton Oven, the pulsating "pause cycle" gives the rest of the molecules time to "Catch up" with the others which are activated faster.

A Hobart version of the microwave oven has two magnetrons with two mode stirrers which maintain the microwaves at a uniform rate. This model has several advantages over the microwave oven that has only one magnetron. Using a pyrometer, I have tested the temperature of two preplated meals placed side by side in the oven. The oven showed excellent temperatures at a range between 150°F. and 180°F. One thing I especially liked about this model was that there were no "cold spots." The reason for this is the presence of two magnetrons with two mode stirrers which eliminate possible "cold spots." This new version of the microwave oven has also shortened reconstitution time.

INTEGRAL HEATING
FOOD SERVICE SYSTEM

The Integral Heating Food Service System is a new concept developed by 3M Company for plating, heating, and serving refrigerated or frozen meals on a volume basis.

The system consists of two elements: (1) special dish/ovens in which the food is both heated and served, and (2) a control module that provides electrical energy to the dishes.

The dishes contain built-in sensors which monitor the amount of heat they deliver to the food within, insuring that each meal—regardless of size—is heated to just the right serving temperature and then is held there until removed from the module for service to the patient.

Special dish ovens for heating and serving frozen food are held in module

The module provides electrical energy to heat up to 24 standard 10-ounce refrigerated meals to over 160°F. in about 14 minutes. A single control setting completes the entire process.

The dish/ovens consist of an inner porcelain ceramic eating surface bonded to an outer shell of polysulfone plastic to provide a thermally sealed unit. Metal buttons built into the bottom of the outer shell provide electrical contact when the dish is placed on conductor rails in the module. A sensitive coating on the bottom of the inner porcelain ceramic shell converts the electrical energy into heat which is transmitted through the inner shell directly into the food. Air space between inner and outer shell acts as an insulator to keep the outside of the dish cool to the touch. This construction makes the system extremely efficient, with some 90 percent of the heat generated going directly into the food.

Heat Balance Chart for Converting
Food from 0° to 180°F.
(10 ounces of food)

Process	BTU	Percent Total
Heat to raise from 0°F. to 32°F.		
$(10/16) \times 0.5 \times 32$	10	4.8
Heat to thaw		
$(10/16) \times 144$	90	43.1
Heat to raise from 32°F. to 180°F.		
$(10/16) \times (180-32)$	92.5	44.3
Heat to casserole		
$0.9 \times 0.1 \times 180$	16.3	7.8
Total	208.8	100.0

The 3M system converts electric power to heat only in the area where items are to be heated. It also permits determination in advance of "heat balance" or number of BTU's required to heat mass of food to proper temperature as well as permitting the use of low capacity thermal materials.

Results of the 3M test showed that reconstitution from the 3M oven was better than from a microwave. Some of its advantages are: greater heat retention, quality of flavor and texture after heating, and reduced dehydration of the less dense products on the pre-plate.

Some other discoveries made during our experimentation may also be helpful in setting up a system.

• Certain breaded items will not stick to the plate if surface is sprayed with a vegetable-based agent (Pam). This step also prevents extra work later in cleaning the dish.

• A new bowl design that will be deeper and provide better heat retention than the bowls used in our testing.

• The amount of moisture retained by the vegetables can be controlled during the plating process and can be varied to suit local tastes.

• A variety of covering materials is available for the 3M dishes. One new design would utilize the dish cover first as a "pop-out" (container for freezing).

• The 3M module should be installed on an 18-in. high counter. The inside can then be easily cleaned by dietary employees.

• No warm-up is needed for the 3M module. Late trays may be reconstituted at any time without any excessive power required to energize module components or to heat up the inside cavity.

• The 3M Integral Heating System is 90 percent efficient in utilizing the power supplied. This compares well to the 50 percent (maximum) efficiency of microwave systems and 40 percent (maximum) efficiency of convection ovens. The 3M System uses a maximum of 750 watt-hours to heat 24 meals, compared to at least 1500 watt-hours for microwave or 1700 watt-hours for convection ovens. Also, unlike convection ovens, the 3M module only requires power for the number of meals heated.

There are disadvantages to this system beside the "matching" problems. Additional labor is required to spray Pam to prevent food items from sticking during heating, and to add a teaspoon of water to some pre-plated meals. There is also difficulty in cleaning scorched products from the plates. But, some of these problems will be overcome if foodservice operations review and evaluate their plating and reconstitution techniques regularly.

Our cost analysis proposal from the 3M staff showed a lease cost of $0.09 per meal served in a 3M dish. The following chart explains in detail the process of calculating the total annual cost for both the 430-bed Hennepin County Hospital and for the 1200-bed joint complex.

Service Fee Cost Analysis

I. Number of Beds = 430

II. Occupancy = (Occupancy rate) (Number of beds) =
     (.80) (430) = 344

III. Meals Per Year = (Occupancy) (1095) = (344) (1095) = 376,680

IV. Eat Rate = (Meals per year) (.93) = (376,680) (.93) = 350,312
     (NOTE: 93 percent of bedded patients that actually have meals)

V. Dish Use = (percent meals where plate is used) +
     (percent meals where bowl is used) = (.80) +
     (.40) = 1.20

VI. Total Dish Use = (eat rate) × (dish use) = (350,312)
     (1.2) = 420,375

VII. Service Fee = (Total Dish Use) × (Fee per use) =
     (420,375) ($.09) = $38,833

Estimated Total Annual Service Fee = $38,833 for 430 beds

NOTE: Estimated Total Annual Service Fee = $105,582 for 1200 beds

Note: This fee schedule does not include the cost of dish covering material. Since covering materials must be used on all dishes, this cost is carried as a packaging expense under the supplies budget of the Food Service Department.

The ovens may be purchased or leased from the 3M Company. The oven specifications for each model is given below:

Ovens (Model HI–I)
One 24–unit 220V 3 HP
(Complete with controls—8 trays)

Trays (Model HPI–I)
One set—8 trays (for 8 ¼-in. plate)
(Electro-polished stainless steel)

Trays (Model HSI–I)
One set—8 trays (for 5 ¾-in. × 8 ¼-in. soup dish)
(Electro-polished stainless steel)

General Instructions for Preparation of Meals Using 3M Hospital Foodservice System

The 3M Hospital Food Service System provides for the reconstitution of pre-plated meals, including the meat, vegetable, and starch items, from either a chilled or frozen initial temperature. It also heats single menu items such as eggs, hot cereal, or soup. The 3M soup dishes are used for cereals and soups; the casserole plates for most other meals.

Cooking Time—a 10 oz. general diet meal will be reconstituted in 12 to 14 min. from a chilled starting temperature or in 22 to 24 minutes from a frozen temperature. The time settings are the same for any 10 oz. meal regardless of the ratio of meat, starch, and vegetable used. Smaller weight meals such as breakfasts or special diets require less reconstitution time.

Preparing Food for Plating—most of the food items are fully or partially precooked prior to plating. Fully cooked foods would include well–done meats and poultry, mixed main dishes, noodles, rice, potatoes, bacon, etc. Foods which overcook easily (scrambled eggs, fish, etc.) are only partially precooked. Steaks and lamb chops which are to be of a rare or medium doneness are only browned before plating. Cooked cereals can be partially precooked or, if the "instant" variety is used, can be mixed with water right in the soup dish, then heated.

Most vegetables are plated right from the frozen package. Upon reconstitution, the vegetable is crisp. If a less firm texture is desired, vegetables can be partially precooked.

Plating the Food—plating is the most important step in providing a meal that is evenly heated and looks attractive. Several procedures will assure proper plating:

1. Drain greasy or watery foods well before plating.
2. Place fast cooking foods (i.e., vegetables) toward the edges of the casserole; slower cooking ones (large pieces of meat), near the center.

3. Spread meals that weigh little evenly over the center of the casserole for quick cooking without overheating the dish.

4. Limit the size of the meal. Twelve ounces is the maximum that can be reconstituted well.

5. Leave some spaces between food items for air and steam circulation. For reconstituting frozen food, leave an air space between cover and food.

6. Use small food pieces rather than large ones for more uniform heating. Flatten scoops of food for quicker reheating.

7. Place small amount of water (1 to 2 tsp.) under dry meats. Put water in casserole whenever cups of food are to be heated within it.

8. Use an anti-scorch spray on the casserole with foods that stick easily.

During 1973, ours was the first hospital to experiment with reconstitution from the frozen state. This 3M oven was advantageous in that it had the capability to reconstitute frozen, precooked, pre-plated meals. The pre-plated meals resulted in good quality food products without desiccation, dehydration, or sogginess.

In the following pages, I am presenting the cooking and plating instructions that we developed and implemented for the 3M Integral Heating Foodservice System.

Research continues on these ovens. At the time of this writing, the 3M Company is testing an oven that accommodates fewer trays and does have the flexibility to reheat one tray for late or "hold" trays.

Instructions for Cooking and Preplating Meals

The recipes referred to in this section appear in Volume 2, Blast Freezing Quantity Recipes.

Thursday, May 10

Lunch
Pre-plated Turkey Meal

Cooking Instructions:

1. Turkey to be done but not overdone.

2. Frozen peas to be uncooked—to be thawed only enough to serve on plate.

3. Marshmallow to be uncooked—to be placed on top of sweet potato as the plate is served.

Plating Instructions:

Regular Pre-plated Turkey Meal—*20 meals* to be frozen. Use 3 oz. of sliced turkey; overlap slices slightly. Make sure the turkey is moist. Place No.30 scoop of dressing to one side of turkey, depress top slightly, and put ½ oz. of gravy over dressing. Put a No.12 scoop of frozen peas (uncooked) next to dressing. Place two 1-oz. peices of candied sweet potato next to turkey and place a marshmallow between the two pieces of potato.

Preparing Individual Portions of Potato, Vegetable, and Turkey

Cooking Instructions:

1. Carrots to be slightly underdone. Do not use pepper to season carrots.
2. Salt-free mashed potatoes—not too thin.
3. Turkey to be portioned into 1-oz. portions—cook until done but not over-done.

Portioning Instructions:

1. Freeze 20 1-oz. portions of sliced turkey as follows: Place a 1-oz. slice of turkey in a small plastic bag; make sure turkey meat is moist. To assure moist meat, just before serving, dip slice of turkey in broth.
2. Freeze 15 1-oz. portions of salt free sliced turkey. Place a 1-oz. slice of SF turkey in a small plastic bag; make sure turkey meat is moist. To assure moist meat, dip slice in SF chicken broth before serving.
3. Freeze 20 portions of SF mashed potatoes. Place a No.16 scoop of SF mashed potatoes in a small plastic bag; depress top of potatoes slightly so that mound of potatoes will not be too high.
4. Freeze 20 portions of SF carrots. Place a No.12 scoop of slightly under-done SF carrots in a small plastic bag.
5. Freeze 20 portions of buttered carrots with no pepper. Place a No.12 scoop of slightly underdone buttered carrots in a small plastic bag.

Friday, May 11

Breakfast
Pre-plated Pancakes and Sausage Links

Cooking Instructions:

Pancakes are to be done and nicely browned, allow 2 pancakes per serving. Sausage links (3 per serving) are to be *browned* but underdone.

Plating Instructions:

Pre-plated Pancake and sausage link meals—30 meals to be frozen. Place 2 pancakes on plate, one on each side with 3 sausage links in the center of the plate.

Lunch
Pre-plated Tuna Rice Casserole

Cooking Instructions:

Rice to be fluffy with well separated grains, moist and slightly underdone.

Vegetables for the tuna rice casserole (Regular and SF) to be slightly under-done when sauteed; frozen peas and pimiento to be uncooked.

Plating Instructions:

1. Regular tuna rice casserole—30 meals to be plated. Place a one cup portion of regular tuna rice casserole on each plate. Garnish with a sprig of parsley. Label.

2. Salt-free tuna rice casserole—15 meals to be plated. Place a one cup portion of salt-free tuna rice casserole on each plate. Garnish with a sprig of parsley. Label.

Preparing Individual Portions of Parsley Buttered Rice in Bags:

1. Freeze 10 bags of regular rice. Place a No.16 scoop of parsley buttered rice in a plastic bag so that it lies loose and flat rather than in a high mound. Label.

2. Freeze 5 bags of SF parsley buttered rice. Place a No.16 scoop of SF parsley buttered rice in a plastic bag so that it lies loose and flat rather than in a high mound. Label.

Saturday, May 12

Lunch
Pre-plated Halibut Meal; Individual Ground Chuck Patties

Cooking Instructions:

1. Halibut and Salt Free Halibut—cut fish neatly in 1½ oz. (45-gram) portions before cooking. Cook only until half done; halibut should be moist, not dry. Sprinkle paprika over top of fish.

2. Candied sweet potatoes—cook till just done; potatoes should not be mushy.

3. Frozen mixed vegetables to be uncooked and unsalted. Should be thawed.

4. Weigh 45 grams ground chuck and make individual patties (1 oz. when cooked). Brown quickly but do not cook completely (Regular and SF).

Instructions For Freezing Individual Portions:

1. Bag 5 portions of SF Halibut, each portion weighing 1 oz., by placing 1 oz. of SF halibut in each bag. Label. Freeze with the top side of the fish up.

2. Bag 5 portions of Regular Halibut, each portion weighing 1 oz., by placing 1 oz. of Reg. Halibut in each bag. Label. Freeze with the top side of the fish up.

3. Bag 20 portions of Regular candied sweet potatoes. Use either two 1 oz. pieces of sweet potato or one 2 oz. piece and place in each bag with 1 tbsp. of syrup.

4. Bag 30 portions of frozen mixed vegetables. Place a No.12 scoop of frozen mixed vegetables in each bag. Vegatables should be loose and flat in the bag.

5. Bag 5 Ground Chuck Patties (regular) by placing a 1–oz. patty in a small plastic bag. Dip in broth first to be sure patty is moist. Label.

6. Bag 5 SF Ground Chuck patties by placing a 1–oz. SF patty in small plastic bag. Dip in SF broth first to make sure it is moist. Label.

Sunday, May 13

Dinner
Individual Portions New Potatoes; Broccoli Spears

Cooking Instructions:

1. Quarter new potatoes. Prepare same as Regular and SF persillade potatoes on menu. No pepper.

2. Broccoli spears—thaw only (½ minute in steamer).

Bag and Freeze as follows:

1. Bag 10 portions Regular new potatoes by placing 4 quarters of potato in each bag. Label.

2. Bag 5 portions of SF potatoes by placing 4 quarters of potato in each bag. Label.

3. Bag 20 individual portions of Broccoli Spears by placing 1 large spear or 2 small spears in each bag.

Monday, May 14

Dinner
Pre-plated Salisbury Steak Meal

Cooking Instructions:

1. Salisbury steak to be shaped a little more flat and oval rather than round and oval and to be slightly underdone.

2. Mixed vegetables to be thawed only, not cooked or heated.

3. Noodles—cook until just done, mix with butter and chopped parsley.

Plating Instructions:

1. Plate 25 meals. Place salisbury steak on the plate; put 1 oz. of mushroom gravy over the steak. Put ⅓ cup of noodles on the plate and place a No.12 scoop of mixed vegetables next to the noodles. Place a sprig of parsley between the noodles and the steak.

Wednesday, May 16

Dinner
Individual Chopped Sirloin Patties

Cooking Instructions:

1. Weigh 4 oz. of chopped sirloin and shape into patty. Prepare 10 regular and 10 SF patties. Brown well but do not cook completely done.

Bagging Instructions:

1. Bag 10 3-oz. Regular chopped sirloin patties by placing each patty in a small plastic bag; label bag. Freeze.
2. Bag 10 3-oz. SF chopped sirloin patties by placing each patty in a small plastic bag; label bag. Freeze.

Breakfast
Pre-plated Pancakes

Cooking Instructions:

1. Salt free pancakes should be done and well browned.

Pre-plating Instructions:

1. Plate 15 SF pancake meals. Place 2 SF overlapping pancakes toward one corner of the plate. Leave room in opposite corner for hot cereal if needed. Place 2 tsp. of water on the plate, and a sprig of parsley. Freeze flat on the tray. Label.

Friday, May 18

Lunch
Pre-plated Scrambled Eggs and Bacon

1. Cook scrambled eggs until set (regular and salt free).
2. Cook bacon until brown and almost done.

Plating Instructions:

1. SF scrambled eggs—15 plates. Put 1 tsp. of water on each plate; leave room in one corner of plate to place hot cereal. Label.
2. Regular scrambled eggs and bacon—30 plates. Place 1 egg scrambled and 2 strips of bacon on each plate. Place the eggs in one corner, the 2 strips of bacon well separated from the scrambled eggs so that hot cereal could be placed on the plate if necessary. Label.

Dinner
Pre–plated Beef Stew

1. Plate Beef Stew—30 plates. Place 1 cup of beef stew on each plate. Make sure there are at least 5 pieces of meat on each plate. Garnish will be added when ready to serve.

Saturday, May 19

Lunch
Pre–plated Swedish Meatball Meal; Spaghetti with Meat Sauce

Cooking Instructions:

1. Prepare 30 servings of Swedish Meatballs and sour cream gravy. Allow 3 meatballs per serving.
2. Prepare 30 servings parsley buttered egg noodles; cook until just done, wash well with cold water to separate, then add butter and chopped parsley, and toss.
3. Canned baby carrots do not need to be cooked at all.
4. For spaghetti, cook spaghetti noodles till just done and wash with cold water so that the noodles are well separated.

Pre–plating Instructions:

1. Plate 30 dinners—Swedish Meatballs with sour cream gravy over parsley buttered egg noodles with miniature cooked carrots. Place a small amount of gravy on plate; put ⅓ cup noodles over the gravy; then put 3 Swedish meat-balls and 1 oz. of gravy over the noodles. Place 5 small baby carrots toward opposite corner of plate. Garnish with a sprig of parsley and place a pat of butter over the carrots.
2. Plate 30 plates of spaghetti with meat sauce. Place a small amount of spaghetti sauce on the center of the plate. Place ½ cup of spaghetti noodles over the sauce. Portion ½ cup of spaghetti meat sauce over the spaghetti noodles. Garnish with a sprig of parsley.

Monday, May 21

Lunch
Pre–plated Veal Cutlet

Cooking Instructions:

1. Baked veal cutlet, Regular and SF. Brown quickly but do not cook until done (20 SF and 20 Reg.).

2. Escalloped potatoes, Regular and SF. Cook until done (10 SF and 10 Reg.)
3. Frozen Garden Mixed Vegetables. Thaw at room temperature. Do not cook or heat (10 servings).
4. SF canned peas and carrots—do not cook or heat (10 servings)

Pre-plating Instructions:

1. Plate 10 meals—SF baked veal cutlet, SF escalloped potatoes, SF canned peas and carrots. Place SF baked veal cutlet at one corner of plate; put No. 12 scoop of SF escalloped potatoes next to the veal and a No. 12 scoop of SF canned peas and carrots between the veal and potatoes. Place a sprig of parsley between the veal and the potatoes. Label.
2. Plate 10 meals—low calorie baked veal cutlet, escalloped potatoes, frozen mixed vegetables. Place a veal cutlet at one corner of the plate. Place a No.12 scoop of escalloped potatoes next to the veal, and a No.12 scoop of frozen mixed vegetables between the veal and the escalloped potatoes. Place a sprig of parsley between the veal and the potatoes. Label.

Individual Portions Veal Cutlet

Bagging Instructions:

1. Freeze 10 portions Regular veal cutlet by placing 3 oz. Regular veal cutlet in a small plastic bag. Label and freeze flat.
2. Freeze 10 portions SF veal cutlet by placing 3 oz. SF veal cutlet in a small plastic bag. Label and freeze flat.

Wednesday, May 23

Breakfast

Pre-plated Scrambled Eggs; Scrambled Eggs and Bacon; Waffle with Sausage Links

Cooking Instructions:

1. Cook enough scrambled eggs until just set (SF and Reg. scrambled eggs) for 20 servings SF and 20 servings regular.
2. Cook sausage links until brown but not well done (3 sausage links per serving). 40 servings needed.
3. Frozen waffles are in Annex 4 freezer. 20 servings needed.
4. Cook bacon until brown and almost done. 20 servings needed.

Pre-plating Instructions:

1. Plate (20) SF scrambled eggs by placing one serving of SF scrambled eggs on a plate; leave room on plate for hot cereal if ordered. Garnish with sprig of parsley.

2. Plate (20) servings of Regular scrambled eggs with 2 bacon strips each. Place one scrambled egg in one corner of plate with 2 strips of bacon across the center of the plate. Garnish with sprig of parsley.

3. Plate (20) servings of frozen waffles with sausage links. Place one waffle on each plate with 3 sausage links. Garnish with a sprig of parsley.

4. Bag 20 individual servings of sausage links by placing 3 sausage links in each small plastic bag.

Lunch
Pre-plated Turkey Meal

Cooking instructions:

Regular—1. 28 servings of sliced Roast Turkey—can be plated cold.
2. Sage Dressing and Giblet Gravy—30 servings of each.
3. Candied Sweet Potatoes, 2 small pieces of potato per serving—20 servings needed.

SF
4. 20 servings SF sliced roast turkey—can be plated cold.
5. SF sage dressing; No gravy—20 servings.
6. SF candied sweet potatoes, 2 small pieces per serving—20 servings.
7. SF buttered green beans (canned), do not cook or heat—15 servings.

Pre-plating Instructions:

1. Plate 30 regular turkey plates. Place 3 oz. of roast turkey at one corner of plate. Place a No.30 scoop of dressing next to turkey; put 1 oz. of giblet gravy on the dressing, and put 2 small pieces (1 oz. each) of candied sweet potato next to dressing with a marshmallow between the 2 pieces of sweet potato. Put No.12 scoop of buttered green beans between the turkey and the sweet potato. Label.

2. Plate 20 SF turkey plates. Place 3 oz. roast turkey at one corner of plate. Place No.30 scoop of SF dressing next to turkey. Place 2 small pieces of SF candied sweet potato next to dressing. Put a No.12 scoop of SF green beans between the turkey and the sweet potatoes. Put a marshmallow between the 2 pieces of SF sweet potato. Label.

Thursday, May 24
Dinner
Pre-plated Baked Cod Fillet Meal; Chopped Sirloin Meal

Cooking Instructions:

1. Regular baked cod (15 servings) and SF baked cod (15 servings). Each serving to be 3 oz. cooked and should be cooked until almost done. Prepare

regular lemon butter sauce (15 servings) and SF lemon butter sauce (15 servings).

2. Oven browned potatoes, quartered—15 servings regular and 15 servings SF. Should be cooked through and well browned.

3. Frozen peas and pearl onions—15 servings regular, should be thawed but not cooked.

4. SF canned peas and pearl onions—15 servings, do not cook.

5. SF chopped sirloin patties—10 servings, and regular chopped sirloin patties—10 servings. 4 oz. raw—brown well but do not cook until done.

6. Parsley buttered potato quarter—10 servings regular and 10 servings SF. Cook potatoes until just done. Season with regular and SF butter and chopped parsley.

7. Frozen broccoli, thaw ½ minute in the steamer. Do not season—10 servings.

8. Frozen mixed vegetables, thaw—10 servings. Do not cook.

Pre-plating Instructions:

1. Plate 15 regular baked cod fillet meals. Place 3 oz. baked cod fillet on one corner of plate. Put 1 oz. regular lemon butter sauce over the fish. Place 4 quarters of regular oven browned potato next to the fish. Put No.12 scoop of regular frozen peas and pearl onions next to the potato quarters. Put a sprig of parsley between the potato and the fish. Label.

2. Plate 15 SF baked cod fillet meals. Place 3 oz. of SF baked cod fillet on one corner of the plate. Put 1 oz. of SF lemon butter sauce over the fish. Place 4 quarters of SF oven browned potato next to the fish. Put No.12 scoop of SF canned peas and pearl onions next to the potato quarters. Put a sprig of parsley between the fish and the potato. Label.

3. Plate 10 soft chopped sirloin meals. Place chopped sirloin patty on one corner of plate. Put ½ cup parsley buttered potatoes next to sirloin patty. Put No.12 scoop of mixed vegetables between meat and potatoes. Place a pat of butter on top of the mixed vegetables. Label.

4. Plate 10 SF chopped sirloin meals. Put an SF chopped sirloin patty on one corner of the plate. Put a No.12 scoop of SF parsley buttered potatoes next to the meat. Put 1 large spear or 2 small spears of SF broccoli on the plate between the potatoes and the meat. Put a pat of SF butter on top of broccoli. Label.

Friday, May 25

Breakfast
Pre-plated Bacon

Cooking Instructions:

1. 20 orders of bacon, 2 strips per order. Brown to almost done.

Pre-plating Instructions:

1. Prepare 20 plates by placing 2 strips of bacon on each plate with sprig of parsley.

Lunch
Pre-plated Salisbury Steak Meal
(see page 222 for cooking and plating instructions)

Dinner
Pre-plated Roast Pork Meal

Cooking Instructions:

1. Roast Pork, well done and tender—30 servings Reg. and 15 SF.
2. Regular sage dressing—30 servings
3. Mashed potatoes—30 servings, not too moist; add pork gravy. Baked potatoes, thoroughly cooked and cut in half lengthwise—15 servings.
4. 1 oz. Cinnamon Applesauce in souffle cup—45 servings.
5. SF frozen spinach, thaw only, do not cook—15 servings.

Pre-plating Instructions:

1. Plate 30 Regular meals. Place 3 oz. Regular roast pork at one corner of plate. Place 1 oz. sage dressing next to roast pork. Place No.16 scoop of mashed potatoes next to dressing. Make a depression on top of mashed potatoes and put 1 oz. pork gravy over potatoes and 1 tbsp. of gravy over sage dressing. Put a souffle cup of cinnamon applesauce at one corner of plate. Garnish with a sprig of parsley. Label.
2. SF roast pork dinner—15 meals. Place 3 oz. SF roast pork at one corner of plate. Place ½ baked potato (cut lengthwise) next to roast pork. Cut potato along center and slip a pat of SF butter in the cut. Put ⅓ cup of leaf spinach on plate with ½ slice of lemon on top. Place 1 oz. cinnamon applesauce on one corner of plate. Label.

Saturday, May 26

Dinner
Pre-plated Meat Loaf Meal

Cooking Instructions:

1. Meat loaf should be shaped so that the slices will be approximately 4 inches high, 3 inches wide and ½ inch thick and provide 3 oz. of cooked meat—30 orders regular meat loaf and 20 servings SF meat loaf.

2. Regular au gratin potatoes—20 servings. SF au gratin potatoes—15 servings.

3. SF mixed vegetables, frozen mixed veg. to be thawed only, not cooked—15 servings.

4. Regular frozen lima beans to be thawed-not cooked. 20 servings.

Pre-plating Instructions:

1. Plate 20 regular meat loaf meals as follows: Place 3 oz. slice of Regular meat loaf toward one corner of plate. Place 1 tbsp. of meat juice over slice of meat loaf. Put No.12 scoop of au gratin potatoes next to meat loaf. Put No.12 scoop of lima beans between meat loaf and potatoes. Put a pat of butter on top of lima beans. Label.

2. Plate 15 SF meat loaf meals. Place 3 oz. SF meat loaf toward one corner of plate. Put 1 tbsp. SF meat juice over the meat. Put No.12 scoop of SF au gratin potatoes next to meat loaf. Put No.12 scoop of SF mixed vegetables next to the potatoes. Put a pat of SF butter on top of the mixed vegetables. Label.

Bagging Instructions:

1. Bag 10 individual 3 oz. servings of regular meat loaf by placing each serving in a small plastic bag. Label.

2. Bag 5 individual 3 oz. servings of SF meat loaf by placing each serving in a small plastic bag. Label.

Tuesday, May 29

Lunch
Pre-plated Tuna Noodle Casserole

Cooking Instructions:

1. Prepare 40 servings Regular tuna noodle casserole and 20 servings SF tuna noodle casserole. Be sure sauce is not too thin as sauce does not thicken in the 3M oven.

2. Prepare Regular and SF buttered crumbs for garnishing.

Pre-plating Instructions:

1. Plate 40 meals of Regular tuna noodle casserole. Put one cup of Regular tuna noodle casserole on each plate. Garnish with Regular buttered crumbs. Place a sprig of parsley at one corner of plate. Label.

2. Plate 20 meals of SF tuna noodle casserole. Put 1 cup of SF tuna noodle casserole on each plate. Garnish with SF buttered crumbs. Place a sprig of parsley near the corner of the plate. Label.

June 12

Lunch
Pre-plated Roast Beef Meal

Cooking Instructions:

Regular—1. Roast beef meal—30 meals; Cook roast until medium rare, don't
let it get too dry. Allow 3 oz. per meal.
2. Mashed potato, should not be too runny. Allow ½ cup per meal.
3. Brown Gravy—1 oz. per meal.
Green Beans, defrost only, don't cook or heat—½ c. per meal.

LC SF
Soft—   1. Roast Beef Dinners—10 meals each. Cook roast until medium
rare, should not be dry. Allow 3 oz. per meal.
2. Mashed potato, should not be too runny—½ c. per meal.
3. Green beans, defrost only, don't cook or heat—½ c. per meal.
Plan to use 60 tomato wedges as garnish.

Plating Instructions:

All roast beef meals—arrange slices of roast (overlapping if necessary) on
plate. Place ½ c. (No.8 scoop) potato next to meat, place ½ c. beans on plate
next to potato. Garnish with tomato wedge. Cover as much of plate as
possible. For regular roast beef meals, put 1 oz. gravy on meat and potato.

Dinner
Pre-plated Chili; Pre-plated Baked Fish

Cooking Instructions

Regular:

1. Chili—20 meals. Cook as usual, don't make too runny.
2. Baked fish with lemon butter sauce, oven brown potato, and peas and
onions—30 meals.
3. Fish portions should weigh 3 oz. after cooking. Should be only half
cooked so flesh is moist not dry. Sprinkle with paprika.
4. Sauce—make with lemon crystals and butter. No starch.
5. Potato—cut in quarters lengthwise then brown in oven. Allow 4 quarters
per meal.
6. Peas and onions—defrost only, don't cook.

Salt Free:

1. Fish, lemon butter sauce, oven brown potatoes, peas and onions—20
meals.
2. Fish portions should weigh 3 oz. after cooking. Should be only half
cooked so flesh is moist, not dry. Sprinkle with paprika.

3. Sauce—Make with lemon crystal and salt free butter, no starch.

4 Potato—cut in quarters lengthwise and then brown in oven. Allow 4 quarters per meal.

5. Peas and onions, defrost, don't cook.

Low Cal:

1. Fish with lemon, oven brown potato, peas and onions—20 meals.

2. Fish portions should weigh 3 oz. after cooking, should be only half cooked, so not dry. Sprinkle with paprika.

3. Potato—cut lengthwise in quarters, then browned. Should be fully cooked. Allow 4 quarters per meal.

4. Peas and onions, don't cook, just defrost. Plan to use 1 lemon slice (not cut too thin) per serving (70 slices).

Plating Instructions:

1. Chili—place 1 full cup of chili on plate, spreading it out to cover as much of the plate as possible.

2. Baked fish meal, Regular and Salt Free—place 3 oz. baked halibut on one corner of plate. Put 1 oz. regular lemon butter sauce over the fish. Place 4 quarters of potato next to fish. Put No.8 scoop (½ cup) peas and onions next to potato and the fish. Place lemon slice over fish.

3. Low Cal—place 3 oz. baked halibut on one corner of plate. Place 4 quarters of potato next to fish. Put No.8 scoop (½ cup) peas and onions next to potato and the fish. Place lemon slice over fish. Label.

THE TREXO OVEN

Another method of reconstituting blast frozen preplated meals utilizes a Trexo oven. This is a "heat finishing" automatic oven for completely prepared foods. It operates on an even, relatively low temperature. Each of the 14 shelves is basically an individual oven with separate power input. The oven was engineered to be calibrated on a weight-time ratio so that the average "full entree" placed in the oven at 34°F. to 38°F. will reach 165°F. internal temperature within 30 minutes.

The oven discussed here is 24¼ inches wide, 36 inches deep and 64¼ inches tall and is on 5 inch casters (total height 69¼ inches). The two compartments, upper and lower, each contain 7 shelves with the total capacity being 14 bun pans, 18 inches × 26 inches standard size, or 28 half trays 14 inches × 18 inches. Each compartment has a door which opens from left to right and is constructed so that only one compartment need be opened at a time, minimizing heat loss.

By design, then, the oven functions consistently whether all shelves or a few shelves are used, though, for greatest efficiency each shelf should be loaded fully before proceeding to the next shelf. There is only one "on-off" switch and the shelves do not have individual switch controls.

Each shelf has an indicator light which is coordinated with the power input. The oven operates on 220 volts and draws on two levels of heating power. During the preheating of the oven and during the initial heating of the food, the lights are out. As the pre-set ambient temperature of a shelf is reached, the indicator light comes on signalling that the power input has cycled from the high stage to the standby stage, and is using only enough power to maintain the structured ambient temperature. The reset button on the side of each compartment is used to activate the high power input after the oven is preheated and the chilled food is put into the oven.

Trexo Operation

The unit discussed here has 14 shelves, 7 in each of two compartments: top and bottom. Each compartment has a START button, or RESET button on the left side. Each shelf will hold one sheet (bun) pan, 18- by 26-in.

Each bun pan will accommodate 11 Temp-Rite hospital entrees or 6 platters which fit the Metro Server. This is a total of 154 entrees in the standard dish or 6 platter entrees.

For some entree items, it is best to cover the sheet pan with aluminum foil, though it need not be tightly crimped over the pan edges. For easier identification of special diet items, individually cover and identify the plates. If using purchased pre-plated items, they may be already marked. Oven-film need not be removed before the item is heated, depending on the procedure best suited to the hospital's preferences. When an oven-film is used, it should be punctured over such foods as bacon, potato croquettes, etc., to maintain crispness. Foil, if loosely placed over the entire sheet pan, will allow moisture to escape maintaining product crispness.

The pan should be loaded in the following pattern if it will not be completely filled: right side, left side, center section.

You can determine the order in which the entrees will be needed for tray service and completely fill one pan with a single selection of entrees, or you may wish to place an assortment of items on a pan, loading them in order of removal according to room number and menu selection.

It is suggested that the shelves on the very top and very bottom be used for the least popular items.

If the meal service is sufficiently rapid, a whole bun pan can be removed from the oven at one time allowing entrees to be quickly placed into Servers. Frequent opening and closing of the doors may affect the oven temperature.

Procedures for Using Trexo Oven

1. Preheat oven for at least 30 minutes when practicable. Cooking time is lessened if oven is thoroughly heated.

a. Indicator lights will come "on". All lights on indicates complete preheating.

b. In emergency, preheat time can be shortened with the knowledge that longer time will be needed for actual heating of food.

2. Place dishes of food on sheet (bun) pans.

a. If less than a full sheet pan is anticipated, load pan on right side, left side, and center section in that order.

b. Partial pan loads do not offer benefits in quicker cooking time so load each pan fully before proceeding to the next pan.

3. Sheet pans of food can be covered with foil or oven film, if desired.

a. Moist foods must be covered to retain moisture.

b. If foods are to be loaded on sheet pans and refrigerated before placing in the oven, it is best to cover them to prevent food contamination.

c. Foil and/or oven films perform well in this oven. Non-heat resistant films must be removed before placing pans of food in the oven.

4. Load pans into the oven. Use one unit of oven to full capacity and then begin to place food into second unit.

a. Model of oven discussed here heats both top and bottom module when switch is "on."

b. Each unit performs best when loaded at one time rather than at random times.

i. Heat loss is minimized if doors are not opened after loading until food is heat-finished.

ii. Pans can be marked for identification of food or shelf markings can be noted for placement of foods requiring separate identification; i.e., diet foods, etc.

5. Push red "RESET" button.

a. Indicator lights coming on during preheat process indicate that the current is in "standby" condition and will maintain rather than increase temperature.

b. Reset button activates power input to accommodate food load and provide the needed heat input for heating foods.

c. Indicator lights go out when reset is pushed.

6. Lights indicating "standby" condition will come on when a shelf reaches the proper temperature level.

a. Heat input is steady until indicator light is on.

b. Lights indicate the 220 current is cycling to maintain temperature rather than to markedly increase heat.

c. Food temperatures will slowly increase until the internal temperature is about 180°F. A Dun-Rite probe or an electronic temperature probe can be used to verify internal temperatures.

7. Foods can be safely left in oven on "standby" until time for loading into the Servers if time is not unreasonably long.

a. "Reasonable" length of time is about 1 hour after indicator lights come on.

b. This time limitation is set to assure best quality of food, not for safety. However, foods should be safe for eating after the longer period of holding time (1 hour).

Oven Features

1. No current of air which can dry foods.
2. Low ambient temperature which will not damage food quality.
3. Each shelf is independent of the others which means less than full oven loads will be handled properly.
4. Each shelf is removable for cleaning and maintenance.
   a. DO NOT attempt maintenance on premise. Return entire shelf to A.S.I.
   b. DO NOT immerse shelf in water for cleaning. This will damage electrical connections.
5. Oven will work equally well with Sarite dishes, ceramic casseroles, or aluminum dishes.
6. Since the ambient temperatures are relatively low, oven-cooking, such as for regular cakes needing 350°F., is not feasible. Cooking will take place, but will be so slow that food quality will be damaged. The TREXO is for heat-finishing of prepared foods, whether preplated or prepared bulk foods.
7. For the most efficient operation and best timing for heat finishing, foods should be in a slack-off stage (34°F. to 36°F.) rather than frozen. Make sure that slack-off stage is reached under controlled refrigeration rather than from room-temperature thawing.
   a. Slacking off can be accomplished by controlled microwave heating if the food is not in a metal container.

Experience showed that 75 entree plates of 5 inch by 7 inch dimensions could be placed in this oven. The multi combination of entrees reheated in this unit exhibited good appearance, flavor, temperature, and the proper degree of doneness. This oven has only two disadvantages for hospital foodservice application: it is possible to mismatch the hot food items with the cold; the system is not flexible enough to retain heat in one tray only.

This oven has applications for mental health, rehabilitation, or any other units in a hospital where all patients eat at the same time.

A Trexo oven has been used in the central kitchen for the rethermalization of home delivered meals. Fifty to 100 of these meals are picked up at the same time by the volunteers. The use of this oven to reconstitute 75 pre-plated meals has produced quality entrees such as casseroles, hot sandwiches, and portion controlled meats. We were impressed, during our testing of the oven with a selective menu, by the fact that we were able to place a variety of entrees in the oven and have each of them reach the desired quality and serving temperature.

Cooking and Plating Instructions

Trexo Oven

Thursday, October 3

Breakfast

Pre-plated French toast and Sausage—35 meals;
Pre-plated Scrambled Egg and Sausage—35 meals.

Cooking Instructions:

French Toast should be cut in half diagonally. Should be brown but slightly undercooked. Allow 3 halves per serving.

Scrambled Eggs, cook until just set. Don't overcook. Allow ½ cup per serving.

Sausage should be brown on both sides and completely cooked—1 patty or 2 links per serving.

Plating Instructions:

Use 2 Alladin undivided dinner plates. Plate 35 French toast and sausage meals. 35 scrambled egg and sausage meals. French toast meals—place 2 tsp. water on plate; overlap 3 half slices of toast; place sausage at one end of plate. Scrambled eggs and sausage—place ½ cup egg over 1 pat of butter, spread eggs slightly so not in a mound. Place sausage at end of plate.

Noon

Pre-plated Spaghetti with Meat Sauce meals—35

Cooking Instructions:

Meat sauce—not too runny, lots of meat. Spaghetti—cook spaghetti until just done and wash with cold water so noodles are well separated. Don't forget to butter them.

Plating Instructions:

Use 2 Alladin undivided dinner plates. Plate 35 meals. Place small amount of spaghetti sauce on the center of plate. Place ¾ cup of spaghetti noodles over the sauce. Place ½ cup of spaghetti meat sauce over the noodles.

Saturday, October 5

Dinner

Pre-plated Pork Roast Meals—35

Cooking Instructions:

Roast Pork, well cooked and tender, not dry—3 oz. cooked meat per meal.

Sage Dressing—no special instructions.

Mashed Potatoes, not too moist—⅓ cup per serving (No.12 scoop).

Pork Gravy, use recipe with W–13 starch—1½ oz. per serving.

Frozen Peas, thaw only, don't cook—⅓ cup per serv. (No.12 scoop).

Cinnamon Applesauce in souffle cup—1 oz. per serving.

Plating Instructions:

Place ½ oz. gravy at end of plate. Place pork on the gravy. Place 1 oz. sage dressing next to pork. Place vegetable and mashed potato at the end of plate. Put rest of gravy over meat and dressing.

Monday, October 15

Dinner
Pre-plated Chop, Escalloped Potato, Broccoli—35 meals

Cooking Instructions:

Pork chops—allow 1 large chop per plate, brown on both sides, cook until almost done but don't overcook.

Escalloped Potato, don't make too runny, cook until done, potatoes should not be too firm or mushy—½ c. per serving.

Broccoli—please put broccoli in the steamer for only ½ minute, watching carefully so it doesn't cook any longer.

Plating Instructions:

Place chop at one end of plate, broccoli in middle with pat of margarine on top, and escalloped potato at the other end of the plate.

Thursday, October 18

Dinner
Pre-plated Southern Fried Chicken, Mashed Potato, and Green Beans
35 meals

Cooking Instructions:

Chicken, fry as usual, don't overcook, should retain moisture—2 pieces per serving.

Mashed Potato and Gravy, cook potato as usual. Gravy should be made with W–13 starch.

Green Beans, steam for ½ minute only. Please watch carefully and don't steam longer.

Plating Instructions:

Place chicken at one end of plate. Place mashed potato at opposite end and make a depression for gravy. Pour 1 to 1½ oz. of gravy over potato. Place beans in middle of dish and put pat of margarine on top.

Thursday, October 25

Lunch

Pre-plated Turkey, Mashed Potatoes, Gravy, Dressing, and Green Beans

35 meals

Cooking Instructions:

Cook everything as usual. Do cook green beans, but be careful not to overcook.

Plating Instructions:

Place 3 oz. of turkey at one end of plate. Place a No.30 scoop of dressing next to turkey. Place mashed potato (½ c.) next to dressing. Portion 1 oz. of gravy over dressing and potato. Place green beans at end of plate with 1 pat of margarine on top of beans. Can be plated cold.

Thursday, November 1

Lunch

Pre-plated Hamburger and Fries—33 meals

Cooking Instructions:

Cook as usual.

Plating Instructions:

Place patty at one end of dish with top bun on top of patty. Place fries at other end of plate with bottom bun face down on fries.

Dinner

Pre-plated Lasagna and Peas—33 meals

Cooking Instructions:

Cook as usual, don't overcook.

Plating Instructions:

Place lasagna in large section of dish; place peas in small section. Place pat of butter on peas.

Friday, November 2
Dinner
Pre-plated Stew—35 meals

Cooking Instructions:

Cook stew as you would for the trayline.

Plating Instructions:

Place 1 cup of stew on appropriate dish and spread over the plate. Place a package of saltine crackers in the small section of the dish. Portion size for stew—1 cup.

Saturday, November 3
Breakfast
Pre-plated Omelet; plate one omelet per serving—35 meals
Lunch
Pre-plated Spaghetti with Meat Sauce—35 meals

Cooking Instructions:

Cook meat sauce completely. Don't get sauce too thick or too thin. Cook noodles completely in oiled, salted water. Drain and butter the noodles.

Plating Instructions:

Place a little sauce on the bottom of the plate and portion noodles over it. Place more sauce (¾ cup) over the noodles.
Portion size per serving: Noodles—1 cup
                           Sauce—¾ cup

Dinner
Pre-plated Chicken, Diced Potato, Corn—35 meals

Cooking Instructions:

Cook all the food completely (as you would for the trayline) but do not overcook (chicken should not be dry; corn should not be tough).

Plating Instructions:

Place chicken and potato in the large section of the dish. Place corn in the small section of the plate.
Portion size per serving: Chicken—breast and wing, or thigh and leg, or 3 oz.
                           cooked weight if deboned
                           Potato—½ cup
                           Corn—⅓ cup

Sunday, November 4

Noon

Pre-plated Pot Roast, Mashed Potato, Gravy, Peas and Carrots—30 meals

Cooking Instructions:

Cook all food as usual, cooking as you would for trayline. Please do not over cook vegetables. Gravy should be made with W-13 starch as part of flour.

Plating Instructions:

Place roast in large section of plate. Place small amount of gravy on bottom of plate. Place scoop of potato on gravy. Cover meat and potato with 1 oz. gravy. Place peas and carrots in small section of dish.

Portion size per serving: Meat—3 oz. cooked weight

Potato—½ cup

Gravy—1½ oz.

Vegetable—½ cup

Evening

Pre-plated Veal Cutlets, Mashed Potato and Gravy, Brussels Sprouts
30 meals

Cooking Instructions:

Cook all food completely as you would for the trayline.

Plating Instructions:

Place cutlet in large section of dish. Place a little gravy on bottom of dish and place scoop of mashed potato on it. Pour 1 oz. more gravy over potato and meat. Place vegetable in small section of dish.

Portion size per serving: Veal Cutlet—3 oz. cooked weight

Potato—½ cup

Gravy—1½ oz.

Brussels Sprouts—5 small

Monday, November 5

Noon

Pre-plated Swedish Meatballs w/Gravy, Diced Potatoes, Mixed Vegetables
25 meals

Cooking Instructions:

Cook meat and potato as you would for trayline; do not overcook. If mixed vegetables are frozen, lock steamer so steam can come out fully. Then, turn timer to 3 and back to 1½. If canned vegetables are used, don't cook at all.

Plating Instructions:

Place meat and potato in large sections of dish. Place mixed vegetables in small section of dish. Place pat of margarine on lettuce.

Portion sizes per serving: Cooked Meat—3 oz.

Potato—½ cup

Vegetable—½ cup

Evening

Pre-plated Macaroni and Cheese and Peas, with celery to be served with soup

Cooking Instructions:

Cook macaroni and cheese as usual. Do not overcook. Vegetables—if frozen, lock steamer so steam can come out fully. Turn timer to 3 and back to 1-½. If canned vegetables, do not cook at all.

Plating Instructions:

Place macaroni and cheese in large part of dish. Place vegetables in small part of dish and place pat of margarine on vegetables.

Wednesday, November 7

Lunch

Pre-plated Grilled Cheese Sandwiches with French Fries, with Beets in a side dish—25 meals

Cooking Instructions:

Grill sandwiches on both sides until done but not overdone. Cook fries and sandwiches as you would for the trayline. Do not cook or heat canned beets.

Plating Instructions:

Place sandwich and fries directly into the special Alladin dishes. Place beets in the vegetable side dish (the kind used on the tray line) and place the dish in the Alladin dish.

Portions per serving—Sandwich with 2 slices bread and 2 oz. cheese

Normal (trayline) serving of Fries

Beets—½ cup

Dinner

Pre–plated Chicken Adobo, Buttered Noodles, Carrots—25 meals

Cooking Instructions:

Cook everything except the vegetables as usual for the trayline. Vegetables should (if frozen) be cooked in steamer. Close door until it gets up to full steam, then lock steamer, turn dial to 3 then immediately back to 1½ seconds. Vegetables should cook no more than 1½ seconds. If canned vegetables are used, do not cook or heat.

Plating Instructions:

Place chicken at one end of the plate, with the noodles along side, and place carrots at the other end of the plate.

Portion per serving—Chicken—3 oz. cooked weight without bone or 2 pieces with bone—thigh and leg or breast and wing

Noodles—½ cup

Carrots—½ cup

OTHER RECONSTITUTION SYSTEMS

A Convertible Transport Module can also be used for reconstituting blast frozen pre–plated entrees or individual portions. This system consists of a refrigerated cart which is divided into two parts, one hot and one cold food section. The cart can hold up to 40 meals. The galley hostess turns off the refrigeration cycle and activates the heating circuit 45 minutes prior to meal service. The food products are heated to 160°F. to 175°F. The same disadvantage exists in the possibility of mismatching entrees to trays and there is a lack of flexibility in handling a late tray or a hold tray. It is claimed that toast, hot cereals, soft cooked eggs, poached eggs, and hot beverages can be readily served from the CTM, which gives this system an advantage over other systems.

Sweetheart Serving System represents a newer reconstituting concept in that it overcomes the problem of mismatching. Found in each tray are two individually controlled solid state heating units at the bottom of the tray. The Sweetheart temp tray is completely immersible and dishwasher safe. The galley hostess can activate one or both heaters as desired. The cart can accommodate 20 trays and has an insulated drawer for ice cream and other frozen desserts. The system uses square disposable plastic dinnerware with lids designed to maintain the correct moisture level.

The system has a small module containing 2 trays which becomes a meal holding unit which can be placed wherever needed. The system heats and maintains hot foods in a temperature range of 140°F. to 160°F. The company claims that this gives the system two advantages:

1. Bacterial growth is non-existent.
2. Nutrient destruction, especially of thiamine, does not occur.

Crimsco offers several reconstituting system modules. These include Crimsco hot and cold sections with the oven on top of the cart. But they also have a total tray system with a divided tray that separates the cold food from the hot, but the entire meal can be handled as one unit. The system eliminates mismatching but there is no flexibility in reconstituting a single tray. The cart possesses an independent air convection system resulting in uniform temperature control. It accommodates 20 single trays.

The Alpha System is another excellent total tray system. We have had an opportunity to judge how well the Plastics, Inc., staff has developed not only good product formulation and plating suggestions, but also making possible the service of medium rare steak and a runny yolk in fried eggs. Each tray has its own control switches for the hot section of the tray. In other words, you can put a tray on hold and will be able to maintain its hot temperature. As with the Sweetheart total tray system, there is no matching or rearranging of the hot food items required. While the food is being reconstituted, the galley person can make maximum use of work time.

The system has disadvantages in that it is possible for the galley person to pull the wrong control switches. All the hot sections are in the bottom part of the tray. Another disadvantage is the skimpy look the tray presents when used for liquid and small feedings. For a clear liquid tray, the hot bottom section will be somewhat empty. It is possible that the company can develop a small tray for these meals. Another disadvantage is the lack of flexibility in feeding on a demand basis. This system is quite impressive though when it comes to repair and maintenance, as the heating units are like cartridges. They can be taken out and replaced in 15 minutes.

After analyzing and experimenting with some of the above reconstitution ovens, both the Metropolitan Medical Center and Hennepin County Medical Center have decided to use the Chemetron Votator System. This system is a total tray system. It offers maximum flexibility in meeting the erratic patient feeding schedule due to tests, x-rays, therapies and other medical functions which sometimes must take priority over patient feeding.

Having had five years of experience with microwave ovens, I believe that this system offers a very exciting alternative. I have continually looked for a food system that meets the patient needs at the optimum level. In this system, each tray has a sensor which is the "brain" of the system as it controls the molecular realignment of the food, thus controlling the amount of ionizing waves projected by the magnetron tube.

To ensure that the hot foods are the only items heated by the waves, a shielding device automatically closes on the tray, mating with the tray divider. The sensor also automatically shuts off the oven when adequate heat transfer is completed. It is almost an "idiot proof" system as there are no buttons to push or dials to program. It is almost a totally automated tray system. The food products that we have experimented with were reconstituted in excellent quality.

The only disadvantage to this system is the extra step that must be taken in order to arrive at this optimum quality. Some entrees such as roast beef, beef patties, and roast pork have to be shielded with round sheets cut out of aluminum foil. This disadvantage is outweighed by another good point about the system in that short controlled applications of energy are given to the food to maintain serving temperature until the tray is removed and, therefore, there is no human judgment needed. As a matter of fact, the bell will start ringing after the system has been holding in the "hold" cycle for a given time.

This method of reconstitution has an initial heating period followed by a rest period called the "equalizing cycle," thus making the warmer sections of food heat those which are cooler.

We are anticipating a problem in the handling of trays for isolation patients. The food for the isolation patients will have to be placed in the standard Chemetron Votator tray with the sensor. This will require an extra step in the galley, the transfer of all the food on the Chemetron tray onto a disposable tray. If the company develops a disposable tray with a sensor, this additional operating problem will be alleviated.

Oven and Tray Specifications

Tray   Width 14 inches   Maximum Height 7/8 inches
            Length 18 inches
            Sanitary polyester/fiberglass with integral stainless
                 steel divider.
            Permanently affixed, hermetically sealed sensor assembly.

Oven   Litton Model 70/80 or equal commercially available oven
                 modified in accordance with Votator specifications
                 (Patent Pending).
              Width 32½ inches   Height 24¼ inches
              Depth 27¾ inches   Net Weight 245 lb.

Electrical
  Input   208/240 Vac., 30A.
             Single Phase
  Output   2400 Watts at 2450 mc
  Controls Fully Automatic

Plating Instructions
Chemetron Votator System

Plating arrangement for each of the following entrees:

I.   Meat Loaf

Place 3 oz. (cooked weight) of meat loaf sliced ½ inch thick toward center of plate. Put 1 tbsp. beef glaze over meat. Put 3 oz. of au gratin potatoes toward one corner of plate. Do not use a scoop, use a large serving spoon. Spread the potatoes slightly so that they are not in a high mound. Put 3 oz. of frozen lima beans (uncooked) in an aluminum boat. This should rest flat on the plate. Put a pat of margarine on top of the beans.

II. Baked Fish Fillet

Place 3 oz. (cooked weight) of baked fish fillet toward the center of the plate. Put ½ tbsp. of lemon butter sauce over the fish. Put a thin slice of lemon on top of the fish. Place 3 oz. of oven browned potato (in quarters) toward one corner of the plate. (Each piece of potato should make contact with the plate) Put 3 oz. of frozen peas (uncooked) in an aluminum boat and place one pat of margarine on top of peas. This aluminum boat with peas must rest flat on the plate.

III. Roast Turkey

Place 3 oz. (cooked weight) of sliced roast turkey toward center of plate, overlap slightly and arrange neatly on plate. Place 2 oz. of sweet potato toward one corner of the plate next to the turkey. Put 1 tbsp. syrup over potatoes. Put 3 oz. of frozen peas (uncooked) in an aluminum boat and place one pat margarine on top of peas. Place the aluminum boat flat on the plate next to the sweet potatoes. Put 1 oz. of sage dressing between the peas and the turkey. Make a depression in the center of the dressing and flatten slightly. Put 1 oz. of giblet gravy over dressing and turkey.

IV. Roast Beef

Place two 1½-oz. (cooked weight) slices of roast beef toward center of the plate. Overlap slightly so that the meat is not too thick. Put a No.16 scoop of mashed potatoes next to the roast beef. Make a depression on top of the mashed potatoes to flatten slightly. Put 1 oz. of brown gravy over potatoes and roast beef. Put 3 oz. of frozen green beans (uncooked) in an aluminum boat and put one pat of margarine on top of the beans. Place the aluminum boat next to the mashed potatoes so that it rests flat on the plate.

V.   Broiled Steak

Place 3 oz. (cooked weight) of broiled steak as close to the center of the plate as possible. Put ½ tbsp. au jus over the steak. Put ½ baked potato (cut lengthwise and placed cut side up) toward one corner of the plate. Place 3 oz. of frozen broccoli spears (uncooked) in an aluminum boat and put one pat of margarine on top of the broccoli. Place the aluminum boat with the broccoli at the corner of the plate opposite the baked potato, and make sure it rests flat on the bottom of the plate.

VI. Southern Fried Chicken

Place a 4 oz. portion (cooked weight) of fried chicken breast toward the center of the plate. The chicken must make contact with the plate. Put a No.16 scoop of mashed potatoes toward one corner of the plate. Make a depression in the center of the mashed potatoes to flatten slightly. Put 1 oz. of country gravy over the potatoes. Put 3 oz. of frozen green beans (uncooked) in an aluminum boat and place the boat flat on the plate next to the potatoes. Put one pat of margarine on top of the green beans.

VII. Roast Pork

Place two 1½ oz. slices (cooked weight) of roast pork toward the center of the plate, with the slices overlapped slightly. Put a No.16 scoop of mashed potatoes toward one corner of the plate next to the roast pork, and a No.30 scoop of dressing next to the potatoes. Make a depression on top of the potatoes and dressing and flatten slightly. Put 1 oz. of pork gravy over the potatoes, dressing, and roast pork. Put 3 oz. of frozen whole kernel corn (uncooked) in an aluminum boat and place the boat flat on the plate. Put one pat of margarine on top of the corn.

Diagrams that illustrate correct plate arrangement are helpful in training employees. Examples are shown on pages 246–249.

ADDITIONAL RECONSTITUTION METHODS

Briefly described here are two more pieces of equipment used to reconstitute frozen food:

A Crescor Roll-in Convection Oven, with dimensions of 61 inch width, 63 inch height, 31 inch depth, all stainless steel, with uniform air circulation and steam injection that may be used either for regular baking and roasting or for reconstitution of frozen foods in bulk pans or for pre-plated meals.

A Crescor Forced Air Convection Oven with dimensions of 23 5/8 inch width, 21 inch height, 23 15/16 inch depth, used for reconstitution of frozen pre-plated meals or frozen bulk pans.

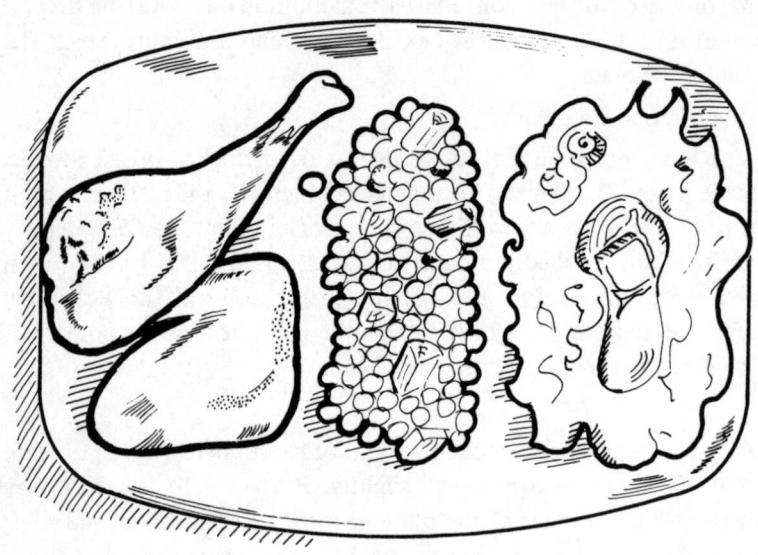

Plate Components and Portion Size:

Entree:	Baked Chicken*	2 pieces (3 oz.)
	Gravy	2 oz.
Starch:	Mashed Potato	3 oz.
Vegetable:	Peas and Carrots	3 oz.

Plating Instructions:

Place chicken pieces on the left side of plate.
Place mashed potatoes on the right (indentation in the center of potatoes for gravy)
Place vegetable in the center.

*USDA Grade A

Plate Components and Portion Size:

Entree:	Baked Fish Fillet*	3 oz.
Starch:	Au Gratin Potatoes	3 oz.
Vegetable:	Vegetable Medley	3 oz.

Plating Instructions:

Place fish on the left side of plate.
Place potatoes on the right side of plate.
Then place vegetables in the center.

*USDA Grade A

Plate Components and Portion Size:

Entree:	Roast Turkey*	3 oz.
	Dressing	2 oz.
	Gravy	2 oz.
Starch:	Sweet Potato	4 oz.
Vegetable:	Green Beans	3 oz.

Plating Instructions:

Place turkey over dressing with gravy on top, on the left side of plate.
Place sweet potato on the right side of plate.
Place green beans in the center.

*USDA Grade A

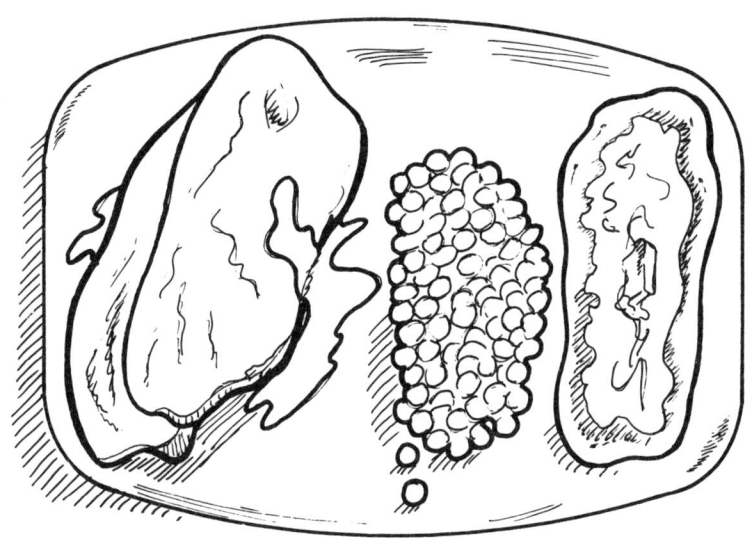

Plate Components and Portion Size:

Entree:	Roast Beef*	3 oz.
	Au jus	2 oz.
Starch:	Baked Potato	4 oz.
Vegetable:	Peas	3 oz.

Plating Instructions:

Place roast beef on the left side of plate, cover with slightly thickened au jus.
Place potato on the right side of plate.
Place peas in the center.

*USDA Choice, sliced ⅓ in. thick.

Comparative Analysis of Three Reheating Systems

It was most difficult for us to make a decision on what type of reconstitution system to use in the galleys of both the Hennepin County Medial Center and the Metropolitan Medical Center. Our consultant, Service Directions, Inc., who assisted us in the final design and layout of the Central Food Preparation Facility prepared a reconstitution systems comparison sheet. (See next page.) This sheet presented and compared three systems which seemed most likely to meet our needs.

After detailed discussions of the various reconstitution system alternatives, we based our decision on the factors revealed by filling out the comparison sheet.

We also used a performance rating form to gather data for use in deciding on a system. (See page 252.)

Before making a final decision on a reconstituting module for use in a blast freezing system for foodservice, there are several basic criteria that should be explored. They are:

1. Food quality must be maintained and enhanced with further cooking; it must release flavor, aroma, and retain juiciness. Reconstitution of foods should permit the more dense materials to be heated simultaneously with the less dense products. This will prevent dehydration and burning of certain parts of the food.

2. Reconstitution must occur in the minimum time possible to maintain maximum staff utilization and patron service.

3. The system must operate with minimum difficulty and require relatively unskilled operators.

4. Reconstitution equipment should allow for reheating of hold trays or late admissions without time or quality loss.

Cost and Quality Analysis
Summary Sheet for Reconstitution Systems Comparison

Financial Administrative Procedure

System	Quality of Rethermalized Food	Flexibility		Operating Complexities	Capital Costs				Annual Direct Operating Costs		
		Multiple Servings	Single Patient Service		Ovens	Trays	Plates/Bowls	Total	Replacement Plates/Bowls	Lease Costs	Total

Chemetron/Votator Total Tray System
Performance Rating Form

	Excellent 15	Good 10	Fair 5	Poor 0	Total
Complexity of Operation	7	7	1		15
Flexibility of Systems Response to Individual Patient Serving Times	4	8	1	2	15
Quality of Rethermalized Foods	2	8	5		15
Tray Presentation	1	8	5	1	15

Please check the appropriate box.

Definitions

Complexity of Operation:	Operating difficulties associated with removing food from trays, sequencing trays, labeling, and related reconstituting activities.
Flexibility of System's Response to Individual Patient Serving Times:	Ability of the system to be flexible in order that events such as x-rays, laboratory tests, and physicians' visits do not prevent the patient from being served a fresh, appetizing, and satisfying meal.
Quality of Rethermalized Food:	Systems' ability to serve hot food at a minimum of 140°F. and cold food at a maximum of 45°F. Systems' ability to reconstitute a variety of foods.
Tray Presentation:	Aesthetic appearance of the patients' tray with specific regard to the entree plate and soup dish.

PART 3

QUALITY CONTROL FOR BLAST FROZEN FOODS

17

The Role of Management

WORKING THROUGH PEOPLE

Management is the process of achieving desired goals through people. Management consists of planning, organizing, controlling, and evaluating available resources, time, and personnel, to meet the institution's and employees' objectives. Therefore, good management is the effective utilization of employee functions to satisfy everyone's goal within the cost parameters.

The role of management in a system of freezing food becomes magnified in the areas where human factors interact with machines within a precise time and raw material framework. When management is able to set the proper environment for all these interactions, the system will work successfully. But what does "setting a proper environment" mean?

There are too many foodservice operations where planning is haphazard and inadequate; consequently, employees are working under a handicap that is built in. In a previous chapter, I discussed the merits of Work Simplification through the use of Industrial Engineering techniques. Various techniques will define and analyze each step of a task or process to determine the easiest, most efficient, and most productive method to reach the desired results.

It would be unfortunate, after reading the chapter on Work Simplification, if you were not able to realize the potential impact of Therblig's Time and Motion Economy on the present greatest challenge in foodservice—the increasing cost of labor. History shows that foodservice institutions rank low in employee productivity. A foodservice system with a factory concept of production feeding using a refrigerator and freezer inventory certainly has merits over a more conventional system. With this mass production concept, it is easier to quantify productivity standards as one can determine how and when to provide for maximum utilization of employees.

Management's function does not end with good planning, and organization of available resources and personnel within a time and cost framework. The most critical aspect is the manager's ability to control and evaluate all of the various processes that are taking place.

Establishing standards of quality and cost control is a very difficult task. One has to determine where, what, how, and when to take steps so that a definite result is achieved. We began with personnel standards, trying to define three things: 1) what the work production standards are based on; 2) the tasks that need to be performed and, 3) what measures can be used to determine qualitatively and quantitatively whether the employee is accomplishing these tasks.

To determine the quantity of tasks to be performed, management has to be astute in determining the estimated workload that needs to be performed. Production forecasting is comprised of past history, food acceptance surveys, and an innovative marketing approach. Armed with a predicted production load, it is easier to develop and control the various standards of quality in the system.

There are several questions one must ask to determine whether management is fulfilling the various standards necessary to run a smooth, efficient operation. The questions I would pose include:

1. Are you purchasing raw materials or semi–processed goods with standards of quality specifications? What are the merits of a bidding process?

2. Are your stock clerks knowledgeable about these quality standards when they are checking and evaluating the goods received?

3. Have you attempted to analyze your preparation techniques as they relate to standardization of recipes?

4. Are your employees trained, motivated, and knowledgeable in the preparation, sanitation, and safety procedures that meet both your and controlling agencies' standards?

5. If you are a menu planner, have you analyzed your menu to ensure good product rotation and freezer shelf-life? Is "first-in, first-out" rotation being followed?

6. Has there been a recent cost analysis of the various steps or processes in recipes? Does it include the rationale behind every decision on the raw-to-ready scale of pre-prepared foods?

7. Have you thought of hiring an industrial engineering consultant to analyze your kitchen design and layout, the adequacy of its flow, and the utilization of equipment and personnel?

8. Have there been time and motion studies on the functions of temperature maintenance and control? Can you further reduce the time between preparation and freezing so time in the danger zone between 40°F. and 140°F. is minimized?

9. Have you researched the merits of good packaging to prevent dehydration and increased rancidity? It is possible that a penny gained is a dollar lost when it comes to packaging.

10. Do you have a freezer and refrigerator preventive maintenance program? Have you considered an outside contract for engineering maintenance if you do not have the talents?

11. What about the quality loss during tempering, and reheating? Have you backed up your methodology and techniques with facts and figures you have collected yourself?

12. Do you know how to tell quality in a product? Is everyone who should be trained and qualified to make final decisions on quality? Do you have a quality testing program?

13. Are you meeting not only your quality objectives, but staying within the service schedule and cost constraints you have been committed to maintain?

INTRODUCTION TO STANDARDS OF QUALITY CONTROL IN FOODSERVICE OPERATIONS

Before measures can be taken to insure the proper maintenance of foodservice quality, it is important to define the *philosophy* of management that one must pursue. For example, it was our basic responsibility to provide a flexible system to meet the needs of both patients and employees of the hospital. It was also the management's responsibility that this objective of achieving good quality food and service in a most economical manner be met. The same challenge is met in all types of foodservice operation.

What is food quality? *Food quality* depends on the quality of the raw materials and their costs, food formulation and preparation, efficiency of equipment, plant layout and design, and labor skills and productivity. All of these factors are vested in the amount and quality of skills management possesses.

Food quality can be measured through the following methods:

1. Chemical method (nutrition assay, fat test, oxidation, etc.).
2. Physical methods (texture, tenderness, odor).
3. Biological method (organoleptic, nutritional, and bacteriological).
4. Consumer acceptance (plate waste, patient and staff questionnaire, palate polls, entree tally by cashiers, taste panel).

To determine whether the standard of good quality control is being achieved, it is best to go directly to the consumers. I feel strongly that "the test of the pudding is in the eating." In a hospital foodservice *patient questionnaires* can determine the degree of satisfaction, the type of items well–liked, quality of service, quality of each food item (portion size, temperature, appearance, flavor, etc.), and patients' eating habits and schedules. This form also helps management develop the menu plan.

A computerized patient questionnaire provides 1) direct feedback on the quality of patient care; and, 2) data input from the patient for a workable menu plan.

Questionnaires can also be developed to secure information from those eating in other types of operations.

Patient Profile Questionnaire
A Sample Patient Survey*

Name _____

Patient No. _____

Form No. _____

Date _____

No. Dependents:

1. none–76%
2. one–16%
3. two–
4. three–6%
5. four–1%
6. five–1%
7. six–
8. seven–
9. eight or more–

Diet:

1. Regular – 45%
2. Soft – 6%
3. Diabetic – 4%
4. Low Calorie –5%
5. Low Sodium –15%
6. Renal – 7%
7. Other Special Diets – 18%

No. Days in Hospital

1. 3 – 4   26%
2. 5 – 9   34%
3. 10 –14 15%
4. 15 +   25%

---

*Hennepin County Medical Center, Nutrition and Food Service Department.

Age:

1. 10-19 8%
2. 20-29 11%
3. 30-39 9%
4. 40-49 18%
5. 50-59 20%
6. 60-69 21%
7. 70 + 13%

Sex:

1. Male -53%
2. Female - 47%

Pay Status:

1. free - 7 - 31%
2. part - 8
3. full - 9 - 69%

Education Level:

1. 0-8 years - 9%
2. 9-11 years; no H.S. diploma - 9%
3. High School graduate - 16%
4. College (at least 1 yr.) - 6%
5. College graduate -
6. unknown, no response - 60%

Financial Class:

1. Medicare - 20%
2. Welfare - 18%
3. Blue Cross-Blue Shield - 2%
4. Other insurance - 9%
5. Dialysis (RKDP) - 9%
6. Workmen's Compensation - 6%
7. none - 36%

Ethnic Group:

1. White - 82%
2. Black - 7%
3. Indian - 7%
4. Mexican - 1%
5. Other -3%

Type of Gov't Aid

1. OAA - 1 - 2%
2. MAA - 8 - 4%
3. AFDC - 2 - 3%
4. AB - 3 - 1%
5. AD - 4 - 7%
6. Title V - 9 -

PLEASE CIRCLE ONE ANSWER FOR EACH OF THE FOLLOWING CONCERNING THE FOOD THAT YOU RECEIVED AT HENNEPIN COUNTY MEDICAL CENTER.

1. Are the hot foods usually . . .
   1. too hot—0
   2. warm enough—67%
   3. too cool—33%
   4. no opinion—0

2. Are the cold foods usually . . .
   1. too cold—0
   2. cool enough—91%
   3. too warm—7%
   4. no opinion—2%

3. How long do you usually have to wait for your tray after the cart reaches the station?
   1. 0–5 minutes—58%
   2. 5–10 minutes—12%
   3. 10–20 minutes—3%
   4. more than 20 minutes—27%
   5. no opinion—0

4. What size are the portions on your tray?
   1. large—22%
   2. just right—69%
   3. small—8%
   4. no opinion—0

5. Choose the word which best describes the appearance of your tray . . .
   1. attractive—78%
   2. plain—18%
   3. unappetizing—1%
   4. no opinion—0

6. How well prepared do you think your food is?
   1. good—61%
   2. average—32%
   3. needs improvement—6%
   4. no opinion—1%

7. Do you receive the foods that you ordered from the menu (within your diet restrictions)?
   1. almost always—61%
   2. usually—14%
   3. seldom—4%
   4. almost never—0
   5. no opinion—21%
      (usually people who did not want to select own food)

8. How much is the meat usually cooked?
   1. overcooked—15%
   2. cooked about right—77%
   3. undercooked—6%
   4. no opinion—2%

9. How much are your vegetables usually cooked?
   1. overcooked—7%
   2. cooked about right—84%
   3. undercooked—5%
   4. no opinion—4%

10. How is the food usually seasoned within your diet restrictions?
    1. overseasoned—5%
    2. seasoned about right—64%
    3. underseasoned—30%
    4. no opinion—1%

11. What is your general concept about the food at Hennepin County Medical Center?
    1. very good—48%
    2. all right for a hospital—45%
    3. needs improvement—7%
    4. no opinion—0

12. How often are you visited by a dietitian?
    1. every day—12%
    2. every other day—13%
    3. once while in the hospital—17%
    4. never—58%
       (people on regular diets are not visited by dietitians)

13. Do you recognize what is in the dish by the name on the menu?
    1. almost always—42%
    2. usually—31%
    3. seldom—5%
    4. almost never—0
    5. no opinion—18%

14. Is the diet clerk available to help you if you have difficulty filling out the menu?
    2. almost always—54%
    2. usually—16%
    3. seldom—5%
    4. almost never—1%
    5. no opinion—24%

15. How many meals do you prefer to eat each day?
    1. one to two—20%
    2. three—73%
    3. four or more—6%
    4. no opinion—1%

WOULD YOU LIKE A SNACK . . .

16. In the mid-morning
    1. yes—21%
    2. no—79%

17. In the afternoon
    1. yes—38%
    2. no—62%

18. In the evening
    1. yes—71%
    2. no—29%

19. PLEASE RATE THE FOLLOWING COOKED VEGETABLES:

	Favorite	Like Well Enough	Dislike But Will Eat	Dislike Don't Eat
Whole Kernel Corn	17%	68%	6%	9%
Beets	7%	51%	22%	20%
Peas	8%	80%	7%	5%
Carrots	9%	66%	19%	6%
Mixed Veg. (peas, carrots, beans)	2%	59%	18%	21%
Green Beans	7%	77%	7%	9%
Broccoli	11%	45%	16%	28%

20. PLEASE RATE THE FOLLOWING ENTREES:

	Favorite	Like Well Enough	Dislike But Will Eat	Dislike Don't Eat
Hamburger on Bun	5%	67%	19%	9%
Toasted Cheese Sandwich	9%	64%	17%	10%
Baked Chicken	14%	77%	8%	1%
Roast Pork	4%	72%	12%	12%
Roast Beef	9%	84%	5%	2%
Salisbury Steak	2%	69%	18%	11%
Baked Fish Fillet	10%	52%	20%	18%
Roast Turkey	9%	78%	10%	3%

Tuna Noodle Casserole	6%	50%	21%	23%
Spaghetti with Meat Balls	8%	67%	13%	12%
Macaroni & Cheese	7%	65%	13%	15%
Beef Stew	8%	73%	10%	9%
Fishwich on Bun	0	49%	22%	29%

21. Are there any foods not offered that you would like to have on the menu?
    Which ones? _____
    _____

22. Are there any foods that you would like offered more often?
    Which ones? _____
    _____

23. Are there any foods that you would like prepared other than how they
    have been offered on the menu?
    Which ones and how? _____
    _____

24. Do you have any suggestions that would improve the efficiency of the
    Foodservice? _____
    _____

    That would improve the menu? _____
    _____

Cafeteria Survey

In order to give you the best possible service in the future facility, please help
us with our cafeteria survey by completing the following questionnaire. Circle
the appropriate number preceding the answer which best fits your situation in
each case. Thank you.

1. About how often would you expect to purchase lunch at the cafeteria?
   1. very seldom or never
   2. once a week
   3. twice a week
   4. three times a week
   5. four times a week
   6. five (or more) times a week

2. About how often would you expect to bring a bag lunch to the cafeteria?
   1. very seldom or never
   2. once a week
   3. twice a week
   4. three times a week
   5. five (or more) times a week

3. If you bring a bag lunch, which of the following items would you purchase? You may circle more than one here.
   1. Beverage
   2. Soup
   3. Salad
   4. Dessert
   5. None of the above

4. If you bring a bag lunch, which of the following beverages would you purchase? You may circle more than one.
   1. Coffee
   2. Milk
   3. Carbonated beverages

5. When you buy your lunch, how much do you typically spend for lunch?
   1. $.00—.49
   2. .50—.99
   3. 1.00—1.49
   4. 1.50—1.99
   5. 2.00—2.49
   6. 2.50—2.99
   7. 3.00 or more

6. How much time in minutes do you personally allocate for your lunch?
   1. 0—14
   2. 15—29
   3. 30—44
   4. 45—60

7. Would it be worth it to you to spend $.10 extra for lunch for the use of permanent ware dishes and stainless flatware?
   1. yes
   2. no
   3. no opinion or not concerned

8. How many people do you usually eat with?
   1. alone
   2. one other
   3. two or three others
   4. four or more

9. Would you be coming from the outside and be needing a coatrack for winter coats or raincoats?
    1. almost always
    2. occasionally
    3. seldom
    4. never

10. What color room would you most enjoy eating in?
    1. vibrant colors such as bright yellow or emerald green
    2. pastel colors such as baby blue or pale yellow
    3. neutral tones such as beige, light brown, or eggshell
    4. black and white
    5. no preference

11. What type of lighting do you like best for dining?
    1. bright
    2. moderately lit
    3. dimly lit
    4. no opinion

12. What shape table do you prefer?
    1. round
    2. square
    3. rectangular
    4. no opinion

13. Do you like to listen to music while eating?
    1. yes
    2. no
    3. sometimes
    4. no opinion

Items 14-19 ask for personal information which we are interested in for statistical reasons; please don't feel obliged to answer this portion of the questionnaire if it offends you.

14. Age
    1. 16–19   3. 30–39   5. 50–59
    2. 20–29   4. 40–49   6. 60 and over

15. Sex
    1. Male   2. Female

16. Ethnic Group
    1. Black   3. Indian   5. Other
    2. White   4. Mexican

17. Education Level
    1. 0–8 years
    2. 9–11 years; no high school diploma
    3. High school graduate
    4. College (at least 1 yr.)
    5. College graduate
    6. Vocational school
    7. No response

18. Personnel Status
    1. Full-time
    2. Part-time
    3. Temporary

19. Income
    1. $ 0—4,999   5. 11,000—12,999
    2.   5,000—6,999   6. 13,000—14,999
    3.   7,000—8,999   7. 15,000 or over
    4.   9,000—10,999

How many times during the past week can you remember purchasing each of the items below for lunch:

Fast Food   *Hot entrees*

20. Hamburger .... _____   37. Baked Chicken .... _____
21. Cheeseburger .... _____   38. Meatloaf .... _____
22. Californiaburger .... _____   39. Pork Chop .... _____
23. Hot dog....................... _____   40. Grilled Liver .... _____
24. Fishwich .... _____   41. Pork or Veal Cutlet .... _____
25. French Fries .... _____   42. Ham .... _____
26. Onion Rings .... _____   43. Roast Meat .... _____
27. Sloppy Joe on Bun .... _____   44. Spaghetti, Lasagna or
                                                 Pasta .... _____
Sandwiches   45. Steak .... _____
28. Sliced Meat Sandwich .... _____   46. Casserole Dishes .... _____
29. Ham and/or Cheese .... _____   47. Chow Mein .... _____
30. Denver .... _____   48. Beef Stew .... _____
31. Cold Cuts (salami, etc.) .... _____   49. Pot Roast .... _____
32. Reuben .... _____   50. Veal Chop .... _____
33. Hot Sliced Meat Sandwich . _____   51. Pizza .... _____
34. Egg or Tuna Salad .... _____   52. New England Boiled Dinner _____
35. Bacon-Lettuce-Tomato .... _____   53. Stuffed Peppers .... _____
36. Grilled Cheese .... _____   54. Chili .... _____

Hot entrees (cont.)

55. Meat Pie .... ———
56. Baked Beans .... ———
57. Fish .... ———
58. Sea Food .... ———

Salads

59. Cole Slaw .... ———
60. Tossed Greens .... ———
61. Gelatin Salad .... ———
62. Fruit Salad .... ———
63. Marinated Bean Salad ..... ———
64. Chef Salad Plate .... ———
65. Cottage Cheese .... ———

Soups

66. Chicken Noodle Soup ..... ———
67. Cream Soup .... ———
68. Vegetable .... ———
69. Minestrone .... ———
70. Split Pea Soup .... ———
71. Tomato Soup .... ———
72. French Onion Soup .... ———
73. Other Soups .... ———

Desserts

74. Pie .... ———
75. Cake .... ———
76. Cookies .... ———
77. Ice Cream .... ———
78. Pudding, custard and/or gelatin .... ———
79. Fruit .... ———
80. Donuts, bismarks, and/or——— other _____
   _____
81. Do you like special ethnic foods?

   1. yes   2. no

82. Which of these ethnic group foods would you like to see occasionally on the cafeteria menu?

   Oriental   1. yes   2. no
   Italian   1. yes   2. no
   Mexican   1. yes   2. no
   German   1. yes   2. no
   French   1. yes   2. no
   Scandinavian 1. yes   2. no

83.	NAME	NO. OF TIMES
Please indicate if you purchased lunch elsewhere during the last week and where you went. (Specify cafe or restaurant)	_____	____
	_____	____
	_____	____
	_____	____

One of the best actual sources of information in determining the quality of service is to determine the *percentage of plate waste* in relation to a normal percentage of waste in other operations of the same size. There are many factors that would contribute to plate waste that can be discovered such as the adequacy of seasoning, meat being tough, or the temperature of the food as served.

Plate Waste Control Sheet

Cycle I		Good 0–10 lb.	Average 11–25 lb.	Bad 26 lb. or more	Patients' Items Observed	Comments	Action Taken
MONDAY	Breakfast						
	Lunch			X	Hot sl. Roast Beef w/BBQ sce.		
	Dinner		X		Roast Pork Loin w/Applesauce		
TUESDAY	Breakfast						
	Lunch	X			Chicken Fricassee	Very Good	
	Dinner		X		Fillet of Cod		
WED.	Breakfast						
	Lunch			X	Egg Salad Sandwich	Too Wet	Recipe changed and standardized
	Dinner	X			Baked Chicken in Tomato Sauce		

Day	Meal		Dish	Note
THURS.	Breakfast			
	Lunch	X	Hamburger on a Bun	
	Dinner	X	New England Boiled Dinner w/Roast Beef	
FRIDAY	Breakfast			
	Lunch	X	Haddock in Cream Sauce	
	Dinner	X	Beef Stew	
SAT.	Breakfast			
	Lunch	X	Prime Rib (New Yr's Day)	Portion too large
	Dinner	X	Salmon Loaf w/Cr. Pea Sauce	
SUNDAY	Breakfast			
	Lunch	X	Pot Roast Jardiniere	
	Dinner	X	Veal Cutlet	

Another source for determining the staff and patients' standard of quality is to use taste panel forms or palate polls when a new recipe is being tested, or a new commercial product is being introduced. This will determine which recipe formulation best suits the patient's palate.

Entree tallies that merely show the totals for individual menu offerings chosen by patients and staff provide no direct measurement of quality. Yet, the degree of acceptance for each item affects forecasting and production and ultimately affects the various productivity standards of the staff. Work production standards are the goals in terms of the amount of work that each staff member is expected to accomplish. Without these standards, there is no way of determining whether an employee is being overworked—with quality of service being compromised—or if the employee is not producing equal work for equal salary.

These methods of determining what the clientele likes to eat are a component of the *menu* control program. The menu offering in any operation is the basic factor that controls the entire operation. The menu pricing structure affects the percentage of profit.

A limited a la carte restaurant menu, including a special of the day, provides several advantages:

1. Simplifies every phase of the operation to the point that a standard of performance can be developed.

2. Standardizes basic food preparation resulting in less waste. A high degree of specialization among the production staff contributes toward a high degree of pride in their work.

3. Simplifies cost accounting; food and labor costs of the items can be based on a standard of performance index.

4. Reduces prolonged inventory of raw materials, thus reducing the amount of cash tied up in the storeroom.

5. Evens out the workload in each preparation and service area. With properly established volume, a production run can be established. As a result, a "production to an inventory system," either chilled or frozen, can be achieved.

18

Product Control

Food has not been the major expenditure in foodservice in the past. But a crucial time is coming where food costs are approaching labor cost as the major portion of total expense.

STANDARD FOOD AND BEVERAGE SPECIFICATIONS

Where does product control start? A tight standard food purchasing specification is the first and most important step. Here is a contract bid with written standard specifications. The price is quoted from the New York market.

Specifications for Eggs
For Various Hennepin County Institutions

1979   Contract No. 5092

1. **INVITATION FOR BIDS:** Sealed bids will be received at the office of the Hennepin County Commissioners, 130 Courthouse, Minneapolis, Minnesota

55415, until 2:00 p.m., Tuesday, November 26, 1978, for the furnishing and delivery of fresh and frozen eggs to various institutions of the County of Hennepin throughout the year 1979, in accordance with the specifications set forth herein and the "Other Terms, Conditions, and Instructions to the Specifications" attached hereto and made a part hereof as though fully set forth herein. Quantities are approximate and as indicated on the attached proposal form. Bids shall prevail for the entire year 1979.

2. SPECIFICATIONS:

a. *Fresh Eggs*

1. The eggs called for herein shall be fresh, white, U.S. Grade A, Large, also described and identified as "white fancy heavy weights." AT LEAST 80% OF EACH 30–DOZ. CASE SHALL BE GRADE A QUALITY AND THE BALANCE GRADE B.

2. The minimum net weight of each 30–dozen case shall not be less than 45 lbs; candling certificate to be enclosed in each case; empty egg cases to be exchanged.

3. Pricing: Bidders shall quote an amount in cents per dozen over or under the New York quotations, with quoted difference to prevail throughout the entire year 1979, price being based upon and to follow the New York Market, LINE #1, *on date of delivery*, as published daily by the *Dairy and Poultry Market Service, Inc.,* 412 Gorham Building, Minneapolis, Minnesota. Price quoted includes all delivery costs and shall prevail for all County institutions.

4. Deliveries: Deliveries to Medical Center shall be made on Tuesdays and Fridays before 10:00 a.m. Deliveries to other County institutions shall be on an as–called–for basis, usually once a week.

b. *Frozen Eggs*—(30 lb/tin)

1. Frozen Eggs, made from pasteurized USDA Grade A whole eggs, minimum net weight 30 lbs per minimum 30 dozen U.S. Grade A, large, no preservatives added, eggs to be packaged in clean sanitary materials.

2. Deliveries to be made as set forth in 2 and 4 above.

Compliance: Successful bidder shall comply with the Minnesota Egg Law rules and regulations in the performance of this contract.

3. INSTRUCTIONS TO BIDDERS:

a. All bids must be written in ink or typewritten.

b. All bids must be enclosed in the envelope provided by the County Purchasing Director for the purpose of submitting bids.

c. All bid envelopes must bear the inscription: "BID FOR EGGS," as well as the name and address of the bidder.

d. The bid envelopes shall be addressed to the Hennepin County Purchasing Director, c/o 130 Courthouse, Minneapolis, Minnesota 55415.

BIDDERS NOTE: Any amplification, modification, insertion, deletion, or changes, except as caused by an addendum, made by *any* bidder to *any* material contained on the proposal sheet(s) shall be cause for rejection of your bid. Should any bidder wish to submit amplifying data with his bid, make a statement on the bottom of the proposal that such amplification matter is a part of the bid and *attach* said matter to the proposal form(s).

4. **BASIS OF AWARD:** Award under this contract shall be based upon, but not necessarily limited to, the factors of: a) net price(s); b) stated conditions and limitations on service, if any; and c) evidence of work experience and performance history in terms of meeting specification requirements.

5. **TERMINATION OF CONTRACT:** The termination date of this contract shall be understood to be December 31, 1979, and all quantities of items not ordered prior to that date shall be considered cancelled as of that date, and County of Hennepin shall not be held liable for any claim by reason of such cancellation.

Hennepin County executes contracts and price agreements through sealed bids, written quotations, and cooperative purchasing with the public schools. Purchasing recommendations I have made include having items delivered directly to a freezer warehouse and our hospital warehouse. This has helped offset cost increases and alleviate availability problems.

ACCURATE RECEIVING, STORING, AND WAREHOUSING

In many foodservice operations, purchase requisitions and purchase orders are used for receiving. These forms carry purchase order numbers to eliminate errors in receiving items that were not ordered or in wrong quantities. The problem is that there is no check on specified quality control by the person receiving. I recommend that a *quality specification* column be added to the forms so the receiving clerk will be aware of any discrepancies in quality, grade, weight, size, and portion.

An accurate, semi-automatic, self-dating machine should be in every food facility. This machine will help in rotating products on a first–in–first-out basis.

Meat is the most expensive item in food cost so it needs extra attention in receiving. A credit or discrepancy report should be written by the storeroom clerk so that a credit memorandum can be executed by the dealer. Our format for meat tagging is this:

Meat Tag No. _____

DATE RECEIVED   DATE RECEIVED

ITEM   GRADE   ITEM   GRADE
WEIGHT_____kilos.   WEIGHT_____kilos.

DEALER_____   DEALER_____
EXTENSION_____   EXTENSION_____

DATE ISSUED_____   DATE ISSUED_____

COMMENTS ON PKG. _____   COMMENTS ON PKG._____
_____   _____
_____   _____
_____   _____

Perforated and self-sticking
(gummed labels)

Storage and Inventory Control

Storage and inventory control is a function of *time and temperature.* These factors affect the shelf life, perishability, and, consequently, quality of the products in storage. Maintenance and repair programs for all compressors, condensers, evaporators for refrigeration and freezer units are important in the control of time and temperature. The Repair and Maintenance Department of any institution should have either a refrigeration expert or a contract with an outside company to do a daily check of all refrigeration and freezer panels in the facility.

Dry Storage Control

Dry storage control must include the following:

a. A thermometer alarm system that will sound off if excessive high temperature is reached.

b. Restricted number of personnel allowed in the storeroom. Storeroom must be locked when no one is present.
c. Dating and marking system.
d. Adequate shelving, with shelves 6 to 10 inches above the floor.
e. Monthly insect and pest control (use of spray).

INGREDIENT CONTROL BASED ON STANDARD RECIPES

Ingredient amounts are given in either weight, volume, or issue units. The formats will depend on the system. Here is our manual format for an ingredient control list and a standarized recipe which can be computerized.

Cycle _____ **Day** _____

Ingredient Control List

Evening

Item	Cnt	Dry Ingred.	Amt.	Wet Ingred.	Amt.
Tuna Noodle		Med. or Wide		Margarine	3#,
Casserole	300	Egg Noodles	18#		12 oz.
		Flour		Canned Cream of	15–
			22½ oz.	Mushroom Soup	#5 cans
		W–13 Starch	3 oz.	Half & Half Cream	3 qts
		Onions, dehydrated	3 oz.	Chicken Broth	3 qts.
				Celery diced (⅓")	12 oz.
Topping		Grated			
		Cheddar Cheese	3#	Frozen Peas	6#
		Dry Bread Crumbs	1# 5 oz.	Pimiento, chopped	12 oz.
				P & S Mushrooms	
		Parsley, dried	1½ oz.	Canned—Drained	3#
		Margarine	12 oz.	Tuna, Flaked	39#
				Lemon Juice	
				(No Crystals)	1½ cups
SF Tuna		Med. or Wide	2#	(for sauce)	
Noodle Cass.	45	Egg Noodles	12 oz.	SF Margarine	14½ oz.
		Flour	12 oz.	SF Chicken Broth	2¾ qts.
		W–13 Starch	27 grams	Half & Half Cream	7 oz.
		Pepper, white	½ tsp.	Lanolac–Mixed	29 oz.
				Onions, fresh	
				chopped	7 oz.

Ingredient Control Sheet (cont'd)

Item	Cnt	Dry Ingred.	Amt.	Wet Ingred.	Amt.
SF Tuna Noodle Casserole (cont'd)				Celery, diced	⅓ cup
				Mushrooms—	
		SF Margarine	2 oz.	Fresh-sliced	14 oz.
Topping		SF Dry Bread		(for sauce)	
		Crumbs	3 oz.	SF margarine	7 oz.
		Parsley—		SF canned	
		frsh. chopped	⅓ cup	peas	1¼ cups
				Pimiento, chopped	2 oz.
				SF Tuna—flaked	5# 13 oz.
				Lemon Juice (no crystals)	3½ oz.
Hot Roast Beef Sand.	125	Salt	5½ Tbsp.	Boneless Top Round	51#, 4 oz.
		Pepper, white	16 grams	Celery, chopped	1# 4 oz.
		Bay Leaves	5 leaves		
		Onions, dehydrated	37 grams		
		Bread White (2#)	4½ lvs		
Au Jus (LC–Diab.)	25			Beef Au Jus	1 qt.
Beef Gravy	100	Flour	14 oz.	Fat	24 oz.
		W–13 Starch	1 oz.	Beef Stock	2 gals.
		Salt	2¼ oz.		
		Pepper, white	1 Tbsp		
Pureed Beef	15			#303 cans Pureed bf	3 cans

A standardized recipe that includes portion size and yield factor is an important factor in cost control.

		Cycle 3
Title TUNA NOODLE CASSEROLE	No.	Sun. Evening
Yield 100	Portion Size	¾ to 1 cup

Ingredients	Weight	Amount
Noodles, wide or medium	6 lbs.	12 qts.
Flour	7½ oz.	1¾ cups

W–13 cornstarch	1 oz.	3 Tbsp.
Margarine	1 lb. 4 oz.	2 ½ cups
Cream of Mushroom Soup	15 lbs. 15 oz.	5 No.5 cans
Half and Half	2 lbs.	1 qt.
Chicken Broth	2 lbs.	1 qt.
Onion, chopped, dehydrated	1 oz.	—
Celery, diced (⅓ in.)	4 oz.	1–¼ cups
Mushrooms, canned, drained	1 lb.	1 pt.
Pimiento, chopped	4 oz.	½ cup
Peas, frozen	2 lbs.	5 ¾ cups
Tuna, flaked	13 lbs.	3 64 oz. cans
Lemon juice (no crystals)	4 oz.	½ cup

Topping

Margarine	4 oz.	½ cup
Bread Crumbs	7 oz.	1 qt.
Grated Cheese	1 lb.	1 qt.
Parsley, dried, chopped	½ oz.	¾ cup

Procedure:

1. Rehydrate onions using ice water. Refrigerate until used.
2. Cook noodles in boiling, salted water. Drain and wash off excess starch with cold water.
3. Make white roux with margarine, flour, and starch. Dilute cream of mushroom soup with half and half and chicken broth. Add to roux, and stir continuously until thickened.
4. Saute onions, celery, and mushrooms for 10 minutes. Add to the sauce in the steam kettle.
5. Add cooked noodles, tuna, lemon juice, frozen peas, and pimientos. Mix lightly but thoroughly so that all ingredients are distributed evenly.
6. Pour into half steam table pans which have been lightly oiled.
7. Bake 30 minutes at 300°F.
8. Prepare topping. Melt margarine; add to bread crumbs and grated cheese.
9. Sprinkle topping and parsley over each pan of tuna noodle casserole. Return to oven and bake 15 minutes longer.

Quality control is achieved through the ingredient control room. Limited access to this room is mandatory for efficient control.

As part of the same system, we can use pressure sensitive labels which identify the ingredients after they are portioned and weighed. The production

cook receives a copy of the ingredient control sheet to check items and procedures. Before the end of each step or process, the production supervisor checks
the labor cost analysis sheet. This sheet indicates whether the time of completion is accurate based on the standard, and allows a check on product quality.
A computer printout of labor standards should show not only the labor or production center, product description, and batch number, but also the various
preparation delays, total operating times, clean-up time, and the size of the
crew.

TEST KITCHEN

In the test kitchen product quality control is checked and maintained through
the following:

a. Sample production run is judged based on taste, flavor, texture, aroma,
color, appearance, and other organoleptic criteria established for the particular product.

Quality Comparison Tests are based on:

Appearance—Does it look like the product you normally associate it with?
Does the food item have satisfactory color?
Is there pleasant eye appeal in its color?
Is the portion of food uniform in size and shape?
Are garnishes properly used?

Flavor— Does it have the flavor the product is supposed to have?
Is there a predominance of one spice over another?
Does any ingredient produce an undesirable or aftertaste
flavor?
Does the product contain a pleasing aroma?
Is the seasoning adequate?

Texture and
Tenderness— Is it crispy in texture as it should be?
Is the meat too tough to chew?
Is the crust soggy?
Are the vegetables overcooked or undercooked?
Is the proper texture identifiable in the product?
Is the product not too soft and/or mushy?

Percentage of Fill Weights—What is the ratio between the meat, sauce and
starch or vegetables?
Is there a good ratio between the meat and the sauce
depending on the portion of meat desired?

Labor Standards

Labor Ctr.	Product Code	Product Desc.	Unit Meas.	Batch	Entry Code	Seq. Code	Operation Desc.	Machine Speed Min.	Machine Delay	Machine Oper Time Min.	Setup Cleanup Min.	Crew Size
042	542028	Lamb Stew 110	EAC	1152	542028	10	Set Up				15	1
					542028	27	Mixing	48	16.1	7		1
					542028	30	Deposit					6
					542028	90	Clean Up				60	1
042	542029	Hungarian Goul	EAC	1152	542029	10	Set Up				15	1
					542029	27	Mixing	58	39.8	7		1
					542029	30	Deposit					6
					542029	90	Clean Up				60	1
042	542030	3 lb. Cream Chicken	EAC	732	542030	10	Set Up				30	1
					542030	30	Deposit			60		5
					542030	90	Clean Up				30	1
042	542031	Corned Beef Hash	EAC	1196	542031	10	Set Up				15	1
					542031	27	Mixing	58	20.7	30		3
					542031	30	Deposit					5
					542031	90	Clean up				60	1
042	542040	Fillet Cod Dinner	EAC	980	542040	10	Set Up				30	2
					542040	30	Deposit			110		6
					542040	90	Clean Up				60	2
042	542041	Whip Cream	LBS	44	542041	10	Set Up				10	1
					542041	27	Mixing			20		1
					542041	90	Clean Up				10	1
042	542043	Chicken Ala King	EAC	1054	542043	10	Set Up				30	1
					542043	30	Deposit			88		5
					542043	90	Clean Up				30	1
042	542044	Stewed Chicken	EAC	1056	542044	10	Set Up				30	1
					542044	30	Deposit			90		5
					542044	90	Clean Up				30	1
042	542045	Macaroni	EAC	1056	542045	10	Set Up				30	1
					542045	30	Deposit			90		5
					542045	90	Clean Up				30	1
042	542046	Mashed Turnips	EAC	1050	542046	10	Set Up				30	1
					542046	30	Deposit			85		5
					542046	90	Clean Up				30	1

b. Laboratory Analysis should be performed on the protein content, type of fat, and the ratio of the polyunsaturated to the saturated fat. For entrees such as casseroles with starches it is sometimes necessary to determine the type of starch used for allergy type diets. In most hospitals the laboratory is able to provide this.

c. A product control sample is prepared and tested to check difference grading in standards with the use of a declared control difference test as indicated.

Declared Control Difference Test

STANDARD	TEST SAMPLES
A	
B	
C	
D	

ARE THE TEST SAMPLES	Score
Same as standard	5
Slightly different	4
Moderately different	3
Very different	2
Extremely different	1

Testers score the samples on the sheet. The unknown samples always contain an undeclared standard. The score of the undeclared standard should be the same as the standard and be compared with the score of the sample which is different.

d. Taste Panel consisting of 10 people chosen from personnel in various departments as well as other users of the facility to average out some errors of human judgment. Samples and score sheets are numerically coded. It is also recommended that a summary of the quality comparison testing be accomplished as indicated in the chart.

Quality Control Comparison Chart

PRODUCT NAME_____

Refer-ence	Item Code	Case Wt.	Units/Case	% Fill Weights			Cost/Case	Cost/Oz.	Panel Scores	Panel Comments
				Meat	Sauce	Starch Veg.				
TOTAL RATINGS										

Comments for Rating_____

_____

_____

_____

_____

_____

THAWING/PORTION CONTROL

a. Time and Temperature Control

Whether frozen food items are premise prepared or purchased prepared, they must be properly thawed before portioning. Once again, the time and temperature control sheets have to be filled in in every area.

Time and Temperature Quality Control
Inspection Sheets

Task	Division	Activity: I Receipt, Warehousing, Thawing	Time	Location or Equip.	Equip.* Temp.	Product* Temp
1	A	Receive and check frozen food and beverage		Freezer	–10°F.	0°F.
	B	Receive and check refrigerated food and beverage		Refrig.	30–38°F.	38°F.
2	A	Remove frozen food and beverage from central freezer warehouse and deliver to kitchen freezer		Refrig. truck	48°F.	0°F.
	B	Receive and transfer from truck into kitchen freezer	15 to 20 min.	Receive. Freez. Dock	65–75°F. –10°F.	0°F. 0°F.
3	A	Remove and thaw frozen food and beverage	48 hr.	Refrig. Thaw rm.	35–40°F.	38°F. 38°F.
	B	Transfer refrigerated food and beverage to food preparation/portion areas	30 min.	Refrig. Prep Area	30–38°F. 55°F.	38°F. 40°F.
4	A	Transfer and portion thawed food from pans into individual portions	1 hr.	Thaw rm.	40°F.	38–40°F.
	B	Transfer and move portioned, thawed food items into assembly, packaging, and staging		Staging Assembly areas	40°F.	38–40°F.
5	A	Transfer thawed and frozen food to food preparation and reconstitution areas for finishing stages of processing	15 min. 20 min.	Food prep areas	65–75°F.	38–40°F.

*All product temperature taken with a portable pyrometer with ½ inch penetration at the center of the product.

Task	Division	Activity: II Food Preparation and Chilling	Time	Location or Equip.	Equip.* Temp.	Product* Temp.
1	A	Transfer meat and potato items from the preparation cart ot the tilting braising pan	15–30 min.	Food prep. area	300–400°F.	140–200°F.
	B	Transfer meat and potato items from the preparation cart to the convection ovens	15–60 min.	,,	325–375°F.	160–200°F.
	C	Transfer meats from the prep. cart to the broiler	15–30 min.	,,	450–550°F.	160–200°F.
	D	Transfer potatoes and vegetables (from the prep. cart) to the steam cooker	15–25 min.	,,	250–280°F.	170–200°F.
	E	Transfer soup, sauces, and gravies to steam jacketed kettles	15–45 min.	,,	250–350°F.	160–200°F.
2	A	Remove food items from various food preparation and reconstituion equipment for blast chilling	10–60 min.	Blast chill	–10°F.	30–38°F.
	B	Remove chilled meats, potatoes, vegetables, soups, sauces and gravies and place in thaw assembly room or process into nitrogen freezer inventory	15–30 min.	Nitrogen freezer	–20°F.	38–40°F. 40°F. 0°F

*All product temperature taken with a pyrometer with ½ inch penetration at the center of the product.

A portable pyrometer with a range of 50°F to 200°F and a 1° scale division (readable to the nearest 0.5°)

Time and Temperature Quality Control
Inspection Sheet

Task	Division	Activity: Thawing and Portioning	Time	Location	Equip. Temp.	Prod. Temp.
1	A	Remove food products from the freezer	15 min.	Freezer	−10°F.	0°F.
	B	Transfer products to a shelving cart	10 min.	Freezer	−10°F.	0°F.
2	A	Move shelving carts to thaw room	10 min.	Thaw rm	35–40°F.	0°F.
	B	Organize and transfer products in the cart to allow air movement and product rotation	20 min.	Thaw rm	35–40°F.	0°F.
3	A	Thaw products in thaw room	48–72 hr.	Thaw rm	40°F.	36–40°F.
	B	Remove thawed products and transfer to portioning carts beside the conveyor belt				
4	A	Gather clean equipment to be ready for portioning	15 min.	Thaw rm	40°F.	
	B	Portion food items into dishes	6 hr.	Thaw rm	40°F.	36–40°F.
	C	Remove packaged and wrapped pre-portioned items from thaw room to trayline inventory or staging area for other accounts	20 min.	Thaw rm Trayline Inven	40°F.	38–40°F.
	D	Remove thawed bulk pans from thaw room into the cafeteria staging refrigerator	15 min.	Thaw Cafe. Refrig.	40°F.	36–40°F.

The importance of speed in handling food and beverage products after being thawed cannot be ignored. Portioning and packaging demands discipline and dispatch.

b. Personal Appearance and Hygiene

Remember that tempered products are at temperatures that are conducive to fast bacterial growth and contamination. Beyond initial high quality and low bacteria count of the raw and prepared ingredients, a commitment toward maximum personal cleanliness by the staff, plus clean equipment and work areas are critical. Here is a personal appearance, hygiene, and work habits checklist that should be posted in the employees' locker room. With this, they can motivate each other towards good hygiene and appearance. Management can encourage compliance with these standards by posting ratings in each department. The department with the highest percentage of employees that passed the average ratings will receive a commendation for the month. As shown in the sample, every area has to accomplish this checklist. You will be surprised to find that "self-inspection" results in a tighter surveillance among peer groups.

Employees' Personal Appearance
Hygiene, and Work Habits Checklist

AREA: Trayline

	10		9		8		7		6		5		4		3		2		1	
Appearance	S	U	S	U	S	U	S	U	S	U	S	U	S	U	S	U	S	U	S	U
1. Uniform free of soil, pressed, good repair																				
2. Proper fit (not too short or tight)		X																		
3. Proper clean stockings or kneehighs																				
4. Soft sole shoes, clean																				
5. Uniform conform to standard			X																	
6. Employee cap clean and being worn																				
7. Hairnet covers head completely																				
8. Hairnet in good repair																				
9. Hairnet worn in all areas																				
10. Beards and mustaches must be kept clean and neat. Face masks must be worn over beard when handling food																				
11. No jewelry should be worn except a watch, wedding band, or small earrings																				
12. Sweaters are not to be worn except under yellow smocks																				
13. No gum chewing																				
Work Habits and Hygiene																				
1. Wash hands before and after using toilet																				
2. Use gloves when touching food																				
3. Wash hands thoroughly and often																				
a. Before starting work																				
b. After using toilet facilities																				
c. After coughing and sneezing																				
d. After using a handkerchief or tissue																				
e. After handling soiled dishes																				
f. After smoking																				
4. Cover coughs and sneezes																				
5. Cleanliness of body is essential																				
Summary of Total Ratings																				

c. Blast Chill Method Control

As products are moved from the food preparation area into the refrigerated blast chill section, a fast drop of internal temperature should occur. At this point the internal product temperature should be checked before the product is moved into the portioning and staging room to make sure the time the product is in the danger zone is less than 5 to 10 minutes. There have been incidents where internal temperature reached 50°F. and clostridium botulinum growth was already occurring.

d. Product Rotation

This is one of the most critical control areas. With an adequate preventive maintenance program for all refrigerators and freezers, the problems caused by a blocked evaporator, frosted coils, or more than a quarter inch of ice accumulation can be alleviated. Defrosting freezer units has to be done at least once a month.

Products in the thaw box must be removed on a first-in, first-out basis. Every package must be date labeled so there is no confusion. Foods that have been thawed should not be refrozen. Bacterial activity increases at thaw temperatures, which causes food spoilage, and the "thaw drip" causes loss of quality.

e. Portioning

A standard portion control sheet needs to be developed. This control lists every item to be portioned in weight (oz.) and volume. A good portion control scale is a basic necessity in this area. These scales will be used to weigh prepared entrees in the portioning and assembly areas.

Effective portion control implementation requires the following:

1. Develop a standard portion size per unit of the product being produced.
2. Make sure the portion control program is implemented and has the necessary follow-through from supervisory personnel to preparation crew.
3. A standard purchasing specification is a good start on portion control for proper size of food items (e.g., 4-oz. steaks and 5-oz. chops with bone in).
4. Adequate portion scales, scoops, and ladles must be available at the right time and in every area where they are needed.
5. Obtain feedback from production and serving personnel on the details of the portion control program. Check out standards and any deviations that occur in practice.

TRAY ASSEMBLY AND STAGING

To be sure that refrigerated thawed products coming from the portioning area are quickly processed without an increase in bacterial growth, a basic design layout must be developed and implemented. The basic design parameters are:

a. Entree, starch, and vegetables are portioned into a plate under refrigerated conditions at 40°F.

b. The location of the freezer, thawing, portioning, and tray assembly lines lends itself to a speedy movement of products. Materials are handled only once after portioning.

c. Tray assembly is based on individual portioning, thus facilitating the handling and movement of the various products.

d. Entree plates individually wrapped or lidded are moved from only one side of the inventory to the trayline operator. Replenishments will be easier as they can be directly and continuously fed from the refrigerated storage area. There are several quality control inspection sheets which can be used in establishing standards of productivity, time schedules, percentage deviations for accuracy, standards of quality for appearance, taste, flavor, and texture, and basic standards and par levels for replenishment of supplies to the trayline. Here is a sample Quality Control Inspection Sheet for the Tray Assembly area with the corresponding standard for quality control including appearance and accuracy ratings.

Quality Control Inspection Sheet
III. Tray and Food Assembly

BREAKFAST   LUNCH   DINNER

DATE:_____
TIME:_____

Category	Trays				Tray Delivery				
	Appear.		Accura.		Leave	Arrive	Leave	Arrive	Time
Diet Type	S	U	S	U	Kitchen	Floor	Galley	Pt.	Diff.
1. General MMC									
2. General HCMC									
3. Bland MMC				X					
4. Bland HCMC									
5. Soft MMC									
6. Soft HCMC									
7. Diabetic MMC				X					
8. Diabetic HCMC									
TOTAL RATINGS									

	COMMENTS FOR UNSATISFACTORY RATINGS
Reference	
3	Wrong entree plate
7	Wrong portion in fruit exchange

Food Service Quality Control
Inspection Standards

ACTIVITY III

Tray Appearance and Delivery Logistics

1. Tray Appearance
   a. Is the standard tray set–up used as in the diagram?
   b. Are the items correctly placed on tray?
   c. Is the food portion of uniform size and shape as stated in the standard?
   d. Are the items neatly placed and portioned?
   e. Is the tray overcrowded?
   f. Are the dishes free from cracks, stains, or dents?
   g. Is the tray attractive in color and shape?
   h. Are the food items correctly placed on dishes?
   i. Are the hot food items to be heated placed on the right side of the tray?
   j. Are the cold food items on their respective side of the tray?
   k. Are the napkins, silverware, condiments, cups or mugs in their respective places?
   l. Do the items on the tray correspond with the coded items listed on the menu?

2. Tray Accuracy
   a. Do the items on the tray correspond with the coded items listed on the menu?
   b. Are the utensils, condiments, cups, saucers provided on the tray?
   c. Does the condiment kit correspond with the coded items listed in the menu?
   d. Is the food on each component of the tray the right item allowed in the diet?
   e. Are there items on the tray that are not supposed to be there?

It is well to develop a standard trayline checking technique, to help the assistant increase accuracy and speed in checking trays. This technique will not be difficult if the menu format as designed supplies a good eye transfer and movement from product on the tray to the menu. The most modern technique to improve trayline accuracy is the optical scanner together with universal product coding. Research may lead to a computerized system where accuracy is checked by the computer through signals from the menu items themselves.

TRANSPORTATION AND GALLEY SERVICE

Product control is achieved through the staging and holding of carts in a walk-in refrigerated area. Any air movement around the trays induces temperature

Blast Freezing System for Quantity Foods

increase which makes the products drier and warmer. Once again, time and temperature control is checked at the point that foods are received in the galley. In the galley, a check on the quality of the food items on the tray needs to be done. Use of a control sheet to determine how many trays per minute are completed in the distribution area will give a clue as to whether some trays are getting cold. This also indicates that the foodservice assistant is reconstituting the trays at too fast a rate and nursing service is not able to catch up.

Quality Control Inspection Sheet
V. Galley Service—Reconstitution and Service
Food Preparation

REF. NO.   BREAKFAST   LUNCH   DINNER

DATE:_____

TIME: _____

Category	Appear.		Taste		Texture		Food Temperature											
							Galley				Floor				Pt. Bedside			
	S	U	S	U	S	U	STD	ACT	S	U	STD	ACT	S	U	STD	ACT	S	U
1 Hot Cereal				X														
2 Fried Egg		X																
3 Ham Slice																		
4 Toast						X												
5 Coffee																		X
1																		
2																		
3																		
4																		
5																		
1																		
2																		
3																		
4																		
5																		
TOTAL RATINGS																		

COMMENTS FOR UNSATISFACTORY RATINGS

4 Soggy
1 Too Salty
2 Greasy   5 Coffee left uncovered at patient bedside

Food Service Quality Control Inspection Standards
Galley Service—Reconstitution and Service

a. FOOD PREPARATION AND RECONSTITUTION

1. *Food Appearance*
   a. Does the food item being checked have satisfactory color?

    b. Is there pleasant eye appeal in the variety of color and texture?
    c. Is the portion of food uniform in size and shape?
    d. Are garnishes properly used?
    e. Is there a right texture for a particular food item?

2. *Food Taste*
    a. Are there any strong or undesirable flavors?
    b. Is the taste desirable as to what is expected of the product?
    c. Is there any ingredient that produces undesirable or after-taste flavor?
    d. Is the seasoning adequate?
    e. Does the product have a pleasing aroma?

3. *Food Texture*
    a. Is the product over or undercooked?
    b. Does the moisture content make the texture suitable to the particular food product?
    c. Is the proper texture identifiable in the product?
    d. Is the product too tough and/or stringy?
    e. Is the product too soft and/or mushy?

Bacteriological Control

A tight bacteriological program has to be developed and implemented in a central food facility of this magnitude. A gross error could mean thousands of lives. Laboratory tests to determine the viable count of micro-organisms must be made at least once a month. The bacteriological standards to be implemented are as follows:

    a. Viable Aerobic bacteria plate count does not exceed more than 50,000 colonies per gram. The count must not indicate the presence or absence of a specific pathogen.
    b. Coliform plate count—5 coliform per milliliter.
    c. Coagulase positive staphylococci—negative.
    d. Perfringens plate count—negative.

    Quick or blast chilling of food products before storing in a refrigerated condition brings the temperature down to 40°F. at a faster rate. Of course, a nitrogen or CO_2 freezer cools the product much faster than the blast chill method, but the rate of freezing through a nitrogen freezer is not economical unless the total output exceeds 1000 pounds per day.

    A low temperature of 0°F. to -10°F. must be achieved in the internal product core to inhibit bacteria growth. A more detailed discussion on the necessary product formulation and manipulation that needs to be done to achieve a fast reduction of internal temperatures has been given in previous chapters.

Quality Control Inspection Sheet
V. Galley Service
Temperature and Time Control

	2E1	2E2	1W1	1W2	3W1	3W2	3W3	3E	2W1
					Stations				
Cart Completed									
Leaves Kitchen									
Arrives at Ward									
1st Tray Passed									
Last Tray Passed									
Number Passing									
Total Trays to Be Passed Per Galley									
Arrive Until Passed									
Total Time									
Total Time Passing									
Trays Passed per Minute									

There are several questions management must ask to maintain good bacteriological control. They are:

a. Is the flow of production structured so there is no criss-crossing or back-tracking?

b. Is there minimum handling of materials from receiving to storage?

c. Is the food prepared, chilled, and frozen so that the danger zone temperature between 40°F. and 140°F. is minimized?

d. Is there a good system to insure that products received first are used first?

e. Are personal hygiene standards being followed?

f. Is there a good equipment sanitation and maintenance program?

g. Is travel minimized from one area to another by duplicating commonly-used small equipment and tools, such as scales, scoops, ladles, and bun pans?

h. Is the time and temperature control always maintained?

Bacteriological control requires that the entire operation has proper maintenance of quality of the foods produced, and proper education and training in sanitation of all production and foodservice personnel.

INGREDIENT CONTROL

Selection of ingredients of the quality specified on the following pages and their use as suggested is important if the recipes in Volume 2, Blast Freezing Quantity Recipes, are incorporated into the system. Those recipes were developed using ingredients of the standards specified here. All other quality controls are based on the foundation of careful ingredient control for blast frozen items.

Herbs and Spices Used in Freezing

Spices derive from the seed, root, bud, or bark of aromatic tropical plants. They have more pungent qualities than herbs, which come from the leafy or soft portions of biennial or annual plants. The most commonly-used spices and herbs that have practical applications for cooking in a freezing system are:

Allspice is usually in ground form. The flavor resembles, tastes, and smells like a combination of cinnamon, nutmeg, and cloves. It is used in stews, soups, boiling or poaching fish, pickling spices, and for ham, stews, and pot roast.

Anise is a licorice-flavored dried seed of a plant belonging to the celery family. It is used on coffee cake, sweet rolls, and cookies, and in sweet pickles, candies, and chocolate cake icing.

Basil, sweet is part of the mint family with a clove-like scent. This is a favorite spice for tomato dishes, soups, and meat dishes, especially lamb, and for peas, potatoes, and cream sauces.

Bay Leaf is a dried leaf of laurel grown in many parts of the world. This adds to tomato dishes, and meats such as chicken, beef sauerbraten, lamb, and pork. It is excellent for stews, relishes, gravies, marinade.

Capers come from a low growing shrub and the green flower buds and berries are used for fish, chicken, potato, and salads. It is also used for lamb, mutton, heart, and tongue.

Caraway Seed is a dried pungent seed from an herb of the carrot family. The seeds are used in rye bread, coffee cakes, sauerkraut, sweet sour beets, and are good for meats such as roast pork, goose, duck, and for cheese and baked goods, such as cakes and cookies.

Cardamon is part of the ginger family. Seeds and pod may be ground together to be used in pickling, with the seed used for danish pastry, coffee cake, and fancy rolls.

Cayenne Pepper is one of the most pungent and strongest items from the red pepper family. It is used with sauces, gravies, and meat dishes, especially sausage, and curry dishes, and seafood items.

Celery Salt is made by grinding salt and celery seed together. It is used in soups, cream sauces, salads (especially chicken), fish or other seafood, and roast meats.

Celery seed is a pungent seed from a plant similar to garden celery. It is good for pickling spices, croquette mixtures, stews, coleslaw, potato salad, salad dressing, cheese, and fish and meat spreads.

Chervil is an aromatic herb of the carrot family used in salads, soups, egg and cheese dishes, and especially in potato salad.

Chili Powder is a blend of chili, red peppers, cumin seed, oregano, garlic powder, salt. It is excellent for tomato dishes and Mexican foods, as well as cocktail sauce, barbeque sauce, meat loaf, and some soups.

Chives is a miniature green onion plant with similar onion-like bulbs. Because of its mild onion flavor, it is added to cottage cheese and cream cheese, egg and potato dishes, soups, and cream cheese/sour cream dips.

Cinnamon is one of the oldest spices. It comes from the bark of a cinnamon tree, and is used for rolls, baked desserts, pastries, pickles, preserves, fruits, hot drinks, and hot after-dinner drinks. I have used it for roast pork, lamb, and beef in a small amount and its sweet flavor has been an effective addition.

Cloves are the nail-shaped, dried flower buds of the clove tree. Rich and pungent in flavor, the bud is used for curing ham, pickling meats, and in hot beverages. It is also good for gravy.

Coriander is an aromatic herb of the carrot family used for curried dishes, pickles, meat products, sausages, and frankfurters.

Cumin is a favorite for Italian and Mexican dishes. It is also good for egg and cheese dishes, sauerkraut, soups, pickles, sausage.

Curry Powder contains turmeric, ginger, red pepper, cumin, coriander, etc., and is used to make Indian style dishes of meat, fish, eggs, and chicken. It can be applied to rice, veal, shrimp, and chicken dishes.

Dill is an aromatic leaf, seed, and stem of the carrot family. The fresh leaves are used in sauces for potatoes, beans, fish, lamb, veal. The seeds are excellent in potato salad, shrimp, seafood, coleslaw, hamburger, macaroni salads, soups, and marinating sauce for vegetables. It is blended with butter or sour cream for fish, seafood, and shellfish.

Garlic has a very potent, clinging flavor, but is delicious used as seasoning for meats, such as beef, pork, lamb, veal, poultry, and game birds. Orientals use it also for seasoning vegetables, rice, and noodle dishes.

Ginger is the dried root of a subtropical plant grown in China, Japan, India, and the British West Indies. It is used in the Orient for hot beverages, pickles, preserves, and chutneys. It can also be used for pot roast, vegetables, steaks, poultry, and duck. It is excellent for making teriyake marinades for meat.

Horseradish is ground to make a sauce which is excellent for meat, fish sauces, marinades, and in seafood salads.

Marjoram is one of the popular mint family members used with veal and other meats, potato, spinach, peas, green beans, and vegetable salads. It is excellent in lamb, poultry stuffings, sausage, stews, and soups.

Mint is a mild herb that has its application as mint jelly for roast lamb, and in glazed carrots and sweet and sour beets.

MSG (monosodium glutamate), which originated in the Orient, is extracted from wheat protein and sugar beets. If used sparingly it has the tendency to heighten flavor in meat, poultry, fish, and vegetable dishes.

Nutmeg is the sweet and spicy kernel of the fruit from the nutmeg tree. Traditionally it has been used in baked custards and desserts, but it is excellent if used sparingly to heighten flavors in cream soups, sauces, stews, gourmet vegetables, Oysters Rockefeller, and other spinach recipes.

Oregano is a sharp fragrant spice, stronger than sweet marjoram. Used for Italian dishes such as spaghetti, Mexican and Spanish dishes, and lentils.

Onion Powder is derived from the strongest and most popular yellow onions and takes the place of fresh onions. There are also freeze dehydrated chopped onions which, if properly rehydrated, are far better to use in recipes for freezing because fresh onions lose their strength during freezing.

Paprika is a red pepper ground to give it a fiery red color and rich flavor.

It is used for color and in fish, shellfish, vegetables, egg dishes, and salad dressings.

Parsley is best for frozen items if it is in its freeze dehydrated form so it will not look wilted and slimy after thawing. It is used to garnish soups, stews, salads, potatoes, and stuffings.

Pepper comes from grinding either black or white berries. White pepper is made from berries with the hulls removed. After salt, pepper is the most commonly used spice for meats, vegetables, fish, egg dishes, potatoes, soup, gravies, and pickling.

Rosemary belongs to the mint family, and is used for tomato, egg dishes, soups, fish, lamb, pork, beef, and duck.

Saffron is one of the most expensive spices; luckily a small amount goes a long way.

Sage is a familiar potent herb. It is used with stuffings, sausage, veal, pork dishes, beans, tomatoes.

Savory is grown in Southern France, and is used for boiling fish. It is also excellent for lentils, dried peas, and beans. Seventh Day Adventists use this for all vegetarian recipes.

Sesame Seeds are used in the U.S. primarily for cookies, rolls, breads, and cakes. But they are excellent with vegetables, salads, and pork or beef dishes. Recipes for Oriental dishes often call for them.

Soy Sauce is made from fermented soybeans. It is used in beef, pork, poultry, soups, vegetables, noodles, and rice dishes. Orientals use soy sauce in almost all of their dishes. Americans associate it with chow mein.

Tabasco is a sauce made from small, hot, Mexican red peppers, salted, cured for three years and blended with vinegar. It is excellent if used sparingly for marinades, egg dishes, gravies, sauces, seafoods (especially clam chowder and oyster stew), chicken and poultry.

Tarragon is an aromatic leaf, delicate in flavor. When combined with vinegar and other spices it produces a most delicious salad dressing. It can also be used for poaching salmon and other fish, chicken dishes, lobster thermidor, and for marinades.

Thyme is one of American's favorite herbs, starting with New Orleans cuisine. With other spices it is used as bouquet garni for seasoning soups, chowders, beef stews, swiss steaks.

Turmeric is the root of a plant belonging to the ginger family and resembles saffron. Mixed into curry powder, it finds several applications with meat and egg dishes.

Vanilla is the seed pod of a rare orchid, and is expensive. It is used mostly for baking. Vanilla extract is used in puddings, cakes, cookies, and confections.

Produce

It would require a long dissertation to include all of the detailed information on quality standards, variety, and grades of perishable fruits and vegetables. Most fresh produce in wholesale houses nowadays are graded by a USDA inspector so customers are assured of standard quality, size, and weight. It is my intent to give you a short summarized version of these quality standards.

Various fruit, fruit juice, and vegetable components included in freezing entrees are given in the following specifications:

STANDARDS OF QUALITY FOR THE COMPONENTS OF THE VARIOUS CONVENIENCE ENTREES:

If the entree contains any FRESH VEGETABLES they must meet the following standards:

Asparagus: USDA No.1 Fresh, moist, tender stems, deep green or bluish green tips, straight, firm, closed, unbroken tips, crisp, 2 inch max. white, brittle at butt end, punctures easily if tender, soft and clinging bracts, round compact tips, at least 2/3 green (not less than 4 ½ inch of stalk length green). Not wilted, spreading tips, angular stalks, tough, seedy shoots. Free from damage, decay and injury. ½ inch min. diameter, 2/3 green unless otherwise specified.

Beans, Dry: USDA No.1. Good natural color, plump, uniform size. Should not be shriveled, off colored, undersized, immature. Free from damage, decay, and injury. Free from foreign materials.

Beans, Dry Pea (Navy): USDA Extra fancy. Center of bean should be soft, glossy, yellowish white (no foreign beans). Free from damage, decay, and injury. Free from defects, good character, typical color.

Beans, Dry Split Peas: USDA Extra fancy. Green. Free from damage, decay, and injury.

Beans, Green: USDA Grade A Fancy. Uniform, bright, clean, fresh, young, tender, firm. Typical color. No leaves or stems. Free from damage, decay, and injury. Crisp, snap readily, grass green, clean, firm, juicy, meaty, immature seeds. Not stringy, without vine, not crooked, bulging pods, dull, wilted.

Beans, Wax: USDA Grade A Fancy. Bright yellow, uniform, clean, fresh, typical color, tender, firm, no leaves or stems. Free from damage, decay, and injury. Crisp, snap readily, firm, juicy, meaty, immature seeds. Not stringy, without vine, not crooked, bulging pods, dull, wilted.

Beans, Lima: USDA Extra No. 1. Free from damage decay and injury. Free from foreign material, clean, fresh. Free from defects, good character, typical color, one variety, fairly well filled. Fresh (not flabby), no yellow or dry pods, small size (4 or more beans/pod) bulging, well-filled pods, dark green, shelled limas should be plump, tender skin, greenish white color. Not overripe, soft, leathery pod (tough), dried, shriveled, or spotted.

Beets Fresh, Tops Off: USDA Grade No. 1. Similar varietal characteristics; firm, fairly smooth, fairly well shaped; free from soft rot and damage. Leaf stems free from damage, well-washed, uniform size, deep red, small or medium size, no large beet, no cracks, not soft, flabby, or shriveled. Free from decay and injury.

Broccoli, Fresh: USDA Fancy. Tender, firm stalks, compact buds in clusters, short stems, hard, top dark or purplish green. No open bud clusters with yellow or purple blossoms, stalks not over 6 in. long. Each bunch closely trimmed. Free from damage, decay or injury.

Brussels Sprouts, Fresh: USDA No. 1. Well-colored (light or dark green), firm, not withered or burst; no soft decay, no seed stems, no damage, no discoloration, insects, or foreign material. Free from damage, decay, and injury, hard, unscarred firm, fresh cut ends, tight buds, medium size. No loose, flabby, puffy riddled leaves, yellow leaves.

Cabbage, Fresh: USDA No. 1, bright heads smooth, round, very hard. Not soft, puffy, withered, free from damage, decay, and injury. Fresh.

Carrots Fresh, Tops Off: USDA Extra No. 1, similar varietal characteristics, well-trimmed, firm, clean; fairly well-colored, fairly smooth, well-formed. No secondary new top growth, no soft rot, or other damage. Not flabby, soft, tough, or stringy center, not green shoulder. Free from damage, decay, and injury.

Cauliflower, Fresh: USDA Grade No. 1, compact, not discolored or overmature, (not loose, open, or turning yellow) no soft or wet decay. Free from damage, decay, and injury. Jacket leaves fresh, green, and free of damage of any kind, hard, tight budded, clean, heavy, firm, white or creamy white head; outer leaves green and crisp, not in separated segments; not yellow, wilted leaves, dark surface spots, yellow color, loose buds, open clusters, not overmature or soft spots.

Celery, Fresh: Colo. Pascal USDA Extra No. 1. Similar varietal characteristics, well-developed, good heart formation, clean, well-trimmed, fairly compact, no black heart, brown stem, or decay. Free from damage, decay, and injury. Fairly well blanched. No wilted leaves, pithy, wilted stalks, not stringy.

Corn, Fresh Sweet: USDA Fancy. One variety, well-trimmed, well-developed, free from decay, damage, and injury, cobs well-filled with plump, milky kernels; well covered with fresh husks. 8 row Golden Bantam or Country Gentleman. Fresh, mature, well-ripened, fresh green husk, well-filled with bright, plump, milky kernels. No loose husks, stunted ears, poorly developed rows, shriveled kernels, wilted or discolored husks.

Cucumbers, Fresh: USDA Extra Fancy or USDA Fancy. Hard, dark green, straight, slim, long, well-colored (¾ green); well formed, not over grown (soft with tough seeds), fresh, no damage, firm, not spongy, no soft ends, not withered, not curved or yellow.

Eggplant: USDA No. 1, heavy, firm, dark purple; glossy, smooth, clear surface, no blemishes, one variety, (not soft or flabby), good type color, no damage, decay, or injury. No light purple or reddened tint; not large (pithy), wilted, wrinkled, immature or old, without dark areas or discoloration. Free from damage, decay, or injury.

Endive, Escarole, Chicory: USDA No. 1. Endive—narrow leaf, finely divided, curly, thick midribs. Escarole—broad-leaved. Chicory—broad leaved, upright spreading. All three should be bright, crisp, fresh, tender, centers creamy white. Endive must be very crisp. Not wilted, decayed, no coarse leaves. Free from damage, decay, or injury. Each should be of one variety, fresh, well-trimmed (roots cut close to outer leaf stem), fairly well-blanched. (Yellowish white to white heart with a spread not less than 4 inches in diameter)

Green Peppers, Fresh: USDA Fancy, hard, unblemished, crisp, sweet, medium size, uniform size, heavy dry stem. Not soft, pliable, thin fleshed, pale color, crooked, blemished. One variety, green but not immature (seeds developed), well-shaped, firm, not soft or shriveled, free from damage, decay, and injury.

Greens, Fresh: USDA No. 1. Beet tops, broccoli, chard, collard, dandelion, kale, mustard greens, turnip tops, all should be fresh, short stems, green leaf, not wilted, coarse, yellow. Free from decay, damage, and injury. No seed stems, no broken, spotted, or discolored leaves, no dirt, or insects.

Lettuce, Iceberg: USDA No. 1. Fresh, solid, crisp, white butt; fresh, green outer leaves. Similar variety, not soft, split or burst; free from damage, dirt, decay, and injury. Well-trimmed, heavy for size, good green color.

Romaine: USDA No. 1. Fairly well-headed, well-trimmed, free from damage, decay, or injury. Tightly bound leaves on head, cone shape size; large tender full leaves, not old, no rust, no oversized butt.

Lettuce, Boston: USDA No. 1. Similar variety. Fresh. Loose heads bright green; crisp, solid; firm, heavy for size, no seed stems inside heads, free from damage, decay, and injury.

Leaf Lettuce: USDA No. 1. Long, loose leaves. Bright green; crisp; brittle when you snap a leaf. Should not be misshapen; or have center seed stem. Free from damage, dirt, decay, or injury and foreign materials.

Lettuce, Bibb: USDA No. 1. Rose-shaped head, compact leaves; pale green, medium size. Should not have misshapen heads, overgrown center coats, outer rust. Free from dirt, damage, decay, injury, and foreign materials.

Mushrooms, Fresh: USDA No. 1. Cultivated, firm, clean, creamy white, moist, closed veils; stem attached to cap pin or flesh colored gills. No spotted tops, dark gills, broken veils, not dry, rubbery, no scars, mold, wet, black caps or open caps. One variety, fresh, not badly misshapen; no spots, no damage.

Okra, Fresh: USDA No. 1. Young, tender, fresh, clean pods, short, rich green type, pods snap easily and are easily punctured. Not withered, old, black tips, dull, or dry. One variety, fresh tender, not badly misshapen. Free from dirt, damage, decay, injury, and foreign materials.

Olives, Green: USDA Grade A (Fancy). Similar varietal characteristics, good typical texture; normal flavor and odor uniform, typical color, uniform size, absence of defects, firm but tender, fleshy texture, mature.

Onions—Bermuda, Globe, Red, Spanish, Yellow: USDA No. 1. One variety, mature, firm, not soft, fairly well-shaped, no soft rot, no doubles, no bottlenecks, no pink onions, no splits, or seed stems. Free from dirt, damage, decay, injury, or foreign material.

Onions, Shallots: USDA No. 1. Good rich green color, straight upright stems; full pod, not wilted or yellow. Well-formed, firm, young, tender, well trimmed bulb, fresh, clean, crisp. Free from damage, decay, and injury. No bruised or yellow leaves. One variety, fairly well blanched.

Parsley, Fresh: USDA No. 1. Fresh, bright green, no yellow leaves, no decay, no seed stems, free from dirt, damage, decay, injury, or foreign matter.

Parsnips, Fresh: USDA No. 1. Clean, firm, smooth, small to medium size, soft not flabby, no large. Well-trimmed, firm, fairly smooth, fairly well-formed, free from damage, decay, injury, and foreign matter.

Peapods, Fresh: USDA No. 1. Bright, green, well-filled pods, young, tender, sweet; pods should be green; pods should crackle when opened, not flat, dark green pods, no swollen pods of poor color flecked with gray specks. Free from damage, dirt, decay, injury, and foreign materials.

Pimientoes: USDA Grade A Fancy, practically whole, firm, fairly uniform in size; not less than 2 inches in length and width when flattened, uniform full red color, free from defects, damage, decay, injury, or foreign materials.

Potatoes, White Fresh: USDA Fancy or USDA Extra No. 1. Should be hard, firm, smooth, clean, no green ring, or second growth, no knobbiness, flabbiness, sunburn, feathering, or chilled. Free from injuries, damage, decay. Free from hollow heart, black heart, deep eye bruises, dark corky spots, slightly green color, also slightly green color under surface. Not wilted, leathery, not frozen.

Potatoes, Red: USDA Fancy or USDA Extra No. 1. Should be hard, firm, smooth, clean, no green ring or second growth, no knobbiness, flabbiness, sunburn, feathering, or chilled. Free from injuries, damage, decay. Free from hollow heart, black heart, deep eye bruises, dark corky spots, slightly green color, also slightly green color under surface. Not wilted, leathery, not frozen and washed.

Potatoes, Sweet, Fresh: USDA Fancy, either Tenn., Ill., New Jersey, kiln dried, smooth, plump, bright, absolutely no bruises. Free from dirt, damage, decay, injury, and foreign materials, one variety, firm, smooth, fairly clean, well-shaped, free from black rot, soft rot, wet breakdown, free from damage, decay, injury, dirt, and foreign materials.

Pumpkin, Fresh: USDA No. 1, mature, clean, fairly well-formed, rich yellow color, thin shell, hard shell, free from damage, dirt, decay, injury, rich yellow color, flesh fine-textured (not coarse or stringy), no large.

Radishes, Fresh: USDA No. 1. Well-formed, smooth, clean, firm, tender, free from damage, decay, and injury. Fresh, hard, crisp, bright color, fresh tops, not spongy, no yellow leaves, not soft or pithy.

Rhubarb, Fresh: USDA Fancy, fresh, firm, tender, crisp, red rich color, pale tops, coarse, deep green leaves. Not wilted, no slimy leaves, not pithy. One variety, very well-colored, fresh, tender, straight, clean, well-trimmed. Free from damage, dirt, decay, injury, and foreign materials.

Rutabagas, Fresh: USDA No. 1, pale yellow, hard, smooth. Fresh, well-trimmed, firm, fairly well-shaped, clean. Free from soft rot. Free from damage, decay, dirt, injury, and foreign materials.

Sauerkraut (Bulk): USDA Grade A, color lighter than olive buff, uniform shreds about 1/32 inches thick; practically free from defects and blemishes; fine; crisp texture, normal, well developed flavor. Free from damage, decay, and injury.

Spinach Fresh: USDA Extra fresh, No. 1, clean, short stem, large flat leaves. Not wilted, not yellow or weeds. One variety, fairly clean, well-trimmed, free from coarse stalk, seed stems, and roots. Free from damage, decay, injury, dirt, and foreign material.

Squash, Fresh—Summer and Winter: USDA No. 1. Young, tender, free from damage, dirt, decay, injury, and foreign materials. Firm, well-developed, not too hard shelled, not spotted or discolored, no damage caused by dirt, and insects. Not pithy. Marrow should be mature, well-formed, good orange color, smooth tapering. Flesh thick, fine grained, dry, mealy, shell thick and hard. No soft shell, cracks, or broken stock. Heavy for size, no blemishes, no soft rind.

Tomatoes, Fresh: USDA No. 1 mature but not operripe or soft, well-developed (not ridged or peaked at stem end), fairly well-formed (not misshapen, fairly smooth, uniform size, few seeds). No dull, puffy, lopsided, cracked, bruises, deep stems.

Tomatoes, Cherry: Ditto except for weight as cherry tomatoes do not weigh more than 1 oz.

Turnips, Tops Off, Fresh: USDA Grade A one variety, pale yellow, firm, (not soft or flabby), fairly smooth, fairly well-shaped, no soft rot, free from damage, dirt, decay, injury, and foreign materials. Tender, close grained, hard, medium size, uniform size, smooth. No crown leaf scars, should be heavy for size, not pithy.

Watercress: USDA No. 1, young, good green color, fresh, crisp leaf, should snap when broken, no yellow or wilted leaves. Well trimmed, free from damage, decay, dirt, injury, and foreign materials, not wilted.

Garlic: USDA No. 1, well-cured, firm (not soft or spongy), compact (kernels not spreading), well-filled, fairly plump, no damage, and each bulb enclosed in its outer sheath with a minimum diameter 1½ in.

Any other fresh vegetables, not listed above, used in making items for blast freezing must be the top quality USDA grade.

If the entrees contain any fresh fruit, they must meet these standards:

Apples: USDA Extra fancy. Mature, not overripe; clean, well-formed, free from damage, decay, and injury.

Banana: USDA Extra Fancy or USDA No. 1 or better, mature, but not overripe or soft. Well-shaped, well-formed, free from damage, decay, and injury.

Blueberries: USDA No. 1, cultivated. Bright, clean, fresh, firm, plump, well-colored, not overripe or underripe. Dry, free from trash, sticky juice, molds. Free from damage, decay, and injury.

Cantaloupe: USDA Fancy or USDA No. 1 or better (melons should have yellow color beneath "netting" and softness at stem end which indicates ripeness, and a heavy, distinctive aroma). Mature, but not overripe. Free from damage, decay, and injury.

Casabas: Mature but not overripe. USDA Fancy or USDA No. 1 or better. Free from damage, decay, or injury.

Cherries, Sweet: USDA No. 1. Mature, but not soft, overripe, or shriveled. Well-colored, well-formed, clean. Free from damage, decay, or injury.

Cranberries: USDA Grade A or better. Fresh, clean, mature, firm, not soft, overripe, or decayed. Free from damage and injury. Fairly well-colored.

Grapes, Almeria: USDA Fancy or USDA No. Extra. Should be plump, firm, full, well-developed, not straggly, should not drop off when shaken. Well-colored, mature, and not overripe; free from damage, decay, and injury.

Grapes, Emperor: USDA Fancy or USDA Extra No. 1 or better. Should be plump, firm, full, well-developed, not straggly, should not drop off when shaken by stem. Well-colored, mature, not overripe. Free from damage, decay, and injury.

Grapefruit: USDA Fancy. Mature, well-colored, firm, well-formed, thin-skinned, and skin of a smooth texture. Free from decay, damage, and injury. Heavy for size and few seeds.

Grapes, Malaga: USDA Fancy or USDA Extra No. 1. Should be plump, firm, full, well-developed, not straggly, should not drop off when shaken by stem. Well-colored, mature, and not overripe. Free from damage, decay, and injury.

Grapes, Seedless, Thompson's: USDA Extra Fancy No. 1. Should be plump, firm, full, well-developed, not straggly, should not drop off when shaken by stem. Well-colored, mature, not overripe. Free from damage, decay, and injury.

Grapes, Tokay: USDA Fancy or USDA No. 1. Should be plump, firm, full, well-developed, not straggly. Should not drop off when shaken by stem. Well-colored, mature, not overripe. Free from damage, decay, and injury.

Honeydew Melons: USDA No. 1 or better. Mature, but not overripe. Free from damage, decay, and injury. Firm, well-formed, well-developed.

Lemons: USDA No. 1. Firm, well-formed, well-colored, skin should have a smooth texture. Mature, but not overripe. Free from damage, decay, and injury.

Limes: USDA No. 1. Firm, well-formed, fairly smooth texture, good green color, clean, free from dirt, damage, decay, injury, and stylar end breakdown.

Nectarines: USDA Fancy or better. Mature, but not soft or overripe, well-formed, clean, well-colored, firm. Free from damage, decay, and injury.

Oranges: USDA Fancy. Well-formed, well-colored, firm, mature, and of smooth texture. Free from damage, decay, and injury.

Peaches: USDA Fancy or USDA Extra No. 1. Should be plump, rosy yellow coloring, free from blemishes, firm, free from damage, decay, and injury. Mature, not soft, or overripe, well-formed.

Pears: (Winter Pears) USDA Extra No. 1 or (Fall Pears) USDA No. 1. Flesh should be delicately smooth, fine-grained, sweet and juicy. Mature, but not overripe, clean; well-formed, free from damage, decay, and injury.

Plums: USDA Fancy. Well-matured, well-formed, clean, not overripe, or soft, or shriveled. Free from damage, decay, and injury. Well-colored.

Raspberries, Red: USDA No. 1. Well-colored, well-developed, mature, but not soft or overripe or broken. Bright, clean, fresh, firm, plump, dry, free from trash, molds, sticky juice, damage, decay, or injury.

Rhubarb, Field: USDA No. 1 or better. Fresh, firm, well-formed, clean, well-colored, crisp shiny stalks, mature, but not overripe. Free from damage, decay, and injury.

Strawberries: USDA No. 1. Should be plump, firm, bright, clean, fresh, firm, dry, mature but not overripe or undeveloped. Free from dirt, mold, damage, decay, and injury. Surface should have a pink or red color.

Tangelos: USDA Fancy. Well-colored, firm, well-formed, mature but not overripe, and of a smooth texture. Free from damage, decay, and injury.

Tangerines: USDA Fancy. Mature, firm, well-formed, free from damage, decay, and injury. Clean, free from dirt, highly colored.

Watermelon, Red: USDA No. 1. Should have bloom or gloss on rind surface, light green color. Mature but not overripe. Free from damage, decay, or injury.

Any other fresh fruit not listed above must be the top quality, USDA Grade.

Frozen Juice Specifications
DETAILED SPECIFICATIONS:

a. Juice Specifications: Group I—Standard specifications for each frozen juice concentrate are to be as follows:

1. Orange juice is to be an all Valencia product, pure and unsweetened, sealed and frozen in vacuum packed cans to prevent spoilage, and to which vitamin C is added in quantities of not less than 30 mg. or more than 60 mg. Juice is to be of USDA Grade A Fancy with good color, excellent flavor, with no less than a score of 95, and no less than 12.8° Brix minimum.

2. Grape juice is to be of pure concord, with very good color, free from defects, coagulation, with excellent flavor, with a 13.3° Brix minimum, and no less than score of 95.

3. Grapfruit juice is to be unsweetened, with very good color, free from coagulation, defects, and with a score of 95, and a 10.6° Brix minimum.

4. Apple juice is to be of USDA Grade A Fancy, clarified, unsweetened with bright color, free from defects (apple pulp, particles, seeds, residues, or pulp coagulation), no less than 12.0° Brix, not less than 0.4 percent nor more than 0.65 percent malonic acid, and no off flavor, oxidized, astringent or disagreeable odor. It must have a normal apple juice flavor.

5. Pineapple juice is to be of USDA Grade A Fancy Hawaiian Pineapple, unsweetened, very good color, free from defects, very good flavor, not more than 1.35 mg. of anhydrous citric acid per 100 ml of juice, not less than 10.5° Brix soluble solid content, and with vitamin C added in quantities not less than 30 mg and not more than 60 mg, and a minimum score of 95.

6. Tomato juice is to be of USDA Grade A Fancy, ripe tomato color, good consistency, typical ripe tomato flavor, free of any reddish brown tints, free of seed pieces, skin, specks or poor flavor, with a minimum score of 95, and a Brix minimum of 6.7°.

7. Cranberry juice cocktail is to be of USDA Grade A Fancy made from cranberry juice and concentrated cranberry juice extracted from mature, well-colored cranberries. Contains not less than 25 percent cranberry juice, with not less than 0.55 gm per 100 mg of citric anhydrous acid, with vitamin C added in

quantities not less than 30 mg and not more than 60 mg, and a Brix minimum of 15.0°.

Juice Specifications: Group II—Standard specifications of individually portioned fresh/or frozen juices (reconstituted):

8. Apricot Nectar is to be of USDA Grade A Fancy, with normal color, not excessively pale yellow, light, bright green, or brown. It must be free of particles, seeds, pits, or other foreign materials capable of being avoided by well-accepted manufacturing practices. Fruit ingredient should not be less than 35 percent by weight of the finished food, with a Brix value of no less than 14.3° Brix.

9. Prune juice is to be of USDA Grade A Fancy, good color, free from defects, good flavor, contain not less than 18.5 percent by weight of water soluble solids extracted from dried prunes. Vitamin C added, in quantities not less than 30 mg and not more than 50 mg, with honey in a quantity of not less or more than 2 to 3 percent.

To secure produce of the quality needed for best results in using the recipes in Volume 2, Blast Freezing Quantity Recipes, carefully written purchasing specification forms are essential. The following samples will be helpful in the development of such specifications:

A Sample Format of Specifications for
Processed Fruits, Vegetables and Potatoes*
GENERAL SPECIFICATIONS:

It is the intent of these specifications to provide for the needs of the various County departments as they arise through the contract period, and no guarantee or statement is given as to the extent and nature of these needs. Accordingly, quantities are estimates, and the right is reserved by the purchaser to order only as department requirements dictate and to increase or decrease these estimates as needed.

INGREDIENTS QUALITY

Bacterial Count: The items as supplied shall not have a bacterial count in excess of the following:

a. Total aerobic bacteria plate count not to exceed more than 7500 colonies in 1 gram.
b. Coliform plate count—50 colonies per gram
c. Coagulose positive type staphylococci—negative count.
d. Salmonella Shigella typhoid—negative count.
e. E coli—negative count.

*Hennepin County, Minneapolis, MN

f. Faecal Streptococci—negative count.

g. Perfringens—negative count.

If samples indicate values in excess of the above, an additional sample will be taken to cross check the first sample. These tests shall be made by a certified, approved, outside laboratory.

ACCEPTABLE ADDITIVES: Manufacturer shall use only currently acceptable additives as generally recognized as safe status (as stated on current GRAS list), as established by the United States Food and Drug Administration. Manufacturer to state all additives used in product.

PRESERVATIVES:

a. Any processed fruit or vegetable (except potatoes) shall be preserved with a minimum ot a 1 percent ascorbic and malic acid mixture.

b. Pre-peeled potatoes shall be preserved with a solution of 0.1 percent sodium benzoate or sodium sulfite.

PROCESSING: Peeled potato products shall be processed through mechanical abrasers; coustic bath peeling is not allowed.

DATING: The date of production shall be marked on all packages.

DETAILED SPECIFICATIONS: Detailed specifications and quantities are cited on the proposal form. Failure to meet the quality contemplated shall be reason for rejection of the item(s) bid.

DELIVERY:

a. Bidders shall quote on the basis of "delivered price," and all quotations, whether for regular or emergency orders, shall include all transportation and delivery charges. The minimum dollar amount of the order placed for delivery shall be Twenty-Five Dollars ($25).

b. Deliveries shall be made, as called for, within one (1) week after receipt of order. Emergency orders shall be delivered in forty-eight (48) hours.

c. The delivery point shall be the Hennepin County General Food Facility, 530 Chicago Avenue, Minneapolis, Minnesota 55415, or any other department designated by the County Purchasing Director.

d. It shall be the successful bidder's responsibility to meet the County's delivery requirements even if such bidder finds it necessary to purchase same on the open market or to incur additional freight costs.

PACKAGING:

a. For items packaged in bags, the bags must be of a medium density polyethylene material.

b. For items packaged in cartons, the cartons must be of Kraft paper with a 14,400 sq. in. per lb. yield strength.

c. For items packaged in cartons and that need to be separated due to the delicateness and fragility of the items so as to prevent them from crushing and/or bruising, it is required that a Kraft waxed board liner be used to separate the layers.

TERM OF CONTRACT: The term of this contract shall be from January 1, 1979 through Decenber 31, 1979. All quantities of items not ordered prior to expiration date shall be considered cancelled as of that date, and the purchaser shall not be liable for any claims for reason of cancellation.

SAMPLES: If requested, all samples shall be delivered to the Hennepin County Medical Center not later than one (1) calendar week from date of request for same.

INSPECTION: All items shall be subject to inspection and testing by Hennepin County to the extent practicable and in any event prior to acceptance. The inspection is to insure that the items meet the requirements of the specifications and the proposal. Any deviation or substitution thereof will not be accepted by the Storekeeper unless prior approval has been given by the Food Buyer or the County Food Service Director.

QUANTITY INCREASES-DECREASES: The County reserves the right to increase or decrease these estimated requirements by any amounts deemed necessary to meet its needs without any adjustment in contract prices, and it shall be understood that the budget estimate herein is an approximation only.

BID AWARD AND ACCEPTANCE: Award will be made by and contract executed by the County on behalf of itself.

Award shall be based on but not limited to the factors of: price; the County's experience with the products proposed; the County's evaluation of the bidder's ability to service the County in terms of its requirements as called for in the specifications; the general reputation and experience of the bidder in the industry; the nature and extent of company data furnished with this bid or furnished upon request by the County at any time prior to bid award; the financial responsibility of the bidder; the County's prior knowledge of and experience with the bidder's past performance; quality of merchandise offered; bidder's ability to meet delivery and stocking requirements; and the needs and requirements of the purchaser's program.

The County Purchasing Director reserves the right to accept or reject any or all bids or any part of any bids and to waive any informality contained herein where the acceptance, rejection, or waiving of such would be in the best interests of the County. The County Purchasing Director also reserves the right to award in whole or in part, by item, group of items, or by section where such action serves the purchaser's best interests.

INSTRUCTIONS TO BIDDERS:

a. All bids must be written in ink or typewritten.

b. All bids must be enclosed in the envelope provided by the County Purchasing Director for the purpose of submitting bids.

c. All bid envelopes must bear the inscription: "PROCESSED POTATOES, FRUITS, AND VEGETABLES" as well as the name and address of the bidder.

d. The bid envelopes shall be addressed to the Hennepin County Commissioners, Government Center, 2400 Administrative Tower, Minneapolis, Minnesota 55487.

BIDDERS NOTE: Any amplification, modification, insertion, deletion, or changes, except as caused by an addendum, made by *any* bidder to *any* material contained on the proposal sheet(s) shall be cause for rejection of your bid. Should any bidder wish to submit amplifying data with his bid, make a statement on the bottom of the proposal that such amplification matter is a part of the bid and *attach* said matter to the proposal form(s).

Proposal

PROPOSAL OF _____

ADDRESS _____

PHONE _____

FOR THE FURNISHING AND DELIVERY OF PROCESSED POTATOES, VEGETABLES, AND FRUITS TO VARIOUS HENNEPIN COUNTY INSTITUTIONS FOR THEIR REQUIREMENTS, FROM JANUARY1, 19__ TO DECEMBER 31, 19__, IN ACCORDANCE WITH THE ATTACHED SPECIFICATIONS AND "OTHER TERMS, CONDITIONS AND INSTRUCTIONS TO THE SPECIFICATIONS" WHICH WERE SUBMITTED WITH THIS PROPOSAL AND UPON WHICH THIS PROPOSAL IS MADE.

Item No.	Est. Quantity	Description	Unit Price	Total
1	1400 doz.	Apples, cored, Jumbo Jonathan or Roman Beauty, USDA Grade A—Fancy	$_____/doz	$_____
2	500 doz.	Apples, ditto above, peeled, cored, USDA Grade A—Fancy	$_____/doz	$_____

3	350 bags	Apples, Winesap, diced 5/8 x 5/8, 10 lb./bag, USDA Grade A—Fancy	$_____/bag $_____
4	350 bags	Apples, Winesap or Delicious, washed, cored, wedged (6 wedges per apple) 10 lb. USDA Grade A—Fancy	$_____/bag $_____
5	20,885	Grapefruit, half, washed, sectioned, 4 inches + 24/box 2 layers, USDA Fancy	$_____/hvs $_____
6	100 bags	Grapes, Thompson seedless, ind., washed, trimmed, 5 lb. bags USDA Extra Fancy No. 1	$_____/bag $_____
7	100 ctn	Cantaloupe or honeydew melon wedges, max. of 3 inches x 5 inches, 10 lb., USDA Grade A—Fancy	$_____/ctn $_____
8	300 ctn.	Cantaloupe or honeydew melon balls, same as above 1 inch diameter 10 lb.	$_____/ctn $_____
9	25 ctn.	Pineapple Spears, max. of 1 ½ inch x 6 inches, 10 lb., USDA Grade A—Fancy	$_____/ctn $_____
10	25 case	Rhubarb, fresh, 1 inch chunks, 10 lb., USDA Grade A—Fancy	$_____/cs $_____
11	50 case	Strawberries, fresh, capped, 12 pts/cs. USDA Grade A—Fancy	$_____/bag $_____
12	100 bags	Watermelon chunks, 3 inches x 4 inches, 5 lb. USDA Grade A	$_____/bag $_____
13	100 bags	Watermelon balls, 1 inch diameter, 5 lb. USDA Grade A—Fancy	$_____/bag $_____
14	500 bags	Cabbage, cored, cut in 1/8, 10 lb. USDA No. 1	$_____/bag $_____
15	50 bags	Cabbage and Apple chunks, mixed 10 lb. USDA No. 1 (equal parts green cabbage, red cabbage, and diced Winesap apples ¾ inch x ¾ inch)	$_____/bag $_____
16	25 bags	Cabbage and Pineapple chunks, mixed 10 lb. (green cabbage and equal part of ½ inch x ¾ inch USDA Grade A—Fancy Pineapple)	$_____/bag $_____

Item No.	Est. Quantity	Description	Unit Price	Total
17	1233 bags	Cabbage, plain, shredded, 10 lb. USDA No. 1	$_____/bag	$_____
18	25 bags	Cabbage, shredded, rainbow, green and red cabbage w/carrots, equal proportions, 10 lb. bags, USDA No. 1	$_____/bag	$_____
19	1585 bags	Carrots, peeled, sliced, ¼ inch slices, USDA Extra No. 1, 10 lb.	$_____/bag	$_____
20	320 bags	Carrot sticks, 3 inches, USDA Extra No. 1, 10 lb. bags	$_____/bag	$_____
21	200 bags	Carrots, peeled, shredded 10 lb. bags USDA Extra No. 1	$_____/bag	$_____
22	550 bags	Carrots, Julienne cut, 3/8 inch x 3/8 inch, 10 lb. bags, USDA Extra No. 1	$_____/bag	$_____
23	350 bags	Celery Sticks, 3 inches, 10 lb. bags	$_____/bag	$_____
24	250 bags	Celery, plain, finely chopped, 3/8 inch x 3/8 inch, 10 lb. bags	$_____/bag	$_____
25	345 bags	Celery, Julienne cut, 3/8 inch x 3 inch 10 lb. bags	$_____/bag	$_____
26	520 bags	Celery, plain, regular chunks, ¾ inch x ¾ inch, 10 lb. bags	$_____/bag	_____
27	50 bags	Celery, cleaned stalks, 3 inch pieces, 10 lb.	$_____/bag	$_____
28	50 doz.	Corn, husked, trimmed, doz. ea., max. 6 inches long	$_____/doz	$_____
29	100 bags	Cauliflowerettes, trimmed, sectioned, buds, 10 lb. bag	$_____/bag	$_____
30	100 bags	Cucumber, sliced, USDA Fancy or Extra Fancy; not to exceed 2 3/8 inch in diameter, and ¼ inch in thickness	$_____/bag	$_____
31	150 bags	Endive, washed, trimmed, 12 ea/bag, USDA No. 1, in indiv. leaves	$_____/bag	$_____
32	200 bags	Lettuce cups, cleaned, trimmed, washed, indiv. leaves, 10 lb. bags, USDA No. 1 Iceberg Lettuce	$_____/bag	$_____

33	70 bags	Lettuce, leaf, cleaned and trimmed, 10 lb. bags, USDA Fancy	$_____/bag $_____
34	1500 bags	Lettuce, plain, chopped, USDA No. 1, Iceberg Lettuce, 10 lb. bags	$_____/bag $_____
35	1000 bags	Potatoes, fresh, pre-peeled raw, medium size boiler, USDA Fancy or USDA Extra No. 1, 15 lb. bag	$_____/bag $_____
36	370 bags	Ditto above, cubes, 15 lb. bags	$_____/bag $_____
37	100 bags	Ditto above, chunks, fresh, pre-peeled, raw, 1 ½ inch x 1 ½ inch 15 lb. bags	$_____/bag $_____
38	200 lbs.	Potatoes, bakers, indiv. foil wrapped, 6 to 9 oz. cleaned and washed 50 lb./ctn, USDA Fancy or USDA Extra No. 1	$_____/lb $_____
39	10,000 lbs.	Potatoes, bakers, 6 to 8 oz., cleaned and washed, not wrapped, 50 lb./ctn USDA Fancy or USDA Extra No.1	$_____/lb. $_____
40	300 bags	Onions, chopped, 3/8 inch cut, 10 lb. bags, USDA No. 1	$_____/bag $_____
41	250 bags	Green Onion, washed, trimmed, and cut into 4 inch lengths, 10 lb. bags USDA No. 1	$_____/bag $_____
42	500 bags	Onions, whole peeled, 10 lb. bags, USDA No. 1	$_____/bag $_____
43	500 bags	Onions, peeled, sliced, ¼ inch slices, 10 lb. bags, USDA No. 1	$_____/bag $_____
44	800 bags	Parsley sprigs, washed, trimmed, 1 lb., of usable size, USDA No. 1	$_____/bag $_____
45	100 bags	Green Peppers, whole, cleaned, trimmed and cored from top for stuffing, 40 lb. bags, USDA Fancy	$_____/bag $_____
46	100 bags	Green Pepper/diced, 3/8 inch x 3/8 inch USDA Fancy, 5 lb. bags	$_____/bag $_____
47	200 bags	Green Pepper Rings, 5 lb. bags, USDA Fancy, Max. of 3 inch diameter x 3/8 inch in width	$_____/bag $_____
48	50 bags	Green Pepper strips, 3 inches long, 3/8 inch wide, cleaned, trimmed 5 lb. bags, USDA Fancy	$_____/bag $_____

Item No.	Est. Quantity	Description	Unit Price	Total
49	500 bags	Radishes, Rosette, 5 lb./bag	$_____/bag	$_____
50	150 bags	Romaine leaves, cleaned, washed, trimmed indiv. leaves, 10 lb. bags, USDA No. 1	$_____/bag	$_____
51	50 bags	Fresh pre–prepared 3 Bean Salad consisting of fresh green beans, wax beans, canned kidney beans, onions of USDA No. 1 quality, marinated 12 hours in vinegar, oil, sugar, salt, Tabasco, and pepper mixture. Salad must be freshly prepared and not to exceed more than 2 days of storage. 10 lb. bags.	$_____/bag	$_____
52	5000 bags	Deluxe Sald Mix, lettuce, radish slices, carrots, red cabbage, 10 lb. bags	$_____/bag	$_____
53	800 bags	Potato Salad consisting of pre-peeled, diced potatoes, with a minimum preservative content of not more than 1% ascorbic and malic acid, mixed with diced celery, onions, green onions, and marinated 12 hours with a dressing consisting of blended cooked egg yolks, mustard, vinegar, sour cream and mayonnaise, salt and and pepper	$_____/bag	$_____
54	200 bags	Potato Salad, parsley (no onions), 10 lb. SALAD DRESSING—same as above, except no pepper	$_____/bag	$_____
55	385 bags	Soup Mix; ½ inch x ½ inch carrot, celery, onions, and potatoes, 15 lb. bags, USDA No. 1, packaged with a ratio of 5 lb. potatoes, 5 lb. carrots, 3 lb. celery, and 2 lb. onions	$_____/bag	$_____
56	600 bags	Squash, peeled, cut 4 inches x 4 inches, 10 lb. bags	$_____/bag	$_____

| 57 | 200 bags | Stew Mix chunks, 1 inch x 1 inch, 10 lb. bags carrots, potatoes, celery, equal mixture, USDA No. 1 w/ratio of 6 lb. potatoes, 5 lb. carrots, 3 lb. celery | $_____/bag $_____ |
| 58 | 2500 box | Tomatoes, stem removed, 5 lb., USDA No. 1 | $_____/box $_____ |

TOTAL AMOUNT OF BID...................$_____

State discount for payment in 20 days.............._____
Amount of additional discount if requirement for a performance bond is waived (see "Other Terms, Conditions and Instructions to the Specifications," Paragraph 2)..................................._____

PROPOSAL MUST BE SUBMITTED IN TRIPLICATE ON THIS FORM ONLY

STATE YOUR FIRM'S
FULL LEGAL NAME_____
(This information is necessary for preparation of contract forms if awarded to your firm)

SIGNATURE_____

INCORPORATED
IN STATE OF _____

Minimum Standards of Quality for Canned Goods, Staples, and Miscellaneous Products

The availability of fresh fruits and vegetables, the cost of these products, the cost of the labor to process them, and the availability of space and equipment to prepare them are some of the factors to consider in making decisions as to whether to purchase fresh, frozen, or canned goods. Yet there are many food-service operators who have slowly been converted to using frozen fruits and vegetables because of the quality of frozen products available in the market.

In the cities where labor cost is high and the operator desires a maximum quality, the use of frozen fruits and vegetables becomes a necessity. However, there are several reasons why we have continued to use some canned fruits and vegetables. First, we find that in the areas where cost has top priority over quality, these items are far cheaper. For all of our correctional institutions, such as the jails and juvenile centers, we use canned vegetables. In Minnesota where these operations are located, available fresh produce lacks quality and the actual edible yield of fresh vegetables ultimately costs more than canned goods. Second, we have discovered from previous trial and experimentation that some of the frozen fruits and vegetables are too tough or too firm, such as frozen green beans or corn for use in items to be blast frozen. After reconstitution in microwave ovens, for example, the green beans become even tougher. Besides, there are not that many frozen fruits or types of frozen potatoes available at the present time so that the system can operate completely with frozen fruits and vegetables.

The majority of canned fruits and vegetables are packed and priced according to grade. Most packers do not show the grade in their labels. Unfortunately, it takes time before one can settle on a quality brand name as part of the final product specifications.

The reason why there are some Grade B and C products in the specifications listed below is that these items are to be used for cooking in soups or for molded gelatin salads. These grades have various degrees of differences, but are somewhat close in quality as shown:

Grade A or Fancy—Top quality, tender, flavor is excellent, and color is typical of the original color.

Grade B or Standard—Vegetables are not as young as Grade A but have good flavor and color.

Grade C or Standard—Vegetables not as tender and do not have as good color and good flavor as B or A.

The above grades do not include the styles of vegetables or fruits, such as whole, sliced, diced, krinkle cut, fancy cuts, short cuts. Depending on the fruit or vegetable, it is safe to assume that whole vegetables cost more than pieces or cut-up vegetables.

Oil and Shortening

Fats are available in liquid or solidified form. In hospitals where the ratio of saturated to polyunsaturated fats is important, we have decided to use pure corn oil with isopropyl citrate added. We also use hydrogenated shortening for frying, which is made of cottonseed and soybean. Hydrogenation is the process of adding hydrogen to the unsaturated carbon bonds of the glycerides during the processing, which makes the fat have better texture, firmness, raises the melting point well over 400°F., makes it odorless, and tasteless. This process makes hydrogenated shortening good for frying. Solid hydrogenated shortening finds its application in the baking of pies, cakes, and other pastries where flaky crusts are needed.

The following specifications cover our total program on canned goods, staples, and other miscellaneous products for our freezing program.

Asparagus, Canned Cuts, USDA Grade C (Standard)—Fairly clear liquor, fairly free of defects; tender, normal flavor and odor. Cut spears, culturally bleached "white"—practically all white or yellow-white. Stalks or spears; medium spears, minimum score of 70. Minimum drained weight 60¼ oz. Approximate net weight 6 lb. 5 oz. 6/No. 10/case.

Beans, Green, Canned, Cut, USDA Grade B (Extra Standard)—Cut ¾ to 2¾ in. in length. Similar varietal characteristics, normal flavor and odor, very young and tender, clear liquor, uniform color, absence of defects, tender and not fibrous, practically uniform. Score 80 points. Minimum drained weight 63 oz.; Approximate net weight 6 lb. 5 oz. (Sieve No.2) 6/10/case.

Beans, Great Northern, USDA Grade A (Fancy)—25 lb. bag.

Beans, Wax, Canned, USDA Grade B (Extra Standard)—Cut ¾ to 2¾ in. in length. Similar varietal characteristics, normal flavor and odor, very young and tender, clear liquor, uniform color, absence of defects. Tender and not fibrous, fairly uniform. (Sieve No. 2) Minimum drained weight 63 oz., approximate net weight 6 lb. 5 oz. Score 80 points. 6/No. 10/case.

Beans, Lima, Canned Baby, (thin seeded), *USDA Grade A* (Fancy)—Normal flavor and odor, good color, free from defects; clear liquor, good character, similar varietal characteristics. 30/64 to 34/64 in. width, size small. Should be green (not chartreuse yellow) color, uniform size; score 90 points. Minimum drained weight 72 oz. Approximate net weight 6 lb. 9 Oz. 6/No. 10/case.

Beans, Oven Baked—Made from USDA Extra Fancy, without any hard foreign beans mixed with the Boston Baked, or New York, or Michigan hand picked, and closely screened, beans; beans when cooked are chewy but soft in the center. 6/No. 10/case.

Beans, Kidney Beans, Dark Red, USDA Grade A (Fancy)—Practically free from defects, good character; typically bright red color, reasonably rich, typical normal flavor, good consistency, score 85 points, net weight 110 oz. 6/No. 10/case.

Beans (Chick Peas) *USDA Grade A* (Fancy)—Practically free from defects (absence of loose skin or broken units); good character (firm, not mushy), typical normal color, reasonably rich, normal flavor. Score 85 points. Net weight 95 to 100 oz. 6/No. 10/case.

Bean Sprouts—(no specs)

Beets, Canned, Krinkle Cut Sliced, USDA Grade A (Fancy)—Practically no defects, tender and succulent; no objectionable flavor, not mushy or fibrous, good flavor, free from defects; no end pieces, medium size, 2 – 2½ in. diameter. Slices should not be more than 5/15 in. in thickness. Minimum score of 85. Minimum drained weight 69 oz.; approximate net weight 6 lb. 8 oz.; 6/No. 10/case.

Beets, Canned, Quartered, USDA Grade A—Practically uniform bright color and size, almost no defects, with min. score 85. No end pieces. Medium size, 2 to 2¼ in. diameter, min. dr. wt. 68 oz., 6/No. 10 cans to case, approx. net wt. If slices, not more than 5/15 in. in thickness. If whole, small in size, count 125 to 175, min. dr. wt. 60 oz., 6/No. 10 Cans/case, approx. net wt. 6 lb. 8 oz., no beets over 2¼ in. in diameter.

Carrots, Canned, Quartered, USDA Grade A—Similar varietal characteristics, normal flavor and odor; good color, no defects, tender, uniform size and shape. Score of 85 or better. Minimum drained weight 69 oz. Approx. net weight 6 lb. 8 oz. 6/No. 10/case.

Corn, Cream Style, Canned, USDA Grade B (Extra Standard)—Made from yellow sweet corn of similar variety, tender, good color, good consistency, no defects, very good flavor, odor, and tenderness. Kernels should be in early cream stage, corn should be 90 percent full. Should not be dull, curdling, watery, doughy, or with firm and hard kernels. Score 80. Net weight 6 lb. 6 oz. 6/No. 10/case.

Corn, Whole Kernel, Canned USDA Grade B (Extra Standard)—Made from yellow variety, reasonably tender, good color, good flavor, well cut, may lack brightness, fairly free from defects. Score 80. Net weight 72 oz.; 6/No. 10/case.

Chinese Vegetables, USDA Grade A Fancy—Made from bamboo shoots, bean sprouts, water chestnuts, pimientos. Net weight 112 oz. 6/No. 10/case.

Mushrooms, Canned, Stems and Pieces, USDA Grade C (Standard)—Fairly similar variety and uniform size; normal flavor and odor, good characteristics; fairly free from defects (no spots or damage, or stems over 1¼ in. long), score 70. Net weight 68 oz. 6/No. 10/case.

Okra, Whole Canned, USDA Grade A (Fancy)—Similar varietal characteristics, tender, practically whole, uniform color, small seeds, reasonably uniform size, not to exceed 3½ in. in length, clear, bright, thin gelatinous liquor, practically free from discoloration, not tough, free from inedible strings or tips, stems, and all other defects. Typical characteristic fresh okra flavor; head space from top of product to underside of lid must not exceed 10 percent of total inside height. Score 85 or better.

Olives, Green, Canned, USDA Grade A (Fancy)—Similar varietal, good typical texture, normal flavor, odor, uniform typical color, uniform size, absence of defects. Score of 90 points or better. Net weight 5 lb. 8 oz. per gallon: Minimum count 100 to 110. 4/1Gal/case.

Olives, Ripe Canned, USDA Grade A (Fancy)—Similar varietal characteristics, practically uniform color, size and symmetry, practically free from defects, firm but tender, fleshy texture; normal flavor and odor; matured olives; treated to remove bitterness, packed in brine. Minimum count 231; 4/1Gal/case.

Onions, Whole, Canned, USDA Grade A (Fancy)—Made from white onions of ¾ in. to 1 in. in diameter. Minimum count 100 to 120. 6/No. 10/case.

Onions, Dehydrated/Chopped—Made from early white globe or other to give a pungency Peale rating of no more than 97 reading, pack 2/15lb./case.

Onions, Dehydrated, Canned—Made of flaked dried onions from US No. 1 Bermuda onions, preferable if freeze dehydrated process used, free from diseased brown spots or off flavors or colors when reconstituted. 6/No.10/case.

Peas, Early June, Canned, USDA Grade B (Extra Standard)—Reasonably of similar varietal characteristics, normal flavor, very tender; neither mushy nor hard. Practically uniform in color, reasonably free from defects and materials such as pea pods or thistle buds, not more than 5 percent broken peas, liquor reasonably clear. Sieve No. 3. Net weight 6 lb. 9 oz. 6/No.10/case.

Pickles—Dill, Hamburger Slices, USDA Grade A, 4/1-gal.

Pickles—Cucumber, Sweet Sliced, USDA Grade A, 6/10/case.

Pickles—Dill, Hamburger Slices, Grade A, 5 gal. tins.

Pickles—Chip, Sweet, USDA Grade A, Fancy, 4/1 – gal./case.

Pickles—Relish, Sweet, USDA Grade A, Fancy, 4/1 – gal./case.

Pimientos, Pieces/Strips, USDA Grade A, Fancy—Area of each portion not less than 1 in. square, practically firm, fairly uniform in size, bright red color, practically free from defects, typical pimiento flavor. Minimum score 80 24/2½/case.

Potatoes, Dehydrated Slices, Idaho (Random Cut)—25 lb. or 30 lb. pack.

Potatoes, Sweet, Canned, Golden Yam, Whole, Packed, Solid or Dry Pack, USDA Grade A, Fancy—All should be of good color, uniform size or consistency, free from defects, good character, normal flavor and odor, score 85 or better. Net weight 4 lb. 8 oz. 6/No. 10/case.

Potato, Sweet, Canned Golden Yam, Whole, Vacuum or Water Pack, USDA Grade A , Fancy—Same as above except packed in water without additional optional ingredients such as syrup dextrose or dextri maltose or corn syrup.

Potato, White Instant Mashed—Made from USDA Grade A Fancy white potatoes of good color, free from defects, good texture, uniform. Score of 85 or better, which will pass, when reconstituted, a specific gravity of not more than 1.07. 6/No. 10/case.

Pumpkin, Canned, USDA Grade A Fancy—Clear and sound varieties of the firm shelled, golden fresh, fine, soft grained pumpkin pulp reduced to heavy consistency, uniform color throughout; smooth fine finish, free from seed particles, rind, or other defects. Typical flavor of well-ripened pumpkin. Minimum score 85. Net weight 8 lb. 10 oz. 6/No. 10/case.

Sauerkraut, Canned, USDA Grade A, Fancy—Light straw color, uniform shred (about 1/32 in. thick), practically free from defects and blemishes, firm, fine texture, well developed; typical sauerkraut flavor, minimum score 85. Net weight 5 lb. 6/No. 10/case.

Squash, Canned, USDA Grade A, Fancy—Fine, soft, thick consistency, uniform color and smooth finish, free from seeds, rind, fiber, etc.; good, ripe squash flavor. Net weight 6 lb. 13 oz. 6/No. 10/case.

Tomatoes, Canned, USDA Grade A, Fancy—Practically free from defects, normal tomato flavor and odor, 90 percent practically uniform tomato red color, without green surface area. 80 percent of tomatoes whole or almost whole, solid pack, drained weight not less than 66 percent of can capacity about 74 ¼ oz. 6/No. 10/case.

Tomatoes, Canned, USDA Grade C (Standard)—Small or large pieces with some whole tomatoes, fairly red, fairly free from defects, normal flavor, minimum score 60. Drained weight 50 percent minimum 54¾ oz. 6/No.10/case.

Tomato Paste, Canned, USDA Grade A, Fancy—Good red, ripe tomato color, practically free from defects, typically tomato paste flavor, minimum score 85, with 33 percent or more salt free tomato solids. Net weight 6 lb. 10 oz. 6/No. 10/case.

Tomato Paste, Vacuum or Water Pack, Canned USDA Grade A, Fancy—Same as above except packed without salt.

Tomato Puree, Canned, USDA Grade A, Fancy—Good red tomato color, practically free from defects, typical flavor, heavy concentration. 12 to 25 percent salt-free tomato solids, score 85 points. Net weight 6 lb. 10 oz. 6/No. 10/case.

Tomato Sauce, Canned, USDA Grade A, Fancy—Good red tomato color, practically free from defects, typical flavor and odor, not more than slight amount of minute particles of seeds, tomato peel, core material, or other similar defects, which do not materially affect the appearance of the product; free from scorched, bitter green tomato flavor or other objectionable flavor or odor. Score not less than 85. Net weight 6 lb. 9 oz. 6/No. 10/case.

Tomato Catsup, USDA Grade A (Fancy)—A good, red, ripe tomato color, of good consistency; only slight separation of free liquid allowed, smooth finish; practically free from specks, particles of seed, skin, core, etc. A clean, aromatic flavor.

SPECIFICATIONS FOR SALT FREE VEGETABLES (canned)

Salt Free Beets, Sliced, USDA Fancy—No added sodium, not more than 52 mg per 4 oz., 24/303/case.

Salt Free Peas, Early June, USDA Fancy—No added sodium, not more than 52 mg per 4 oz., 24/303/case.

Salt Free Tomatoes, Whole, USDA Fancy—No added sodium, not more than 52 mg per 4 oz., 24/303/case.

Salt Free Corn, Whole Kernel, USDA Fancy—No added sodium, not more than 52 mg per 4 oz., 24/303/case.

Salt Free Green Beans—Ditto Above.

Salt Free Carrots—Ditto.

Salt Free Peas and Carrots—Ditto.

SPECIFICATIONS FOR CANNED FRUITS

Apples, Canned-Sliced (more than four segments or quartered) *USDA Grade A Fancy*—Should be similar varietal characteristics with normal flavor and odor; good color, uniform size, practically free from defects; good character, score 85 points, unsweetened. 6/10/case.

Apples, Chips, US Grade C—Smaller pieces of apples preferably from York. West Coast Winesap and Spitzenberg apples to be used should retain practically all normal flavor and odor, practically irregular in size, color, ripeness, and possibly packed in a light syrup. Less than 16 Brix. 6/10/case.

Applesauce, Canned, USDA Grade A Fancy—Heavy consistency, forms mounds when stirred and poured on flat surface, uniform bright color, free from pink tinge or discoloring, finish may be grainy but not pasty or lumpy; practically no peel, or carpel tissue; distinct apple flavor, score not less than 85 points; packed in light syrup. 6/10/case.

Apricots, Canned, USDA Grade A Fancy—(preferably from Blenheim)— Fresh apricots, whole, peeled, unpitted, normal flavor, practically no defects, uniform, bright typical color, practically uniform size and symmetry. Minimum score of 75. No apricots with over 25 percent of a unit being light green allowed. Packed in heavy syrup. 21 Brix minimum. 35/40 count. 6/10/case.

Apricots, Canned, USDA Grade B: (preferably from Blenheim)—Whole, unpeeled, unpitted, reasonably almost uniform in color, size, flavor, and symmetry. No part of contents may have any objectionable flavor. Packed in heavy syrup. 21 Brix minimum. 55/70/count. 6/10/case.

Apricots, Halves, Canned, USDA Grade B: (preferably Blenheim)— Halves unpeeled, not off suture cuts allowed over ¼ of an inch. The weight of the largest halves is not to exceed by more than 65 percent the weight of the smallest half in a can. Almost uniform in color, size, and flavor, with no apricots over 25 percent of a unit allowed to be light green. Heavy syrup. 21 Brix minimum. 95 to 115 count. 6/10/case.

Apricots, Canned, USDA Grade B—Sliced, peeled, reasonably almost uniform in color, size, flavor, and symmetry, practically no apricots over 25 percent of a unit allowed to be light green. Heavy syrup. 21 Brix minimum. 200 to 250 count. 6/10/case.

Cranberries, Canned, USDA Grade A Fancy—Strained, good bright, dark red color; well-formed; good texture, firm, tender gel; practically free from defects, good tart flavor, good odor; no trace of caramelized flavor, score of 85 or better. 6/10/case.

Cherries, Red Pitted, Sour, Canned, USDA Grade A Fancy—Good, bright, typical color, no defects, good normal flavor, not over 5 percent less than 1/16 in. diameter. Packed in water with net weight of 4 lb. 10 oz. 6/10/case.

Cherries, Sweet, Canned, USDA Grade A Fancy—Royal Ann Cherries, Bing, Black Republican and Lambert, well-matured, bright color, practically uniform size, practically free from defects, thick fleshed, tender but not soft, normal flavor, and odor. Minimum score of 90 points. Packed in light syrup. 21 Brix minimum. 250 to 300 count. 6/10/case.

Fruit Cocktail, Canned, USDA Grade A Fancy—Practically free from defects, good color, firm and tender, good texture, normal flavor, minimum score 85. Proportion of fruit: minimum and maximum drained weight equal to 71.15 oz. (4 lb. 9½ oz.) as follows: 30 to 50 percent diced peaches; 25 to 45 percent diced pears; Hawaiian pineapple tidbits 6 to 16 percent of ½ in. cubes not over ¾ in. long; seedless grapes whole 6 to 20 percent, cherries 2 to 6 percent halves. Syrup density, 18 to 20 percent. 6/10/case.

Fruit Salad, Canned, USDA Grade A Fancy—Reasonably good color, practically free from defects and staining (from colored fruits added), each fruit practically uniform size, practically free from defects, tender, good texture, normal flavor, minimum and maximum drained weight equal to 64.5 oz. as follows: 24 to 40 percent yellow cling peaches (peeled and sliced); 18 to 30 percent apricots (peeled or unpeeled halves), 8 to 16 percent pears (sliced or wedge-shaped segments), 6 percent whole seedless grapes; 3 percent red maraschino cherries or grapes (whole, natural or artificially colored); packed in light syrup, minimum score of 85 points. 14 to 18 Brix minimum. 6/10/case.

Grapefruit, Canned, USDA Grade A Fancy—Properly matured fruit, segments separated, most of membrane, core, and seeds removed, packed in light syrup. Drained weight at least 58 percent capacity of can, 75 percent by weight, whole or almost whole segments, practically uniform, bright color, practically no defects, firm fleshy fruit, normal grapefruit flavor, minimum score of 90. 12/50 oz./cs.

Oranges, Mandarin, Canned, USDA Grade A Fancy—Whole sections, properly mature, segments separated, most of membrane, core, and seeds removed. There are no particles of skin in the can, and no dry or mushy segments. Imported from Formosa. The color, size, shape, and flavor closely related to US Tangerine, Packed in light syrup. 14 to 18 Brix minimum. 425 to 450 count, net weight 5 lb. 6/10/case.

Peaches, Yellow Cling, Halves, Canned, USDA Grade A Fancy—Peeled, uniform, good bright yellow or yellow orange, no green or oxidation tints.

Uniform size and shape; not more than 16 slices may be small size. Absence of defects, free from pit material and peel. Fairly fleshy, tender but firm, pit cavity soft, but no fraying or hardness or mushiness, and not more than one unit in a container of less than 20 units crushed or broken. Pack in light syrup. 14 to 18 Brix. Minimum score of 90. 35 to 40 count. 6/10/case.

Peaches, Yellow Cling, Halves, USDA Grade B Choice—Reasonably as above. Allowance of one crushed peach half in 4 cans and two ½-sq. in. or less blemishes in 4 cans, no part of contents may have any objectionable flavor. Minimum score of 75. Packed in light syrup. 35 to 40 count. 6/10/case.

Peaches, Yellow Cling, Slices, USDA Grade B Choice—Reasonably uniform in color, size, and shape as above. Reasonably free from pit material and peel, with an allowance of 2 to 3 broken slices; reasonably fleshy and tender, slightly firm or soft, with no more than slightly frayed edges. Maximum of 8 to 10 slices may be softer or firmer than balance of slices in a can. May not be mushy or rock hard. No part of contents may have objectionable flavor. Packed in light syrup. Minimum score of 75. 120 to 150 count. 14 to 19 Brix minimum, net drained weight 76 oz. 6/10/case.

Peaches, Freestone, Canned, Diced, or Irregular Size and Shapes, USDA Grade C Standard—Fairly uniform in color but variable in size and symmetry; fairly free from defects but may possess mechanical defects and not over ½ in. of peel per pound of contents or not more than one pit per 100 ounces; variable texture but not over 10 to 15 percent of mushy fruit. Normal flavor. Minimum score 60. Packed in slightly sweetened water. 14 to 19 Brix, net drained weight 69 oz. 6/10/case.

Pears, Bartlett Halves, Canned USDA Grade A Fancy (from Bartlett pears)—Practically free from defects, good character, normal flavor and odor, uniform color (white or yellow), none chalky; uniform size, free from damage and defects, ripe, tender, fleshy, no graininess or toughness, not mushy. Packed in light syrup. Minimum score of 90, 14 to 19 Brix minimum, 35 to 40 count, net drained weight 63 oz. 6/10/case.

Pears, Bartlett, Halves, Mixed Pieces of Irregular Sizes and Shape, USDA Grade C Solid Pack—Fairly good color; fairly free from defects; fairly good character with not over 10 to 15 percent of slices and diced pieces to be mushy; normal flavor and odor, packed in lightly sweetened water. 14 to 19 Brix, net drained weight 90 oz. 6/10/case.

Pineapple, Hawaiian Slices Whole, USDA Grade A Fancy—Practically uniform size and symmetry, practically free from defects, practically uniform, fleshy texture; normal flavor. Minimum score 90. Packed in light syrup. 14 to 19 Brix. 50 to 55 count, net drained weight 65 oz. 6/10/case.

Pineapple, Hawaiian Broken Slices, USDA Grade B—Reasonably as above; usually pieces of 3/8 in. thick and 3 1/8 in. diameter consisting of arc-shaped portions cut or broken from slices which portions are not uniform in size and shape. Minimum score 75. Packed in light syrup, net drained weight 65 ounces. 6/10/case.

Pineapple, Hawaiian Chunks, USDA Grade B—Reasonably as specified in slices, consisting of short, thick pieces cut from thick slices, or peeled, cored fruit; may or may not be symmetrical or uniform in shape and size with a thickness greater than ½ in. and a width greater than 9/16 in., but longest dimension not more than 1½ in. No complete mash of chunk allowable. Packed in slightly sweetened water, net drained weight 65 oz. 285 to 310 count. 6/10/case.

Pineapple, Hawaiian Crushed, USDA Grade B—Reasonably uniform color with white markings not noticeable, consisting of shredded or finely cut pieces of fruit flesh, with not more than 1¼ percent of the drained weight of the contents of the can consisting of fragments bearing blemishes such as brown spots, deep fruit eyes, peel, bruise, seed, excessive trimmings or deep gouges or abnormalities that it is possible to detect. Drained weight is not less than 63 percent of the net weight of contents of the container's net drained weight, 98 oz. Packed in slightly sweetened water. 10 to 14° Brix or less minimum. 6/105/case.

Plums, Prune, USDA Grade A Fancy—Whole, unpeeled and unpitted, practically free from defects, normal flavor and color, uniform size; good character, thick fleshed and tender, in heavy syrup 18 to 22° Brix min.

Applesauce, Canned USDA Grade A Fancy—Same as regular except instead of syrup, it is packed in water and has added artificial sweetening agents which include saccharin, sodium saccharin or a combination of both. Such packing medium may be thickened with pectin and may contain any mixture of organic salts or acids as flavor enhancing in a quantity not more than reasonably required for that purpose, and the label shall bear these ingredients. 24/303/case.

Apricot, Halves, USDA Grade A, Pitted and Peeled—Same specifications as regular halves, except packed in water with added sweetening agents as saccharin, sodium saccharin or combination of both and may be thickened with pectin and may contain any mixture of organic salts or acids as flavor enhancing in a quantity not more than reasonably required for that purpose, and the labels shall bear these ingredients. 24/303/case.

Cherries, Royal Anne, USDA Grade A—Same specifications as above. 24/303/case.

Fruit Cocktail—Same as above.

Fruits for Salad, USDA Grade A—Same specifications as regular except packed in water with added artificial sweetening agents as above. 24/303/case.

Grapefruit Sections, USDA Grade A—Same as above. 24/303/case.

Peaches, Yellow Cling, Sliced, USDA Grade B Choice—Same specifications as regular sliced, except packed in water with artificial sweetening agents as mentioned above.

Peaches, Yellow Cling, Halves, USDA Grade A Fancy—Same specifications as regular, except packed in water with artificial sweetening agents as above.

Pears, Bartlett, Halves, USDA Grade A Fancy—Same specifications as regular halves, except packed in water with added artificial sweetening agents as saccharin or sodium saccharin.

Pineapple, Hawaiian, Sliced, USDA Grade B Choice—Same specifications as regular sliced except packed in water with added artificial sweetening agents as saccharin or sodium saccharin.

Pineapple, Hawaiian Crushed—Same as above.

Plums, Prune, USDA Grade A Fancy—Same as regular except packed with water.

Prunes, Stewed, USDA Grade A Fancy— (preferably from Santa Clara Valley)—10 percent defects allowed from C to J; 4 percent from I and J, and 1 percent from J in the following:

Defect category:

A. Skins different color from black, blue–black, or reddish purple.
B. Flesh darker than Mirador Brown (golden red–yellow best).
C. Porous, woody, fibrous, immature air pockets in flesh
D. Fermentation damage
E. Growth cracks, splits, skin breaks, skin damage
F. Scab
G. Sunburn damage; dehydration damage
H. Insect injury or similar
I. Mold, insect infestations, dirt
J. Prunes affected by decay

Pie Cherries, Red Pitted Sour, USDA Grade A Fancy—Good, bright, typical color, no defects, good character, normal flavor, not over 5 percent less than 9/16 in. in diameter. Packed in light syrup, net weight shall be 4 lb. 6¼ oz. 6/10/case.

STANDARDS OF QUALITY FOR FRUIT JUICES

Apple Juice, USDA Grade A Fancy—Clarified, unsweetened, bright color (no dull or off color); free of defects (apple pulp, particles, seeds, residue, or pulp coagulation) not less than 12.5°Brix, not less than 0.4 percent or more than 0.65 percent malonic acid, normal apple juice flavor (no off flavor, oxidized, astringent, disagreeable odor). 12 to 46 oz./case.

Apple Cherry Juice, USDA Grade A Fancy—Clarified, unsweetened, good, bright color (no dull or off color); free of defects (apple or cherry pulp) particles, seeds, residue, or pulp coagulation. No off flavor, oxidized, astringent or disagreeable odor.

Apricot Juice or Nectar, Canned, Unsweetened, USDA Grade A Fancy— Even normal color not excessively pale yellow, light, bright green, or brown. Free from particles, seeds, pits, or other coarse or hard substances capable of being avoided by good canning practices. Fruit ingredient should not be less than 35 percent by weight of the finished food, with a Brix value of 14.2°. 12/46 oz./case.

Cranberry Juice Cocktail, USDA Grade A Fancy—Made from Cranberry juice and concentrated cranberry juice extracted from mature, well-colored cranberries. Contains not less than 25 percent cranberry juice with not less than 0.55 gm per 100 mg of citric anhydrous acid, with vitamin C added in quantities of not less than 30 mg and not more than 60 mg. Not less than 14 to 16° Brix. 12/32 oz./case.

Grape Juice, Unsweetened, Canned, USDA Grade A Fancy—Made from Concord or Catawba; very good color, free from defects, no coagulation, very good flavors. 15° Brix minimum. Score of 85, net weight 46 oz. 12/46 oz./case.

Grapefruit Juice, Canned, USDA Grade A Fancy—Unsweetened, very good color, no coagulation, free from defects. Score of 85, net weight 46 oz. 12/46 oz./case.

Orange Juice, Canned, Florida, USDA Grade A Fancy—Unsweetened, very good color, no coagulation; free from defects, very good flavor, added unfermented juice not more than 10 percent by volume, no seeds (except embryonic seeds that cannot be separated by good manufacturing practices); orange oil and pulp may be adjusted in accordance with good manufacturing practices. Not less than 10° Brix minimum. 12/46 oz./case.

Orange Juice Drink, Canned, Instant, Dried—Obtained from one or more of orange juice constituents specified in orange juice; sealed and dried in containers to prevent spoilage, will include optional sweetening ingredients as sugar, or invert sugar syrup, or dextrose, or dried corn syrup, with orange oil or essence recovered during the concentration of orange juice and acidifiers as lemon citric, malic or fumaric acid, and to which vitamin C is added in quantities not less than 30 mg or more than 60 mg in 4 fluid ounces of finished reconstituted drink; may be colored as long as it conforms with color additives section of Federal Food and Drug and Cosmetic Act, and may contain sodium benzoate and ascorbic acid within the minimum content as specified in the preservative section of the law.

Pineapple Juice, Canned, USDA Grade A Fancy—Unsweetened, very good color; free from defects, very good flavor, not more than 1.35 mg of anhydrous citric acid per 100 ml of juice, not less than 10.5° Brix soluble solid content, and a fill of not less than 90 percent of total capacity of the container. With vitamin C added in quantities not less than 30 mg and not more than 60 mg in each 4 fluid oz. Scores 85. 12/46 oz./case.

Pineapple Juice, Canned, USDA Grade C (Standard)—Fairly as above, good flavor, same specifications with score 70. Net weight 46 oz. 12/46 oz./case.

Prune Juice, Canned, USDA Grade A Fancy—Good color, free from defects, good flavor, contains not less than 18.5 percent by weight of water soluble solids extracted from dried prunes. Vitamin C added in quantities not less than 30 mg and not more than 50 mg in 6 fluid ounces with honey of not less or more than 2 to 3 percent.

Tomato Juice, Canned, USDA Grade A Fancy—Ripe tomato color, good consistency, typical ripe tomato flavor, no reddish brown color, seed pieces, skin, specks, poor flavor. Score 85. Wt. 46 oz., 12/46 oz./case.

Tomato Juice, Canned, USDA Grade C (Standard)—Fairly as above. Avoids reddish brown color, poor flavor, and does not contain seed pieces, skin, specks. Score 70. Net weight 46 oz. 12/46 oz./case.

Tomato Juice, Canned, USDA Grade A Fancy—Same specs as regular except packed without salt or any sodium derivative and not exceeding the preservative additives section of Food and Drug Act. Net weight 46 oz. 12/46 oz./case.

V-8 Juice—12/46 oz./case.

OTHER PRODUCTS AND STAPLES USED FOR FREEZING
Barley w/Beef Soup, USDA No. 1 Specifications, 12/50 oz./cs.
Beef Noodle Soup, USDA No. 1 Specs., 12/50 oz./cs.
Cream of Celery, USDA No. 1 Specs., 12/50 oz./cs.
Cream of Chicken, USDA No. 1 Specs., 12/50 oz./cs.
Cream of Mushroom Soup, USDA No. 1, 12/46 oz./cs. 1 to 1 concentrate
Chicken Noodle, USDA No. 1 Specs., 12/46 oz./cs.
Chicken Noodle, Lipton Dehydrated, 6/10/cs.
Tomato Soup, USDA No. 1 Specs., 1 to 1 concentrate, 12/46 oz./cs.
Vegetable Soup, USDA No. 1 Specs., 12/50 oz./cs.
Pureed Applesauce, no Added Sugar or not more than 52 mg sodium per 4 oz.,
    USDA Fancy, 17 oz., 12/303/cs.
Ditto, Pureed Apricots
Ditto, Pureed Peaches
Pureed Pears, no added sugar or not more than 52 mg. sodium per 4 oz.,
    USDA Fancy, 17 oz., 12/303/cs.

Ditto, Pureed Asparagus

Ditto, Pureed Beets

Ditto, Pureed Carrots

Ditto, Pureed Green Beans

Ditto, Pureed Peas

Ditto, Pureed Beef, 14 oz.

Ditto, Pureed Pork, 14 oz.

Ditto, Pureed Veal, 14 oz.

Baby Strained Applesauce, minimum levels of Sodium, USDA Grade A
  Fancy, 24/4½ oz./cs.

Ditto, Apricots

Ditto, Peaches, 24/4 oz./cs.

Ditto, Pears

Ditto, Beets

Ditto, Carrots

Ditto, Peas

Ditto, Green Beans

Ditto, Beef

Ditto, Lamb

Ditto, Pork

Ditto, Veal

Raisins, Dried, Seedless, USDA Grade B Choice, 30 lb./box

Rice, Converted, Long Grain, US No. 1 Fancy, Uncle Ben's, 25 lb. bag

Kurly Roni, Minimum 5.5 percent Egg Content, 10 lb./boxes

Macaroni Shells, Durum Wheat, Min. 5.5 percent Egg Content, 10 lb./boxes

Elbow Macaroni, Durum Wheat, Min. 5.5 percent Egg Content, 10 lb./boxes

Egg Noodles, Durum Wheat, Min. 5.5 percent Egg Content, Borad,
  10 lb./boxes.

Spaghetti Noodles, 100 percent Durum Wheat, Min. 5.5 percent Egg Content,
  Long Length, 20 lb./boxes

Lasagna Noodles, 100 percent Durum Wheat, Min,. 5.5 percent Egg Content,
  Medium, 10 lb./boxes

Cream of Rye, Semolina, 18/1 lb./cs

Farina, Semolina, 5 lb./bag

Malt O Meal, 12/24 oz./cs

Pettijohns, 12/14 oz/cs

Rolled Oats, Quick Cooking, Purity, 12/42 oz/cs

Pablum Barley, Mead Johnson, 12/8 oz/cs

Pablum Oatmeal, Mead Johnson, 12/16 oz/cs

Pablum Rice, Mead Johnson, 12/8 oz/cs

Rice Krispies, Kellogg, 24/13 oz/cs

Cream of Wheat, 12/28 oz/cs
Cocoanut, fresh, shredded, 10 lb. plastic bag, sealed/carton
Walnuts, shelled, US Grade C, no crumbs, 5 lb. box
Flour, enriched, patent, 50 lb. bag, Best Bakers Special
Crackers, Salt Free, not more than 10 mg sodium, indiv., 1/360/cs.
Chocolate, Semi-Sweet Chips, Blue Ribbon, 10 lb/ctn
Chocolate Syrup, Hersheys, 6/No. 10/cs
Cocoa, 23 percent Plus Cocoa Butter, Bakers, 6/5 lb/cs
Baking Soda, 24/1 lb/cs
Baking Powder, Calumet Double Action, 4/10 lb./cs
Cornstarch, 24/1 lb/cs
Vinegar Cider, Min. 4 percent Acetic Acid, 45 Grain, 4/1 gal/cs
Syrup, corn, dark, Karo, Blue Label, 12/5 lb/cs
Syrup, corn, white Karo, Red Label, 24 pts/cs
Peanut Butter, cream style, 6/3 lb/cs
Devils Food Cake Mix, Pillsbury or Betty Crocker, 6/5 lb/cs
Gingerbread Mix, Pillsbury or Betty Crocker, 6/5 lg/cs
Lemon-Gold Cake Mix, Pillsbury or Betty Crocker, 6/5 lb/cs
Spice Cake Mix, Pillsbury or Betty Crocker, 6/5 lb/cs
White Cake Mix, Pillsbury or Betty Crocker, 6/5 lg/cs
Egg Custard Mix, Delmark, No Baking Variety, 6/3¾ lb/cs
Cherry Pie Filling, USDA Grade A Cherries, 6/No. 10/cs
Blueberry Pie Filling, USDA Grade A Berries, 6/No. 10/cs
Pancake Mix, Buttermilk, Pillsbury, 12/2 lb/cs
Evaporated Milk, unsweetened, Carnation Vit. D Added, 48/14 ½ oz/cs
Honey, light amber, USDA Grade B Choice, 6/5 lg/cs
Salt, iodized, 1 percent carbonate or magnesium, Morton, 25 lb bag
Salt, iodized, 100 lb. sack
Sugar, granulated, 99 percent Sucrose from beet sug., Reg. Grind, 100 lb. sack
Sugar, brown, golden type, 2 B cane soft, 25 lb. bag
Sugar, powdered, std., 25 lb. bag
Soup Base, *low sodium*
Clear Beef Bouillon, instant, granulated
Roast Beef Gravy Mix, clear
Aromat, ½ lb. can
Consomme, Beef, double, 12/2 lb.
Kitchen Bouquet, 1 gal. size
Mustard, prepared, yellow, 4/1 gal/case
Horseradish, 12/1 qt/cs
Tabasco Sauce, McIlhenys, 12 oz btl
Soy Sauce, La Choy, 4/1 gal/cs

Worcertershire Sauce, 4/1 gal/cs

Cooking Wine, sherry, 12/24 oz

Cooking Wine, Claret, 12/12 oz

Lemon Juice, Real, qt. 4/1 gal/cs

Chopped Diced Chives, 12/2½ lb./cs

Bac-O-Bits, 6/22 oz/cs

Strawberry Jam, Home Brand, 6/4 lb./cs

Raspberry Jam, Staleys, 6/4 lb./cs

Grape Jelly, 6/4 lb./cs

Waffle Syrup, Staleys, 4/1 gal/cs

Parmesan Cheese, grated, 1 lb cans

Parmesan Cheese, grated, 5 lb cans

Catsup, USDA Grade A, pkd, in paper foil, cellophane, 200/½ oz/cs

Tunafish, white albacore, US No. 1, solid in water, 6/4 lb/cs

Honey, light amber, USDA Grade B, Choice, ½ oz., 200/cs

Jelly, Apple, Pure, USDA Fancy, 6/4 lb/cs

Dried Egg, 6/10/cs

Powdered Eggs, 32 eggs/1 lb., 25 lb./can

Marshmallows, 12/1 lb./box

Gelatin, plain, Knox or equal, 12/1 lb/cs

Pudding, choc, ind. portions, LOL

Ditto, Butterscotch

Ditto, Vanilla

Gelatin (Jello) Dessert Powder, lemon, orange, lime, strawberry, raspberry, cherry, gel strength take at least 32 g's. Gelatin used to meet U.S. Government specs for bloom strength of 250 to 290 gelometers, 50 lb. drums

Ditto above, 6/4½ lb. pkg/cs

Gelatin dessert powder, instant lime, lemon, black cherry, orange, strawberry, 50 lb. drums

D'Zerta, Gen. Foods, lime, lemon, raspberry, orange, strawberry, 50 lb. drums

Danish Junket Dessert, strawberry flavor 12/1 lb.

Danish Junket Dessert, currant-raspberry flavor, 12/1 lb.

Dietetic Gelatin Dessert, sugar free, low sodium, no sugar or cyclamates, 12/3½ oz/env/box, lime

Ditto, lemon

Ditto, cherry

Ditto, strawberry

Ditto, raspberry

Salad Dressing, Homogenized, egg content, 4/1 gal/cs, Gedney, Cuisine or equal

Salad Dressing, 4 gal carton or plastic tub
Corn Oil, pure with added isopropyl citrate, 5 gal can
French Dressing, Gedney or equal, 4/1 gal/cs

Carefully written specifications, a well-evolved plan for receiving and storing ingredients of all kinds in a controlled set-up, and a quality control system combining taste tests with product inspection testing at all key points are the basis of effective product control.

19

Equipment Control

Factors to consider in setting up controls that assure maximum returns for equipment investment include production scheduling, sanitizing of equipment, and preventive maintenance.

Production scheduling control should produce the following results:

1. A maximum 80 percent to 90 percent utilization of equipment capacity.

2. A minimum of overlapping products in a piece of equipment, thus minimizing forced delays and frequent clean-up periods.

3. A minimum holding time of products before they go to blast chill or freezer.

4. A minimum of byproducts, such as oil and grease, which are difficult to store and hold if not used 100 percent at one time.

5. A minimum of overlapping in the arrival of foods at the assembly line at the same time.

Forms that have been effective in achieving required production scheduling control are reproduced here.

Production Schedule—Salisbury Steak Pre-Plate and Bulk Pack

Mid 11 12 1 2 3 4 5 6 7 8 9 10 11 12 Noon 1 2 3 4 5 6

Salisbury Steaks (3 oz.) 17,600
Broiler—2200/Hour
Pre-Plate: 8800 3 oz. Portions
440–5 Lb. Bulk Packs of Salisbury Steak with Mushroom Gravy
Bulk Pack 440—20 oz. Each Pack

Mushroom Gravy, (1 oz.) 1100 Lbs.
Steam–Jacketed Kettle
Pre-Plate: 8800 1 oz. Portions

Pre-Peeled Quartered Potatoes, (3 oz.) 3300 Lbs.
2 Jet Steamers & 3 Conventional Steamers 615 Lb./Hour
Pre-Plate: 1650 Lb. (8800 3 oz. Portions)
330–5 Lb. Bulk Packs

Buttered Mixed Vegetable (2 oz.)
No Cooking Required for Pre-Plates
Pre-Plate: 1100 Lb. (8800 2 oz. Portions)

Liquid Margarine 275# From Dairy Cooler
Dispense 1 tsp. over Potato and 1 tsp. over Vegetable
Bulk Pack 4 oz. for Each of 330 Bulk Packs
46 Lb. 8800 Portions of 1 tsp.

Chopped Parsley
46 Lbs.—2¼ oz. Per Bulk Pack

All raw foods will be weighed, tagged, and recorded the day before production by Ingredient Control so that production may begin immediately the following day.

Equipment Utilization and Workload Control

Task	Equipment Data	Date	Recipe Code	Portion Unit	Class	Min. Units	Units Day	Min. Day	% Utilization per 6 hr.
11–1	Tilting Braising Pan 60 gallon electric	12/6	3335	Pt	Ck	.50	500	250	60%
		12/7	4680	Pt	Ck	.71	453	322	70%
		12/8	3940	Pt	Ck	.42	400	168	30%
		12/9	3660	Pt	Ck	.80	120	106	20%
		12/10	4000	Pt	Ck	.60	300	180	50%
11–2	Broiler	12/6	6231	Pt	Ck	.10	50	5	1%
		12/7	5842	Pt	Ck	.15	65	10	3%
		12/8	6200	Pt	Ck	.30	180	54	15%
		12/9	6111	Pt	Ck	.65	400	260	72%
		12/10	6427	Pt	Ck	.20	150	30	83%

*Minutes per day of the processing of items in the TILTING BRAISING PAN also can be used to calculate the standard hours spent by the cook per patient day as follows:

TOTAL MINUTES/WEEK	HRS/PATIENT DAY
Cook—16.5	.018
No. Pt. Days—900	

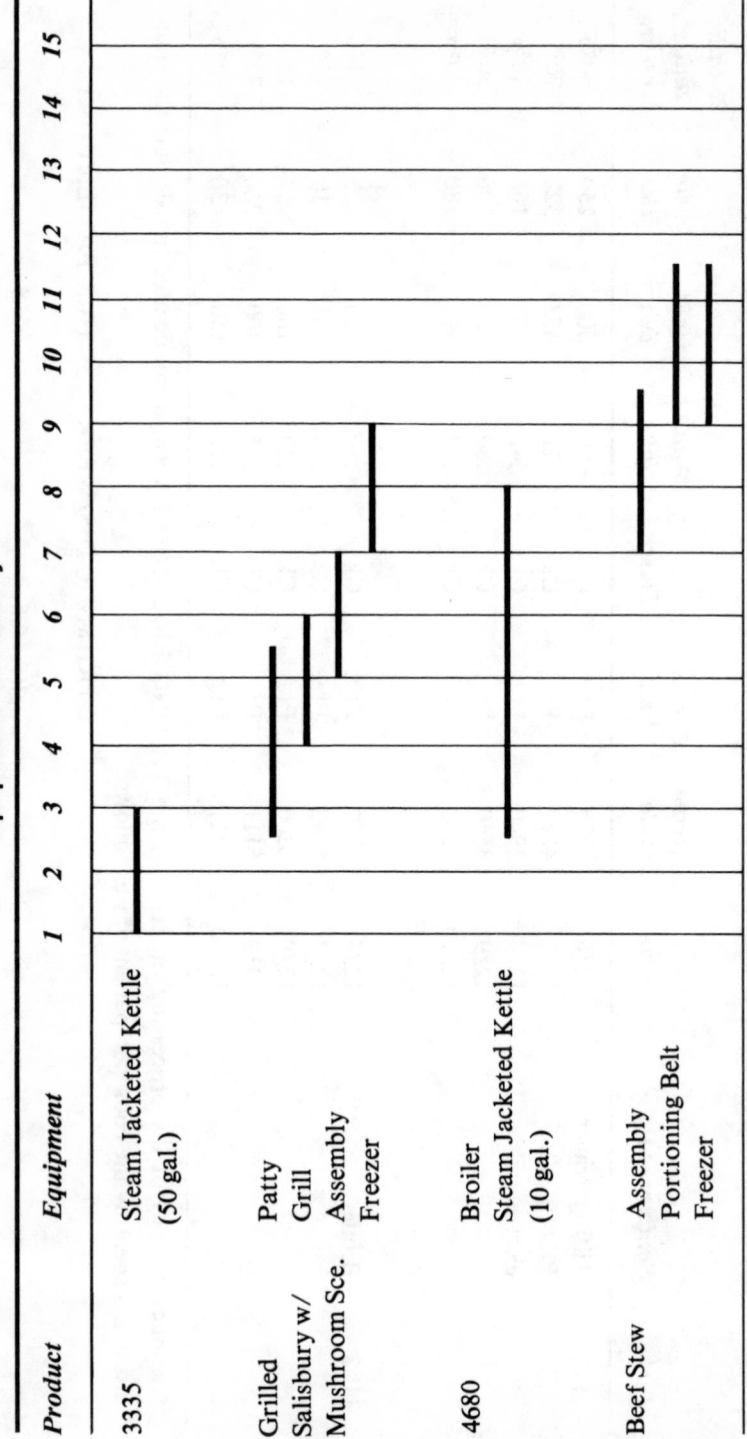

Equipment Availability

Since the gravy is done in the 50 gallon kettle, there is no overlapping in the 100 gallon steam jacketed kettle.

In production, it is important that National Sanitation Foundation codes are an integral part of equipment specifications. Design and placement of equipment should meet not only NSF, but Underwriters' Laboratories standards as well.

Equipment must be easily sanitized, smooth, and free from open seams, cracks, exposed junctions, and sharp corners. This equipment should be placed so that it is accessibile for cleaning around and under, and so inspection is simple. Portable equipment is desirable, but all moving parts must be equipped with guards or casings.

Flat surfaces that rest directly on the floor should be scribed to the surface with a mastic or cement to seal against vermin. Screens and electro–magnetized panels at all receiving and distributing docks will keep flies and other insects away.

A preventive maintenance program for equipment should be developed from the data collected on forms described below and reproduced on the following pages.

1. Preventive maintenance equipment records that give both stocking specifications of spare parts and a record of activity and frequency of repair.

2. A weekly preventive maintenance checklist (see page 335) should be prepared by the maintenance staff. This is routinely done from Monday through Saturday, either night or day.

Centralized Sanitizing

A centralized sanitizing system was designed for the Hennepin County Medical Center Central Food Preparation facility. There are approximately 10 hose stations which are 50 feet in length. Central control of the sanitizing detergent insures a good bacteriological reduction in each area.

An efficient, modern dishwashing system handles the dishes and ware.

All refrigerators and freezers have an alarm buzzer that is activated when temperatures rise above a certain level. The system immediately alerts personnel to report the condition.

Returns on equipment investment that make a blast freezing system cost effective are determined by the controls that are implemented. Productivity is improved when full use of equipment is assured through proper scheduling and maintenance.

Equipment Data Correction Sheet
Preventive Maintenance
Equipment Records

Equipment Description _____
Manufacturer _____
Model Number _____ Serial Number _____ Instal. Date _____
Vendor _____
Contractor _____
Equipment Cost _____
Installation Cost _____
Purchase Order Number _____

Specifications: *Spare Parts to Stock:*

Volt Amp. _____   1. _____

Phase _____   2. _____

H.P. _____   3. _____

R.P.M. _____   4. _____

Belt _____   5. _____

Bearing _____   6. _____

Drive _____   7. _____

Filter _____   8. _____

Lubricant _____   9. _____

Capacity _____   10. _____

Preventive Maintenance (Activity & Frequency)   *Time*   *Code*

1 _____
2 _____
3 _____
4 _____
5 _____
6 _____
7 _____
8 _____
9 _____
10 _____
11 _____

Location Code
Room Code
Equip. Code

WEEKLY PREVENTIVE MAINTENANCE CHECKLIST

Week of _____ to _____

Name_____

P.M. Number	Item Description	P. M. Activity Codes	Weekly Frequency	Day of Week Circle When Completed	In
200	Air Compressor	I03 Fan Belts C05 Motor L02 Change Oil	7	S M T W T F S	
				S M T W T F S	
				S M T W T F S	
				S M T W T F S	
				S M T W T F S	
				S M T W T F S	
				S M T W T F S	
				S M T W T F S	

PART 4

System Testing

20

Cost Comparison and Analysis of Three Foodservice Systems

SYSTEMS DEFINED

Conventional (Preparation for Immediate Service), *Ready Foods* (Preparation, Chilling, and Freezing for Inventory) and *Total Convenience* (Purchase of Ready-to-Eat or Reheat Foods from Vendor)

While these cost comparisons were made in a health care institution, the principles used can be effectively applied to many other types of foodservice operations.

During the past two decades the number of health institutions has increased greatly. And with every new hospital or nursing home there is a commensurate growth in foodservice activities.

Unfortunately, the status quo of low productivity and inefficient operation has resulted in increasing costs for each meal produced and served. During the 1970's, a slow but progressive change has been taking place in the health care industry; every service department in a hospital has made a continuous effort to lower costs.

Foodservice is beset with many complex problems such as rising food costs, food shortages, union demands for increased wages and benefits and, not least, the changing food habits of the customers. Attempts have been made to develop new methods of charging patients or customers to arrive at a break-even cost. Some innovative operators have tried to absorb increasing labor costs through automated food production and/or tray assembly systems.

Where do we, as operators, start on the problem? All kinds of cost analyses have been used to justify the changes from conventional to total convenience, or from conventional to a mixed system, or from conventional to cook-chill and freeze systems.

A systems analysis approach is recommended in planning the type of foodservice system to meet the objectives determined by management.

In a sophisticated health care foodservice system, there are 11 basic sub-systems:

Menu Planning

Purchasing

Receiving and Storage

Ingredient Control

Advance Pre-preparation

Production and Freezing or Chilling

Thawing, Portioning, Tray Assembly

Transportation and Distribution

Holding and Staging

Service in Galleys

Warewashing and Sanitation

We have a choice between three basic systems often described as 1) convenience food system, 2) conventional food system, and 3) Ready Foods System. To some design consultants there are many hybrids of these three. They are:

Conventional

Conventional-Convenience

Total Convenience

Ready Foods

Cook and Chill

Satellite

Catered

Shared Facilities

As for service systems there are:

Ware Kitchens

Match-A-Tray Carts

Combined Hot and Cold Food Cart

Trayveyors

Pellet System

Insulated Component System

Insulated Trays

Disposables

Nursing Unit Pantries

Developing a customer or patient profile in terms of menu preferences cannot be done overnight. There are regional preferences, food idiosyncracies, likes and dislikes, and food faddism to consider. At Hennepin County Medical Center, a computerized patient and cafeteria questionnaire was developed, (See pages 258-267.) This questionnaire was distributed on a random sampling, and the returns monitored individually by dietetic trainees. Based on these surveys, a menu was designed that almost automatically incorporates low cost items. We discovered our patients and customers liked fish and chicken and a variety of salads. Therefore an effort was made to include fish, chicken, and cheese in the menu at least five times a week as part of our selective cycle menu.

Role of Ingredient Room in Ready Foods System

The advent of a mass feeding, central preparation facility made it possible to demonstrate the advantages of a central ingredient room. The foodservice director at Ford Motor Company in Dearborn, Michigan, once compared cost and quality performance of company-operated units with catered foodservice operations within the company. He reaffirmed a fact generally agreed upon—the skilled chef and first cooks are the highest labor cost in the kitchen. Moreover, quality control was a problem because the chef in each unit tried to outdo the others by adding a pinch here and there to the company's good set of recipes.

Quality control is one of the most important reasons our present operation installed an ingredient control room as soon as it was feasible. We elected to purchase convenience desserts and free up the bakery area for this room. After purchasing special equipment, such as highly efficient scales, polyethylene bags, plastic containers, and a locked cabinet for expensive spices and staples, we were on our way to a manually operated ingredient control system. Adequate preparation of our production and service personnel paved the way towards a sound implementation.

PURCHASING

The type of menu design determines the complexity of purchasing procedures in any system. To a person responsible for purchasing in a selective, 3–week cycle menu, it would seem that function in a total convenience food system is simple and easy. But if purchasing includes development of specifications based on product testing and evaluation, this assumption is erroneous. Without rigid product specifications, any convenience food system will fail in its objective of serving quality foods. One must work hard to develop specifications for frozen entrees and desserts because there are no USDA or FDA regulations governing frozen food processors, though some of these component items are covered under the Meat and Poultry Products Act. Testing available products to arrive at acceptable items has been an agonizing experience. To meet the requirements of our future a la carte menu with a daily special item on a nine day cycle, we have had to go to at least 20 frozen food processors for entrees. It would have been simple to purchase all of the entrees from one or two processors. This would simplify our purchase orders, invoices, etc., and give us access to mass purchasing advantages with discounts on truckload shipments. But, the fact is that the availability of acceptable products differs from one processor to another, making it very difficult to do the right job of purchasing.

In a convenience food system, there is still minimal preparation of items such as breakfast cereals, eggs, and special diet items that needs to be done. For these, the purchasing function exists as in a conventional food system. Since there is a tight schedule between delivery, preparation, and service, purchasing becomes involved with daily pressures in meeting deadlines. Whereas in a cook–chill and freeze system, the purchasing of a few items for preparation into an inventory is less chaotic, and there is less time pressure. In a Ready Foods System, the purchasing of a few items in larger quantities results in discounts which affects overall food costs. It has been my experience that this affects the negotiation position with suppliers, especially in a larger hospital. Making use of seasonal food items which are low cost during certain periods makes the Ready Foods System advantageous in that you can hoard these items for later use.

RECEIVING

With the advent of frozen convenience foods such as whipped toppings, vegetables and fruit, and other items used in a conventional system, many hospitals found they had insufficient freezer space. In an almost total convenience food system, the receiving clerk has a greater problem in juggling delivery schedules with the available freezer space. In a Ready Foods System, the greatest economy is achieved when seasonal items are purchased and delivered to the freezer or dry storage when there is a good buy on these items.

Because of the nature and complexity of the items to be prepared immediately prior to serving in a conventional system, the delivery schedule is very tight and close. The quantity needed for both the patient and the cafeteria is only approximate. These estimates are sometimes difficult to forecast. The success of a good receiving clerk in any system depends on his problem solving and decision making when commodities are substituted, exchanged, and short-ordered or back-ordered for three months. So not only is the accuracy of estimated needs important, but the intricate and delicate problems associated with delivery and receiving as well.

STORAGE AND INVENTORY

From studies made at Veterans' Hospitals in West Haven, Connecticut, and Gainesville, Florida, it was learned that total space allocations for receiving, storage, and ingredient control areas differ very little between a conventional system and the almost total convenience food system!

The storeroom clerk must view product rotation as one of his important responsibilities regardless of the system. One can compare the systems by the varying degrees of control he has to master. In a conventional food system, the product rotation of frozen convenience entrees, potatoes, and other processed items is very delicate during the tempering stages. Time and temperature control is a must for frozen foods. Perishability and quality deterioration of these items needs to be watched closely. Food remaining at a thawed state for over three days is susceptible both to increased microbial growth and the "burning" dehydration effect of prolonged refrigeration that causes the items to be mushy looking.

Management has a responsibility to maintain close control over refrigerator and freezer temperatures in all systems. With a large inventory of frozen prepared foods, lack of temperature control could bring about a catastrophe.

INGREDIENT CONTROL

The key to successful food preparation is the mastery of the central nucleus of the kitchen—ingredient control. Anyone not thoroughly convinced of the merits of a central ingredient control room, should devote more time to studying it.

Production control is achieved through a simple change into an ingredient control system. The reason most hospitals have had a cost savings in foodservice after a computer assisted management system has been implemented is due to the installation of a standardized recipe file and a central ingredient room.

There is just no quality control in conventional or Ready Foods Systems if the cook is given the opportunity to change recipes on his own and manipulate the quantity of items that go into his recipes. There are too many times when these judgements depend on his mood that day.

The main advantage of conventional, and cook-chill, and freeze combination systems is the complete control of the recipes by the dietitians. This control gives them the flexibility to program nutritional specifications. Some dietitians feel that the protein content of each entree portion has to be consistent and uniform to assure that patients are getting their allowance of protein. This uniformity is even more important when the specific needs of patients on special diets can be met only by manipulating the standard recipes to achieve nutritional control.

HOT AND COLD FOOD PRODUCTION

One of the major differences between the three food production systems is found in the areas of production employee costs. The Veterans' Hospital studies mentioned earlier illustrate how the number of employees assigned to processing and preparation differ in a convenience food system. About 5 percent of the total time required to prepare and serve a meal in a general hospital is spent in food processing and preparation as contrasted to 13 percent in a conventional system. Unfortunately, a total convenience system is difficult to implement. One of the hindrances to maximum reduction in cooking staff is the preparation still necessary for hot cereals and breakfast items such as scrambled, poached, and fried eggs, and pancakes. Freezing cereals results in a mush or a thick scum which is difficult to reconstitute, and it is difficult to find acceptable versions of the other items. The same conditions exist, of course, in a cook-chill-freeze system where these same items need to be prepared on premise. And there are many other items that do not lend themselves to the frozen convenience concept such as grilled sandwiches, meats without gravy or glaze due to special dietary restrictions, some pre-prepared potatoes, and pasta. At this point, it is difficult to forecast how soon we can arrive at a total convenience food system. The unavailability of a good variety of special diet items makes it impractical at this time.

Because a conventional food system requires continuous small scale production, the disadvantages are many. First, the production requirements necessitate cooks at all three meals. This type of staffing results in high and low peaks of productivity. During the low peaks, as serving and cleaning occur, there is also a loss in preparation. There is wastage of food from over-ordering or under-ordering. One of the problems we have in hospital foodservice is not being able to forecast how many patients are eating and how many are to be away from their rooms for tests at each meal.

In a convenience food system payroll savings from reduction of the cooking staff must equal or offset the increase in food cost that results from purchasing items that have built-in labor. A major advantage in purchasing this "built-in" labor is that most frozen food processors can afford highly skilled chefs, whereas a small hospital cannot. I wonder, though, whether it is worth the additional cost if the items are too fancy or elaborate for a patient's taste buds. Besides, due to regional preferences certain dishes, such as shrimp creole made in San Francisco, might not be the right recipe for patients from New Orleans, or vice versa.

Several foodservice directors swear they are never going back to conventional production. I always ask "why?" One reason they give is the improvement in employee morale with the absence of the "time schedule crisis" in a conventional system. This improved morale has been reflected in reduced turnover rate.

In a cook-chill and freeze system, the advantages of a convenience food system—fewer crises in meeting deadlines, improved quality control, and flexibility in meeting patient needs—will also accrue. Of course, the problems will still be there if the hospital is not able to find the talent necessary to make the system work. Since the production in a ready foods system is on a large scale, there will be problems of greater magnitude if quality control and testing are not done by a skillful, competent staff. Cost economy is achieved through a maximum utilization of both the staff and the equipment. Because of inherent good utilization, productivity, measured in meals per manhour, increases at a rate reflecting the amount of inventory desired. Millrose and Glew[1] concluded that a facility programmed to produce 700 meals per day in a conventional system can produce more than 2000 meals per day in a cook-freeze system with only the addition of a blast freezer, freezer storage facilities, and packaging equipment.

It is logical that the use of pre-prepared food will reduce processing time. The study done by Zolber and Donaldson[2] showed there is no direct relationship between the percentage of foods used in each state and either total or direct labor time, processing time, or delay time. They concluded that there was no significant shift in re-allocation of work functions and no direct relationship between the processed state of the purchased food and time spent in processing in the institution.

FREEZING, CHILLING, THAWING, AND STAGING

In a conventional food system, these functions do not exist. But the heart of a conventional system lies in the control of keeping hot foods hot and cold foods cold within a definite schedule. Distribution of food in this system is a function of time and temperature. It is difficult to estimate how fast trays are distributed to patients by the nursing or foodservice personnel. The tight scheduling required from the time materials are received to the time patients receive their trays makes the conventional system a difficult one to implement and control.

In a convenience food system, the person in charge of thawing and staging has a key role in making the system work. Also, the receiving clerk must know the quality specifications and proper method of handling perishable products.

In a Ready Foods System, freezing and chilling are the two processes that have been added to a conventional food system. As with the convenience system, more product research and development data is needed on freezing techniques to make it successful. The advantage of a Ready Foods System over a convenience food system is that recipes that are well liked in your institution can be converted easily to your own convenience food. A lack of standardized recipes for on-premise freezing in hospitals and other institutions has been a problem.

For this reason the recipes appearing in Volume 2, Blast Freezing Quantity Recipes, were tested and standardized. They were checked further when used in other operations. Among them: St. Elizabeth's Hospital, Lincoln, Neb. (under Chuck Beyer's direction) and West Jersey Hospitals in Camden (under Paul Doyer's direction).

PLATING

Plating has long been associated with the conventional system since salads, desserts, and special diet items are portioned and plated ahead of the tray assembly schedule. Thus, with the exception of a total convenience system, where every item including pre-plated frozen meals is received, reconstituted and served to the patients, a good portion control program is a must. Effective portion control requires that the following steps be taken:

1. Determine size per portion through patient and cafeteria surveys and plate waste studies.
2. A tight product specification is a good start on portion control (e.g., 5 oz. pork chop—bone in)
3. Make sure that portion sizes known and adhered to by personnel.
4. Have adequate portioning equipment, such as scales, scoops, and ladles, readily available.
5. Regularly check, evaluate, and update your standard portion control procedures.

In a total convenience food system, portion control is done for you by an outside vendor. Even so, it is important that steps 1, 2, and 5 are part of the procedure. You must emphasize rigid product control specifications to vendors so there is no problem in interpretation. If a total convenience food system ever exists in the future, one of the major advantages will be the transfer of this function from hospital management to an outside management.

TRAY ASSEMBLY

Tray assembly using foods produced in a conventional food system produces too much pressure to make such a system practical if there are other alternatives. Since tray assembly is required only in health care operations, this discussion is related to their problems. The tight schedule in meeting patient mealtime deadlines makes the employee more prone to mistakes and inaccurate portion control, and produces a constant strain on employee–supervisor relationships. The calls from the nursing station for holds, diet changes, late trays, and cancelled trays does not make the trayline assembly an efficient method of preparing and assembling food.

In a convenience food system or Ready Foods System, the tray assembly can start at 9 or 10 in the morning. Tray assembly is continuous except for breaks. The personnel assembling foods on the tray do not have a tight schedule. The employees working on the trayline need not be involved in portion control as this can be done in a separate area or pre-plated meals may be purchased.

TRANSPORT SYSTEMS

Historically, in a conventional food system the trays have been assembled in the wards from a hot bulk transport cart. This is the decentralized transport system. Delays in the arrival of the bulk transport cart often occur, because of elevator problems, delays in the main kitchen, or the absence of a cart pusher. Whatever the problem, the delayed arrival of meals, especially breakfast, is not well received by patients.

In the last ten years, these carts have been modified to a hot and cold food cart. As a result the portioning and setting of trays was taken away from the wards and put back in a central tray assembly area for better quality control.

With the advent of microwave ovens, the food carts with completely assembled trays began to be distributed to galleys where hot foods are reconstituted and served immediately. Reconstitution is flexible because it is done only when the patients are ready for their meals. This was when convenience food systems in hospitals finally emerged. There were problems in serving coffee, toast, and poached eggs. In a more recent version of this system, these items have been prepared right in the galleys. But a few years later, even more items appeared to present problems, such as steaks, roast beef, fish, and other items. Microwave reheating became associated with overdoneness, burned edges, and with cold spots in the center of the food. However, equipment companies responded to the problems with a vigorous campaign of research and development. With this interest and enthusiasm, a new generation of reconstitution equipment for galley service was introduced.

To solve the elevator problems which occur in all systems, whether conventional, convenience, or Ready Foods, an automatic cart transport system was devised and implemented in several hospitals. There are now several systems available, and all move the carts not only vertically, but horizontally.

An almost ideal cart transport system has been adopted by one operation. After proper programming, the food will be delivered as required without human hands pushing the cart. The only exception is in the cart staging for tray assembly at the central food facility where it must go to the upper floor manually.

CART DISTRIBUTION AND STAGING

Hot foods hot, and cold foods cold is one of the largest hurdles in the conventional food system. Many factors contribute to the improper temperature of food when it is received by the patient or customer. Some of these are: heat loss through poor initial temperature when it leaves the kitchen; long distance from kitchen to the patient; inadequate personnel to pass trays; and delays in elevators.

There is no patient programming and their schedule is so erratic that even nursing personnel sometimes do not know where patients are. There are also menu items which do not react well when transported long distances, such as coffee, teas, soups, and other liquids where temperatures drop rapidly.

Flexibility in the delivery and distribution schedules is one of the inherent advantages in both the convenience foods and Ready Foods Systems. There are many cart systems available where the transportation of foods to be served hot as well as those to remain cold is done in a chilled state. Variations within the cart design allow the food to remain at 38°F. to 40°F. until it is ready to be transported to the patient galleys to be reheated.

GALLEY SERVICE

The galley service function is characteristic of both the convenience food system and the Ready Foods System. The transfer of this function from a centralized kitchen to the numerous locations required in a decentralized system necessitates the development of a highly specialized group of employees. Members of this group are sometimes referred to as "galley hostesses" or "dietitian assistants." This role requires knowledge of the basic diets and how each applies to a patient's therapeutic needs. An employee filling this role is also responsible for final tray assembly in systems where the hot and cold foods are separated in the transport cart.

RECONSTITUTION IN FLOOR GALLEYS

Some foodservice consultants and designers, and even some dietitians and foodservice directors, feel that final quality control is lost when reconstitution takes place in the galley. Some are afraid of mismatching of trays, or believe the union of hot and cold food is time-consuming. Several innovative food-service operators decided to ask the help of equipment manufacturers in designing fool proof reconstituting systems where the trays remain untouched until the nursing or foodservice personnel is ready to pass them. This system offers not only flexibility and accuracy, but maximum quality control.

WAREWASHING AND SANITATION

In all of these three systems, there are no major advantages or disadvantages, except that in the Ready Foods System every step and precaution has to be taken to achieve bacterial control.

In any foodservice system, warewashing functions occur in almost the same methodology and, therefore, one system has no advantage over another. The exception is a total disposable ware system, normally associated with a total convenience food system, where warewashing and sanitation are limited to the galley areas. The components and the tray itself are discarded at the nursing stations where they are thrown in a chute for compaction or some other waste removal technique.

In summary, here is a graphic comparative analysis of the three systems.

Comparative Analysis of Systems

	Conventional	*Ready Food*	*Convenience*
Menu planning	difficult	easy	easy
Purchasing	difficult	somewhat easy	somewhat easy
Receiving	difficult	good control possible	good control possible
Storage/Inventory	difficult	good control possible	good control possible
Ingredient Control	good control possible	good control possible	
Hot & Cold Food Production	difficult	easier to control	easier to control except on molded salads & breakfast
Freezing & Chilling		difficult to control	
Thawing & Staging		good control possible	good control possible
Plating	difficult to portion control	easy to control w/automated equipm.	same
Tray Assembly	difficult to control	good control possible & easier to achieve	good control possible & easier to achieve
Cart Distribution & & Staging	difficult	easy to control T & T	easy to control T & T
Galley Service		good control possible	good control possible
Warewashing & Sanitation	timetable always hectic	same	same

Comparison of Systems as They Relate to
Quality and Cost Control

Management concerns for effective cost control in any system have grown in recent years. Quality control is more difficult, perhaps partly because quality, compared to cost, is relative. Quality, for example, is hard to define when it comes to feeding patients in a hospital. Quality is associated with the total well-being of the patient, not only from the physio-chemical and nutritional standpoint but also as it affects morale. There is no better indicator that a patient is getting well than when his appetite improves.

The small-scale production in a conventional system makes it difficult to achieve high quality. Managers and supervisors need to be keenly aware of the productivity of each person.

In a convenience system it is not difficult to maintain quality and cost control if the original cost guidelines and product specifications have been formulated correctly. One must develop tight specifications to assure the product is not compromised or sacrificed for cost. It is practical to check the percentage of fill weights, fat content, protein content, and such other quality factors as appearance, flavor, color, and texture. We have had difficulty obtaining a nutritional analysis for most of our entrees. Continuous product testing and research to arrive at uniform product data will be necessary.

In the previous chapter on Quality Control, there was a form called a Quality Control Inspection Chart that should be developed for each product. A test panel is the only acceptable methodology for evaluting products prepared from recipes, or for judging samples of pre-prepared products.

Quality compared to cost is not only relative, but also changes with time. We have to reach a continuity where quality becomes an integral part of cost effectiveness. A more responsible and effective dialogue has to occur between health care foodservice operators, food processors, and design consultants to effect a "cost effective system." What we need now is not divisiveness but mutual respect and cooperation to provide meals that will meet both patient needs and our cost. Let us not wait until we are forced to do this by governmental regulatory agencies.

Let us get together and take time to analyze some of the basic underlying causes of our present problems in foodservice systems. Many are obvious to us as we deal with them from day to day, but no one has taken the time to initiate the preventative solutions. We are in a rut and it's time we do something about it. What are some of these basic problems in foodservice systems?

1. Lack of uniform standardized principles of diet therapy—as they apply to the basic standard diets—which processors and operators can work from.

2. Lack of good productivity indexes in hospitals and other health care institutions.

3. Lack of system analysis in patient schedule programming due to the erratic demand schedules by the medical staff. This reflects in uneven workloads for the service departments because almost all of the orders for diet, treatment, x-rays, etc., occur after the medical staff rounds. In private hospitals, these orders occur before noon; in teaching hospitals after grand rounds in late afternoon or evening.)

4. Lack of a quality monitoring system for costs. In recent years there has been improvement in quantifying costs, but these have yet to be related to levels of quality.

5. Lack of energy consciousness in foodservice.

6. Lack of quality standards in the food processing industry. Perhaps the solution to this problem will come when USDA or FDA develop a set of regulatory standards. But why wait? The experts in pre-determining and judging what these standards ought to be should be professionals in foodservice operations. It is sometimes easy to see the forest but not the trees. In this case, the overall cost is the forest and the components to quality service are the trees.

Once we have made a committment to develop standards, it is easy to project the overall cost of the menu design by determining at which point of the raw-to-ready scale one wants to be.

There are several methods by which an operator can project the budget for his raw food cost. The following formula explains how a patient food cost (basics) is pre-determined for budget calculation. Using this cost summary, the entree cost can be determined as shown in the following calculation.

Once the entree cost is determined, the rest of the raw food cost figures are not difficult to define.

Patient Food Cost Formula
(Ancillary Meal Components)

Food	Portion Cost	Times Used Per Day	Sub Total	Daily Total
Salt	.0019	3	.005	
Pepper	.003	3	.009	
Sugar	.003	4	.012	
Milk	.0735	2	.147	
Beverage	.015	3	.030	
Bread	.0268	2	.053	
Butter	.012	2	.024	

Food	Portion Cost	Times Used Per Day	Sub Total	Daily Total
Cream	.0119	.5	.005	
Juice	.06	1	.060	
Cereal	.04	.8	.032	
Egg	.06	.5	.030	
Roll	.07	.5	.035	
Jelly	.0156	1	.016	
Bacon/Saus.				
Ham Slice	.06	.5	.030	.488
French Tst				
Pancakes				
Ancillary Meal Components				.488
Nourishments	.15	1		
Soup, Juice Appetizers	.06	1	.06	.060
Salad	.10	1.5	.15	.225
Dessert	.10	2	.20	.410
				1.183

Based on Entree Food Cost of   .80/Meal   2.8/day = 2.240
(Total minus lunch and dinner entrees)   − 1.183
                                                              1.057

Entree 1.057 divided by 2 =   .528 cost per
                                          L & D Entree

SUMMARY:
Entree = 0.528
Other = 1.183
Total Food Cost Per Patient Tray 1.711

The first step in cost control is to obtain quality labor cost data. Labor costs are the principal drain on foodservice budgets in health care institutions. In 1977, labor costs rose an average of 10 percent for non–commercial operators. If labor costs are to set the pace for effective cost control, we must provide leadership in developing Time and Motion Studies. These will help us analyze productivity and thus ultimate labor cost.

Each recipe must be broken down into various activities, and each activity assigned a cost. These labor component costs, plus raw food and overhead costs, reveal the true cost of each step in the recipe. With this method, you can evaluate whether purchasing a ready-to-serve product is cheaper than preparing an item on premise. Of course, cost is not the only factor to consider. The range and format of the menu are dependent also on quality, availability, and adaptability of these items to the type of reconstitution system you have selected. One has to remember that cost cannot make up for a difference in quality. One has to be a keen student in learning when and how to compromise. Acceptability and quality do not always go hand in hand, or our life would be simple to manage.

With conventional and ready foods, the quality control of preparation and processing has to be continuously evaluated in terms of productivity, and meeting goals and objectives for patient service. A well-developed menu is not going to be effective unless controls are established for its evaluation.

Every foodservice system requires a program of monitoring quality and cost. This program has to provide managers and employees with specific tools and guidelines so a definite evaluation can be accomplished. Not only is setting up the program important, but there must also be a procedure for written records to be kept.

Because the liability for the safety of patient meals rests with foodservice management, you must keep records of what products you received and where they were purchased, and what happened to these products subsequently. If a patient sues you for a cooked worm found in spinach, you are liable unless you can pass the liability on to the distributor or canner who produced the can of spinach. The new law states that any product is considered foreign material as long as an average group of persons would agree that the extraneous item is not identified with the item being sold. In past years a chicken bone in chicken salad was not considered foreign, as it comes from the chicken. Under the new law, chicken bone is a foreign material, and you may be sued. If a guest visiting your kitchen slips on the floor and you do not have a written record of when that floor was mopped and pictures to show that the floor has been mopped and dried, there is no legal evidence to prove that you are not liable. Whatever your system, you have to follow basic controls:

• *Purchasing control* by Specification—Surveys have shown that a majority of the orders in both commercial and noncommercial operations are placed without the use of written or verbal specifications. A lot of operators rely on brand labels or a supplier's reputation.

- *Receiving Control.* It is important that the person receiving merchandise have the knowledge, expertise, and responsibility to assure that items received meet standard specifications that include not only product data but also temperature and packaging of the products received. Also, a bacteria count has to be taken at this area to insure the safeness of the products.

Foodservice Quality Control Standards are maintained by using a simple checklist that every galley service employee must go over when he or she receives the completed trays from the kitchen or the caterer. A daily written report for each meal service must be sent to the main kitchen. In this way, personnel have a method to determine how efficiently they are performing the other functions.

Once a qualitative program is established and implemented (and constantly reviewed and updated), a quantitative cost analysis program is easy to develop, based on the qualitative objectives established by management. Since labor cost is one of the factors most difficult to control and evaluate, I would like to review some methods of defining costs in terms of productivity.

- *Productivity* is a function of four variables: time, energy, motion economy, and temperature. If we are able to overcome all the obstacles associated with these factors, we will automatically reduce our operating costs. Any change to effect an increase in productivity rate means that effective manpower utilization needs to be established.

According to Dr. Gerald Lattin, Dean of the School of Hotel, Food and Travel Service, Florida International University, productivity is a function of *competency* and *motivation.*

$$P = C + M$$

Competency level is established by developing job expectations and objectives that are mutually agreed upon, and then evaluating these expectations in an equitable and consistent manner.

Most employees suffer from inadequate training and information, inherent lack of skill and aptitude, and behavioral problems that affect their performance. Management also has its faults. These include poor communication skills, inconsistent, unfair and biased evaluations, and inadequate knowledge of the employee needs as far as security and social/psychological and self–fulfillment goals. There are five basic rules to remember in communication, Dr. Lattin states. They are:

1. Communicate good news
2. Communicate bad news
3. Listen
4. Handle complaints fairly and consistently
5. Be approachable

I often remember this analogy, used by Thomas H. Lawrence, Lawrence-Dietert and Co., management consultants: "Personnel management is like managing a bank—you make deposits and withdrawals on each employee's account. If you make withdrawals all the time, the employee's security and anxiety increases every time. It will come to a point where his sense of security is so mutilated that he completely loses pride and interest in his job, thereby causing his productivity to drop to zero."

QUALITY AND COST CONTROL AS RELATED TO PRODUCTIVITY

One of the most serious problems affecting productivity is the uneven workloads in a conventional food system. This problem will be alleviated with a convenience food or a Ready Foods System. In these systems, the work scheduling and labor assignments are on smooth, continuous, well-programmed schedules (e.g., tray assembly is continuous in a Ready Foods System, in contrast to a conventional system where between meal lows contribute to decreased productivity).

In a Ready Foods System, the productivity rate in the preparation and processing areas is increased. This is due to the continuous processing, thus reducing waste in storage loss, trim waste, and leftovers from over-production or under-production. Since preparation and processing are continuous in a Ready Foods System, it is possible to schedule personnel on a standard, 40 hour week period. With this schedule, morale and interest in performing at a high rate of productivity increases.

COST CONTROL

Most of us feel secure in making decisions on whether to make or buy food items. A common pitfall is to compare the selling price of ready-to-serve chicken a la king with the food and labor cost to prepare it on-premise, without considering supply and other indirect costs which amount to a substantial figure. A food processor's cost as it is given here is a more realistic method of comparison. I would like to reiterate the importance of costing each recipe component both for labor and food. Of course there is a problem with the constant updating of unit prices; the way to overcome this is through computerization of the data and information system.

FOOD PROCESSOR'S COST

Raw Food Cost
Labor Cost
Supply Cost
Packaging Cost *
General and Administrative Cost

---

*Costs that food processors need to add to the selling price of food items.

Marketing Costs *
   – Merchandising/Advertising
   – Product Samples
   – Storage and Inventory
   – Sales Commissions
   – Profit
Indirect Costs
   Laboratory Analysis *
   Distribution & Transportation
   Fringe Benefits
   Depreciation
   Debt Service
   Buildings and Grounds
   Product Liability Ins.*
   Utilities
   Compactor/Trash Removal
   Computer Service
   Accounting Audit
   Communications
   Linen/Laundry
   Maintenance & Repair
   Housekeeping & Cleaning
   Payroll
   Training
   Bad Debts*
   Taxes .property*
         .income   *
*Costs that food processors need to add to the selling price of food items.

We have been led down a primrose path if we believe we are efficient managers as long as we know the overall cost per patient meal. Never underestimate the impact of also knowing the cost per tray, including specifications, portion size, unit cost per edible portion, total labor cost, and total cost per portion of each component of the tray.

In hospital foodservice, the most critical aspect of cost accounting is determining the cost of each patient tray. Based on our experience, I have developed three methods of determining the cost per tray or cover (for restaurant applications).

In order to compare the three different systems, a comparative cost analysis of total foodservice systems must be made. Each operation has different variables for each line depending on the goals or objectives set forth by management.

Comparative Cost Analysis of
Total Foodservice Systems

I.   CAPITAL COST
     A. BUILDING
     B. EQUIPMENT

II. OPERATING COST
     A. FOOD COST
     B. LABOR COST
         FRINGE BENEFITS
     C. SUPPLY COST
     D. PACKAGING COST
     E. INDIRECT COSTS
         Training/Personnel Dev.
         Laboratory Analysis
         Debt Service (Interest Bond)
         Depreciation–Building
         Depreciation–Equipment
         Interest (lease)
         Product Liability Ins.
         Bldg. & Grounds Rep. Main.
         Utilities
         Product Research & Dev.
         Accounting/Payroll
         Communications
         Transport. & Distrib.
         Linen/Laundry
         Housekeeping/Cleaning

Despite the limited experience of hospitals with Ready Foods Systems and convenience food systems, compared to conventional systems, here are some observations:

1. The operating cost of a total convenience food system is much higher than either conventional or Ready Foods.

2. The initial capital investment is lowest in a convenience food system.

3. The initial capital investment in Ready Foods is somewhat higher than convenience food, but a bit lower than conventional.

4. A total convenience system has a greater food cost but that is somewhat outweighed by a decrease in labor cost.

5. The raw food cost of a Ready Foods System is somewhat lower because of volume purchasing and the ability to purchase and store seasonal foods when their price is lowest.

6. A mixture of cook–chill–freeze combinations with a convenience food system is practical due to the unavailability of a variety of good quality special diet items. But this system will work only if management stays on top with up-to-date labor and food cost evaluations through industrial engineering techniques and computer assisted information systems.

Here are two formats to use to determine which system is most feasible and cost effective for a particular operation.

In determining the cost effectiveness of the various systems, we must consider two parameters:

1. The cost of operating the different systems, including the cost of building and equipment, during the first year of operation.

2. The quality of the food and the quality of service to the consumer or client.

There are several alternatives in choosing between the three major systems. These alternatives affect the type of final service required to achieve the objective. These alternatives consist of:

Total Convenience	Prepared Outside	Preserved & Stored	Decentralized Reconstituted
		Reheated & Served Directly	Centralized Reconstitution
Raw Food	Prepared Inside	Preserved & Stored in Freezer	Decentralized
			Centralized
		Chilled & Served Directly	Decentralized
			Centralized
	Prepared Inside	Served Hot	Centralized

The first format to be used is given in the chart (p. 357) titled Comparative Cost Analysis of Foodservice Systems. The cost of alternatives 1 through 7 will be divided into two basic costs: *capital cost* and *operating cost*.

The second format to be used accounts for predicted future changes in operating costs using different inflationary rates for the prices of labor, food, and supplies. The present trend for the various alternatives is based on these assumptions:

Annual labor inflationary rate   = 5%
Annual food inflationary rate   = 3%*
Annual supplies inflationary rate = 3%
Discount rates   = 4%

The discount rates apply to the discount factor and to the projected costs in determining the present value of future expenses.

The cost difference between each system as it relates to quality has to be assigned a weighted value. This value is given dollar figures to determine the difference in quality of the system alternatives in question.

Cost Per Tray or Per Cover is an excellent gauge to estimate the projected food cost per patient meal or per customer meal.

In both commercial and institutional operations, an almost similar technique or methodology can be used. In the case of patient food cost per tray, there are three allocation formulas I have developed. They are:

1. Determination of cost per tray by costing each individual component of the tray.

The form on page 360 is similar to a PER MEAL CHARGE system that can be computerized and thus be easier to manage. The data can be used to determine an estimated cost figure by multiplying the cost per tray by the anticipated number of patients or customers in a day, month, and year.

2. Determine weighted average cost of entrees based on past usage. If the usage factor is not available, calculate from a general formula:
1. Find anticipated percentage of various diets:
   General, e.g., 40%
   Soft—Bland
   etc.

2. Out of general trays percentage calculate possible total number of meals; e.g. 1200 × 40 % = 480 patients on general diets.

---

*   The annual *food inflationary rate* was given a smaller percentage than experienced in the past. If the inflationary prices of food equal or surpass that of the inflationary prices of labor, then a cost advantage might be given to Ready Foods Systems in general.

Cost Analysis per Tray or Cover

Item Specification	Size Portion	Unit Cost	Total Cost per Portion	Total Labor Cost per Portion	Total Cost per Portion
Hormel 2240 Chicken Ala King	8 oz.	.53	.53	.10	.63
Hart 3208 Prepared Biscuits (2)	2 oz.	.08	.16	.05	.21
R20A Fruit Cup	2 oz.	.10	.10	.05	.15
R40D Salad—Toss #1	4 oz.	.06	.06	.02	.08
Oleo 1	1 ea.	.007	.007	.004	.011
Crackers	2 pkg.	.015	.015	.004	.019
R60B Gelatine Dessert #4	3 oz.	.033	.033	.056	.089
Milk carton	8 oz.	.080	.080	.004	.084
Parsley	Sprig	.001	.001	.001	.002
Plastic Wrap (Entree, soup, salad, gelatine)			.002	.004	.006
Condiments	(1 ea.)				
Sugar Salt Pepper Napkins		.006	.006	.006	.012

Total Cost _____

Selling Price _____

Operation _____   Menu_____

Date Typed_____   Effective Date_____

3. Calculate percentage acceptance of each luncheon and dinner or breakfast entree; e.g.

     Entree No. 1—18% × 480 = 86.4 patients who chose Entree No. 1
     Entree No. 2—15% × 480 = 72.0
     Entree No. 3—14% × 480 = 67.2

4. Cost each entree and weight each by percentage of acceptance to arrive at a weighted average cost *per tray* for patients on general *diet entrees*. Calculate cost by multiplying number of patients on general diets who chose entree No. 1 by the cost of entree No. 1 and arrive at total cost figure allocation for this particular item. Proceed with the rest of the tray components until the USAGE FACTOR is less than 1. In this case, multiply the total cost by whatever usage factor is used.

3. Determine weighted average cost of milk, appetizer, salad, dessert, and diet kits.

1. Find the average weighted cost of a dessert based on acceptability percentages for each.

2. Do the same for the rest of the meal components.

3. Calculate usage factor for each component and obtain total cost of the above basic meal excluding the entree.

The method stated below is a "future generation" type of forecasting in which computerization will play an important role.

Method of determining food cost and total cost per item on order.

1. Cost each menu item for all categories
General entrees No. 1
SF Entree No. 11

2. As patients *order an item* the patient *menu list* will be *computed* automatically at the selling price agreed upon.

3. All items will be priced depending on food cost, labor cost, supply cost, indirect cost, and overhead.

SAMPLE COST

Patient A		*Patient A Nourishments*	
Trays	B–1.10	10:00 a.m.	.50
	L–1.75	2:00 p.m.	.75
	D–2.50	8:00p.m.	1.25
	5.35		2.40

Parallels are easily drawn between conventional, Ready Foods, and total convenience systems if the analysis includes the factors detailed in this chapter. Those factors should be assessed in terms of the unique requirements of the institution making the analysis.

21

Comparison Testing for Quality

USE OF SURVEYS

To campare the quality of frozen precooked foods with on-premise prepared foods, the operator should conduct surveys through a taste panel as an initial pre-screening technique. After several brands (a minimum of three) have been chosen by the panel, then a scientific analysis of the pre-cooked product should be made. This analysis should determine:

1. The percentage of fill weights.
2. The fat content.
3. The quality and percentage of protein content.
4. The percentage of meat extenders.
5. The grades for each component of the frozen precooked foods (if possible).

A continuous product testing and research program should be developed, implemented, and evaluated so that quality comparison testing becomes realistic.

A Quality Control Comparison Chart like the one reproduced here is helpful in presenting collected data in an easy to analyze form.

Quality Control Comparison Chart

PRODUCT NAME _____

Reference	Item Code	Case Wt.	Units/ Case	% Fill Weights			Cost/ Case	Cost/ Oz.	Panel Scores	Panel Comm.
				Meat	Sauce	Starch/Veg.				
TOTAL RATINGS										

Comments for Rating: _____

Remember, there are several standards for each component of these products; e.g., canned fruits have USDA grade standards based on color, texture, flavor, and appearance.

There are laboratory or instrument measurements for some of the standards. To learn the nutritional content of a pre-prepared food, a laboratory analysis can be made. A bacteria count analysis is a measurement of sanitation and freshness of the components and the processing. The color and viscosity of the product can be measured through spectrophotometer or gas chromatography; the desired color is the color expected by an average individual viewing the product. A tenderometer is an instrument that measures shearing cutting movement which is similar to chewing action and measures that factor in a pre-cooked item.

A flavor standard is harder to qualify than texture or color. The standard for flavor is based on test panel acceptance by persons consuming the item rather than by instrument measurement.

Test panels should consist of a random sampling of persons to average out biases in taste. Usually, it is desirable that a testing room be well lighted and ventilated, and free from distractions.

Another scientific method of product testing is a "declared control difference test" in which a standard product is compared with the items being tested. It is challenging to develop a standard other than the recipe you are using. The declared control standard might be a product from another hospital. In this way your standard will not come from a product that might have lower quality than desirable.

In grading differences in standards of quality of various products, strive to compare these items not only on cost, but also on percentage of fill weights, nutrient content, bacteria count, packaging, and reconstitution directions. We should try to determine objectively scores for each of the products being tested. The following chart is a comparison of fill weights by percent for com-

Comparison of Fill Weights by Percent

Brand A —CHICKEN A LA KING
　　Meat—22%
　　Sauce—73%
　　Vegetalbes—5%

FRESH CHICKEN A LA KING
　　Meat—35.5%
　　Sauce—50.0%
　　Vegetables—14.5%

mercially prepared chicken a la king and a freshly prepared product. You will note that the on-premise prepared product contains 13% more meat than the chicken a la king prepared commercially.

To be assured of good quality frozen precooked food from outside vendors, one must develop tight specifications. Here are some examples:

A. INGREDIENT SPECIFICATIONS—ENTREES

1. *Percent Animal Protein*: Convenience Entrees that are mixed dishes (e.g., chicken chow mein, lasagna, or beef stew) shall have a minimum of 14 grams of *Animal Protein* per serving size indicated by specifications. Convenience Entrees that are meat type (e.g., Roast Turkey and Dressing, Veal Parmesan, or Swiss Steak) shall have a minimum of 21 grams of *Animal Protein* per serving size indicated by specifications. Acceptable variance of 20 percent in animal protein will be allowed. Processor to state grams of animal protein per 100 grams of product.

2. *Percent Meat Extenders*: Convenience Entrees shall contain not more than 5 to 7 percent meat extenders to meat ratio.

3. *Acceptable Meat Extenders*: Texturized vegetable protein and its derivatives.

4. *Meat Specifications*: All beef and veal used in the product formulation shall be USDA Choice; processed meats shall be the top packers brand, (but equivalent to USDA Good or above); all poultry shall be USDA Grade A; pork shall be USDA No. 1, and fish shall be USDA Grade A.

5. *Vegetable Specifications*: Canned, fresh, or frozen vegetables used in the products' formulation shall meet the specifications outlined in Part III, Chapter 17.

B. LABELING

1. *Name of Product*: Processor to state name of product on each individual package and shipping case.

2. *Ingredients*: Processor to state all ingredients in descending order of quantity on each individual package.

3. *Expiration Date*: Processor to state the lot number and expiration date on each individual package.

4. *Storage Requirements:* Processor to state the proper storage procedures on each individual package to maintain the quality and shelf life of the product.

5. *Tempering Requirements*: Processor to state proper tempering procedures on each individual package.

6. *Heating Instructions*: Processor to state heating instructions for both conventional and convection heating methods on each individual package if item requires it.

7. *Product Weight*: Processor to state product weight on each individual package.

8. *Shipping Case*: Processor to state product pack on shipping case.

C. OTHER PRODUCT INFORMATION (BROCHURES, MANUALS, LEAFLETS)

1. *Special Handling Instructions*: Processor to state any special handling requirements on each individual package.

2. *Nutritional Content*: Processor to provide a complete nutritional analysis using the RDA's Nutritional Component Categories to include: calories, protein (percent animal and percent vegetable proteins) fat, carbohydrate, vitamins, and minerals. Processor to state cholesterol, saturated and unsaturated fatty acid contents. It is desirable and highly recommended that a thorough and complete laboratory analysis of nutrients be made and sent with the products.

3. *Other Instructions*:

a. Entrees: Processor to provide the percentage of meat, starch, vegetables, and gravy used in product. Processor to state additives and thickening agents used.

b. Desserts: Processor to state percent fruit and filling in pies.

D. MICROBIOLOGICAL STANDARDS

The following are the recommended bacteriological specifications for frozen foods:

a. As prescribed by the standards within the foodservice industry, certification from an outside laboratory must be furnished by the food processor.

Pre-cooked or partially cooked frozen foods shall not have a bacteria count in excess of the following:

1. Total aerobic bacteria plate count not to exceed more than 7,500 colonies/gram
2. Coliform plate count—50 colonies per gram
3. Coagulase positive type staphylococci—negative count
4. Salmonella shigella typhoid—negative count
5. E coli count—negative
6. Faecal streptococci—negative
7. Perfringens—negative

If samples taken from a case lot exceed the above mentioned plate count, another random sampling will be taken to cross–check the lot. Said tests shall be made by a certified, approved outside laboratory.

E. ACCEPTABLE ADDITIVES

Processor shall use only currently acceptable additives generally recognized as having safe status, from current GRAS (generally recognized as safe) list, established by the U.S. Food and Drug Administration. Processor to state all additives used in product.

F. PACKAGING AND PACKING

Unless otherwise specified, all items shall be packaged in accordance with acceptable commercial standards. Where special or unusual packing is specified in the order, but not specifically provided for by contract, such packing details must be the subject of an agreement independently arrived at between the ordering agency and the contractor; provided:

1. Each shipping container of each item in a shipment is of uniform size and content, except for residual quantities.

2. The gross weight of each shipping container does not exceed 50 lb. except when the weight of a single item within the shipping container is of a higher weight.

3. Shipping containers comply with requirements of the National Motor Freight classification (issue in effect at time of shipment).

G. ENTREE PACKAGING

1. *Convenience General Entrees*: Shall be packed in a rigid Ekco or equal aluminum foil half-, third-, or full-size steamtable pan (as requested) with aluminum foil lids, or packed in a polyethylene bag contained in a corrugated fiberboard box of packing sizes as stated in the specifications. The convenience entree shipping case shall be properly labeled with the minimum requirements of the Food and Drug Administration.

H. DELIVERY

To safeguard the quality of these frozen foods, it is recommended that a temperature device be given to the Food Buyer showing a record of the external temperatures to which these frozen products have been exposed. The internal temperature of these products will be checked by the receiving Storekeeper and must meet a minimum of 0°F. or lower.

Upon delivery, the items shall be inspected to verify the general specifications of these products. Any deviation or substitution thereof will not be accepted by the stock clerk without prior approval from either the Food Buyer or the Foodservice Director.

The elements to be considered in comparison testing for quality can frequently be presented in chart form. This makes it easier to determine the preferred item and to defend the choices made. It also provides data that simplifies systems comparison.

Appendix

Specifications for A Three Door Blast Freezer for Dietary Department

1. *INVITATION FOR BIDS:* Sealed bids will be received for furnishing the necessary labor, materials, equipment, and supervision to install a three (3) Door Blast Freezer in the Dietary Department on the first floor and in the basement of the Main Building, in accordance with the specifications set forth herein and the "Other Terms, Conditions, and Instructions to the Specifications" attached hereto and made a part hereof as though fully set forth herein.

2. *GENERAL SPECIFICATIONS:*
   a) Delivery and installation shall be made on the site and must be completed by _____. Bidders must quote on a delivered and installed price.
   b) Bidder shall visit the site to determine the conditions under which he will have to work and all other considerations and limitations imposed by the physical layout of the building. In visiting the site, bidder should contact _____. Contractor shall verify all dimensions and conditions at the installation site.
   c) All cartons, containers, metal, debris, dust and dirt will be removed promptly from the building and will be disposed of by the contractor.

d) All work embodied in this operation shall be done subject to the inspection and approval of the Hospital Administrator or his designated representative. Payment will be made after final inspection and acceptance by the County of all work included under these specifications.

e) Contractor shall warrant all materials and workmanship from all defects and deficiencies in material, construction, or installation for a period of one (1) year from date of installation, and any defects or deficiencies shall be promptly corrected at no cost to the County.

3. *DETAILED SPECIFICATIONS:*

a) Contractor shall furnish and install a Blast Freezer approximately 6'10" wide, 2'11" deep, 6'8" high (without legs) but 6" stainless steel legs to be included, Model #3SLFR Koch as manufactured by Hobart Manufacturing Co. of Troy, Ohio.

b) Cabinet shall be constructed of all steel exterior with the front and sides of 18-8 finished stainless steel and the back, top, and bottom of zinc-coated steel. The interior of the cabinet shall be constructed of one-piece, smooth, seamless, satin-grained 18-8 stainless steel.

c) Insulation shall be of polyurethane plastic, poured, expanded, and bonded in place and completely filling all cavities between the inner and outer surfaces of both the cabinet and the doors.

d) Doors shall be full height—approximately 58" high and 21½" wide. Door faces are to be of seamless construction, 18-8 finished stainless steel. Door drums are to be of seamless styrene plastic. Door gaskets and breaker strips around the doors are to be of extruded vinyl plastic.

e) All exterior hardware is to be chrome plated. Door fasteners are to be equipped with cylinder locks. Forty-eight wire shelves are to be included with the unit. Shelves are to be of plated and sealed steel, supported by stainless steel clips which mount on stainless steel vertical shelf supports with shelf adjustment on 1" centers. A properly calibrated thermometer shall be mounted inside and outside the cabinet in such a way that it is easily visible.

f) Unit is to be complete with fans and motors and defrost controls (thermostat and defrost time clock) for use with a remote condensing unit. Unit must also include a condensate drain outlet. This Blast Freezer shall include the installation of an adequate self-defrosting freezing coil and an adequate water-cooled compressor to maintain a box temperature of at least $-40°F$. (minus forty degrees Fahrenheit) when supplies at temperatures of $150°F$. are put into it.

g) Bid price must include freight with deliver to _____.
Contractor shall warrant all materials and workmanship from all defects

and deficiencies in materials, construction, or installation for a period of one year from date of installation; and any defects or deficiencies shall be promptly corrected at no cost to the County. Detailed instruction on operation and maintenance must be provided to personnel operating this equipment throughout the one year warranty period. Two copies of operating instructions and parts list must be provided.

h) Installation shall be complete with all necessary refrigerant, refrigeration connections, controls, water connections, regulating valve, condensate drain lines, crankcase pressure regulator, contactor, dehydrator, sight glass, electrical connections, pipe insulation, terminal valves, regulating devices, and any other necessary accessories required for a complete installation.

i) Adequate electrical service to a breaker switch near the compressor installation site and a cooling water supply line and return line for the condenser shall be installed by owner.

j) Electrical service shall be 208 volt—three phase.

k) The installed freezer and all related accessories supplied by seller shall be guaranteed against defects in material and workmanship for a period of one year from the date of completed installation. In addition, the compressor will be guaranteed against defects in material and workmanship for a period of five years from the date of completed installation.

4. *BASIS OF AWARD:* The award of this contract shall be based upon but not necessarily limited to the factors of: a) net cost; b) installation–completion date and ability of bidders to meet completion date; c) evidence of harmonious labor relation to insure work continuity; and d) evidence of work experience and performance history in terms of meeting specification requirements.

5. *TIME SCHEDULE:* Successful bidder shall agree to begin work and to prosecute and complete the project in such fashion as will ensure meeting the time schedule required herein.

6. *AWARD OF CONTRACT:* The right is reserved to send to the successful bidder the necessary contract and bond forms and a notice that the contract has been awarded to him at any time within 15 days after the date on which proposals are received.

Bibliography

PART 1, CHAPTER 1

1. Glew, George, *Cook-Freeze Catering, An Introduction to its Technology,* Faber & Faber, Queen Square, London, 1973.
2. Rappole, Clinton L., Feasibility of On-Premise Production of Frozen Entrees under Institutional Conditions, a monograph for the degree of Master of Professional Studies, 1970.
3. Deignan, Paul B., A Food Service Operator's Approach to Ready Foods, a monograph for the degree of Master of Professional Studies, December, 1973.

PART 1, CHAPTER 2

1. Pinkert, Michael S., Basic Planning Concepts for Ready Foods Systems, *Canadian Hospital Journal,* June, 1972, pp. 32-34.
2. Cain, Howard, Kitchen, William, Private Design Consultants Hired by Medical Facilities Associates, Architect, Private Communication.
3. Peterson, Alice, Pickett, Rex, Hennepin County Central Food Facility Staff, 1975, as submitted specifications for purchasing.

PART 1, CHAPTER 4

1. Tressler, D.K., Van Arsdel, W.B., Copley, M.J., *The Freezing Preservation of Foods,* The AVI Publishing Company, Inc., Vol. 4, 1968.
2. Technical Service Bulletin No. 243: Purity 69, Chicago, National Starch & Chemical Corp., 1951, p. 1.

3. Technical Information: AMA120 W–13, Stabilizer, Hammond, Indiana, American Maize Products Company, 1975, p. 1–10.

PART 1, CHAPTER 5

1. Treat, N., Richards, L., *Quantity Cookery*, Little, Brown and Company, Boston, Toronto, Fourth Edition, 1966.
2. Rogers, John L., *Production of Pre-Cooked Frozen Foods for Mass Catering*, Food Trade Press, Ltd., London, England, 1969.

PART 1, CHAPTER 6

1. Wenzel, George L., *Wenzel's 1964 Menu Maker,* Boston, CBI Publishing Company, Inc., 1964.
2. Beyer, Chuck, Consultant, Hysen and Associates, Detroit, Michigan, Private Communication.
3. Doyon, Paul, Director of Food Services, Camden, N. J., Hospitals, Camden, New Jersey, Private Communication.
4. Rappole, Clinton, Feasibility of On–Premise Production of Frozen Entrees Under Institutional Conditions, a thesis presented to the faculty of the Graduate School of Cornell University for the Degree of Master of Science, 1971, pp. 91-99.

PART 1, CHAPTER 8

1. Bulletin 244, Freezing Foods for Home Use, Agricultural Extension Service, University of Minnesota, 1972.

PART 1, CHAPTER 9

1. Gould, Wilbur A., Professor and Lecturer, Ohio State University, as part of lecture when author was a student under Dr. Gould.

PART 1, CHAPTER 10

1. Tressler, Donald K., Van Arsdel, Wallace B., Copley, Michael J., *The Freezing Preservation of Foods*, The AVI Publishing Company, Inc., Westport, Connecticut, 1968.

2. Harder, Rudolph, Private Communication, former baking instructor, Dunwoody Institute, Minneapolis, Minnesota.

PART 1, CHAPTER 11

1. Weiser, H. H., Mountney, G. J., Gould, W. A., *Practical Food Microbiology and Technology*, The AVI Publishing Co., Inc., Westport, Connecticut, 1971.

2. Rappole, Clinton L., Feasibility of On-Premise Production of Frozen Entrees under Institutional Conditions, a Masters Degree Thesis for Advanced Professional Studies.

3. Glew, George, *Cook/Freeze Catering, An Introduction to its Technology*, Faber and Faber, London, England, 1973.

4. Litksky, W., Fagerson, I.S., and Tellers, C.R., *A Bacteriological Survey of Commercially Frozen Beef*, Pontly and Tina Pres. J. Milk Food Technology, vol. 20, pp. 216–219, 1957.

5. Saleh, M. A. and Ordal, Z. J., *Studies on the Growth and Toxin Production of Clostridium Botulinum in a Precooked Frozen Food*, Food Research Vol. 20, pp. 340–350, 1955.

6. Harder, E.L., Developing and Effective Food Sanitation Program, *Hospitals, J.A.H.A.*, vol. 49, Feb. 16, 1975.

7. Tressler, D. K., Van Arsdel, N. B., Copley, M. J., *The Freezing Preservation of Foods*, The AVI Publishing Co., Inc., Westport, Connecticut.

8 Rogers, J. L., *Production of Pre-Cooked Frozen Foods for Mass Catering*, Food Trade Press, London, W.C.2, pp. 63–64, 1969.

9. Deignan, Paul B., A Food Service Operator's Approach to Ready Foods, presented for the degree of Master of Professional Studies, School of Hotel Administration, Cornell University, 1973.

10. Glew, G., University of Leeds and the United Leeds Hospitals: An Experiment in Hospital Catering Using the Cook-Freeze System. Procter Department, University of Leeds, Leeds LS295T, England, 1970.

11. Raj, H., and Liston, J., The Detection and Enumeration of Fecal Indicator Organisms in Frozen Seafoods, *Applied Microbiology*, vol. 9, pp. 295–303, 1961.

12. TEC Service Bulletin, Victory Metal Manufacturing, Plymouth Meeting, Pennsylvania.

PART 1, CHAPTER 12

1. Glew, George, *Cook/Freeze Catering, An Introduction to its Technology*, Faber & Faber, 3 Queen Square, London, 1973.

2. Pinkert, M., Hysen, Paul, Packaging Procedures for Ready Foods, *Canadian Hospital: Journal of Canadian Hospital Association*, Vol. 49:9:46–50, 1972.

3. *Factors Affecting Quality of Frozen Prepared Food Products*, a publication of the American Society for Hospital Food Service Administrators, American Hospital Association, 1972

4. Harder, Eulalia L., "Packaging for Health Care," Symposium: Packaging Needs of the Food Service Industry; *Food Technology*, vol. 26, No. 9, pp. 42–52, 1972

5. Tressler, D. K., Van Arsdel, W. B., Copley, M. J., *The Freezing Preservation of Foods*, Vol. 4, The AVI Publishing Co., Westport, Connecticut, pp. 116–117, 1968.

6. Rappole, Clinton L., Feasibility of On–Premise Production of Frozen Entrees Under Institutional Conditions, A Masters Degree Thesis for Advanced Professional Studies.

7. Dorney, David C., Millross, Janice, Glew, George, Packaging Storage and Transport, *Hospitals, J.A.H.A.*, 48:81 July 16, 1974, pp. 81–84.

8. Livingston, G. E. and Mario, T., Why Not Standardize Institutional Prepared Frozen Food Packaging? *Food Technology*, 24:978, Sept. 1970.

9. Solberg, Myron, Microbial Considerations of Packaging, *Food Technology*, 21:758, May, 1967.

PART 2, CHAPTER 13

1. Glew, George, *Cook–Freeze Catering, An Introduction to its Technology*, Faber & Faber, Queen Square, London, 1973.

2. Tressler, D.K., Van Arsdel, W.B., Copley, M.J., *The Freezing Preservation of Foods*, The AVI Publishing Company, Inc., Vol. 4, 1968.

PART 2, CHAPTER 14

1. Maclinn, Walter A., Frozen Foods Under Adverse Temperature Control, *Journal of Environmental Health*, Vol. 25, pp. 15–20, January 26, 1963.

2. Peterson, A. C., Karlson, K. E., Gunderson, M. F., Time & Temperature Effect on Food Quality, *Cornell Hotel and Restaurant Administration Quarterly*, Vol. 4, pp. 25–36, May, 1963.

3. Uncle Ben's, Inc., Food Service Division, *New Kettle Cookery Entrees* (Houston, Texas).

4. Decareau, Robert V., *Microwave Energy Applications Newsletter*, The Cabinet Press, Inc., vol. IV, No. 4, pp. 6-7, July – August, 1971.

5. Decareau, Robert V., *Microwave Energy Applications Newsletter*, The Cabinet Press, Inc., vol. IV, No. 5, pp. 13-14, September – October, 1971.

6. Weiser, H. H., Mountney, G. J., Gould, W. A., *Practical Food Microbiology and Technology*, The AVI Publishing Co., Inc., Westport, Connecticut, 1971.

PART 2, CHAPTER 15

1. Decareau, Robert V., Equipment for Heating Pre-Cooked Frozen Food for Food Service, *Microwave Energy Applications Newsletter*, vol. IV, No. 6, November – December, 1971.

2. Glew, George, *Cook/Freeze Catering, An Introduction to its Technology*, Faber & Faber, 3 Queen Square, London, 1973.

3. Olsen, C. M., Microwave Inhibits Bread Mold, *Food Engineering,* vol. 37, No. 7, pp. 51-53, 1965.

4. Lasey, B. A., Winners, H. I., McLellan, M. E., and Bogshawe, K. D., The Effects of Microwave Cookery on Baterial Counts of Food, *Journal of Applied Bacteriology*, vol. 28, No. 2, pp. 331-335, 1965.

5. Pinkert, Michael S., The Ready Foods System for Health Care Facilities, *Institutions/Volume Feeding Magazine,* Chicago, Illinois, pp. 82-83, 1973.

6. Fenton, F., and Gleim, E., Dinners Frozen Right on the Plate, *Farm Research*, vol. 14, No. 1, p. 5, 1948.

7. Napleton, Lewis, *A Guide to Microwave Catering*, Northwood Industrial Publications Limited, Elm Street, London, 1967.

8. Causey, K., and Fenton, F., Effect of Reheating on Palatability, Nutritive Value and Bacterial Count of Frozen Cooked Foods (1) vegetables (2) meat dishes, *Journal of American Dietetic Association*, vol. 27, 390, p. 491, 1951.

PART 2, CHAPTER 16

1. Rappole, Clinton, Feasibility of On-Premise Production of Frozen Entrees Under Institutional Conditions, a monograph for Masters Degree in Advanced Professional Studies.

2. Tressler, D. K., Van Arsdel, W. B., Copley, M. J., *The Freezing, Preservation of Foods*, The AVI Publishing Company, Inc., Vol. 4, 1968.

3. Livingston, Guy E., Chang, Charlotte M., Second Generation Reconstitution Systems, *Cornell Hotel and Restaurant Association Quarterly*.

PART 4, CHAPTER 20

1. Millross, J. & Glew, G., "Staff, Equipment and Wastage," *Journal of the American Hospital Association*, August 16, 1974, vol. 48, pp. 72–74.

2. Zolber, K. B. & Donaldson, B., "Distribution of Work Functions in Hospital Food Systems," *Journal of the American Dietetic Association*, January, 1970.

Index